# SOLARO
## STUDY GUIDE

**English Language Arts 5**

**SOLARO Study Guide** is designed to help students achieve success in school. The content in each study guide is 100% curriculum aligned and serves as an excellent source of material for review and practice. To create this book, teachers, curriculum specialists, and assessment experts have worked closely to develop the instructional pieces that explain each of the key concepts for the course. The practice questions and sample tests have detailed solutions that show problem-solving methods, highlight concepts that are likely to be tested, and point out potential sources of errors. **SOLARO Study Guide** is a complete guide to be used by students throughout the school year for reviewing and understanding course content, and to prepare for assessments.

FARMINGDALE PUBLIC LIBRARY

Copyright © 2013 Castle Rock Research Corporation

All rights reserved. No part of this book covered by the copyright hereon may be reproduced or used in any form or by any means graphic, electronic, or mechanical, including photocopying, recording, taping, or information storage and retrieval systems without the express permission of the publisher.

Rao, Gautam, 1961 –
**SOLARO STUDY GUIDE –** English Language Arts 5 (2013 Edition) Common Core State Standards

1. English Language Arts – Juvenile Literature. I. Title

Castle Rock Research Corporation
2410 Manulife Place
10180 – 101 Street
Edmonton, AB T5J 3S4

1  2  3  MP  15  14  13

Printed in the United States of America

**Publisher**
Gautam Rao

*Dedicated to the memory of Dr. V. S. Rao*

# THE *SOLARO STUDY GUIDE*

The *SOLARO Study Guide* is designed to help students achieve success in school and to provide teachers with a road map to understanding the concepts of the Common Core State Standards. The content in each study guide is 100% curriculum aligned and serves as an excellent source of material for review and practice. The *SOLARO Study Guide* introduces students to a process that incorporates the building blocks upon which strong academic performance is based. To create this resource, teachers, curriculum specialists, and assessment experts have worked closely to develop instructional pieces that explain key concepts. Every exercise question comes with a detailed solution that offers problem-solving methods, highlights concepts that are likely to be tested, and points out potential sources of errors.

The *SOLARO Study Guide* is intended to be used for reviewing and understanding course content, to prepare for assessments, and to assist each student in achieving their best performance in school.

The *SOLARO Study Guide* consists of the following sections:

## TABLE OF CORRELATIONS

The Table of Correlations is a critical component of the *SOLARO Study Guide*.

Castle Rock Research has designed the *SOLARO Study Guide* by correlating each question and its solution to Common Core State Standards. Each unit begins with a Table of Correlations, which lists the standards and questions that correspond to those standards.

For students, the Table of Correlations provides information about how each question fits into a particular course and the standards to which each question is tied. Students can quickly access all relevant content associated with a particular standard.

For teachers, the Table of Correlations provides a road map for each standard, outlining the most granular and measurable concepts that are included in each standard. It assists teachers in understanding all the components involved in each standard and where students are excelling or require improvement. The Table of Correlations indicates the instructional focus for each content strand, serves as a standards checklist, and focuses on the standards and concepts that are most important in the unit and the particular course of study.

Some concepts may have a complete lesson aligned to them but cannot be assessed using a paper-and-pencil format. These concepts typically require ongoing classroom assessment through various other methods.

## LESSONS

Following the Table of Correlations for each unit are lessons aligned to each concept within a standard. The lessons explain key concepts that students are expected to learn according to Common Core State Standards. As each lesson is tied to state standards, students and teachers are assured that the information will be relevant to what is being covered in class.

## EXERCISE QUESTIONS

Each set of lessons is followed by two sets of exercise questions that assess students on their understanding of the content. These exercise questions can be used by students to give them an idea of the type of questions they are likely to face in the future in terms of format, difficulty, and content coverage.

## DETAILED SOLUTIONS

Some study guides only provide an answer key, which will identify the correct response but may not be helpful in determining what led to the incorrect answer. Every exercise question in the *SOLARO Study Guide* is accompanied by a detailed solution. Access to complete solutions greatly enhances a student's ability to work independently, and these solutions also serve as useful instructional tools for teachers. The level of information in each detailed solution is intended to help students better prepare for the future by learning from their mistakes and to help teachers discern individual areas of strengths and weaknesses.

For the complete curriculum document, visit www.corestandards.org/the-standards.

*SOLARO Study Guide*s are available for many courses. Check www.solaro.com/orders for a complete listing of books available for your area.

For more enhanced online resources, please visit www.SOLARO.com.

*Student-Oriented Learning, Assessment, and Reporting Online*

## solaro

SOLARO is an online resource that provides students with regionally and age-appropriate lessons and practice questions. Students can be confident that SOLARO has the right materials to help them when they are having difficulties in class. SOLARO is 100% compliant with each region's core standards. Teachers can use SOLARO in the classroom as a supplemental resource to provide remediation and enrichment. Student performance is reported to the teacher through various reports, which provide insight into strengths and weaknesses.

# TABLE OF CONTENTS

**KEY TIPS FOR BEING SUCCESSFUL AT SCHOOL** .................................................. 1
   Key Factors Contributing to School Success ........................................................ 2
   How to Find Your Learning Style ............................................................................ 3
   Scheduling Study Time ........................................................................................... 4
   Creating Study Notes .............................................................................................. 5
   Memorization Techniques ....................................................................................... 7
   Key Strategies for Reviewing .................................................................................. 7
   Key Strategies for Success: A Checklist ................................................................ 8

**CLASS FOCUS** .................................................................................................... 9
   **Table of Correlations** ........................................................................................ 10
   **Concepts** ........................................................................................................... 24
      Key Ideas and Details ...................................................................................... 24
      Craft and Structure .......................................................................................... 40
      Integration of Knowledge and Ideas ................................................................ 58
      Presentation of Knowledge and Ideas ............................................................. 76
      Comprehension and Collaboration .................................................................. 79
      Range of Reading ............................................................................................ 84
      Vocabulary Acquisition and Use ...................................................................... 89
      Fluency ........................................................................................................... 101
      Conventions of Standard English .................................................................... 110
      Knowledge of Language .................................................................................. 156
      Text Types and Purposes ............................................................................... 160
      Production and Distribution of Writing ............................................................. 239
      Research to Build and Present Knowledge .................................................... 260

**PRACTICE EXERCISES** ..................................................................................... 275
   **Table of Correlations** ........................................................................................ 276
   **Exercise #1—Reading Informational** ............................................................... 278
   **Table of Correlations** ........................................................................................ 300
   **Exercise #2—Reading Informational** ............................................................... 302
   **Table of Correlations** ........................................................................................ 322
   **Exercise #1—Reading Literature** ..................................................................... 324
   **Table of Correlations** ........................................................................................ 347
   **Exercise #2—Reading Literature** ..................................................................... 349
   **Table of Correlations** ........................................................................................ 372

Exercise #1—Language Arts .................................................................................................. 374
Exercise #1—Answers and Solutions—Reading Informational ................................. 384
Exercise #2—Answers and Solutions—Reading Informational ................................. 389
Exercise #1—Answers and Solutions—Reading Literature ........................................ 393
Exercise #2—Answers and Solutions—Reading Literature ........................................ 397
Exercise #1—Answers and Solutions—Language Arts ................................................ 401

## WRITING .................................................................................................................................. 405
Exercise #1—Writing ............................................................................................................... 406
Sample Responses—Writing Exercise #1 ........................................................................ 408
Exercise #2—Writing ............................................................................................................... 414
Sample Responses—Writing Exercise #2 ........................................................................ 416

## APPENDICES ........................................................................................................................... 423
Credits ........................................................................................................................................ 424

# Key Tips for Being Successful at School

# KEY TIPS FOR BEING SUCCESSFUL AT SCHOOL

## KEY FACTORS CONTRIBUTING TO SCHOOL SUCCESS

In addition to learning the content of your courses, there are some other things that you can do to help you do your best at school. You can try some of the following strategies:

- **Keep a positive attitude:** Always reflect on what you can already do and what you already know.

- **Be prepared to learn:** Have the necessary pencils, pens, notebooks, and other required materials for participating in class ready.

- **Complete all of your assignments:** Do your best to finish all of your assignments. Even if you know the material well, practice will reinforce your knowledge. If an assignment or question is difficult for you, work through it as far as you can so that your teacher can see exactly where you are having difficulty.

- **Set small goals for yourself when you are learning new material:** For example, when learning the parts of speech, do not try to learn everything in one night. Work on only one part or section each study session. When you have memorized one particular part of speech and understand it, move on to another one. Continue this process until you have memorized and learned all the parts of speech.

- **Review your classroom work regularly at home:** Review to make sure you understand the material you learned in class.

- **Ask your teacher for help:** Your teacher will help you if you do not understand something or if you are having a difficult time completing your assignments.

- **Get plenty of rest and exercise:** Concentrating in class is hard work. It is important to be well-rested and have time to relax and socialize with your friends. This helps you keep a positive attitude about your schoolwork.

- **Eat healthy meals:** A balanced diet keeps you healthy and gives you the energy you need for studying at school and at home.

## How to Find Your Learning Style

Every student learns differently. The manner in which you learn best is called your learning style. By knowing your learning style, you can increase your success at school. Most students use a combination of learning styles. Do you know what type of learner you are? Read the following descriptions. Which of these common learning styles do you use most often?

- **Linguistic Learner:** You may learn best by saying, hearing, and seeing words. You are probably really good at memorizing things such as dates, places, names, and facts. You may need to write down the steps in a process, a formula, or the actions that lead up to a significant event, and then say them out loud.

- **Spatial Learner:** You may learn best by looking at and working with pictures. You are probably really good at puzzles, imagining things, and reading maps and charts. You may need to use strategies like mind mapping and webbing to organize your information and study notes.

- **Kinesthetic Learner:** You may learn best by touching, moving, and figuring things out using manipulatives. You are probably really good at physical activities and learning through movement. You may need to draw your finger over a diagram to remember it, tap out the steps needed to solve a problem, or feel yourself writing or typing a formula.

## SCHEDULING STUDY TIME

You should review your class notes regularly to ensure that you have a clear understanding of all the new material you learned. Reviewing your lessons on a regular basis helps you to learn and remember ideas and concepts. It also reduces the quantity of material that you need to study prior to a test. Establishing a study schedule will help you to make the best use of your time.

Regardless of the type of study schedule you use, you may want to consider the following suggestions to maximize your study time and effort:

- Organize your work so that you begin with the most challenging material first.
- Divide the subject's content into small, manageable chunks.
- Alternate regularly between your different subjects and types of study activities in order to maintain your interest and motivation.
- Make a daily list with headings like "Must Do," "Should Do," and "Could Do."
- Begin each study session by quickly reviewing what you studied the day before.
- Maintain your usual routine of eating, sleeping, and exercising to help you concentrate better for extended periods of time.

# CREATING STUDY NOTES

## MIND-MAPPING OR WEBBING

Use the key words, ideas, or concepts from your class notes to create a mind map or web, which is a diagram or visual representation of the given information. A mind map or web is sometimes referred to as a knowledge map. Use the following steps to create a mind map or web:

1. Write the key word, concept, theory, or formula in the centre of your page.
2. Write down related facts, ideas, events, and information, and link them to the central concept with lines.
3. Use coloured markers, underlining, or symbols to emphasize things such as relationships, timelines, and important information.

The following mind map is an example of one that could help you develop an essay:

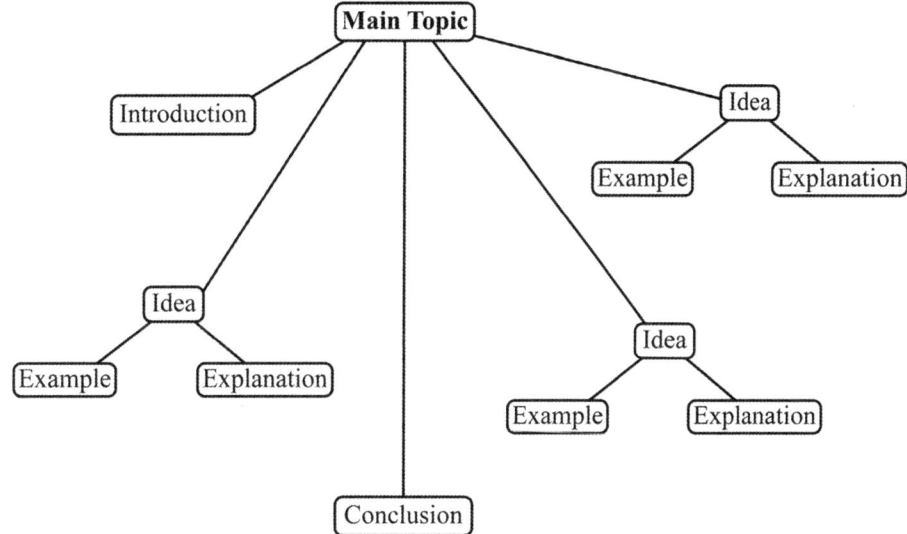

**INDEX CARDS**

To use index cards while studying, follow these steps:

1. Write a key word or question on one side of an index card.
2. On the reverse side, write the definition of the word, answer to the question, or any other important information that you want to remember.

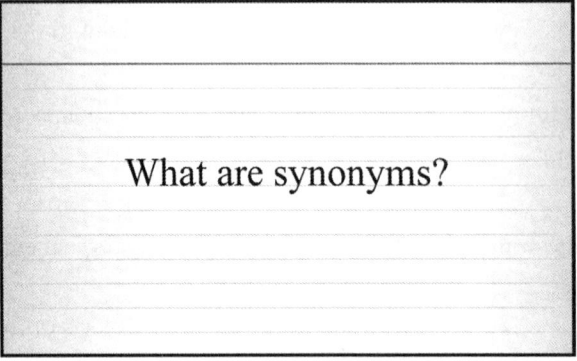

**SYMBOLS AND STICKY NOTES—IDENTIFYING IMPORTANT INFORMATION**

Use symbols to mark your class notes. The following are some examples:

- An exclamation mark (!) might be used to point out something that must be learned well because it is a very important idea.
- A question mark (?) may highlight something you are not certain about
- A diamond (◊) or asterisk (*) could highlight interesting information that you want to remember.

Sticky notes are useful in the following situations:

- Use sticky notes when you are not allowed to put marks in books.
- Use sticky notes to mark a page in a book that contains an important diagram, formula, explanation, or other information.
- Use sticky notes to mark important facts in research books.

## MEMORIZATION TECHNIQUES

- **Association** relates new learning to something you already know. For example, to remember the spelling difference between dessert and desert, recall that the word *sand* has only one *s*. So, because there is sand in a desert, the word *desert* has only one *s*.

- **Mnemonic** devices are sentences that you create to remember a list or group of items. For example, the first letter of each word in the phrase "Every Good Boy Deserves Fudge" helps you to remember the names of the lines on the treble-clef staff (E, G, B, D, and F) in music.

- **Acronyms** are words that are formed from the first letters or parts of the words in a group. For example, RADAR is actually an acronym for Radio Detecting and Ranging, and MASH is an acronym for Mobile Army Surgical Hospital. HOMES helps you to remember the names of the five Great Lakes (Huron, Ontario, Michigan, Erie, and Superior).

- **Visualizing** requires you to use your mind's eye to "see" a chart, list, map, diagram, or sentence as it is in your textbook or notes, on the chalkboard or computer screen, or in a display.

- **Initialisms** are abbreviations that are formed from the first letters or parts of the words in a group. Unlike acronyms, an initialism cannot be pronounced as a word itself. For example, GCF is an initialism for **G**reatest **C**ommon **F**actor.

## KEY STRATEGIES FOR REVIEWING

Reviewing textbook material, class notes, and handouts should be an ongoing activity. Spending time reviewing becomes more critical when you are preparing for a test. You may find some of the following review strategies useful when studying during your scheduled study time:

- Before reading a selection, preview it by noting the headings, charts, graphs, and chapter questions.

- Before reviewing a unit, note the headings, charts, graphs, and chapter questions.

- Highlight key concepts, vocabulary, definitions, and formulas.

- Skim the paragraph, and note the key words, phrases, and information.

- Carefully read over each step in a procedure.

- Draw a picture or diagram to help make the concept clearer.

## KEY STRATEGIES FOR SUCCESS: A CHECKLIST

Reviewing is a huge part of doing well at school and preparing for tests. Here is a checklist for you to keep track of how many suggested strategies for success you are using. Read each question, and put a check mark (✓) in the correct column. Look at the questions where you have checked the "No" column. Think about how you might try using some of these strategies to help you do your best at school.

| Key Strategies for Success | Yes | No |
|---|---|---|
| Do you attend school regularly? | | |
| Do you know your personal learning style—how you learn best? | | |
| Do you spend 15 to 30 minutes a day reviewing your notes? | | |
| Do you study in a quiet place at home? | | |
| Do you clearly mark the most important ideas in your study notes? | | |
| Do you use sticky notes to mark texts and research books? | | |
| Do you practise answering multiple-choice and written-response questions? | | |
| Do you ask your teacher for help when you need it? | | |
| Are you maintaining a healthy diet and sleep routine? | | |
| Are you participating in regular physical activity? | | |

Class Focus

# CLASS FOCUS

## Table of Correlations

| Standard | | Concepts | Page |
|---|---|---|---|
| 5RL | Reading Standards for Literature | | |
| 5RL.1 | Quote accurately from a text when explaining what the text says explicitly and when drawing inferences from the text. | Quoting Information From Print | 24 |
| 5RL.2 | Determine a theme of a story, drama, or poem from details in the text, including how characters in a story or drama respond to challenges or how the speaker in a poem reflects upon a topic; summarize the text. | Summarizing Text after Reading | 27 |
| | | Recognize a Theme within a Text | 29 |
| | | Understand How A Situation Causes Character's Actions | 33 |
| | | How Setting Causes a Character's Actions | 34 |
| | | Understand How Traits Cause Character's Actions | 34 |
| | | How Motivations Cause a Character's Actions | 35 |
| | | How Poetry Achieves an Author's Purpose | 36 |
| | | Demonstrate an Understanding of the Main Idea within a Text | 64 |
| | | Identifying the Main Idea and Supporting Details | 65 |
| 5RL.3 | Compare and contrast two or more characters, settings, or events in a story or drama, drawing on specific details in the text. | Compare and Contrast Information | 38 |
| 5RL.4 | Determine the meaning of words and phrases as they are used in a text, including figurative language such as metaphors and similes. | What is a Metaphor? | 40 |
| | | What is a Simile? | 41 |
| | | Figurative Language | 42 |
| 5RL.5 | Explain how a series of chapters, scenes, or stanzas fits together to provide the overall structure of a particular story, drama, or poem. | Locating Chapters within a Text | 44 |
| | | What Is A Play? | 47 |
| | | What Is a Novel? | 48 |
| | | What Is Poetry? | 49 |
| | | Identify Sequential/Chronological Pattern in Text | 69 |
| | | Proposition and Support | 70 |
| 5RL.6 | Describe how a narrator's or speaker's point of view influences how events are described. | What Is Point of View? | 51 |
| | | Identifying the Speaker or Narrator in a Text | 55 |
| 5RL.7 | Analyze how visual and multimedia elements contribute to the meaning, tone, or beauty of a text. | The Purpose of Visual and Graphic Materials | 58 |

| | | | |
|---|---|---|---|
| | | How Format Makes Information Accessible | 72 |
| | | How Graphics Make Information Accessible | 74 |
| | | How Sequence Makes Information Accessible | 76 |
| | | How Diagrams Make Information Accessible | 77 |
| | | How Illustrations Make Information Accessible | 77 |
| | | Asking and Answering Questions to Convey Information | 79 |
| 5RL.9 | Compare and contrast stories in the same genre on their approaches to similar themes and topics. | Compare and Contrast Information | 38 |
| | | How Authors Develop Themes | 59 |
| | | Compare Information on One Topic from Many Sources | 60 |
| | | Contrast Information on One Topic From Many Sources | 60 |
| 5RL.10 | By the end of the year, read and comprehend literature, including stories, dramas, and poetry, at the high end of the grades 4–5 text complexity band independently and proficiently. | What Is A Play? | 47 |
| | | What Is a Novel? | 48 |
| | | What Is Poetry? | 49 |
| | | What is a Myth? | 62 |
| | | What is a Legend? | 62 |
| | | What is a Fantasy? | 63 |
| | | What Is Fiction? | 64 |
| 5RI | Reading Standards for Informational Text | | |
| 5RI.1 | Quote accurately from a text when explaining what the text says explicitly and when drawing inferences from the text. | Quoting Information From Print | 24 |
| 5RI.2 | Determine two or more main ideas of a text and explain how they are supported by key details; summarize the text. | Summarizing Text after Reading | 27 |
| | | Recognize a Theme within a Text | 29 |
| | | Understand How A Situation Causes Character's Actions | 33 |
| | | How Setting Causes a Character's Actions | 34 |
| | | Understand How Traits Cause Character's Actions | 34 |
| | | How Motivations Cause a Character's Actions | 35 |
| | | How Poetry Achieves an Author's Purpose | 36 |

|  |  | Demonstrate an Understanding of the Main Idea within a Text | 64 |
|---|---|---|---|
|  |  | Identifying the Main Idea and Supporting Details | 65 |
| 5RI.3 | Explain the relationships or interactions between two or more individuals, events, ideas, or concepts in a historical, scientific, or technical text based on specific information in the text. | Compare and Contrast Information | 38 |
| 5RI.4 | Determine the meaning of general academic and domain-specific words and phrases in a text relevant to a grade 5 topic or subject area. | What is a Metaphor? | 40 |
|  |  | What is a Simile? | 41 |
|  |  | Figurative Language | 42 |
|  |  | Understand Content-Specific Vocabulary | 68 |
| 5RI.5 | Compare and contrast the overall structure of events, ideas, concepts, or information in two or more texts. | Locating Chapters within a Text | 44 |
|  |  | Identify a Compare/Contrast Pattern in Informational Text | 69 |
|  |  | Identify Sequential/Chronological Pattern in Text | 69 |
|  |  | Proposition and Support | 70 |
|  |  | Identifying Cause-and-Effect Patterns in Informational Text | 71 |
| 5RI.6 | Analyze multiple accounts of the same event or topic, noting important similarities and differences in the point of view they represent. | What Is Point of View? | 51 |
|  |  | Identifying the Speaker or Narrator in a Text | 55 |
|  |  | Compare Information on One Topic from Many Sources | 60 |
|  |  | Contrast Information on One Topic From Many Sources | 60 |
| 5RI.7 | Draw on information from multiple print or digital sources, demonstrating the ability to locate an answer to a question quickly or to solve a problem efficiently. | The Purpose of Visual and Graphic Materials | 58 |
|  |  | How Format Makes Information Accessible | 72 |
|  |  | How Graphics Make Information Accessible | 74 |
|  |  | How Sequence Makes Information Accessible | 76 |
|  |  | How Diagrams Make Information Accessible | 77 |
|  |  | How Illustrations Make Information Accessible | 77 |
|  |  | Asking and Answering Questions to Convey Information | 79 |

| 5RI.8 | Explain how an author uses reasons and evidence to support particular points in a text, identifying which reasons and evidence support which point(s). | Identify Evidence that Supports the Main Ideas in a Text | 81 |
|---|---|---|---|
| 5RI.9 | Integrate information from several texts on the same topic in order to write or speak about the subject knowledgeably. | Compare and Contrast Information | 38 |
| | | How Authors Develop Themes | 59 |
| | | Compare Information on One Topic from Many Sources | 60 |
| | | Contrast Information on One Topic From Many Sources | 60 |
| | | Combine Information from More than One Source | 79 |
| 5RI.10 | By the end of the year, read and comprehend informational texts, including history/social studies, science, and technical texts, at the high end of the grades 4–5 text complexity band independently and proficiently. | What Is Non-Fiction? | 84 |
| | | Media Texts | 86 |
| **5RF** | **Reading Standards: Foundational Skills** | | |
| 5RF.3a | Know and apply grade-level phonics and word analysis skills in decoding words. Use combined knowledge of all letter-sound correspondences, syllabication patterns, and morphology to read accurately unfamiliar multisyllabic words in context... | Using Context to Understand Unfamiliar Words | 89 |
| | | Using Inferencing to Understand Unfamiliar Words | 91 |
| | | Understanding Words by Finding Familiar Words Within Unknown Words | 92 |
| | | Using Prefixes and Suffixes to Understand New Words | 95 |
| | | Using the "Does it Make Sense" Strategy to Understand Text | 98 |
| | | Use Phonetic Knowledge to Figure Out Words | 99 |
| | | What are Homograph Words? | 180 |
| 5RF.4a | Read with sufficient accuracy and fluency to support comprehension. Read on-level text with purpose and understanding. | Read Aloud Fluently | 101 |
| | | Read Aloud Accurately | 102 |
| | | Using Appropriate Strategies for Full Comprehension | 103 |
| 5RF.4b | Read with sufficient accuracy and fluency to support comprehension. Read on-level prose and poetry orally with accuracy, appropriate rate, and expression on successive readings. | Read Aloud Fluently | 101 |
| | | Read Aloud Accurately | 102 |
| | | Using Appropriate Strategies for Full Comprehension | 103 |
| | | Read Aloud with Appropriate Pacing | 104 |

| | | Read Aloud with Appropriate Intonation | 106 |
|---|---|---|---|
| | | Read Aloud With Appropriate Expression | 107 |
| 5RF.4c | *Read with sufficient accuracy and fluency to support comprehension. Use context to confirm or self-correct word recognition and understanding, rereading as necessary.* | Using Context to Understand Unfamiliar Words | 89 |
| | | Using the "Does it Make Sense" Strategy to Understand Text | 98 |
| | | Using Appropriate Strategies for Full Comprehension | 103 |
| | | Using the Re-Read Strategy to Determine Unfamiliar Words | 109 |
| **5W** | **Writing Standards** | | |
| 5W.1a | *Write opinion pieces on topics or texts, supporting a point of view with reasons and information. Introduce a topic or text clearly, state an opinion, and create an organizational structure in which ideas are logically grouped to support the...* | Create a Written Piece to Convince | 207 |
| | | Create an Introductory Paragraph | 208 |
| | | Use Similarities and Differences to Convey Information | 209 |
| | | Use Chronological Order for Conveying Information | 236 |
| | | Use Cause and Effect for Conveying Information | 238 |
| 5W.1b | *Write opinion pieces on topics or texts, supporting a point of view with reasons and information. Provide logically ordered reasons that are supported by facts and details.* | How Sequence Makes Information Accessible | 76 |
| | | Create a Written Piece to Convince | 207 |
| | | Create Support Paragraphs with Facts, Details, and Explanations | 210 |
| 5W.1c | *Write opinion pieces on topics or texts, supporting a point of view with reasons and information. Link opinion and reasons using words, phrases, and clauses.* | Combining Sentences Using Participial Phrases | 160 |
| | | Combining Sentences with Prepositional Phrases | 164 |
| | | Create a Written Piece to Convince | 207 |
| | | Use Connecting Words to Link Ideas in Sentences | 211 |
| | | Develop Sentence Fluency | 212 |
| 5W.1d | *Write opinion pieces on topics or texts, supporting a point of view with reasons and information. Provide a concluding statement or section related to the opinion presented.* | Create a Written Piece to Convince | 207 |
| | | Create a Concluding Paragraph That Summarizes Main Points | 213 |

Class Focus — Castle Rock Research

| | | | |
|---|---|---|---|
| 5W.2a | Write informative/explanatory texts to examine a topic and convey ideas and information clearly. Introduce a topic clearly, provide a general observation and focus, and group related information logically; include formatting, illustrations, and... | How Format Makes Information Accessible | 72 |
| | | How Illustrations Make Information Accessible | 77 |
| | | Create an Introductory Paragraph | 208 |
| | | Use Similarities and Differences to Convey Information | 209 |
| | | Revising Your Non-Fiction Writing Piece to Provide Focus | 214 |
| | | Create a Written Piece to Inform | 216 |
| | | Create a Written Piece to Explain | 217 |
| | | Use Chronological Order for Conveying Information | 236 |
| | | Use Cause and Effect for Conveying Information | 238 |
| 5W.2b | Write informative/explanatory texts to examine a topic and convey ideas and information clearly. Develop the topic with facts, definitions, concrete details, quotations, or other information and examples related to the topic. | Create Support Paragraphs with Facts, Details, and Explanations | 210 |
| | | Create a Written Piece to Inform | 216 |
| | | Create a Written Piece to Explain | 217 |
| | | Including Details | 218 |
| 5W.2c | Write informative/explanatory texts to examine a topic and convey ideas and information clearly. Link ideas within and across categories of information using words, phrases, and clauses. | Combining Sentences Using Participial Phrases | 160 |
| | | Combining Sentences with Prepositional Phrases | 164 |
| | | Use Connecting Words to Link Ideas in Sentences | 211 |
| | | Develop Sentence Fluency | 212 |
| | | Create a Written Piece to Inform | 216 |
| | | Create a Written Piece to Explain | 217 |
| 5W.2d | Write informative/explanatory texts to examine a topic and convey ideas and information clearly. Use precise language and domain-specific vocabulary to inform about or explain the topic. | Create a Written Piece to Inform | 216 |
| | | Create a Written Piece to Explain | 217 |
| | | Use Content-Specific Vocabulary in your Writing | 219 |
| | | Choose Precise Words for Writing Tasks | 221 |
| 5W.2e | Write informative/explanatory texts to examine a topic and convey ideas and information clearly. Provide a concluding statement or section related to the information or explanation presented. | Create a Concluding Paragraph That Summarizes Main Points | 213 |
| | | Create a Written Piece to Inform | 216 |
| | | Create a Written Piece to Explain | 217 |

| | | | |
|---|---|---|---|
| 5W.3a | Write narratives to develop real or imagined experiences or events using effective technique, descriptive details, and clear event sequences. Orient the reader by establishing a situation and introducing a narrator and/or characters; organize... | Identifying the Speaker or Narrator in a Text | 55 |
| | | Create a Story with a Logical Sequence | 222 |
| | | Create a Story with Relationships between Characters and Plot | 224 |
| | | Narrative-Descriptive Writing | 227 |
| 5W.3b | Write narratives to develop real or imagined experiences or events using effective technique, descriptive details, and clear event sequences. Use narrative techniques, such as dialogue, description, and pacing, to develop experiences and events... | Understand How A Situation Causes Character's Actions | 33 |
| | | Narrative-Descriptive Writing | 227 |
| | | Write a Story Beginning that has Action | 227 |
| | | Create a Story Beginning Using Dialogue | 228 |
| 5W.3c | Write narratives to develop real or imagined experiences or events using effective technique, descriptive details, and clear event sequences. Use a variety of transitional words, phrases, and clauses to manage the sequence of events. | Create a Story with a Logical Sequence | 222 |
| 5W.3d | Write narratives to develop real or imagined experiences or events using effective technique, descriptive details, and clear event sequences. Use concrete words and phrases and sensory details to convey experiences and events precisely. | Narrative-Descriptive Writing | 227 |
| | | Create Narratives to Relate Ideas, Observations, Recollections | 230 |
| | | Create Narratives that Use Concrete Sensory Details | 231 |
| | | Create Narratives to Provide Insight About Memorable Experiences | 232 |
| 5W.3e | Write narratives to develop real or imagined experiences or events using effective technique, descriptive details, and clear event sequences. Provide a conclusion that follows from the narrated experiences or events. | Narrative-Descriptive Writing | 227 |
| | | Ending a Story with a Whole Story Reminder | 234 |
| | | Create an Ending for a Multi-Paragraph Narrative Composition | 234 |
| 5W.4 | Produce clear and coherent writing in which the development and organization are appropriate to task, purpose, and audience. | Select a Paragraph Focus Based on Purpose | 239 |
| | | Select a Paragraph Focus Based on Audience | 240 |
| | | Paragraph Focus Based on Format Requirements | 240 |
| | | Set a Purpose for Writing | 242 |

| | | | |
|---|---|---|---|
| 5W.5 | With guidance and support from peers and adults, develop and strengthen writing as needed by planning, revising, editing, rewriting, or trying a new approach. | Revising Your Non-Fiction Writing Piece to Provide Focus | 214 |
| | | Thinking of a Story Topic | 243 |
| | | Using a Checklist to Edit your Story | 245 |
| | | Generating Ideas For A Non-Fiction Topic Using A Word Web | 247 |
| | | Generating Ideas for a Non-Fiction Topic Using the KWL Chart | 249 |
| | | Generating Ideas for a Non-Fiction Topic Using Mind Mapping | 250 |
| | | Using A Checklist to Edit your Non-Fiction Writing | 253 |
| | | Revise Your Non-Fiction Writing to Expand on Relevant Ideas | 256 |
| | | Use the Appropriate Graphic Organizer to Sort Information | 257 |
| | | Use Knowledge of a Rubric to Enhance Writing | 258 |
| 5W.6 | With some guidance and support from adults, use technology, including the Internet, to produce and publish writing as well as to interact and collaborate with others; demonstrate sufficient command of keyboarding skills to type a minimum... | Use Electronic Dictionaries and Thesauruses | 260 |
| 5W.8 | Recall relevant information from experiences or gather relevant information from print and digital sources; summarize or paraphrase information in notes and finished work, and provide a list of sources. | Use the Appropriate Graphic Organizer to Sort Information | 257 |
| | | What is a Bibliography? | 261 |
| | | Create a Bibliography | 262 |
| | | Gather Facts using Primary Resources | 263 |
| | | Gather Facts Using Secondary Resources | 263 |
| | | Analyze Details and Information from Reference Material | 264 |
| 5W.9a | Draw evidence from literary or informational texts to support analysis, reflection, and research. Apply grade 5 Reading standards to literature. | Making Inferences While Reading | 266 |
| | | Making Inferences About Characters | 266 |
| | | Supporting Generalizations about Text with Textual Evidence | 268 |

| | | Supporting Conclusions about Text with Textual Evidence | 268 |
|---|---|---|---|
| *5W.9b* | *Draw evidence from literary or informational texts to support analysis, reflection, and research. Apply grade 5 Reading standards to informational texts.* | Identify Evidence that Supports the Main Ideas in a Text | 81 |
| | | Supporting Generalizations about Text with Textual Evidence | 268 |
| | | Supporting Conclusions about Text with Textual Evidence | 268 |
| *5W.10* | *Write routinely over extended time frames (time for research, reflection, and revision) and shorter time frames (a single sitting or a day or two) for a range of discipline-specific tasks, purposes, and audiences.* | Select a Paragraph Focus Based on Purpose | 239 |
| | | Select a Paragraph Focus Based on Audience | 240 |
| | | Set a Purpose for Writing | 242 |
| **5SL** | **Speaking and Listening Standards** | | |
| *5SL.1a* | *Engage effectively in a range of collaborative discussions (one-on-one, in groups, and teacherled) with diverse partners on grade 5 topics and texts, building on others' ideas and expressing their own clearly. Come to discussions prepared...* | Working in a Group: Adding Your Part to a Discussion | 188 |
| | | Making a Class Plan to Get Information | 189 |
| *5SL.1b* | *Engage effectively in a range of collaborative discussions (one-on-one, in groups, and teacherled) with diverse partners on grade 5 topics and texts, building on others' ideas and expressing their own clearly. Follow agreed-upon rules...* | Use Questioning for Communicating | 191 |
| | | Clarifying Meaning in a Group Discussion | 192 |
| | | Working with Others by Negotiating | 194 |
| | | Working With Others: Compromising | 195 |
| | | Working in a Group: The Presenter Role | 196 |
| *5SL.1c* | *Engage effectively in a range of collaborative discussions (one-on-one, in groups, and teacherled) with diverse partners on grade 5 topics and texts, building on others' ideas and expressing their own clearly. Pose and respond to...* | Asking and Answering Questions to Convey Information | 79 |
| | | Working in a Group: Adding Your Part to a Discussion | 188 |
| | | Use Questioning for Communicating | 191 |
| | | Make and Share Connections when Interacting with Others | 197 |
| *5SL.1d* | *Engage effectively in a range of collaborative discussions (one-on-one, in groups, and teacherled) with diverse partners on grade 5 topics and texts, building on others' ideas and expressing their own clearly. Review the key ideas...* | Working in a Group: Reflecting | 198 |

| | | | |
|---|---|---|---|
| 5SL.2 | *Summarize a written text read aloud or information presented in diverse media and formats, including visually, quantitatively, and orally.* | Summarizing Text after Reading | 27 |
| 5SL.3 | *Summarize the points a speaker makes and explain how each claim is supported by reasons and evidence.* | Summarizing Text after Reading | 27 |
| | | Identify Evidence that Supports the Main Ideas in a Text | 81 |
| 5SL.4 | *Report on a topic or text or present an opinion, sequencing ideas logically and using appropriate facts and relevant, descriptive details to support main ideas or themes; speak clearly at an understandable pace.* | How Sequence Makes Information Accessible | 76 |
| | | Read Aloud Accurately | 102 |
| | | Read Aloud with Appropriate Pacing | 104 |
| | | State a Position in Support of a Proposal | 199 |
| | | Support a Position with Relevant Evidence | 200 |
| | | Create a Written Piece to Convince | 207 |
| | | Create Support Paragraphs with Facts, Details, and Explanations | 210 |
| 5SL.5 | *Include multimedia components and visual displays in presentations when appropriate to enhance the development of main ideas or themes.* | Use Visuals to Engage an Audience | 201 |
| | | Use Visuals to Sustain an Audience Throughout a Presentation | 202 |
| | | Use Visuals to Engage an Audience at the End of a Presentation | 203 |
| | | Use Audio to Engage an Audience | 203 |
| 5SL.6 | *Adapt speech to a variety of contexts and tasks, using formal English when appropriate to task and situation.* | Demonstrate Voice Through Word Choice | 205 |
| | | Understand Language Appropriate for Variety of Contexts | 206 |
| **5L** | Language Standards | | |
| 5L.1a | *Demonstrate command of the conventions of standard English grammar and usage when writing or speaking. Explain the function of conjunctions, prepositions, and interjections in general and their function in particular sentences.* | Identify Common Conjunctions | 110 |
| | | Using Conjunctions in Your Writing | 111 |
| | | Identifying Prepositions | 112 |
| | | Using Prepositions In Your Writing | 114 |

| | | | |
|---|---|---|---|
| 5L.1b | Demonstrate command of the conventions of standard English grammar and usage when writing or speaking. Form and use the perfect verb tenses. | What are Verb Tenses? | 115 |
| | | Using Appropriate Verb Tenses in your Writing | 117 |
| 5L.1c | Demonstrate command of the conventions of standard English grammar and usage when writing or speaking. Use verb tense to convey various times, sequences, states, and conditions. | What are Verb Tenses? | 115 |
| | | Using Appropriate Verb Tenses in your Writing | 117 |
| | | What is a Verb? | 119 |
| | | How Do I Use a Verb Properly in my Writing? | 120 |
| | | Identify Correct Subject-Verb Agreement | 121 |
| | | Use Correct Subject-Verb Agreement | 122 |
| | | What is an Irregular Verb? | 123 |
| | | Using Irregular Verbs in Your Writing | 124 |
| | | Correctly Use Verbs (lie/lay;sit/set) | 125 |
| 5L.1d | Demonstrate command of the conventions of standard English grammar and usage when writing or speaking. Recognize and correct inappropriate shifts in verb tense. | Editing Your Work for the Proper Verb Tenses | 127 |
| | | Editing Your Non-Fiction Work for the Appropriate Verb Tenses | 129 |
| 5L.1e | Demonstrate command of the conventions of standard English grammar and usage when writing or speaking. Use correlative conjunctions. | Identify Common Conjunctions | 110 |
| | | Using Conjunctions in Your Writing | 111 |
| 5L.2a | Demonstrate command of the conventions of standard English capitalization, punctuation, and spelling when writing. Use punctuation to separate items in a series. | Use Commas in a List | 131 |
| | | Using a Colon to Introduce a List | 132 |
| 5L.2b | Demonstrate command of the conventions of standard English capitalization, punctuation, and spelling when writing. Use a comma to separate an introductory element from the rest of the sentence. | Identify Commas Following Introductory Words | 133 |
| | | Use Commas in Introductory Words | 134 |
| 5L.2c | Demonstrate command of the conventions of standard English capitalization, punctuation, and spelling when writing. Use a comma to set off the words yes and no, to set off a tag question from the rest of the sentence, and to indicate direct address. | Identify Commas Following Introductory Words | 133 |
| | | Use Commas in Introductory Words | 134 |
| | | Identify Commas Between Describing Words | 135 |
| | | Use Commas Between Describing Words | 135 |
| | | Using Commas in Direct Quotations | 136 |

Class Focus       Castle Rock Research

| 5L.2d | Demonstrate command of the conventions of standard English capitalization, punctuation, and spelling when writing. Use underlining, quotation marks, or italics to indicate titles of works. | Quotation Marks to Show a Title in Writing | 138 |
|---|---|---|---|
| | | Use Quotation Marks to Show a Title in Writing | 139 |
| | | Using Underlining to Identify Titles of Documents | 140 |
| | | Using Italics to Identify Titles of Documents in Your Writing | 141 |
| 5L.2e | Demonstrate command of the conventions of standard English capitalization, punctuation, and spelling when writing. Spell grade-appropriate words correctly, consulting references as needed. | Spell Correctly One-Syllable Words that have Blends | 142 |
| | | Spell Correctly One-Syllable Words that have Contractions | 143 |
| | | Spell Two-Syllable Compound Words Correctly | 144 |
| | | Spell Correctly One-Syllable Words with Orthographic Patterns | 145 |
| | | Spell Correctly One-Syllable words that are Common Homophones | 146 |
| | | Spell Root Words Correctly | 146 |
| | | Spelling Inflections Correctly | 148 |
| | | Spell Suffixes Correctly | 150 |
| | | Spell Prefixes Correctly | 151 |
| | | Correctly Spell Syllable Constructions | 152 |
| | | How to Use a Dictionary | 153 |
| | | How to Use a Thesaurus | 155 |
| 5L.3a | Use knowledge of language and its conventions when writing, speaking, reading, or listening. Expand, combine, and reduce sentences for meaning, reader/listener interest, and style. | Use a Variety of Sentence Beginnings | 156 |
| | | Use a Variety of Sentence Lengths in your Writing | 157 |
| | | Combining Short Related Sentences With Appositives | 158 |
| | | Combining Sentences Using Participial Phrases | 160 |
| | | Combining Sentences With Adjectives | 162 |
| | | Combining Sentences with Adverbs | 163 |
| | | Combining Sentences with Prepositional Phrases | 164 |

| | | | |
|---|---|---|---|
| 5L.3b | Use knowledge of language and its conventions when writing, speaking, reading, or listening. Compare and contrast the varieties of English used in stories, dramas, or poems. | Compare and Contrast Information | 38 |
| 5L.4a | Determine or clarify the meaning of unknown and multiple-meaning words and phrases based on grade 5 reading and content, choosing flexibly from a range of strategies. Use context as a clue to the meaning of a word or phrase. | Using Context to Understand Unfamiliar Words | 89 |
| | | Using the "Does it Make Sense" Strategy to Understand Text | 98 |
| 5L.4b | Determine or clarify the meaning of unknown and multiple-meaning words and phrases based on grade 5 reading and content, choosing flexibly from a range of strategies. Use common, grade-appropriate Greek and Latin affixes and roots as clues to the... | What are Word Origins? | 167 |
| | | Define Unfamiliar Words Using Word Origins | 167 |
| 5L.4c | Determine or clarify the meaning of unknown and multiple-meaning words and phrases based on grade 5 reading and content, choosing flexibly from a range of strategies. Consult reference materials, both print and digital, to find the... | Using a Thesaurus to Determine the Meaning of an Unfamiliar Word | 169 |
| | | Using a Dictionary to Determine Unfamiliar Words | 170 |
| | | Using a Picture Dictionary to Determine an Unfamiliar Word | 172 |
| | | Using a Glossary to Determine an Unfamiliar Word | 172 |
| 5L.5a | Demonstrate understanding of figurative language, word relationships, and nuances in word meanings. Interpret figurative language, including similes and metaphors, in context. | Understand Figurative use of Words in Context | 173 |
| | | Explain Figurative use of Words in Context | 174 |
| | | Evaluate Influence of Figurative Language on Readers | 175 |
| 5L.5b | Demonstrate understanding of figurative language, word relationships, and nuances in word meanings. Recognize and explain the meaning of common idioms, adages, and proverbs. | What Are Idioms? | 178 |
| | | Demonstrate Knowledge of Idioms | 179 |
| 5L.5c | Demonstrate understanding of figurative language, word relationships, and nuances in word meanings. Use the relationship between particular words to better understand each of the words. | What are Homograph Words? | 180 |
| | | Demonstrate Knowledge of Homograph Words | 181 |
| | | What are Synonym Words? | 183 |
| | | Demonstrate Knowledge of Synonym Words | 184 |
| | | What are Antonym Words? | 185 |
| | | Demonstrate Knowledge of Antonym Words | 186 |

| 5L.6 | Acquire and use accurately grade-appropriate general academic and domain-specific words and phrases, including those that signal contrast, addition, and other logical relationships. | Understand Content-Specific Vocabulary | 68 |
| --- | --- | --- | --- |
| | | Use Content-Specific Vocabulary in your Writing | 219 |
| | | Choose Precise Words for Writing Tasks | 221 |

*5RL.1  Quote accurately from a text when explaining what the text says explicitly and when drawing inferences from the text.*

## Quoting Information From Print

Quoting information from another source is important. When you quote another's words, information, or ideas, you are informing others that you are using someone else's original statement, or use of words, to support your own work.

A **direct quotation** uses the exact words of another author or source and must be identified in your own writing.

There are two types of direct quotes that you may use. A **short quote** (less than four lines long) or a **long quote** (more than four lines long).

Let's look at some examples of the two different types.

## Short Quotes

A short quote must be shown in your text through the use of quotation marks. The quotation marks begin at the start of the direct quote and end after the quote.

*Example*
Macy, the head owner for Rick's Superstore, was excited to find that "the success of the company is run on good energy and positive team work" (299).

---

Notice in this short quote, the period does not fall within the quotation marks, but rather, comes at the end of the sentence, after the bracket.

### What are the brackets for?

The brackets and the number inside the brackets state what page number the quote can be found on, in the text you are quoting from.

**Please Note:** If you need information about the format for quoting each individual text and how to put them in a list for quoting purposes at the end of your project, you need to search a new lesson regarding making a bibliography or a reference list.

Let's look at another short quote example.

Mark Johansson laments, "We will not be free until we start looking at who we truly are, and where we truly want to go" (45).

Not for Reproduction

## Long Quotes

Long quotes are more than four lines long. When this is the case, you do not use quotation marks to indicate the quote. Instead you set it off from the rest of the text by indenting the quote. You must also indicate the beginning of the long quote by using a colon.

Let's look below for an example.

*Example*

Elliot Johns sums up the company meeting, that determined the fate of many, in the following passage, as he compares the drama which occurred that day to that of a jungle:

> The people were on the edge of their seats like a tiger ready to pounce on its prey. Anything might set them off. Nobody knew what to expect, or what was going to come next. The entertaining monkeys, the big guns of the company, were on one side of the table, confident they would still be having a good time swinging from the rooftops, after the meeting was finished. Everything always seemed to go their way. Then there were the kangaroos, the people who were bouncing all over the place because no one ever knew whose side they were on, or whose side they might take. Then there were the meek birds at the end of the table, nervous as ever as to how this final meeting would go. Would they be joining a new flock or flying as fast as they could out of here? The boardroom jungle was full of intense energy, and we were all just waiting for the Lion King to arrive to determine everyone's fate.
>
>

## It's Your Turn

Which of the following quotes are being properly presented? Once you think you know, check the answers below.

*Try This!*

1. Marsha was always excited to see her parents when they came to visit and she was always saying, "My parents are the absolute best. When they visit, its always a great time with tons of shopping trips and good chats. Where would I be really, without my parents? They are everything to me" (78).
2. Nicholas won a tennis match in Santa Barbara and, smiling after the win, he was quoted saying, "It was a tough one. I fought hard and long. The battle was great but the victory was even greater." (45)

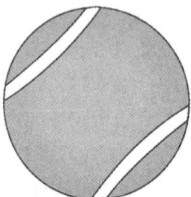

3. Never mind the childish games that the junior high students were playing, the teacher was a wreck. "Never have I felt so disrespected in all my years. I only want the best for my students but they are not understanding that I need them to work" (12).

How do you think you did? Were you able to identify which short quotes are properly done? If so, check your answers below.

Numbers 1 and 3 are quoted properly. Number 2 is not.

In numbers 1 and 3, the quotation marks are in the right place, the brackets and the numbers are in the right place, and the only period that is used, is at the end of the entire sentence, after the bracket. There is no period before the final quotation mark, which is correct.

Have a look.

1. Marsha was always excited to see her parents when they came to visit and she was always saying, "My parents are the absolute best. When they visit, its always a great time with tons of shopping trips and good chats. Where would I be really, without my parents? They are everything to me" **(78)**.
3. Never mind the childish games that the junior high students were playing, the teacher was a wreck. "Never have I felt so disrespected in all my years. I only want the best for my students but they are not understanding that I need them to work" **(12)**.

In number 2, there was a period incorrectly placed before the final quotation mark. There should be no period there. The period only falls at the end of the entire sentence, after the final bracket, that encloses the page number. Highlighted is the incorrect period.

2. Nicholas won a tennis match in Santa Barbara and smiling after the win he was quoted saying, "It was a tough one. I fought hard and long. The battle was great but the victory was even greater." (45).

*5SL.3  Summarize the points a speaker makes and explain how each claim is supported by reasons and evidence.*

*5RL.2  Determine a theme of a story, drama, or poem from details in the text, including how characters in a story or drama respond to challenges or how the speaker in a poem reflects upon a topic; summarize the text.*

## Summarizing Text after Reading

When you summarize a text, you give a shortened version of it in your own words. You need to be sure that you have the main idea and the important supporting details so that you can recall (remember) the information. There are many ways to organize ideas from a text.

You can use:

- Classification—grouping the same ideas together
- Sequencing—arranging ideas in order (e.g., first, second, third)
- Illustrations—pictures, graphs, diagrams, lists

Whatever you find that helps you the most is the method that you should use. Read the following passage about whales carefully, taking note of the main ideas.

*Example*

> ### Diving to the Depths
>
> Northern bottle-nosed whales are wonderful divers, as are sperm whales. They can stay submerged for up to 70 min at a time and can dive as deep as 800 m. Cetaceans are mammals, so they have lungs. Proportionally, their lungs are smaller than those of humans. So, how do they manage to set those diving records?
>
> When a northern bottle-nosed whale comes to the surface to breathe, it exhales and then inhales 90% of all the air its lungs can contain, compared with the 75% that a human does. It has more available oxygen than a human does because it is better at emptying and refilling its lungs, not because its lungs contain proportionally more air.
>
> The oxygen captured during inhalation is then stored in its blood in a protein called hemoglobin. Cetaceans have a higher volume of blood than humans, so they have more hemoglobin in their blood vessels and muscles. This means they can accumulate more oxygen reserves and stay underwater longer.

A summary of this passage might read something like this:

Northern bottle-nose whales are such wonderful divers that they can dive to a depth of almost half a mile and can stay underwater for as long as 70 minutes. They are such great divers because they can almost completely empty and then refill their lungs with air and they can store large amounts of oxygen in their blood.

You can also summarize a text in chart form.

In a summary chart, you can organize your thoughts to help you stay focused and on topic. Here is an example of a summary chart.

TOPIC:_____

| What I Know | What I Want to Know | What I Learned |
|---|---|---|
|  |  |  |

*5RI.2  Determine two or more main ideas of a text and explain how they are supported by key details; summarize the text.*

## Recognize a Theme within a Text

The theme is what an author wants his or her readers to remember the most. It is the underlying message or idea of the work.

Identifying the theme is not always easy, so some detective work may be necessary.

*Example*

For instance, the theme of lost friendship and how it can be like losing a part of yourself in the story "A Secret for Two" may be more difficult to identify than the clear theme in O. Henry's "The Gift of the Magi", which is that the thought behind a gift is more important than the gift itself.

---

**A Secret for Two**

Montreal is a very large city, but, like all large cities, it has some very small streets. Streets, for instance, like Prince Edward Street, which is only four blocks long, ending in a cul-de-sac. No one knew Prince Edward Street as well as did Pierre Dupin, for Pierre had delivered milk to the families on the street for thirty years now.

During the past fifteen years the horse which drew the milk wagon used by Pierre was a large white horse named Joseph. In Montreal, especially in that part of Montreal which is very French, the animals, like children, are often given the names of saints. When the big white horse first came to the Provincale Milk Company he didn't have a name. They told Pierre that he could use the white horse henceforth. Pierre stroked the softness of the horse's neck; he stroked the sheen of its splendid belly and he looked into the eyes of the horse.

"This is a kind horse, a gentle and a faithful horse," Pierre said, "and I can see a beautiful spirit shining out of the eyes of the horse. I will name him after good St. Joseph, who was also kind and gentle and faithful and a beautiful spirit."

Within a year Joseph knew the milk route as well as Pierre. Pierre used to boast that he didn't need reins —he never touched them. Each morning Pierre arrived at the stables of the Provincale Milk Company at five o'clock. The wagon would be loaded and Joseph hitched to it. Pierre would call "Bon jour, vieille ami," as he climbed into his seat and Joseph would turn his head and the other drivers would smile and say that the horse would smile at Pierre. Then Jacques, the foreman, would say, "All right, Pierre, go on," and Pierre would call softly to Joseph, "Avance, mon ami," and this splendid combination would stalk proudly down the street.

The wagon, without any direction from Pierre, would roll three blocks down St. Catherine Street, then turn right two blocks along Roslyn Avenue; then left, for that was Prince Edward Street. The horse would stop at the first house, allow Pierre perhaps thirty seconds to get down from his seat and put a bottle of milk at the front door and would then go on, skipping two houses and stopping at the third. So down the length of the street. Then Joseph, still without any direction from Pierre, would turn around and come back along the other side. Yes, Joseph was a smart horse.

Pierre would boast at the stable of Joseph's skill. "I never touch the reins. He knows just where to stop. Why, a blind man could handle my route with Joseph pulling the wagon."

So it went on for years—always the same. Pierre and Joseph both grew old together, but gradually, not suddenly, Pierre's huge walrus mustache was pure white now and Joseph didn't lift his knees so high or raise his head as much. Jacques, the foreman of the stables, never noticed that they were both getting old until Pierre appeared one morning carrying a heavy walking stick.

"Hey, Pierre," Jacques laughed. "Maybe you got the gout, hey?"

"Mais oui, Jacques," Pierre said a bit uncertainly. "One grows old. One's legs get tired."

"You should teach that horse to carry the milk to the front door for you," Jacques told him. "He does everything else."

He knew every one of the forty families he served on Prince Edward Street. The cooks knew that Pierre could neither read nor write, so instead of following the usual custom of leaving a note in an empty bottle if an additional quart of milk was needed they would sing out when they heard the rumble of his wagon wheels over the cobbled street, "Bring an extra quart this morning, Pierre."

"So you have company for dinner tonight," he would call back gaily.

Pierre had a remarkable memory. When he arrived at the stable he'd always remember to tell Jacques, "The Paquins took an extra quart this morning; the Lemoines bought a pint of cream."

Jacques would note these things in a little book he always carried. Most of the drivers had to make out the weekly bills and collect the money, but Jacques, liking Pierre, had always excused him from this task. All Pierre had to do was to arrive at five in the morning, walk to his wagon, which was always in the same spot at the curb, and deliver his milk. He returned some two hours later, got stiffly from his seat, called a cheery "Au 'voir" to Jacques, and then limped slowly down the street.

One morning the president of the Provincale Milk Company came to inspect the early morning deliveries. Jacques pointed Pierre out to him and said: "Watch how he talks to that horse. See how the horse listens and how he turns his head toward Pierre? See the look in that horse's eyes? You know, I think those two share a secret. I have often noticed it. It is as though they both sometimes chuckle at us as they go off on their route. Pierre is a good man, Monsieur President, but he gets old. Would it be too bold of me to suggest that he be retired and be given perhaps a small pension?" he added anxiously.

"But of course," the president laughed. "I know his record. He has been on this route now for thirty years and never once has there been a complaint. Tell him it is time he rested. His salary will go on just the same."

But Pierre refused to retire. He was panic-stricken at the thought of not driving Joseph every day. "We are two old men," he said to Jacques. "Let us wear out together. When Joseph is ready to retire—then I, too, will quit." Jacques, who was a kind man, understood.

There was something about Pierre and Joseph which made a man smile tenderly. It was as though each drew some hidden strength from the other. When Pierre was sitting in his seat, and when Joseph was hitched to the wagon, neither seemed old. But when they finished their work, then Pierre would limp down the street slowly, seemingly very old indeed, and the horse's head would drop and he would walk very wearily to his stall.

Then one morning Jacques had dreadful news for Pierre when he arrived. It was a cold morning and still pitch-dark. The air was like iced wine that morning and the snow which had fallen during the night glistened like a million diamonds piled together.

Jacques said, "Pierre, your horse, Joseph, did not wake up this morning. He was very old, Pierre, he was twenty-five and that is like being seventy-five for a man."

"Yes," Pierre said slowly. "Yes. I am seventy-five. And I cannot see Joseph again."

"Of course you can," Jacques soothed. "He is over in his stall, looking very peaceful. Go over and see him."

Pierre took one step forward, then turned. "No… no… you don't understand, Jacques."

Jacques clapped him on the shoulder. "We'll find another horse just as good as Joseph. Why, in a month you'll teach him to know your route as well as Joseph did. We'll…" The look in Pierre's eyes stopped him. For years Pierre had worn a heavy cap, the peak of which came low over his eyes, keeping the bitter morning wind out of them. Now Jacques looked into Pierre's eyes and saw something which startled him. He saw a dead, lifeless look in them. The eyes were mirroring the grief that was in Pierre's heart and his soul. It was as though his heart and soul had died.

"Take today off, Pierre," Jacques said, but already Pierre was hobbling off down the street, and had one been near one would have seen tears streaming down his cheeks and have heard half-smothered sobs. Pierre walked to the corner and stepped into the street. There was a warning yell from the driver of a huge truck that was coming fast and there was the scream of brakes, but Pierre apparently heard neither.

Five minutes later an ambulance driver said, "He's dead. Was killed instantly."

Jacques and several of the milk-wagon drivers had arrived and they looked down at the still figure.

"I couldn't help it," the driver of the truck protested, "he walked right into my truck. He never saw it, I guess. Why, he walked into it as though he were blind."

The ambulance doctor bent down. "Blind? Of course the man was blind. See those cataracts? This man has been blind for five years." He turned to Jacques, "You say he worked for you? Didn't you know he was blind?"

"No….no…." Jacques said, softly. "None of us knew. Only one knew—a friend of his named Joseph…. It was a secret, I think, just between those two."

—*by* Quentin Reynolds

Try not to confuse theme with topic or subject. These are what a work is about, while theme is the author's underlying message about a topic or subject. Here is an example from "The Gift of the Magi".

*Example*

Topic: When you love someone, you are willing to give up prized possessions.

Theme: The thought behind the gift is more important than the gift itself.

---

Find theme in three steps:

1. Find the BIG IDEA
   The "Big Idea" of a passage is the same as the main topics of the passage. Ask yourself, what are the common ideas that appear throughout a passage? One helpful hint would be to list the topics that reoccur in a passage. This will help you focus on the theme of the passage.
2. Listen to what the characters do and say.
   Know that you have determined a main topic focus on how the characters' react to the idea. This step will give you good insight to help you understand the theme.
3. Write a statement.
   A theme statement should be a complete sentence that defines the passage's main idea.
   The statement should be general and should relate to the entire passage. Remember that the theme statement should not summarize the passage.

*5W.3b Write narratives to develop real or imagined experiences or events using effective technique, descriptive details, and clear event sequences. Use narrative techniques, such as dialogue, description, and pacing, to develop experiences and events...*

## UNDERSTAND HOW A SITUATION CAUSES CHARACTER'S ACTIONS

An author needs to create a situation for the characters in his story, a situation that causes the story to unfold. If the situation or problem is easily resolved, then the story is over.

The following story is a great example of how a situation caused a character's actions.

*Example*

We all know the story of Cinderella. The story begins with Cinderella being placed in a bad situation when her father dies and she's left to live with her mean stepmother and terrible stepsisters. A ball is being held at the palace so that the prince can find a bride, and Cinderella wants to attend but has nothing to wear. Suddenly, her Fairy Godmother appears and turns her rags into a beautiful dress and a pumpkin into a carriage. She arrives at the ball, dances with the Prince and has to quickly leave before the magic wears off. As she runs away from the palace, she loses one of her glass slippers. The Prince searches far and wide until he finds the girl who wore the slipper. Cinderella and the Prince live happily ever after.

The situations which led to Cinderella's happily ever after are shown in chart form below.

| Situation | Character's Actions |
| --- | --- |
| Her father died. | She became a servant girl. |
| A visit by her Fairy Godmother. | She goes to the Palace Ball. |
| She meets the Prince. | She falls in love. |
| The clock strikes midnight. | She runs out but drops her slipper. |
| The Prince finds the slipper and begins to search for Cinderella. | She is unhappy until he finds her and she fits the shoe. |

Each situation caused the characters to react to what was happening. The more situations that arise, the longer your story will be.

---

No matter what kind of situation a character is put in, they will react in a certain way. If a character is put in a scary situation, they will probably act scared and their reaction might be to run or scream.

## How Setting Causes a Character's Actions

The setting of a story can strongly influence the character's choices. Sometimes, it limits what a character can and cannot do.

For example, consider the setting suggested by the following phrase:

"It was a dark and stormy night…"

This type of setting shows the reader that the characters are probably not out for a stroll in the park. Setting affects what a character is doing and ultimately begins that character's journey.

A person is shaped by where the person comes from. For example, living in the 1920s versus the 1990s makes a profound difference to the lives of the characters. In the 1920s, the characters might more polite, and discrimination was common at that time.

Think about the story "Little Red Riding Hood". The setting is in a village near the forest. Little Red Riding Hood must go through the woods to get to her grandmother's house, and it is in the woods that she encounters a big, bad wolf.

If Little Red Riding Hood lived in a city, that setting would change the story line because big, bad wolves do not usually live in the city!

## Understand How Traits Cause Character's Actions

Traits are the qualities that a character possesses like being happy, lovestruck, or embarrassed. These traits are revealed through the character's actions.

*Example*

| Character's Action | Traits Revealed |
| --- | --- |
| The Big Bad Wolf blew down the First Piggy's house. | The Big Bad Wolf is mean, nasty, and heartless. |
| The witch gave Snow White a poison apple. | The witch is wicked, jealous, and evil. |
| The Beast saved Belle when the wolves began attacking her. | The Beast was courageous, helpful, and fierce. |

The Gingerbread man was driven by fear but his courage enabled him to jump up from the pan and run away instead of being eaten. However, another of his traits was foolishness. He was too foolish to see through the fox's tricks enough to run away again at the river, and this caused him to be eaten later. This is one of many examples showing how a character's traits cause a character's actions.

## How Motivations Cause a Character's Actions

A character needs motivation to take action. Motivation is what drives the character to act the way he or she does. Characters can be motivated by all sorts of different things. Consider the following examples.

*Example*
In *Romeo and Juliet*, Juliet was motivated by her love for Romeo. Her motivation was so strong that she chose to go against her parents' wishes and marry him anyway.

*Example*
In *The Wizard of Oz*, Dorothy was motivated by her desire to be reunited with her family in Kansas. Throughout the story, she stayed strong.

*Example*
In "Three Billy Goats Gruff", the billy goats were motivated to cross the bridge by their hunger for fresh, green pastures.

In each of the given stories, characters were motivated by a strong desire that led them to act in a certain way throughout the story.

# How Poetry Achieves an Author's Purpose

An author may write for the purpose of expressing an opinion or feelings about something. Letters, journals, and poetry often express opinions or feelings.

*Example*

In the poem below, the author's purpose seems to be expressing some feelings about fond memories associated with growing older and taller.

---

**The Birthday Wall**

In Daddy's bedroom down the hall,
there's a special place, The Birthday Wall.
Every year, about this time,
he hugs me then he draws my line.

We look at where I used to be
when I was small and only three.
Much higher, then, the one for four,
then five, then six, and now one more.

On the wall two names I see,
my little sister's, then there's me.
Sissy's line comes to my nose.
To look at mine, she's on tiptoes.

Sometimes when I am feeling small,
I go down to see The Birthday Wall
to see how big I'll be next time
Daddy hugs me and he draws my line.

—*by* CJ Heck

http://www.barkingspiderspoetry.com/poetry8page.html

What if the author's purpose is to entertain or amuse the reader? Do you think the author of the following poem achieves this purpose?

*Example*

### A Snake Named Rover

Mom wouldn't let me have a dog
"With all the mess they make!"
So, if I couldn't have a dog,
I said I'd like a snake.

My mother gasped quite audibly,
But Dad approved the plan.
"A snake," he gulped, "a real live snake…
Well, sure, I guess you can."

We went to Ralph's Repulsive Pets
And bought a yard of asp.
It coiled inside a paper bag
Held firmly in my grasp.

I put him in a big glass tank
And dubbed my new pet Rover,
But all the fun of owning it
Was very quickly over.

For all he did was flick his tongue
Once or twice each minute,
While nervous Mom rechecked the tank
To make sure he was in it.

Then one fine day, we don't know how,
My Rover disappeared.
My father told me not to fret,
But Mom was mighty scared.

We searched the house from front to back
And gave the yard a sweep.
By midnight we had given up
And tried to get some sleep.

At three AM my dad arose
To answer nature's call.
I heard him scream, I heard him swear,
And then I heard him fall.

For Dad had found the wayward pet
I'd given up for dead
Curled up inside his slipper,
Lying right beside his bed.

Now Rover's living back at Ralph's
With frogs, and newts, and guppies,
And now I have a dog named Spot—
She'll soon be having puppies.

—by Maxine Jeffris

---

As you read the poem above, could you think of some ways this author tried to achieve her purpose of entertaining the reader? See the list below for some possible ways:

- catchy rhyme scheme
- amusing situation
- amusing suspense when the snake disappeared
- amusing word picture of the horrified mom
- unexpected ending with the dog about to have puppies
- exaggeration of the dad's reaction to finding the snake, especially him falling
- amusing phrasing like "To answer nature's call"
- the snake having a dog's name
- the amusing alliteration in the name of the pet store (Ralph's Repulsive Pets)

*5L.3b* *Use knowledge of language and its conventions when writing, speaking, reading, or listening. Compare and contrast the varieties of English used in stories, dramas, or poems.*

*5RI.9* *Integrate information from several texts on the same topic in order to write or speak about the subject knowledgeably.*

## COMPARE AND CONTRAST INFORMATION

When you *compare* two things, you look at the ways in which two or more things are alike. When you *contrast* two things, you look at the ways in which they are different. The overlapping circles below form a Venn diagram. This kind of diagram is used to compare and contrast two things—in this case, fiction and non-fiction. The space where the circles overlap contains similarities, or things that are common to both fiction and non-fiction. The separate parts contain the things that are different.

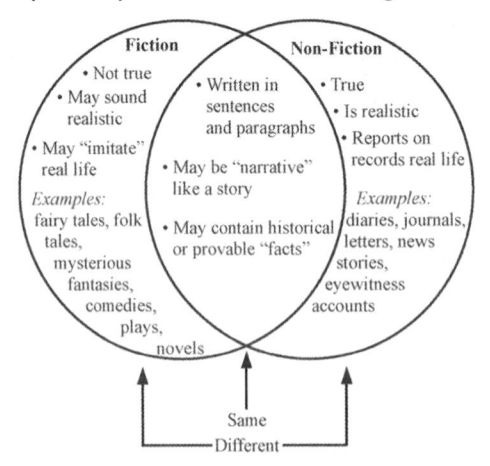

**Fiction**
- Not true
- May sound realistic
- May "imitate" real life

*Examples:* fairy tales, folk tales, mysterious fantasies, comedies, plays, novels

**Both (Same)**
- Written in sentences and paragraphs
- May be "narrative" like a story
- May contain historical or provable "facts"

**Non-Fiction**
- True
- Is realistic
- Reports on records real life

*Examples:* diaries, journals, letters, news stories, eyewitness accounts

## Comparing and Contrasting Wolves and Dogs

Another way of comparing and contrasting is to list the similarities and differences.

### Comparing Wolves and Dogs

- similar appearance
- can interbreed
- carnivorous (meat eaters)
- give birth to pups
- four-footed mammals
- have coats of fur that thicken in winter

### Contrasting Wolves and Dogs

- wolves are wild; dogs are domestic
- wolves are unpredictable, would not make good pets
- wolves are hunters and scavengers; dogs depend on humans to feed them
- dogs can be trained to work for humans: guide dogs, sled dogs, sheep dogs, retrievers, etc.

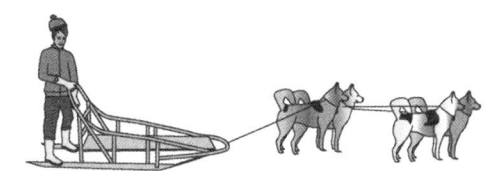

*5RL.4  Determine the meaning of words and phrases as they are used in a text, including figurative language such as metaphors and similes.*

## WHAT IS A METAPHOR?

A metaphor is a comparison of two objects or ideas. Unlike a simile, it does not use the words "like" or "as" to compare.

*Example*
After the argument, Blake was SMOLDERING for days.

The word SMOLDERING, is being compared to Blake's attitude after the argument.

---

*Example*
"Life is a zoo in a jungle."
(Peter De Vries)

Life is being compared to a "zoo in a jungle." Notice it is a comparison, but it is not using the words "like" or "as" like in a simile.

---

The next example shows how the author compares himself to a sword.

*Example*
I am a sword,
sharper than a tongue
nobody can defeat me,
because I am a sword,
I cannot be hurt by what people say about me,
I will not show my anger against someone else.

~By Alex ~

---

## NOW IT'S YOUR TURN

Can you determine which sentences contain metaphors?

1. We all would have eaten more pizza if Tammy wasn't such a hog.
2. Mark was such a mule. We could not get him to change his mind.
3. The mouse didn't stand a chance as our cat, the lightning bolt, got him right away.
4. The baby was a feather to carry.
5. Misty was bouncing off the walls like a hyper child on sugar.

Think you have them figured out? Do you know which of the above sentences are metaphors? Check your answers below.

## ANSWERS

The following sentences did contain metaphors:

1. **We all would have eaten more pizza if Tammy wasn't such a hog.** TAMMY is being compared to a HOG, because she ate like a hog.
2. **Mark was such a mule. We could not get him to change his mind.** MARK is being compared to a MULE, because he is being stubborn.
3. **The mouse didn't stand a chance as our cat, the lightning bolt, got him right away.** The CAT is being compared to a LIGHTNING BOLT, because of how fast it is.

4. **The baby was a feather to carry.** The BABY is being compared to a FEATHER, because it is so light.

The following example was not a proper metaphor:

5. Misty was bouncing off the walls like a hyper child on sugar.

The above sentence did not contain a proper metaphor. It contained what we call a simile, a comparison using "like" or "as". Metaphors do not use "like" or "as". **Metaphors will state something is something else.**

*5RI.4  Determine the meaning of general academic and domain-specific words and phrases in a text relevant to a grade 5 topic or subject area.*

## WHAT IS A SIMILE?

A **simile** is a figure of speech where you compare two unlike things using the words, "like" or "as". You can use a simile in a sentence to draw attention to certain characteristics of the subject being described.

*Example*
The woman was as **busy as a beaver** when she was getting ready for son's birthday party.

*Example*
Our dog dived into the big wave and **swam like a fish** until we pulled him out.

## FIGURATIVE LANGUAGE

Writers often use figurative language to make their writing more descriptive and interesting and to show meaning in different ways. Figurative language can be used to describe the setting of a story and the characters' feelings. It can also be used to set the mood in a piece of writing.

There are many different types of figurative language. Some of the most common types are listed are follows:

*Alliteration* is the repeated use of the first letter or sound in two or more words set closely together.

*Example*
**S**ally **s**ells **s**eashells by the **s**eashore.

**P**atty was the **p**rettiest **p**ig in the **p**en.

**Onomatopoeia** is the use of a word that imitates the sound it describes.

*Example*
The bird **squawked** endlessly.

The sound of the drums **boomed** in my head.

---

**Simile** is the use of the words *like* or *as* to compare two unlike things.

*Example*
The kite flew **like** a bird.

She was **as** quiet **as** a mouse.

---

*Metaphor* is the comparison of two unlike things without the use of the words *like* or *as*.

*Example*
**The stars** were **diamonds in the sky**.

To little Toni, **the wading pool** was a **vast sea**.

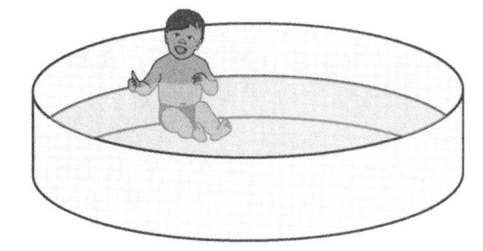

*Personification* is giving human qualities or characteristics to animals or non-living objects.

*Example*

**The wind whispered** soft poems in my ear.

**The raccoon scolded** her babies like a mother in a supermarket. (Hint: Think of the word "person," and you will remember that *personification* means to give an animal or an object the characteristics of a person.)

---

*Hyperbole* is great exaggeration.

*Example*

We ate **a mountain** of ice cream at the party.

---

5RL.5   *Explain how a series of chapters, scenes, or stanzas fits together to provide the overall structure of a particular story, drama, or poem.*

5RI.5   *Compare and contrast the overall structure of events, ideas, concepts, or information in two or more texts.*

## LOCATING CHAPTERS WITHIN A TEXT

The easiest way to find a chapter in a text is to go to the beginning of the book and find the "Table of Contents"

Under the table of contents there will be a list all the chapters in the text, along with their page numbers. The chapters may be listed under section headings as well, depending on the text and the topic. In most fiction stories, there is usually only the title of the book, with the chapters and the page numbers listed below.

Think you understand?

In the book, *Junie B. Jones Has a Peep in Her Pocket* by Barbara Park, The first page after the title and dedication page is the "Contents" page. It looks like the following example:

*Example*

| | |
|---|---|
| Confusing Stuff | 1 |
| Stubby | 9 |
| Pictures | 16 |
| Cockle-Doodly-Doo | 26 |
| E-I-E-I-O | 36 |
| Farmer Flores | 44 |
| Spike | 56 |
| Confusion | 64 |

In the above example, if you were looking for chapter 5, you would locate it on page 36. Do you see that right beside the title of the chapter E-I-E-I-O is the number 36? This number is showing you the page number the chapter will begin on.

What page would Chapter 7 "Spike" fall on?

If you said page 56, you would be correct! On the right side of the chapter's name is the number 56, which shows you the page number.

If you had finished reading your story in the middle of the chapter, but you knew you were on Chapter 4, what page would you start looking from to find your spot?

If you said page 26, you are right! On the right side of Chapter 4's title, "Cockle-Doodly-Doo" is the number 26, and this will tell you the page number Chapter 4 starts on.

## YOUR TURN TO PRACTICE

Do you think you understand now how to locate a chapter within a book? Try the questions below and see how you do.

The following **Table of Contents** example is from the book titled *Roxie's Mall Madness* by Hilda Stahl.

| Families | 9 |
| A Good Deed | 18 |
| The Sleepover | 30 |
| Eli | 41 |
| Secrets | 52 |
| Julie Pieron | 64 |
| Sunday Night | 74 |
| No More School | 84 |
| More Information | 94 |
| Help | 105 |
| Trouble | 114 |
| Julie | 123 |
| Secrets Revealed | 135 |
| Eli's Adventure | 149 |

Questions

1. How many chapters are in this book?
2. What chapter starts on page 74?
3. What is the title of chapter 13?
4. What page would chapter 11 start on?
5. If I had quit reading in the middle of Chapter 3, "The Sleepover", what page might I start looking from to determine where I had quit reading?

Answers
Think you answered them all correctly? Let see. Check your answers below.

1. How many chapters are in this book? **There are 14 chapters in this book.**
2. What chapter starts on page 74? **Chapter 7, titled, "Sunday Night" starts on page 74.**
3. What is the title of chapter 13? **Chapter 13's title is called "Secrets Revealed"**
4. What page would chapter 11 start on? **Chapter 11 would start on page 114.**
5. If I had quit reading in the middle of Chapter 3, "The Sleepover" what page might I start looking from to determine where I had quit reading? **I would start looking at page 30 and look all the way up to page 40 (Because Chapter 4 starts on page 41!)**

*5RL.10 By the end of the year, read and comprehend literature, including stories, dramas, and poetry, at the high end of the grades 4–5 text complexity band independently and proficiently.*

## WHAT IS A PLAY?

A play is a type of drama, or literary form used in theater. It is usually written in a "script", where the characters speak dialogue back and forth to each other. Plays are usually written for performing, rather than for reading. Plays are stories that we see and hear, rather than read.

*Example*

### from Pygmalion, Act I

**The Daughter:** *(in the space between the central pillars, close to the one on her left)* I'm getting chilled to the bone. What can Freddy be doing all this time? Hes been gone twenty minutes.

**The Mother:** *(on her daughter's right)* Not so long. But he ought to have got us a cab by this.

**A Bystander:** *(on the lady's right)* He wont get no cab not until half-past eleven, missus, when they come back after dropping their theater fares.

**The Mother:** But we must have a cab. We cant stand here until half-past eleven. It's too bad.

**The Bystander:** Well, it aint my fault, missus.

**The Daughter:** If Freddy had a bit of gumption, he would have got one at the theater door.

**The Mother:** What could he have done, poor boy?

**The Daughter:** Other people got cabs. Why couldnt he?

*Freddy rushes in out of the rain from the Southampton Street side, and comes between them closing a dripping umbrella. He is a young man of twenty, in evening dress, very wet around the ankles.*

**The Daughter:** Well, havnt you got a cab?

**Freddy:** Theres not one to be had for love or money.

**The Mother:** Oh, Freddy, there must be one. You cant have tried.

**The Daughter:** It's too tiresome. Do you expect us to go and get one ourselves?

**Freddy:** I tell you theyre all engaged. The rain was so sudden: nobody was prepared; and everybody had to take a cab. Ive been to Charing Cross one way and nearly to Ludgate Circus the other; and they were all engaged.

**The Mother:** Did you try Trafalgar Square?

**Freddy:** There wasnt one at Trafalgar Square.

**The Daughter:** Did you try?

**Freddy:** I tried as far as Charing Cross Station. Did you expect me to walk to Hammersmith?

**The Daughter:** You havnt tried at all.

**The Mother:** You really are very helpless, Freddy. Go again; and dont come back until you have found a cab.

**Freddy:** I shall simply get soaked for nothing.

**The Daughter:** And what about us? Are we to stay here all night in this draught, with next to nothing on. You selfish pig—

**Freddy:** Oh, very well: I'll go, I'll go.

*He opens his umbrella and dashes off Strandwards, but comes into collision with a flower girl, who is hurrying in for shelter, knocking her basket out of her hands. A blinding flash of lightning, followed instantly by a rattling peal of thunder, orchestrates the incident.*

**The Flower Girl:** Nah then, Freddy: look wh' y' gowin, deah.

**Freddy:** Sorry. *(he rushes off)*

**The Flower Girl:** *(picking up her scattered flowers and replacing them in the basket)* Theres menners f' yer! Te-oo banches o voylets trod into the mad.

—*by* George Bernard Shaw

## WHAT IS A NOVEL?

A novel is a fictional piece of writing that tells a story. It is greater in length than a short story, so the story has more twists and turns in the plot, and usually has a larger number of characters.

Most of the time, a novel will tell a story through character development and a series of events that allow the reader to understand the message or theme through a story line structure.

Novels are read by people of all ages, especially for their entertainment value. There are all types of genres of novels and graphic novels (a novel with pictures) to be read by all types of readers. Examples of these genres include the following:

- Mystery
- Adventure
- Fantasy
- Science fiction
- Historical

## WHAT IS POETRY?

Poetry refers to poems. Poems often have rhythm, and they sometimes rhyme, especially those that are written for children. They often use very colorful and expressive language to explain an idea or event. Songs are examples of poetry, as are nursery rhymes, limericks, and many picture books. Poetry can often be recognized by the way that it looks on the page. Writers often choose to either group the text in verses or shape the printed words in interesting patterns.

These two verses are from a traditional folksong and use both rhythmic words and rhymes.

*Example*

---

**from The Fox**

The fox went out on a chase one night,

He prayed to the moon to give him light,

For he had many a mile to go that night

Before he reached the town-o, town-o, town-o

He had many a mile to go that night

Before he reached the town-o.

He ran 'til he came to a great big pen,

Where the ducks and the geese were kept therein.

He said "A couple of you are gonna grease my chin

before I leave this town-o, town-o, town-o!

A couple of you are gonna grease my chin,

before I leave this town-o!"

## CONCRETE POEMS

A poem about the sun might be written with the words forming the circular shape of the sun. A poem that visually represents its topic is called a **concrete poem**.

*Example*

burns!
hot so hot
bright so bright
sun sun sun sun
warms all it touches
eye in the sky
watching plants grow
life!

## LIMERICKS

A five line poem (in which lines 1, 2, and 5 rhyme and lines 3 and 4 rhyme, following an *aabba* rhyme pattern) is called a **limerick**.

*Example*

There was a young lady from Niger,
Who smiled as she rode on a tiger!
They came back from the ride
With the lady inside
And the smile on the face of the tiger!

## HAIKUS

A non-rhyming, three line poem with a total of 17 syllables is a called a **haiku**.

*Example*

A red ladybug
Lands on my jelly sandwich
Catcher in the rye!

Here is another haiku. The Japanese are known for creating hundreds of these simple but elegant poems.

*Example*

The first snow this year
Dusted the forest with white
World of cool beauty.

*5RL.6  Describe how a narrator's or speaker's point of view influences how events are described.*

*5RI.6  Analyze multiple accounts of the same event or topic, noting important similarities and differences in the point of view they represent.*

## WHAT IS POINT OF VIEW?

**Point of View** is the way the author chooses to tell a story. The author can choose from three different types of views to make readers "see" and "hear" the story. The three types are:

1. First person: *I, me, my, mine*
2. Second person: *you, your*
3. Third person: author's voice tells the story

The **first person point of view** is used when one character explains the story as the action happens. The author will use *I, me, my,* or *mine* whenever the narrator is speaking or thinking.

*Example*

## The New Boy

The desks in our classroom are arranged in a sort of circle, so we all face each other. Mr. Donaldson had squeezed in an extra desk with the name *Jean-Pierre* printed on a card to match the others. I watched, steaming, while Alyssa guided the poor boy to his place as if he were blind.

"I speak English," I heard him say. "And I can see."

His voice was a bit husky, which made his accent sound like someone in a movie. He was even cuter close up, with hazely eyes and long lashes. Alyssa just kept standing there, staring at him. Her pal Megan leaned over and poked her to stop making a fool of herself.

"Take your seats, people. Settle down. Welcome back, everyone. I'd like to officially welcome our newcomer, Jean-Pierre de LaTour."

Jean-Pierre saluted and smiled a crooked smile. His desk was directly opposite mine, so I caught the main shine. Hubert is next to me, and Alyssa is three over, well out of smile range.

"You'll have plenty of time during the day to show Jean-Pierre how friendly New Yorkers can be." Mr. Donaldson looked around. "Ah, Hubert? Would you be Jean-Pierre's buddy for today?"

Hubert blushed and nodded at Jean-Pierre to introduce himself. In our class, it is well known that Hubert does not like to speak out loud. Especially not to strangers. Mr. D picked him on purpose—an exercise in torture disguised as social encouragement.

"Show him around, make sure he finds the cafeteria and other essential facilities…."

Mr. Donaldson always calls the bathroom "the facilities."

Jean-Pierre nodded back at Hubert and spun his yo-yo like a top across his desk.

"Toys are not allowed in the classroom," said Mr. Donaldson, with a laser-beam squint. "Since it's your first day, I'll let you off with a warning." He laughed to try to show he was a nice guy, but we all knew he was dying to add that yo-yo to the collection of our treasures in his bottom drawer.

"All right then, listen up, people. We have a busy quarter ahead of us, with the first focus on your projects about medieval life. We have a couple of field trips coming up, starting this week—"

"Are we going on a school bus or the subway?" asked Josh

"—with an excursion, on a school bus, to the Cloisters. That's Friday, leaving first thing. We'll be seeing a marvelous reconstruction of medieval architecture as well as—yes Josh?"

"Do we have to bring a lunch?"

"You'll need to bring a bag lunch, no glass bottles, no candy—yes, Josh?"

"Can we have soda, sir?"

"Yes, you *may* have soda. Eyes on me, people. This trip will be very instructive for all who—"

I noticed Hubert was watching Jean-Pierre instead of the teacher. I guess we all were.

I wrote a note and passed it along with my elbow.

*Don't worry. I'll help you with the new kid.*

Hubert and I waited after class while Jean-Pierre collected a stack of textbooks from Mr. D. and stuffed them into a plastic shopping bag. Alyssa hovered at the door, trying, as usual, to barge in where she's not wanted.

Jean-Pierre saw us looking at the plastic bag.

"I was waiting to see what the other kids use," he said shrugging. "I want to look like a New Yorker!"

"We all have backpacks." I turned around to show him.

"Billie would probably die without her backpack." Alyssa giggled, tugging on my strap.

I yanked away from her.

"See? Taking Billie's backpack would be like ripping a shell off a turtle."

Alyssa has been suspicious of my backpack ever since the day last fall when my puppy, Harry, came to school inside it. Thanks to my secret weapon, he was invisible at the time, but he wiggled enough to nearly give himself away. Now Alyssa pokes my pack whenever she can, just in case it will move. She won't give up the hope that she might uncover something to get me in trouble.

What if she knew the truth? I have to keep it hidden from my ever-curious little sister, so I carry it with me at all times. In my backpack is enough Vanishing Powder to make Alyssa disappear from my life.

—from *The Invisible Enemy* by Marthe Jocelyn

The **second-person point of view** is used when the author is talking directly to the reader. The author will use *you* and *your*. This point of view is rare. As you read the example below, the story may appear to be written from the third person point of view (Princess Pea, she, etc.), but watch for lines in the story where the author is speaking directly to you, the reader.

*Example*

### What Furlough Saw

THE PRINCESS PEA looked down at Despereaux. She smiled at him. And while her father played another song, a song about the deep purple falling over sleepy garden walls, the princess reached out and touched the top of the mouse's head.

Despereaux stared up at her in wonder. The Pea, he decided, looked just like the picture of the fair maiden in the book in the library. The princess smiled at Despereaux again, and this time, Despereaux smiled back. And then, something incredible happened: The mouse fell in love.

Reader, you may ask this question; in fact, you *must* ask this question: Is it ridiculous for a very small, sickly, big-eared mouse to fall in love with a beautiful human princess named Pea?

The answer is … yes. Of course, it's ridiculous.

Love is ridiculous.

But love is also wonderful. And powerful. And Despereaux's love for the Princess Pea would prove, in time, to be all of these things: powerful, wonderful, and ridiculous.

"You're so sweet," said the princess to Despereaux. "You're so tiny."

As Despereaux looked up at her adoringly, Furlough happened to scurry past the princess's room, moving his head left to right, right to left, back and forth.

"Cripes!" said Furlough. He stopped. He stared into the princess's room. His whiskers became as tight as bow-strings.

What Furlough saw was Despereaux Tilling sitting at the foot of the king. What Furlough saw was the princess touching the top of his brother's head.

"Cripes!" shouted Furlough again. "Oh, cripes! He's nuts! He's a goner!"

And, executing a classic scurry, Furlough went off to tell his father, Lester Tilling, the terrible, unbelievable news of what he had just seen.

—from *The Tale of Despereaux* by Kate DiCamillo

Not for Reproduction

**Third person point of view** occurs when the author is telling the story instead of one of the characters.

*Example*

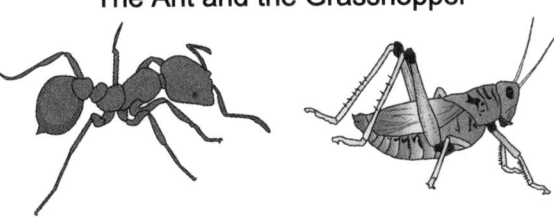

### The Ant and the Grasshopper

One fine summer's day, a Grasshopper was hopping about, chirping and singing most happily. An Ant passed by, dragging an ear of corn he was taking to the nest.

"Come and play with me," said the Grasshopper, "instead of working so hard."

"I am helping to store food for the winter," said the Ant. "I suggest you do the same."

"Why worry about winter?" asked the Grasshopper. "We are surrounded by all the food we could want." But the Ant went on his way and continued his toil.

When winter came, the ants were snug in their hill, eating from the stores they had saved up during the summer. The Grasshopper, however, found himself cold and dying of hunger.

Then the Grasshopper knew ... it is best to prepare for the days of need.

---

*5W.3a Write narratives to develop real or imagined experiences or events using effective technique, descriptive details, and clear event sequences. Orient the reader by establishing a situation and introducing a narrator and/or characters; organize...*

## IDENTIFYING THE SPEAKER OR NARRATOR IN A TEXT

An author writing a story is rather like a person using a camera taking to shoot a video. A person shooting a video decides where to stand and what to capture. What an author tells and how he or she decides to tell it are the author's point of view. There are three main points of view (or perspectives).

Sometimes as a reader it is very clear what the point of view in the story is and who is telling the story. Sometimes it is not so clear. Getting to know the different points of view and the clue words that are used to determine the point of view the author is using, is important and can directly affect your full understanding and comprehension of a text.

In **first person** point of view writing, the author decides to have one of the characters in the story tell about the events and what is said. The pronouns *I, me, my, mine, we,* and *us* are used. When a first person point of view is used, the reader usually knows only what the person who is telling the story thinks and feels.

*Example*
"I was scared because I thought I might fall when I climbed the tree to get the coconuts for our family's supper that night."

---

When an author uses a second person point of view, he or she talks directly to the reader. The pronouns *you* and *your* are used. This point of view is often used in choose-your-own-adventure stories and when an author wants to give directions, and sometimes in poetry.

*Example*
"When you are baking, you need to make sure you have all the ingredients ready before you start."

---

Stories written in **third person** point of view are told through the eyes of a narrator. The pronouns *he*, *she*, *his*, *her*, *they*, and *their* are used. When third person point of view is used, readers can sometimes know a great deal about the story because the narrator tells what is happening in many different places.

*Example*
"While John was playing with his friends at the park, Mary was having trouble trying to fix the car so that they could all go to visit their grandmother."

---

*Try This!*
Now it's your turn. Do you think you understand the different points of view an author or narrator can have in their texts? Try and determine which point of view is being used in each to the following questions. Once you think you have got them all correct, check your answers below.

1. Next, when you understand the first task, then you and your team will move onto task number two.
2. I enjoy all types of cakes.
3. Macy was clear on what she had to do. She knew her friends would not understand, but she had to do what was right for everyone.
4. I feel really sad when my friends don't say good-bye to me after school.

How do you think you did? Were you able to determine which point of view each sentence was written in? If you think you have got them all correct, check your answers below.

1. Next, when you understand the first task, then you and your team will move onto task number two.
   This is **second person point of view**. Notice how it uses the pronouns *you* and *your*.
2. I enjoy all types of cakes.
   This is **first person point of view**. Notice how it speaks with *I*.
3. Macy was clear on what she had to do. She knew her friends would not understand, but she had to do what was right for everyone.
   This is **third person point of view**. Notice how it speaks from a more general perspective, using the pronouns, *her* and *she*.
4. I feel really sad when my friends don't say good-bye to me after school.
   This is **first person point of view**. Notice how it speaks with *I* and *me*.

*5RL.7   Analyze how visual and multimedia elements contribute to the meaning, tone, or beauty of a text.*

*5RI.7   Draw on information from multiple print or digital sources, demonstrating the ability to locate an answer to a question quickly or to solve a problem efficiently.*

## THE PURPOSE OF VISUAL AND GRAPHIC MATERIALS

Have you ever heard the saying, "A picture is worth 1,000 words"? Well, many authors have thought of that very saying. Many people are visual learners, and sometimes need a picture or a graphic to help them understand a topic a little better. For example, if you were learning about an eclipse of the moon, you might want some graphics to help show you where the moon, earth and sun are positioned, instead of just reading about it, and trying to create your own mental picture in your mind.

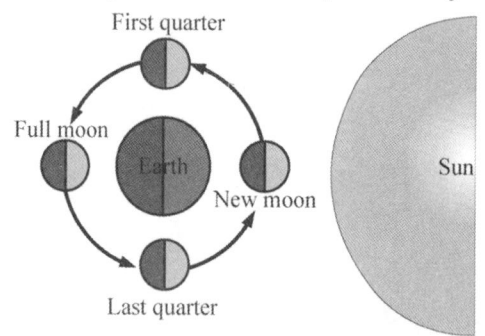

Sometimes authors will use illustrations in their story books to help the reader have a clearer idea of what the characters and setting actually look like.

Graphics in a text are usually used to add important information or enhance the learning or enjoyment of the text.

Graphics will be used to add to the information or to enhance the message in a particular text. Depending on the purpose for the graphic, there are many different types of graphics that can be used. A graphic may come in the form of a:

- picture
- photograph
- diagram
- table
- chart
- graph
- time line
- flow chart
- web diagram
- Venn diagram

Suppose you were trying to describe to your mother how you want to rearrange your room after she paints the walls. Would it be easier to just show her what you mean with a diagram?

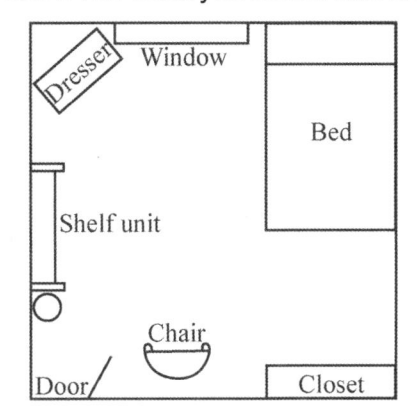

A graphic in a text may be used to help relay the information being taught using one particular image, or by using meaningful patterns or sequences. For example, a diagram may use one particular image, while a flow chart may arrange its information in a sequential order using a few different images.

Some graphics may be used to purely add enjoyment or humor to the text.

*5RL.9 Compare and contrast stories in the same genre on their approaches to similar themes and topics.*

## How Authors Develop Themes

*Themes* are the main ideas, beliefs, or values that are shown in stories. You can often figure out a theme in a story by thinking about what is important to a main character—even though the author may not state the theme in words. Astrid Lindgren is the author of a well-known series for children featuring a main character called Pippi Longstocking. Astrid Lindgren includes themes in her books that are important to children. Some of the themes found in all of the Pippi Longstocking books include beliefs about:

- **justice and fair play**— Although Pippi is "street smart" and often annoying to many adults, she shows respect, in her own way, to people who treat her and other children fairly.
- **friendship and loyalty**— Pippi would never bring harm to her two best friends, Tommy and Annika. She values their friendship above almost anything else in her life.
- **using physical strength to conquer obstacles**— The idea of strength also includes inner strength.

## Ways of Showing Themes

Authors use different methods to express themes in literature. They may develop themes by:

1. describing the theme as a message: "The best things in life are free."
2. showing what is important to a character
3. showing an important change in a character: In "How the Grinch Stole Christmas", a greedy character becomes generous.
4. letting a character speak the theme
5. showing the theme through symbols placed in a story: white horses, knights in shining armor, roses for love, etc.
6. saying the theme through the narrator of the story

## Compare Information on One Topic from Many Sources

If you are assigned a research project on endangered animals, you are going to review many resources such as books and videos before deciding what information to use. One book might list the White Rhino as the most critically endangered animal on earth, while other sources might state it as number two on the list of most endangered animals.

Your job is to compare the information in each of the sources, and decide which source is more credible and reliable. Determine which information is conflicting and which is consistent. Also, if 10 resources state the White Rhino as the second most endangered animal, and only 2 resources state it as the most endangered, then you can choose to go with the majority.

If you are researching information on the Giant Panda from three different sources, it is important to compare the information from all three sources before using it. This will help you determine accurate and reliable information.

## Contrast Information on One Topic From Many Sources

Contrasting information on one topic from many sources allows you to develop a broad view of the topic, and also helps you to eliminate inaccurate or questionable information and facts from your notes.

If you are assigned a research project on endangered animals, you are going to review many resources such as books and videos before deciding what information to use. One book might list the Bengal tiger as the fastest animal on earth, while other sources might state it as number two on the list of the world's fastest animals.

Your job is to compare the information in each of the sources and decide which is more credible and reliable. Decide which information is conflicting and which is consistent. Also, if 10 resources state the Bengal tiger as the fastest animal and only 2 resources state it as the second fastest, then you should choose to go with the most consistent resources. In this case, it would be the 10 resources that state the Bengal tiger is the fastest animal on earth.

*Example*

Let's say you are researching information on African elephants and you use several resources for your research. You will notice that many of the resources will repeat the same information. However, some resources may show contrasting information. It is during this time that you will need to determine which information is more credible. You may choose to search out other resources to continue to compare with the one containing the contrasting information.

Once you have collected multiple resources with enough information, you must determine which information is the most relevant to your research topic and/or assignment given.

## WHAT IS A MYTH?

A myth is a story of heroes and gods that helps to explain events and natural occurrences like lightning.

Most of the myths that still exist today came from either Greek or Roman times—both were a very long time ago. For example, the story of Demeter and Persephone is a Greek myth that explains the origins of the four seasons. As you read the summary below, remember that the Greeks did not have scientists like we have today, to help people understand what happens in Nature. The Greeks, though, had wonderful storytellers. Their stories or "myths" were full of powerful gods and goddesses who caused magical things to happen in the blink of an eye. It worked! Greek people did not worry about things they did not fully understand. They just depended on their wonderful stories to explain it all away.

## SUMMARY OF HOW THE SEASONS CAME TO BE

In the myth, Demeter, goddess of agriculture, has a beloved daughter, Persephone. Persephone disappears one day while taking a walk. It turns out that the Earth has opened and swallowed the girl. Down, down into the Underworld she has fallen, captive of Hades, god of the Underworld. Her mother is crazy with grief. Zeus, king of the gods, sends his messenger to fetch her back. Before letting Persephone go, Hades tricks her into swallowing six pomegranate seeds. Forever, she will have to return to him for six months out of each year. When Persephone returns to the Underworld, the chill winds of autumn and winter cover the earth. Six months later, the first blossoms of spring announce her arrival back to the welcoming arms of her mother, Demeter. That is how we have spring and summer.

## WHAT IS A LEGEND?

A legend is a type of story that helped to pass on the history and culture of a people. Legends were not written down, but were "told" by older members of a group. They often contained animals and were used to explain things in nature. For example, the legend of Sedna, Mother of the Sea Animals, tells the story of the creation of seals, walruses, and whales. You can read a summary of the legend below. Because it was not written down, there are many versions of the story.

## SUMMARY OF THE SEDNA LEGEND

As a young Inuit woman, Sedna lived in the Arctic with her parents. She had no wish to marry. Her father was a good hunter and provider. Sedna had plenty of warm furs and tasty food. She finally married, only because her husband tricked her. He was really a bird dressed as a man! Sedna escaped from the Birdman's island after her father killed her bird husband. Angry birds followed the kayak out to sea. Flapping their wings in revenge, they created a huge storm. Sedna's father threw her overboard so the birds would leave. As Sedna clung to the kayak, seals, walruses, and whales were "born" from her fingertips. Sedna ended up living on the ocean floor, where she still rules over all the animals of the sea.

## WHAT IS A FANTASY?

A fantasy is a type of genre. It is a fictional story that usually takes place in strange, imaginary worlds. The writer uses their creative imagination to tell the story. Unicorns, mythical creatures, mermaids, heroes, and magic are some of the elements found in a fantasy.

*Example*
- The Harry Potter Series
- The Chronicles of Narnia (including *The Lion, the Witch, and the Wardrobe*) by C.S. Lewis
- *Alice in Wonderland* by Lewis Carroll
- *The Secret World of Og* by Pierre Berton
- *Lord of the Rings* by J.R.R. Tolkien

## WHAT IS FICTION?

Fiction is a story that is not true. The author uses his or her imagination to tell a story that is not based on facts. You do not read fiction to gain information but rather to enjoy a story. *Pinocchio* and *Tom Sawyer* are examples of popular fictional stories.

## DEMONSTRATE AN UNDERSTANDING OF THE MAIN IDEA WITHIN A TEXT

If you were asked to explain in one sentence what a reading passage was about, this would be the main idea. Very often the title gives the reader the main idea, but not always. Sometimes the title is to short to give enough information.

*Example*

For example, if you were given a passage with the title "Dolphins Are Our Friends," the main idea might well be something like "Dolphins are our friends and it is important to protect them." If the same passage were just called "Dolphins," you would definitely have to read further to figure out what the author's main point about dolphins would be.

If the passage does not have a title, thinking about what title you would give it may help you to come up with the main idea.

Very often the main idea is given in one strong sentence either near the beginning or at the end of the passage. In the dolphin passage we just imagined, the last sentence of the passage might be something like "You can see how important it is to protect these wonderful creatures from fishermen and from pollution of their ocean homes." This probably sums up the whole passage.

You can also think about why you think the author wrote the text to help give you the main idea.

Class Focus             Castle Rock Research

## Identifying the Main Idea and Supporting Details

Can you pick out the main ideas and the supporting details in the following article?

When you read each paragraph, ask yourself these questions:

- What is the topic or central idea in this paragraph?
- Which sentence expresses the central idea? (Hint: often the first sentence, but not always)
- What are the details that explain, support, or expand that main idea?

## from "Monster Waves, Tsunamis"

### Tsunamis

Tsunamis are caused by underwater earthquakes and volcanic eruptions, and they are the largest waves of all. Earthquakes occur when two **tectonic plates** collide or slide past each other. When an earthquake occurs under the ocean, the ocean bottom shakes. This movement causes the water above to become **displaced**. Waves of energy spread out in all directions from the source of the vibrations in ever-widening circles. As the tsunami approaches shore, the waves rub against the sea floor. **Friction** causes the waves to slow down and build from behind, creating huge piles of water that crash onto the shore.

### Rogue Waves

Sometimes, groups of large ocean waves caused by a storm slam into a powerful ocean current passing in the opposite direction. When this happens, several storm waves pile up to form gigantic waves called rogue, or freak, waves. These waves can be more than 100 feet (30 meters) tall and can bury cargo ships beneath the sea. Rogue waves are most common off the coasts of Japan, Florida, and Alaska. Currently, a project known as WaveAtlas monitors the oceans with satellites. Over the next few years, oceanographers hope to analyze these satellite images to help them better understand why freak waves occur.

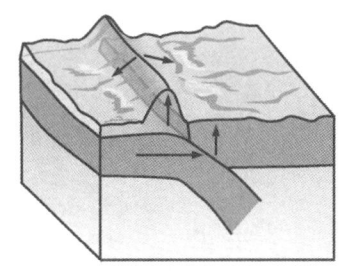

In the open ocean, tsunamis can be 100 miles (161 km) long and travel up to 500 miles per hour (805 km/h). Tsunamis pass under ships easily because the waves do not build until they approach land.

## Whirlpools

Whirlpools are revolving currents formed by the meeting of opposite-moving ocean currents, the collision between currents and tides, or tides moving along uneven coasts. When churning, whirlpools make a loud sucking noise. Small ships may become trapped and wrecked by the force of the revolving water. Larger ships find steering difficult. The best-known whirlpool is the Maelstrom, off the coast of Norway. Here, currents flowing through **fjords** around islands create the whirlpool. Another well-known whirlpool is named the Old Sow and is formed between New Brunswick and Maine.

*Physical barriers in the water can create whirlpools because they disrupt the regular flow of water.*

## Krakatoa

On August 27, 1883, an undersea volcano called Krakatoa erupted in the Indian Ocean. The force of the explosion caused a tsunami with waves more than twelve stories high. The waves were so powerful that small islands were washed away and thousands of boats were sunk. As the waves circled the southern tip of Africa, they entered the Atlantic ocean, traveling at 400 miles per hour (640 km/h). The tsunami destroyed more than 300 communities and killed over 36,000 people.

*Scientists believe that the waves from Krakatoa circled the globe two or three times before running out of energy.*

## AN EXAMPLE TO USE AS A MODEL

The paragraph below is about tsunamis, one of the main topics in the article. The main idea of the paragraph is underlined. The numbered sentences contain supporting details about the main idea.

Sometimes, groups of large ocean waves caused by a storm slam into a powerful ocean current passing in the opposite direction.(1) When this happens, <u>several storm waves pile up to form gigantic waves called rogue or freak waves.</u>(2) These waves can be more than 100 feet (30 meters) tall and can bury cargo ships beneath the sea.(3) Rogue waves are most common off the coasts of Japan, Florida, and Alaska.(4) Currently, a project known as WaveAtlas monitors the oceans with satellites.(5) Over the next few years, oceanographers hope to analyze these satellite images to help them better understand why freak waves occur.(6)

## TRY IT YOURSELF

You could try to make brief notes for each paragraph. Put the main idea at the top of the list of supporting details as a heading. Under that heading, list the supporting details. The notes on the first main paragraph might look something like the example below.

*Example*
**Main Idea:** Tsunamis are largest the waves:

- Caused by underwater earthquakes and volcanoes
- Tectonic plates move and displace water
- Wave energy meets friction from sea floor
- Friction causes waves to pile up as they near land
- Piled up waves crash over the land

## ANOTHER WAY TO LOOK AT MAIN IDEAS AND SUPPORTING DETAILS

If you do not want to put the ideas in lists, you could try a method that is more like a diagram. Below you can see the main ideas and supporting details from an article about poisonous spiders. Even though you have not read the article, you can clearly see the important information arranged in a detail map. The main ideas are on the left. The supporting details are to the right in boxes. For example, the first main idea is that there are several types of poisonous spiders. The supporting details are a naming of the main types of poisonous spiders: black widows, brown recluse, hobo spiders, and yellow sac spiders.

In a main idea or detail map, you list the main ideas on the left, with the details going across the page. Here is an example of a detail map made from an article about poisonous spiders:

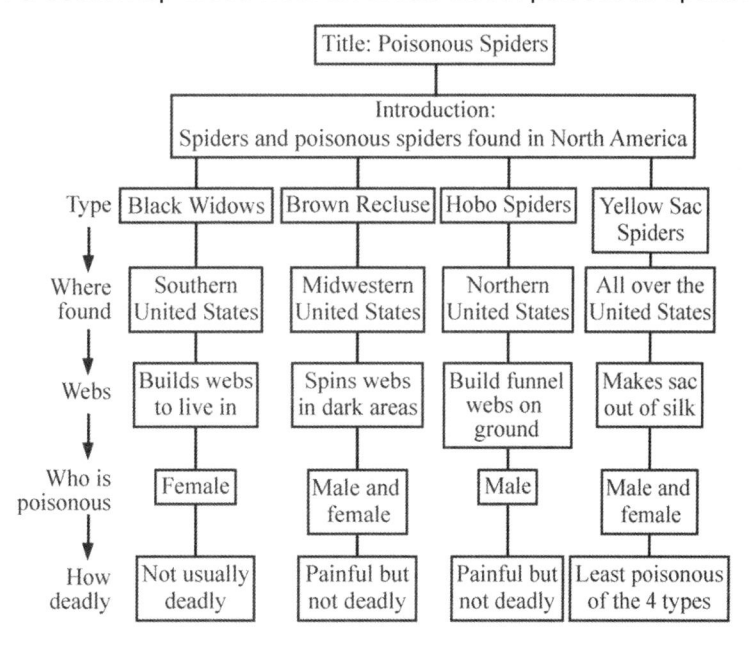

| | Black Widows | Brown Recluse | Hobo Spiders | Yellow Sac Spiders |
|---|---|---|---|---|
| Type | Black Widows | Brown Recluse | Hobo Spiders | Yellow Sac Spiders |
| Where found | Southern United States | Midwestern United States | Northern United States | All over the United States |
| Webs | Builds webs to live in | Spins webs in dark areas | Build funnel webs on ground | Makes sac out of silk |
| Who is poisonous | Female | Male and female | Male | Male and female |
| How deadly | Not usually deadly | Painful but not deadly | Painful but not deadly | Least poisonous of the 4 types |

Title: Poisonous Spiders
Introduction: Spiders and poisonous spiders found in North America

If you are able to pick out the main ideas and supporting details from what you read, you have mastered one of the most important skills in good reading comprehension. Remember, good readers make great students, because they feel successful in school.

*5L.6    Acquire and use accurately grade-appropriate general academic and domain-specific words and phrases, including those that signal contrast, addition, and other logical relationships.*

## UNDERSTAND CONTENT-SPECIFIC VOCABULARY

Often, you can understand the meaning of a word by reading it in context. The word context refers to the words in the sentence around a word. The *context* of a word will help you to understand the word.

This means you may need to **re-read the sentence or even the paragraph that contains the word**. You also may need to **read ahead** a bit, to try figuring out what is being talked about in the passage. When you understand the context, you will be more likely to figure out what the unknown word might mean. When you reread or read ahead, look for familiar words or ideas that may give you a hint about the unfamiliar word.

*Example*
The lady was always very *generous*. She gave the children toys to play with and homemade cookies to eat.

If you did not understand the meaning of the word generous when you read that the woman gave toys and cookies to the children, you could probably guess that *generous* means almost the same as *kind* or *giving*.

As a student, you have to read all the time in most of your subjects. Most of these subjects are presented in units or chapters. Most units, no matter what the subject is, will have some terms you will have to learn. Before you can understand the unit, you must understand central vocabulary terms. Often, subject-specific terminology is introduced at the beginning of a new unit or chapter. For instance, before beginning a poetry unit, most English teachers will review terms such as *simile*, *lyric*, *metaphor*, and so on, because these terms are often used with poetry.

## VOCABULARY SIGNALS

- **bolded** in math, social studies, and science textbooks
- defined at the beginning of a new chapter
- defined at the bottom of the page or at the back of the textbook
- used by the teacher on the board, overhead, or for assignments

Learning new words helps you better understand and remember information, ideas, and concepts.

## TRICKS FOR LEARNING TERMS

Some strategies for adopting new words are to

- add them to your personal vocabulary list
- learn the meaning of the words in the content area
- practice spelling them correctly, even if you have to check back in the textbook
- use them in answers and assignments
- give them a permanent home in your "mental computer" (brain) so you can retrieve them as needed

## IDENTIFY A COMPARE/CONTRAST PATTERN IN INFORMATIONAL TEXT

It is important to be able to recognize a compare/contrast pattern in information passages and articles. This is a way of organizing information and facts in a way that shows similarities and differences between two things, groups, animals, places, etc.

Read the passages below to see if you can identify which one contains the **compare/contrast pattern**.

*Example*

---

### Jaguars and Leopards

Jaguars and leopards are close cousins that are very similar in appearance. The jaguar has a thicker body than the leopard, with shorter legs and a shorter tail. The spots on a leopard are smaller and closer together than on a jaguar. The spots on a jaguar are larger and uneven. One of the most significant differences between the two animals is that the jaguar lives primarily in North and South America, whereas the leopard lives in Africa and Asia. Both animals have cat-like qualities and are excellent predators that can run at tremendous speeds.

---

### The Cheetah

The cheetah is a member of the cat family. It is well known for its tremendous speed, reaching up to 65 mph. A cheetah has a tan-colored coat with small black spots; however, a cheetah does not have spots on its belly. The cheetah only lives to be about 12 years old in the wild. Its favorite foods include gazelles and hares. The cheetah can be found in Africa, Asia, and the Middle East.

---

## IDENTIFY SEQUENTIAL/CHRONOLOGICAL PATTERN IN TEXT

A sequential/chronological pattern in text is important because it helps the reader make sense of what's happening. A story that follows a fixed order of events is more likely to be understood and remembered by the reader.

Can you identify which of the following paragraphs has a sequential/chronological pattern?

### Paragraph #1

As I was packing my suitcase, I wondered how long I would be gone. Suddenly, I heard the taxi pull up in my driveway. I grabbed my luggage, purse and tickets and hurried out the door. It took about 15 minutes to get to the airport. I unloaded my luggage, checked-in, and headed to the terminal to await my flight. It was finally time to board the flight. I was excited and scared all at the same time. Hours passed and I was about to arrive in a different land. I never thought I'd have the courage to put my life on hold and help re-build a town that had been so badly damaged by an earthquake. They needed me and I was finally here to help.

### Paragraph #2

I was excited and scared all at the same time. I grabbed my luggage, purse and tickets and hurried out the door. As I was packing my suitcase, I wondered how long I would be gone. Hours passed and I was about to arrive in a different land. Suddenly, I heard the taxi pulled up in my driveway. They needed me and I was finally here to help. I unloaded my luggage, checked-in, and headed to the terminal to await my flight. It took about 15 minutes to get to the airport. I never thought I'd have the courage to put my life on hold and help re-build a town that had been so badly damaged by an earthquake. It was finally time to board the flight.

If you chose paragraph #1, then you are correct. If a story has clearly organized ideas that follow a consistent pattern, then the reader will be able to easily follow and understand the story.

## PROPOSITION AND SUPPORT

Most of the time, writers organize their information to best persuade readers to agree with their ideas or opinions. Their opinions are supported by several reasons or arguments. Read the paragraph below to see how persuasive information can be organized.

Logging companies should choose selective logging over clear-cut logging in order to benefit the environment. In selective logging, only certain trees are cut, but clear-cut logging is easier, cheaper and knocks down every single tree. Just one tree is probably home to hundreds of insects, and there are birds and mammals who live at different levels in the forest. Many wildlife species, such as lynxes and snowshoe hares, need an old growth forest with a mixture of live, dead, and rotting trees. People, however, need forest wood for houses and furniture. Selective logging not only provides wood for people, it also protects the forest habitat by leaving some trees standing.

You could summarize the proposition and support like this:

**Proposition**: Selective logging is better for the environment than clear-cut logging.

**Support** (arguments or reasons):

1. Selective logging leaves some trees standing
2. Insects, animals, and birds need live, dead, and rotting trees in their habitat
3. Clear-cut logging removes all live trees
4. With selective logging, people can still have lumber and wildlife can still have some trees
5. Both groups benefit, making the extra expense worthwhile

## IDENTIFYING CAUSE-AND-EFFECT PATTERNS IN INFORMATIONAL TEXT

Writers use cause and effect to develop paragraphs. These paragraphs tell why events happened and why things are as they are. A cause-and-effect pattern is often used in writing that informs, explains, or persuades.

Some cause-and-effect words and phrases are *because*, *as a result*, *why*, *when*, *therefore*, *so*, *for this reason*, and *if… then*.

*Example*
It was Games Day at school, and the children were looking forward to a day of playing games outside.

However, at 11:30 A.M., a thunderstorm with lightning, strong winds, and heavy rains began, which resulted in all the children having to go indoors. Because the afternoon activities were canceled, the children had to stay in their classroom.

You can put the examples you have found into a table.

| Cause | Effect |
|---|---|
| Thunderstorm | Children went inside. |
| Activities canceled | Children stayed in the classroom. |

*5W.2a Write informative/explanatory texts to examine a topic and convey ideas and information clearly. Introduce a topic clearly, provide a general observation and focus, and group related information logically; include formatting, illustrations, and...*

## How Format Makes Information Accessible

The way that a passage is organized is called *format*. The format of a research paper is different from the format of poem. The format of your writing should make it easier for readers to follow and understand what you have written.

Following are some examples of information books that are recognizable by their formats.

- Dictionary
- Encyclopedia
- Thesaurus
- Atlas
- Manual

Illustrated below are some examples of formats that make the type of information being presented very accessible.

## Business Letter Format

The format of the letter is set up to clearly show dates, addresses, the sender and receiver of the letter, and its purpose.

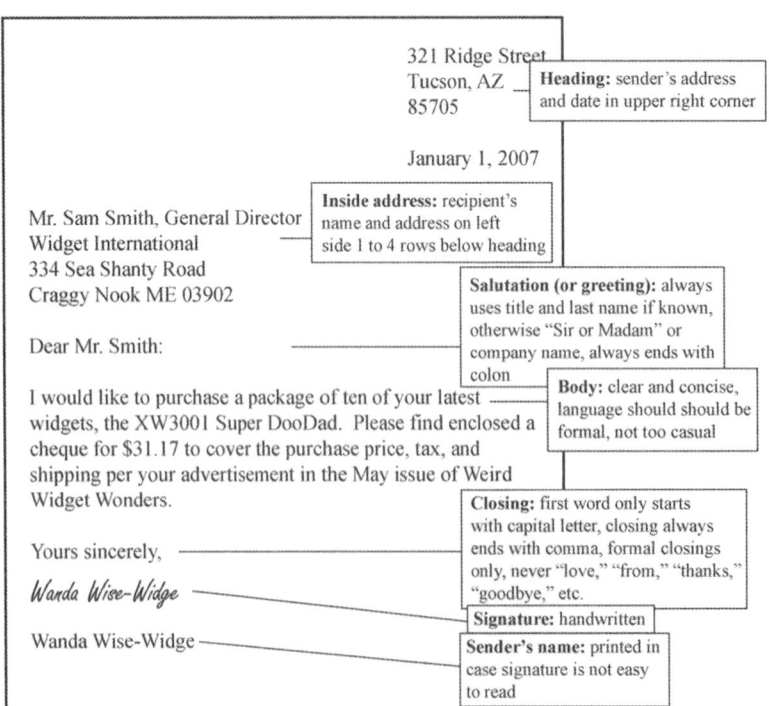

```
                                321 Ridge Street
                                Tucson, AZ          Heading: sender's address
                                85705               and date in upper right corner

                                January 1, 2007

Mr. Sam Smith, General Director    Inside address: recipient's
Widget International               name and address on left
334 Sea Shanty Road                side 1 to 4 rows below heading
Craggy Nook ME 03902
                                                    Salutation (or greeting): always
                                                    uses title and last name if known,
Dear Mr. Smith:                                     otherwise "Sir or Madam" or
                                                    company name, always ends with
                                                    colon
I would like to purchase a package of ten of your latest    Body: clear and concise,
widgets, the XW3001 Super DooDad. Please find enclosed a    language should should be
cheque for $31.17 to cover the purchase price, tax, and     formal, not too casual
shipping per your advertisement in the May issue of Weird
Widget Wonders.
                                                    Closing: first word only starts
                                                    with capital letter, closing always
Yours sincerely,                                    ends with comma, formal closings
                                                    only, never "love," "from," "thanks,"
Wanda Wise-Widge                                    "goodbye," etc.
                                                    Signature: handwritten
Wanda Wise-Widge                                    Sender's name: printed in
                                                    case signature is not easy
                                                    to read
```

## DIAGRAM FORMAT

When diagrams are formatted clearly in your science text, with arrows and labels, it is easy for you to learn the information. You can see at a glance that this diagram demonstrates the water cycle.

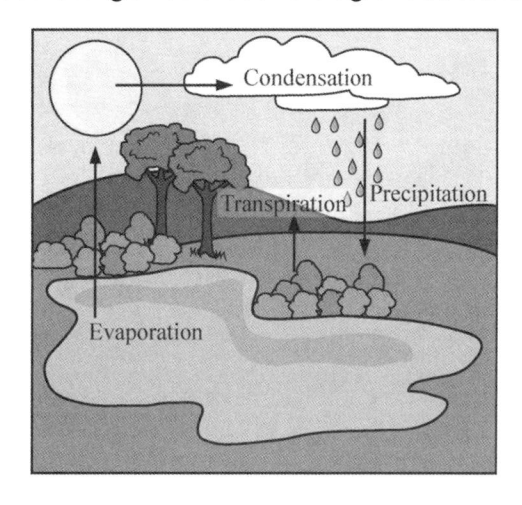

## NEWSPAPER FORMAT

Headlines, subheads, and photographs help readers to locate information quickly in a newspaper. Those items help to make up the format of a newspaper.

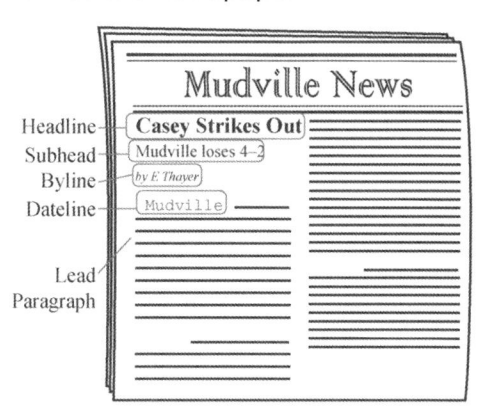

## CALENDAR FORMAT

When you check the calendar, you want to be able to quickly spot the day and date of your next baseball game, or whether your birthday falls on a weekend. The format of a calendar is clear and easy to use for daily events and special occasions.

# Brochure Format

The format of a brochure presents information in columns and colorful pictures to help readers scan the information quickly and efficiently.

> **TEXAS**
> Yours to Discover
>
> **On the Wild Side**
> Padre Island boasts over 300 species of birds. Rattlesnakes, coyotes, deer, and rabbits live in the dunes. You might even spot a rare and endangered sea turtle!
>
> *Heron*     *Laughing gulls*
>
> **Lots to Do!**     **Easy to Find!**
>
> Observe spectacular sunrises; sunbathe, swim, fish, or windsurf. Moderate land and sea temperatures make this an ideal year-round vacation spot. Try camping on the beach, collecting shells, and fishing (with a Texas licence) at Padre Island National Seashore.
>
> From Corpus Christi, it's a short drive across the John F. Kennedy Causeway to North Padre Island Village, a beachfront town with holiday homes, hotels, a campground, nature trails, a boat launch, and miles of empty sand dunes.
>
> *Padre Island*
> **Beautiful. Affordable. Right here.**

# How Graphics Make Information Accessible

Graphics are visual additions to a story, article or book, like photographs, illustrations, charts, or graphs. When you are reading a fiction or non-fiction book that has graphics to accompany the text, it is important to recognize that the graphics are there to add to your understanding.

If the graphics are in a story book, they may have more details then the text mentions. These graphics can help in your understanding of the story line or the characters within the story.

*Example*
A picture book story says: Mary received the important letter from her mother and as she read it, she cried and cried.

This story may have a graphic that has picture of the letter her mother wrote, or other pictures that help you as a reader to understand the effect of the letter on Mary.

*Example*

If a short story or chapter book has a story about a group of friends who were fund raising for their club, a graphic in this fictional story may be a chart of their total earnings, as the book continues, and as they raise more and more money.

This graphic can give you more information and further support the text. It can also give more of a visual understanding to those who need it. Some students learn more from pictures than they do from the printed text.

---

These are just a few examples of how graphics can make information accessible in a fictional story.

If there are graphics in a non-fiction text, these graphics can be informative about the topic being discussed or explained.

*Example*

If a text book you are reading is talking about the provinces of Canada, a graphic that might accompany the text could be a map of Canada with the provinces outlined.

This graphic can be beneficial to you the reader, as it shows a visual of where the provinces are located within Canada and what they may look like in comparison to one another.

*5SL.4 Report on a topic or text or present an opinion, sequencing ideas logically and using appropriate facts and relevant, descriptive details to support main ideas or themes; speak clearly at an understandable pace.*

## How Sequence Makes Information Accessible

When information follows a deliberate order or sequence, it is usually easier to follow. Examples of information that follows a sequence include recipes, instructions for games, classroom rules, and instructions for fixing things.

## Look for the Sequence

Look for the sequence below as you read the instructions for exploring a website. The information would make the most sense if you followed the instructions in the order they are given. Look for clue words like *then*, *when*, and *now*.

If you start a Google search, you can visit a special site for curious kids that is based on the Telkom Exploratorium Museum. The museum has put some great exhibits and experiments online so that you can explore them. Each month, the website is updated, which means that you can find something new, no matter how often you visit.

Are you ready? Type exploratorium in the Google Search bar. Then click Search. The first 10 results are the ones that are most often used. The following two headings are good starting points:Exploratorium: the museum of science, art and human perception, and Exploratorium: "a world where technology and fun meet" Try clicking on the heading "Exploratorium: 'a world where technology and fun meet." When the website homepage appears, click on "background" to read a little bit about the Exploratorium and its location in Cape Town, South Africa. Click on "the itinerary" at the bottom of this page. Click on "Come See" and then click Start to begin a journey through some of the exhibits and activities. Now, go back to the beginning of the instructions, and try to follow them. Step by step, you can explore this interesting website yourself.

## Numbering the Sequence

The information is even more accessible if you can read it in a numbered sequence. Somehow, the numbers make it easier to keep an "order in mind".

1. Typeexploratorium in the Google Search bar.
2. Then click Search. The first 10 results are the ones that are most often used.
3. Try clicking on the heading "Exploratorium: 'a world where technology and fun meet."
4. When the website homepage appears, click on "background" to read a little bit about the Exploratorium and its location in Cape Town, South Africa.
5. Click on "the itinerary" at the bottom of this page.
6. Click on "Come See" and then click Start to begin a journey through some of the exhibits and activities.
7. Now, go back to the beginning of the instructions, and try to follow them. Step by step, you can explore this interesting website yourself.

## How Diagrams Make Information Accessible

A **diagram** is a simple drawing of an object or a process. It can be used to explain what happened in an experiment. It can be used to explain how something works. A diagram is sometimes easier to understand than words. All parts of the diagram should be labeled.

This student-drawn diagram shows how water goes through different states in the water cycle. Sometimes it might be necessary to draw a diagram to show how you arrived at an answer or conclusion.

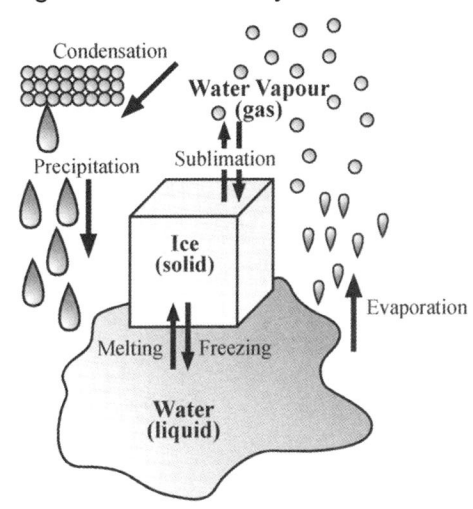

You can make a map diagram to show where something is. For example, a student drew a map to show the location of a pond. This is the pond that the student used to perform a nature study for her science project.

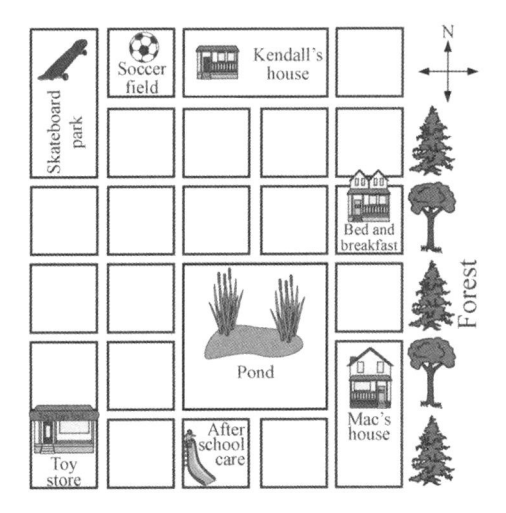

## How Illustrations Make Information Accessible

When you are reading a fiction or non-fiction book that has illustrations to accompany the text, it is important to recognize that the illustrations are there to add to your understanding.

If the illustrations are in a story book, they may have more details then the text mentions. These illustrations can help in your understanding of the story line or the characters within the story.

*Example*

A picture book story says, "Jack was always getting into trouble."

What might come to your mind as a visual in your head?

Without looking at the illustration in the book, you may think this story was talking about a young, mischievous boy.

To your surprise, the illustration has a picture of a little puppy dog eating a child's shoe.

Jack is not a boy, he is a puppy!

---

This is just one example of how illustrations can make information accessible in a fictional story.

If there are illustrations in a non-fiction text, these illustrations can be informative about the topic being discussed or explained.

*Example*

In a book all about kangaroos, one page may be talking about how mother kangaroos carry their babies in their pouch.

If you have never heard of, or seen a kangaroo pouch, you may not be able to understand what a pouch is.

In the illustration that accompanies this page there is a picture of a mother kangaroo carrying the baby kangaroo in her pouch.

This illustration would be very helpful to understand what a kangaroo's pouch looks like.

*5SL.1c Engage effectively in a range of collaborative discussions (one-on-one, in groups, and teacher-led) with diverse partners on grade 5 topics and texts, building on others' ideas and expressing their own clearly. Pose and respond to...*

## Asking and Answering Questions to Convey Information

When you are reading a textbook or studying for a test, it is helpful to be able to use various reading strategies to help you remember what you have read. Asking yourself questions is one such strategy. To do this, think of questions about your reading to help you focus.

Take headings, key words, or topic sentences and turn them into questions. Suppose you were reading a book about Earth. Think of all of the questions you could ask, using what you already know, what you might like to know, and what you are learning through the information in the book. Asking questions and then using the text to answer them is a great way to study and remember the information you have read.

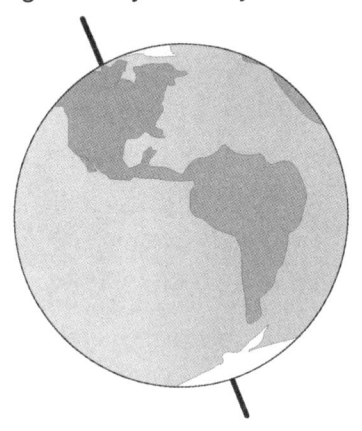

## Write to Answer a Question

Posing a question is a smart way to begin your paragraph or writing project, especially if you are presenting information. Below are some sample questions that you could answer in a paragraph, report, or essay:

- What are the most seriously endangered animals on our planet?
- How can you design your own web page?
- How exactly would you go about creating a blog?
- How can we eat healthy now so that we won't suffer problems like obesity and diabetes later?
- What are the most important things for a babysitter to know?
- What should you do if you hear a tornado warning?
- Why are dolphins such amazing mammals?

## Combine Information from More than One Source

When you are learning about a topic, it is a good idea to read several articles. What information gets repeated? What information is different or new? After you read, you can write down some of the comparisons (similarities) and contrasts (differences) that you find. As you see what facts get repeated, it becomes easier to combine the information from different sources.

Imagine that you have a research topic: "The California Gold Rush." You have found the following three articles:

- "The California Gold Rush"
- "California Gold Rush"
- "The Rush for Gold"

As you read each article, you could underline interesting or important facts or ideas.

You can then compare the articles by creating a chart with the information that you have read. On the chart, use only words that you understand. This will make it easier for you to combine and present your research.

| | |
|---|---|
| **Article 1: The California Gold Rush** | Jan 24, 1848, James Marshall finds nuggets near building site for John Sutter's mill |
| | Half a million people came |
| | 1849: found gold in quartz, led to underground mine lasting 100 years |
| | 1852: gold production reached $81 million |
| | Lasted from 1848 to 1864 |
| **Article 2: California Gold Rush** | Jan 1848 gold discovered at Sutter's mill |
| | Lasted from (1848 to 1855) |
| | 300,000 people came |
| | Gold seekers called "forty-niners" |
| | Faced many hardships |
| | Simple panning led to more complicated methods |
| | Great wealth for a few |
| | Good Effects: San Francisco, roads, churches, schools, towns, laws, new state (1850), railroads |
| | Bad Effects: Native Americans attacked, environment |
| **Article 3: The Rush for Gold** | Many did not find expected gold |
| | Started businesses they had been in before |
| | Lasted 1849 to mid-1850s |
| | Ended in 1859 when silver was discovered in Nevada |
| **Same in All 3 Articles** | Started in 1848 (Article 3 says "By 1849 the rush was on.") |
| | Started in California |
| | People came from all over the U.S. |

Here are some ways that you can think critically about this information:

1. Notice the information that differs in the three articles, like the actual dates of the gold rush. You could conclude that dates are rough estimates, especially when different observers attach them to different important research questions, like "What event started the California Gold Rush?"
2. Notice the different information from each article that you could include in a report under your own headings.
3. Notice that you have many facts about the Gold Rush. These often include names of people and places, and dates of specific events like discoveries.
4. Notice that the articles contain opinions of the writer, like "a half million people from around the world descended upon California" and "some 300,000 people came to California." Opinions of the writer may or may not be true.
5. Come up with a main topic for your research, for example: "The Gold Rush helped create the state of California." Pick a topic that you can support with facts, evidence, or knowledge from the ideas and information in the articles.

As you think about the information you have collected, using guidelines similar to those above, you will be able to combine your information in a report or writing piece, using your own subtopics and without repeating information.

## IDENTIFY EVIDENCE THAT SUPPORTS THE MAIN IDEAS IN A TEXT

Authors must have a logical story line, that usually has events which build upon one another to make an engaging plot. There are key events or ideas within the text that are used to help support the main ideas. Authors may use specific details in the descriptions of the characters, the setting, the plot line, etc., that give evidence about the main ideas of the entire text.

In the following passage, the author, Aaron Taouma, provides evidence throughout about the main idea of the story.

As you read the passage, try to pick out details in the story which help support the main idea.

The main idea is based around the fact that the narrators's uncle is a crazy cab driver who never fails to entertain the people who get a ride with him.

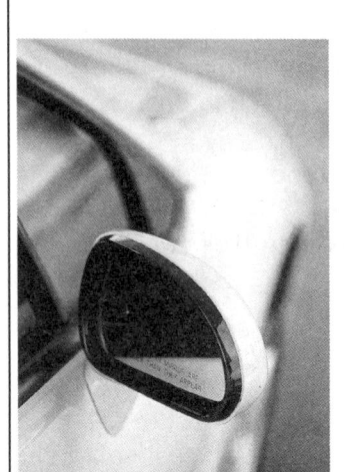

## An Invite from Uncle

Driving in Uncle's taxi was like entering another world, a crazy, mixed-up world where anything could and did happen. This world is my Uncle's home, not a taxi but a rolling chariot of dreams and tales and you as his special guest.

Just getting into Uncle's taxi, you knew this was something different. He would decorate the inside of his taxi with all kinds of frilly bits, a mix between kitsch and FOB, Christmas lights, pictures of Jesus, hanging tennis balls and even a disco ball.

Uncle also played a mix of Island and rock and roll music on his tape deck and you could be forgiven for thinking that you were riding in a rolling disco or even an evangelist tour bus. But this simply was Uncle, a part of him.

Uncle loved telling stories. He especially loved the one about the Elvis impersonator who jumped into his taxi and instead of paying for his fare plugged a microphone into Uncle's sound system and sang for the entire ride. Apparently, things got so carried away that when they stopped at the lights the impersonator jumped out and danced and sang on the street. Uncle turned up the sound and the whole street stopped to look and listen. It was a real traffic-stopper, Uncle would say.

Yep, Uncle had all the celebs in his taxi and it was funny how whoever was in the news at the time, Uncle just happened to have picked them up the night before: Mini-Me from *Austin Powers*, Mr. T from *The A-Team*, even Michael Jackson and his monkey. My Uncle had them all and with each there was a story, a fantastic story to be told.

Uncle's driving was a whole other experience too, a scary and nerve-racking one. He wouldn't drive as such but let his taxi drive while he sat and talked. Uncle would turn and look you straight in the eyes and have whole conversations, including hand gestures and self-applause, while the taxi swerved from side to side, over the median strip, towards parked and oncoming cars and back again. The whole time you would sit holding on for dear life, with a look of horror on your face as you screamed, "Look at the road!"

Then Uncle would drop you off, shaken and yet exhilarated. He would smile and say, "See you soon," and you would stand on the street dumbfounded at the very thought.

> But you know what? Uncle never ever had an accident and driving with him was cheaper and more exciting than an amusement park or a show. So, if you're looking for an experience in the city, look for a taxi, the one with the flashing lights and a disco ball. There you'll find my Uncle. He'll invite you into his world, his home and an experience you won't soon forget.
>
> —by Aaron Taouma

Some of the evidence in the text that helps support the main idea from the story, "An Invite From Uncle" is as follows:

- "Driving in Uncle's taxi was like entering another world, a crazy mixed up world, where anything could happen."
- "You as his special guest."
- "Just getting into Uncle's taxi, you knew this was something different."
- "Uncle loved telling stories."
- "… the whole street stopped to look and listen."
- "My uncle had them all and with each there was a story, a fantastic story to be told."
- "Uncle's driving was a whole other experience too, a scary nerve wracking one."
- "Then Uncle would drop you off, shaken and yet exhilarated."
- "Driving with him was cheaper and more exciting than an amusement park or a show."
- "He'll invite you into his world, his home and an experience you won't soon forget."

Do you see how these specific lines in the passage really help give evidence that supports the main idea of the text? Do you see that the narrator's uncle was an entertaining cab driver who made a difference in the many people's lives he met?

These sentences directly affect the ideas presented in the story. They help build and support the main idea, and the text would not be the same without them.

*5RI.10 By the end of the year, read and comprehend informational texts, including history/social studies, science, and technical texts, at the high end of the grades 4–5 text complexity band independently and proficiently.*

## WHAT IS NON-FICTION?

Non-Fiction is meant to be factual information. Non-fiction is true.

## TYPES OF NON-FICTION TEXTS

There are many types of non-fiction texts. Some of these are listed below:

- Essays
- Recipes
- Diagrams
- Journals
- Biographies
- Autobiographies
- Travel books
- Scientific papers
- User manuals
- Blueprints
- Histories
- Documentaries
- Text books
- Memoirs
- Book reports

*Example*

Below is a non-fiction piece about weather forecasting:

### Weather Lore

Weather forecasting is a modern science. Years ago (before 1930), predicting tomorrow's weather was little more than a guessing game. From experience, farmers and fishermen learned what to watch for. They made up easy-to-remember rhymes and sayings about ways to predict weather. Some of their notions are still with us today. A few of them are based on scientifically valid concepts. But most are wrong as often as they are right.

Each February 2, we are reminded faithfully about the story of the groundhog and his shadow. If the groundhog comes out of his burrow at noon on that day and sees his shadow, we are in for six more weeks of winter. If not, according to the legend, mild weather can be expected. Weather records have proved the groundhog wrong many, many times.

However, some animal behavior is a good predictor for the weather, at least during the next few hours. Some farm animals know when a storm is coming and will seek shelter; others become agitated and restless. Ants and spiders scurry at top speed to complete their tasks. Bees return to the hive.

Today, most weather lore is simply quaint—not very useful in modern life, but fun.

"Squirrel's tail fluffy, winter will be blustery" is one of hundreds of weather rhymes about animals, birds and insects. Another supposed predictor is the wooly caterpillar: if the black band on the caterpillar's back is wide in autumn, the winter will be severe. Scientists say, however, that neither squirrels' tails nor caterpillars' backs predict winter weather.

"A coming storm your shooting corns will presage" is one of many old sayings suggesting that aches and pains are worse when a storm is approaching. This may be true. Some aches could be aggravated because humidity is maximum and atmospheric pressure minimum just before and during a storm.

"If the sun red should set, the next day surely will be wet." Well, it depends on where you live because the following rhyme says the opposite: "Red sky in the morning, sailors take warning; red sky at night, sailors' delight."

"If wooly fleeces spread the heavenly way, be sure no rain disturbs the day." This rhyme refers to a sky of small puffy cumulus clouds. It tells us that no rain will fall that day. This would be true most of the time, but a cumulonimbus cloud can develop, bringing thunderstorms.

Another legend states that rain will arrive soon if frogs creak louder than usual. This is probably true, because frogs are most active in damp weather.

"It's raining cats and dogs" is a very old expression. In mythology, cats were associated with rain and dogs with wind. So a windy rainstorm was called a cat-and-dog storm.

—from *Exploring the Sky by Day: The Equinox Guide to Weather and the Atmosphere* by Terence Dickinson

---

Non-fiction is meant to be true information which can be presented in many different forms.

## MEDIA TEXTS

**Media texts** are products whose purpose is to communicate with others. You will understand the meaning better if you look at a list of examples:

- Radio programs
- Television programs
- Movies
- Billboards
- Television commercials
- Magazine advertisements
- Books
- Paintings
- Photographs
- Comics
- Cartoons
- Web pages
- Travel brochures
- Magazines
- Newspapers

Now, consider a few examples from the list.

## TRAVEL BROCHURES

The purpose of a travel brochure is to persuade tourists to visit a certain place. Attractive photographs, exciting descriptions, and important information are used to attract tourists to the intended destination.

Look at the following example of how a travel brochure for Arkansas might persuade people to go there for their annual holiday.

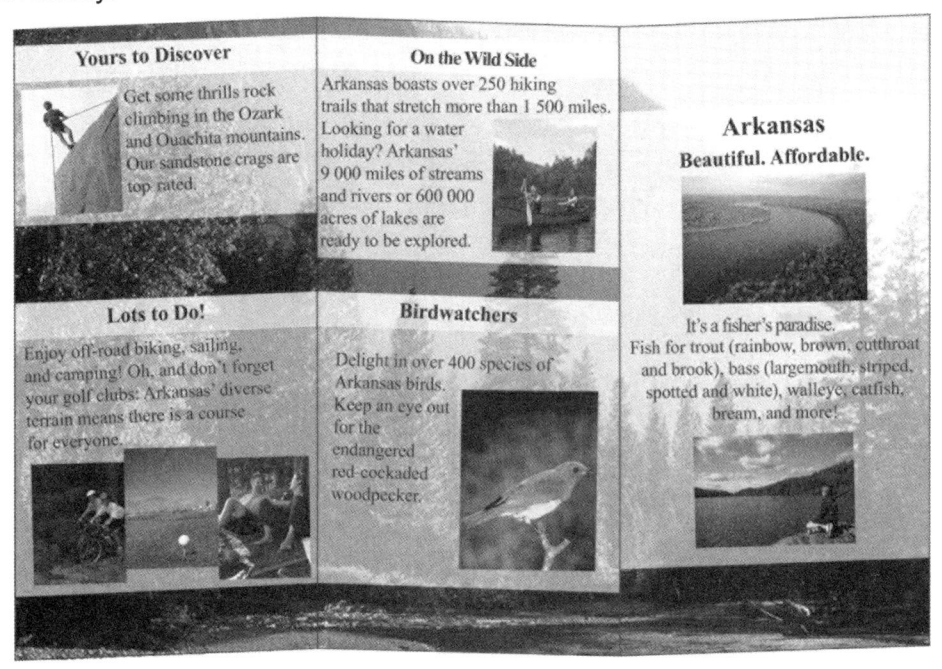

## NEWSPAPERS

Newspapers have different kinds of writing, but their main purpose is to report news exactly as it happened. The kind of factual writing answers the five Ws (who, what, where, when, and why) and one H (how).

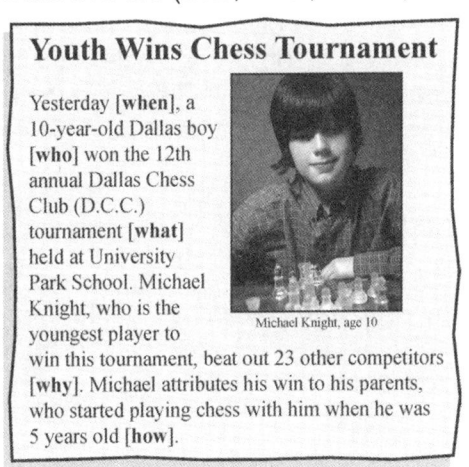

**Youth Wins Chess Tournament**

Yesterday [**when**], a 10-year-old Dallas boy [**who**] won the 12th annual Dallas Chess Club (D.C.C.) tournament [**what**] held at University Park School. Michael Knight, who is the youngest player to win this tournament, beat out 23 other competitors [**why**]. Michael attributes his win to his parents, who started playing chess with him when he was 5 years old [**how**].

Michael Knight, age 10

## Paintings

Paintings are examples of media texts because they can interact with others in the following ways:

- People can enjoy or dislike the paintings
- Viewers can interpret themes and messages
- People can view and purchase paintings in stores or galleries
- Viewers can discuss what they see or how the paintings make them feel
- A collection of paintings can be compared and offer contrasting messages

Artists use different techniques to communicate emotions and moods. They also consider the composition, distance, and perspective. Composition refers to the arrangement of the subject matter in a drawing or a painting. Artists can create a sense of distance and depth using a line that indicates where the sky and the ground meet. This line is known as the horizon line. Objects in the picture that are closer to the horizon line appear to be in the background and farther away. Objects in the picture that are farther away from the horizon line appear to be closer to the front of the painting. This imaginary space is called the foreground.

## The Language of Media Texts

People often think of a "text" as something with words. Some media texts, such as newspapers and magazines, certainly use words. However, a "text" can be visual without words, such as a picture of a soft kitten playing with a "soft" brand of toilet paper. Media text can be sound effects and exaggerated actions in a commercial for a popular new toy. Media text is different from other text because it can "speak" without words.

*5RF.3a Know and apply grade-level phonics and word analysis skills in decoding words. Use combined knowledge of all letter-sound correspondences, syllabication patterns, and morphology to read accurately unfamiliar multisyllabic words in context...*

*5RF.4c Read with sufficient accuracy and fluency to support comprehension. Use context to confirm or self-correct word recognition and understanding, rereading as necessary.*

*5L.4a Determine or clarify the meaning of unknown and multiple-meaning words and phrases based on grade 5 reading and content, choosing flexibly from a range of strategies. Use context as a clue to the meaning of a word or phrase.*

## Using Context to Understand Unfamiliar Words

Sometimes, when you are reading, you will come across a word that you do not understand or know. Often, you will not have a dictionary on hand when you are reading, but the you will want to know what a word means. When this happens, it is important that you stop and try a few different strategies to figure it out. If you do not, it could affect your comprehension of the whole text.

One strategy is to see the word in its context. This means you may need to reread the sentence or even the paragraph that contains the word. You also may need to read ahead a bit, to try figuring out what is being talked about in the passage. When you have a solid understanding of the context, you will be more likely to figure out what the unfamiliar word might mean. When you are rereading or reading ahead, it is important that you look for familiar words or ideas that may give you a hint as to what the unfamiliar word means. These hints are called *context clues*.

If this still has not helped, you could try asking yourself, "What word do I know that would make sense in the place of the new word in this sentence?" Then try substituting the familiar word in the sentence and read the passage to see if the word makes sense in the text.

*Example*
Using the nonsense word TALIBUSIXA, see if you can give a logical meaning to it by using the context clues in the following paragraph.

What kinds of things were in this paragraph that help give clues to the context of the word TALIBUSIXA?

Jacob traveled for a long time to get to his friend's home in Toronto. The TALIBUSIXA took four days on the bus. He was so tired when he arrived in Toronto. He was so happy that the bus ride had come to an end. Jake was so relieved to find his friend waiting for him at the bus station.

Some of the context clues in the passage might be the words *traveled*, *bus*, *distance*, and *Toronto*.

You could come to a conclusion that the word might mean trip or journey just by looking at the context clues.

When you read the sentence over using your inferred words or ideas, the paragraph still makes sense, and it has not changed the meaning of what is being relayed to the reader. It fits!

---

*Example*

Try to figure out the following highlighted word's meaning without using a dictionary. See if there are any context clues that can help you figure out what the word might mean.

Marla was good at many sports. She excelled in fencing, target shooting, swimming, running, and horsemanship. She decided to compete in the PENTATHLON rather than having to choose one of the events.

Some of the words that might give context clues in this paragraph are: *excelled*, the list of the five sports (*fencing*, *target shooting*, *swimming*, *running*, and *horsemanship*) *compete*, and *events*.

Do you think you figured out the meaning of the word PENTATHLON by using the context clues in the paragraph?

You can infer, by looking at the context clues, that the word PENTATHLON has something to do with a sporting event. You can infer that Marla was going to be involved in all five of the listed sports she excelled in because she did not want to have to choose only one of the events.

Class Focus        Castle Rock Research

The meaning of the word PENTATHLON actually means a contest featuring five different events. It is usually a track and field event, and incorporates the skills of shooting, swimming, fencing, equestrian (horsemanship) and running.

---

## Using Inferencing to Understand Unfamiliar Words

Sometimes when you are reading, you will come across a word that you do not understand or do not know. When this happens, it is important that you stop and try a few different strategies to figure it out. If you don't, your comprehension of the story or passage could be affected.

One strategy is to use **inferencing** skills to figure out what an unfamiliar word might mean, by seeing it in its context. **Inferencing** means making your best educated guess about a word by using your background knowledge and ideas to help figure out an answer. You will need to figure out what a word might mean from the clues the author gives you, as well as using your own knowledge and experience.

You may need to **reread the sentence or even the paragraph that the word falls in**, or **read ahead** a bit to try figuring out what is being talked about in the passage. When you have a solid understanding of the context, you will be more likely to figure out what the unfamiliar word might mean, and begin thinking of different similar words that could fit in its place.

If this still has not helped, you could try asking yourself, "What word do I know that would make sense in the place of the new word in this sentence?" Then try substituting the familiar word in the sentence and read the passage to see if the word makes sense in the text.

## Trying Out the Strategy

Using a nonsense word, **MAXORIUM**, let's see if we can give a logical meaning to it, by using it in the context of the paragraph.

Jacob could hardly wait for the **MAXORIUM**. Five more days! Feverishly, he worked every waking minute to complete his model rocket. Last year, he had placed 2nd. Jacob was sure that this Saturday, he would be taking home the winner's trophy!

What word could you put in the place of the nonsense word, **MAXORIUM** in this sentence, based on the clues in the paragraph?

Some of the clues in the passage might be: **worked, complete, model rocket, winner's trophy**.

We could conclude that the word might mean a science fair or contest.

Now, read the sentence using our predicted word meaning and see if it makes sense. It fits!

## Now It's Your Turn

Read the following passage and see if you can infer a meaning for the unfamiliar highlighted word. Remember to see what other words in the passage may be giving you clues as to what the word might mean.

Sally woke up from her deep sleep. She could not believe she had slept for so long. She got out of her bed, got dressed and headed down to the kitchen. "Man, I am thirsty," she thought to herself. She reached up into the cupboard, grabbed a **BRIDA** and then poured herself some orange juice. "Delicious!" she thought.

Do you think you have any guesses as to what the nonsense word **BRIDA** might mean?

Here are some clues if you need some help: She's in the **kitchen**. She's **thirsty**. She went into the **cupboard**, grabbed a **BRIDA**. She **poured** herself some **orange juice**.

We could probably come to the conclusion that the word **BRIDA** might mean, **cup** or **mug**.

Replace our mystery word **BRIDA** with the word **cup**.

Sally woke up from her deep sleep. She could not believe she had slept for so long. She got out of her bed, got dressed and headed down to the kitchen. "Man, I am thirsty," she thought to herself. She reached up into the cupboard, grabbed a **CUP** and then poured herself some orange juice. "Delicious!" she thought.

The word **cup** would easily fit in place of **BRIDA**. It would make sense in the context and does not change the meaning of the passage.

## Understanding Words by Finding Familiar Words Within Unknown Words

Sometimes when you are reading, you will come across a word that you do not understand. Often we do not have a dictionary on hand when we are reading, and we want to know what a word means. When this happens, try a few different strategies to figure it out. It could affect your comprehension of the text.

One strategy is to break the unfamiliar word down into smaller more familiar parts, because the word itself can give you clues about its meaning.

You are a detective trying to decode smaller words in the big, unfamiliar word! Figuring out each part of the word can help you determine its meaning. Breaking the word into separate parts, like its root word, the prefix and the suffix, can help unlock the actual meaning of the word.

*Example*
1. Look for familiar root words in a word. (For example: *Unfamiliar* - the root word is *familiar*)
2. Look at the the prefixes or suffixes of a word. (For example: *Unfamiliar* - the **un** is the prefix of the word)

In the word *unfamiliar* - we can determine the root word is *familiar*, meaning common or well known, and the prefix is UN - which usually means "not" or "opposite". Therefore, we can determine that the word *unfamiliar* means "not common".

## TRY THIS STRATEGY

In the sentence below, TRIPOD is the word we are trying to figure out.

*Example*

Sophie took her camera out of its case and put it on the her TRIPOD to get ready to take a picture of herself and her friends.

When you look at the word *tripod*, you can see the prefix of the word is "TRI". Where else have you seen the prefix "TRI" in other words? Have you seen *triangle, tricycle, triceratops*? What would you guess TRI might indicate?

A triangle has three sides

A tricycle has three wheels

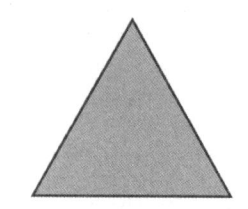

A triceratops dinosaur has three large horns

We can assume "TRI" means three. Now seeing the word TRIPOD in its sentence, we might assume it was a stand with three legs to hold the camera.

Once you have broken the word into smaller parts or words, see if it would make sense in its context. Our guess of a TRIPOD being a stand with three legs would make sense in the context of the sentence.

## Now It's Your Turn

Can you figure out the meaning of the unfamiliar word, *rearrange*, in the following sentence? First, remember to find the root word, then see if you can find a familiar prefix or suffix.

My mom was upset with the renovations in our living room. She said she was going to have to REARRANGE all the new furniture so it would all fit inside.

Can you identify the root word? How about the prefix in the word? What other words have you heard of that have the same prefixes?

Think you have it? Check your answer below.

The root word of *rearrange* is "ARRANGE" and the prefix is "RE" Have you heard of the word of *arrange* before? It means to organize.

Have you ever heard of any other words that have the prefix "re" in them? How about these words: *rebuild, replay, rewrite, remake*? They all mean to do something over again; therefore, we can assume that the prefix "RE" means to do again or do over.

## USING PREFIXES AND SUFFIXES TO UNDERSTAND NEW WORDS

Sometimes when you are reading, you will come across a word that you do not understand. Often you do not have a dictionary on hand when you are reading, and you want to know what a word means. When this happens, it is important that you stop and try a few different strategies to figure it out. It could affect your comprehension of the text.

One strategy is to break the unfamiliar word down into smaller, more familiar parts, because the word itself can give you clues about its meaning.

You are a detective trying to decode smaller words within a bigger, unfamiliar word. Figuring out each part of the word can help you determine its meaning. Breaking the word into separate parts, and looking at the prefix and the suffix, can help unlock the actual meaning of the word. The root word is the core of the word, the prefix is at the beginning of a word and a suffix is at the end of a word.

First, you want to look for familiar root words in a word. (For example: unfamiliar - the root word is familiar) Then you will also want to look at the the prefixes or suffixes of a word. (For example: unfamiliar - the 'un' is the prefix of the word)

In the word *unfamiliar* - we can determine the root word is *familiar*, meaning common or well known, and the prefix is UN - which usually means "not" or "opposite" So therefore we can determine that the word *unfamiliar* means "not familiar."

Below is a table of commonly used suffixes and prefixes. It would be useful for you to get to know these prefixes and suffixes, as that will help you with your word comprehension for years to come.

| Common Suffixes | Common Suffix Word Meaning | Suffix Word Example |
|---|---|---|
| able | tells what kind | suitable, lovable |
| al | having to do with something | magical, national |
| ance | act, process of, state of | disappearance |
| ant | having the quality, manner or condition of a person, "one who…" | assistant, observant |
| ary | belonging to, connected with | legendary, momentarily |
| en | made of | wooden |
| ful | full of, or characterized by | hopeful, sorrowful |
| hood | the state of being | manhood, falsehood |
| ion | the act of | expression, perfection |
| less | unable, without | needless, regardless |
| ly | in what way or manner | lovely, gladly |

| Common Prefixes | Common Prefix Word Meaning | Prefix Word Example |
|---|---|---|
| ab | from | abnormal |
| ad | to | admit, adhere |
| be | by | before |
| com | with, together | compact |
| de | from | deduct |
| dis | apart | disappear, disengage |
| en | in | enjoy |
| ex | out | exhale |
| in | in | inhabit |
| in | not | incorrect |
| pre | before | preview, prediction |
| pro | for, forward | propel, pronoun |
| re | back | renovate, reconsider |
| sub | under | submarine |
| un | not | unhappy, uncommon |

## TRY THIS STRATEGY

In the passage below, *abolishable* is the word we will try to figure out.

The undercover cop told his partner that once he read the police report, it would be ABOLISHABLE. No one could ever see what he was about to read, and therefore he knew it had to be destroyed and never found again.

When you look at the word *abolishable*, you can see the root word is *abolish*? The suffix is ABLE. Where else have you seen words with the suffix "ABLE"? *Lovable, huggable, avoidable, comfortable*. What might ABLE indicate? *Lovable* means "able to love", *Huggable* means "able to hug", *avoidable* means "able to avoid", and *comfortable* is "able to have comfort". Therefore we might assume *abolishable* might mean "able to abolish". Abolish means to destroy.

Seeing the word *abolishable* in its sentence above, we might assume it means to destroy or get rid of.

It is safe to say that that meaning would make sense in the context of the paragraph.

## NOW IT'S YOUR TURN

Can you determine the meaning of the word, *recover*, in the following sentence? First remember to find the root word, then look for a familiar prefix or suffix.

My mom was upset with the pop stains on the easy chair in our family room. She said she was going to have to RECOVER it before Grandma arrived for her visit.

Need a hint?

Can you identify the root word? How about the prefix in the word? What other words have you heard of that have the same prefixes?

Think you have it? Check your answer below.

The root word of *recover* is "COVER" and the prefix is "RE". Have you heard of the word of "COVER" before? It means to hide something from view.

Have you ever heard of any other words that have the prefix "re" in them? How about these words: *restore, refocus, restate, return*? They all mean to do something over again; therefore, we can conclude that the prefix "RE" means to do again or do over.

# Using the "Does it Make Sense" Strategy to Understand Text

Sometimes when you are reading, you may come across words that you are unfamiliar with. There are many great strategies you can use to try figuring out these unknown words. One strategy is called the "Does it make sense?" strategy. What this strategy involves, is stopping your reading when you come to a part that is unfamiliar to you. It is at this time that you must ask yourself, "Does this make sense?"

If your answer is "no," you must go back and read over the text again.

*Example*
Read the following passage carefully. Ask yourself, "Does it make sense?"

Suzie gazed at the fridge for a long moment. "I wonder if it's done yet," she muttered.

Finally, she could wait no longer. She was so hungry! Suzie opened the fridge door, and there sat the huge piece of chocolate cake that she had been thinking about. "Aww...," whispered Suzie. "It needs to cook a little longer." Disappointed, she closed the fridge door and went back outside to play.

At first, the story may seem normal - a small girl opens the fridge because she is hungry, finds a piece of cake.... But, wait! Why would she say that the cake needs to cook longer, if it is in the fridge? Maybe if she was looking in the oven, it would make sense, but the cake is already cooked. The only food that might need more time in the fridge would be something like jello, or pudding, or perhaps some popsicles that her mother was freezing for a snack later. In other words, the story so far does not make sense.

Although the example above is quite silly, it shows the importance of text "making sense" to the reader. If what you are reading does not make sense to you, always reread that part. Sometimes you have:

- misunderstood a word
- misread a word that has a similar spelling
- read something into the sentence that wasn't there
- skipped over a few words or even a whole line

This strategy also works to help you understand strange new words that you encounter in text.

*Example*
"Tim's mother said he would have to visit an ophthalmologist before school started in September."

If you came across the word *ophthalmologist* in your novel, it might not make sense at first, because it is a strange word. However, if an earlier chapter mentioned that the main character, Tim, was looking at TV and complaining to his mother that the picture was "fuzzy", you could think of a phrase like "eye doctor", and try substituting it for the unfamiliar word. Would the sentence make sense now?

## USE PHONETIC KNOWLEDGE TO FIGURE OUT WORDS

Phonetic knowledge refers to your knowledge of word and letter sounds. As a beginning reader, you learned the sound of long and short vowels, all the consonants, plus blends of many letters such as *oo*, *ea*, *ck*, *cl*, *fr*, and so on. You learned about syllables, which contain one vowel sound each. Sounding out each letter or letter chunk in a word is a very common strategy to figure out an unfamiliar word.

When sounding out a word you should first look to see if there are smaller words inside the word that you recognize. Letter chunks like the "ch" sound or the "sh" sound are usually easy to recognize.

When you sound out a word, you should start with the first letter, and say each letter sound out loud. Then, blend the sounds together. Try to say the word to see if you can recognize it.

*Example*
"It rained so hard that I got on my rain boots, ran outside and splashed in the puddles."

If you were unfamiliar with the word *splashed*, you would start by sounding out the first letter and continue to sound out each of the letters in the word.

Note: If you recognize a blend such as "sh", you know that those two letters, when placed together, make a different sound than if they were apart.

## YOUR TURN

Look closely at the words below. Which words do you think are real words and which are alien words (meaning not real words)? You will need to use the "sounding out" strategy to help you decide.

- swamp
- kinter
- spectacular
- wunto
- karmpooa
- zebra
- terprimjo
- windy
- chocolate
- raggit

## ANSWERS

Check your answers below. The words listed are real words.

- swamp
- spectacular
- windy
- chocolate
- zebra

Alien words are listed below:

- kinter
- wunto
- karmpooa
- terprimjo
- raggit

*5RF.4a Read with sufficient accuracy and fluency to support comprehension. Read on-level text with purpose and understanding.*

*5RF.4b Read with sufficient accuracy and fluency to support comprehension. Read on-level prose and poetry orally with accuracy, appropriate rate, and expression on successive readings.*

## READ ALOUD FLUENTLY

Reading is a skill. When you become a master reader, you will be able to read with **fluency**, **accuracy** and **expression**. All three of these elements can affect each other.

In this lesson we are going to concentrate on reading with **fluency**.

Fluency in reading can be described as "reading with an effortless flow that is not choppy or broken." You should be aware of the punctuation within the text to help with your fluency, especially the periods and the commas.

- Periods in a text help you transition from one sentence or idea to the next. When you are reading aloud, the period will signal you that you must stop and take a breath.
- Commas in a text also help with transition **within** a sentence. When you are reading aloud, the comma will signal you to take a short breath, or at least a quick pause, and continue on.

A fluent reader does not take breaks within their reading to figure out an unfamiliar word. If you are a fluent reader, all or almost all of the words should be recognizable, allowing you to read them with ease.

Fluency is not about reading fast; it is about reading at a controlled, enjoyable and understandable pace.

## WORK ON YOUR FLUENCY

Imagine that this symbol (*) is a breath or a pause in someone's reading. Read the following passage out loud, taking a breath each time you see the symbol (*).

*Example*

Mary and Joe were excited(*) for their first trip to the (*) mountains. (*) Joe had never seen so much snow in his life.(*) Mary(*) had not been (*)skiing in over 10 years (*)and could not wait to get onto the ski(*) hill. (*) They packed(*) up all of their clothes(*) and their (*)equipment(*) and set off for their (*) wintry (*)adventure.(*) The snow(*) seemed to(*) blow from every(*)direction and it became more and more(*) difficult to see the road as they (*)drove.(*) Suddenly, the car began to swerve.(*)

Mary (*)yelled, "Joe! (*)What is going on?"(*)

Joe (*) quickly(*) and (*)carefully pulled (*) over to the side of the road.(*) He got of the (*)vehicle and to his (*)horror, the front tire(*) was completely flat.(*)

How do you think that example sounded with all of those breaths? Very choppy, don't you think? Did it sound enjoyable to you? Do you think your audience might have a hard time understanding what you are reading? Probably so.

Let's look at the next example to see where you should take the appropriate breaths, for proper fluency while you read.

*Example*

Mary and Joe were excited for their first trip to the mountains.(*) Joe had never seen so much snow in his life.(*) Mary had not been skiing in over 10 years and could not wait to get onto the ski hill.(*) They packed up all of their clothes and their equipment and set off for their wintry adventure.(*) The snow seemed to blow from every direction and it became more and more difficult to see the road as they drove.(*) Suddenly, (*) the car began to swerve.(*)

Mary yelled,(*) "Joe!(*) What is going on?(*)"

Joe quickly and carefully pulled over to the side of the road.(*) He got of the vehicle and to his horror, (*) saw that the front tire was completely flat.(*)

How do you think that example sounded with the pauses only happening at the appropriate times (at the punctuation)? Do you hear the difference? The fluency is much better in the second example.

## READ ALOUD ACCURATELY

Reading is a skill. When you become a master reader, you will be able to read with **fluency, accuracy** and **expression.** All three of these elements can effect each other.

In this lesson we are going to concentrate on reading with **accuracy**.

Accuracy in reading can be described as "reading without error." You must be aware of the words and the punctuation within the text to help with your accuracy while reading.

- Periods in a text help you transition from one sentence or idea to the next. The period will signal to you as the reader that you must stop and take a breath.
- Commas in a text also help you to make transitions **within** a sentence. The comma will signal you as the reader to take a short breath and continue on.
- An accurate reader does not take breaks within their reading to figure out an unfamiliar word. If you are an accurate reader, all or almost all of the words should be recognizable and read with ease.

## WHAT AN ACCURATE READER DOES NOT DO

1. Omit words in the text
2. Add words into the text
3. Incorrectly read words in the text
4. Mispronounce words in the text
5. Repeat words in the text

## Your Turn to Try

Let's look at the following passage with several errors included that were made by the reader:

*Example*

My sister and I were going on a horseback riding trip trip through the mountains. We could only take one one small back each. What would I need? I knew a first kit would be important. I also need plenty of water. After I finished packing I picked up my sister and set off on our adventure we arrived at the camp four hours later. It was freezing! I didn't antapate how much cold it would be in the mountains. I am wished I would have squeezed a sweater into my packed pack. I was immediately introduced to my horse Lucy who seemed by her kicking and panting.

How do you think that example sounded with all of those errors? Very choppy and confusing, don't you think? Did it sound enjoyable to you? Do you think your audience might have a hard time understanding what you are reading? Probably so.

The passage below is what the reader actually saw. Let's look at the correct version to see the difference when the errors in accuracy do not occur as the passage is read aloud.

My sister and I were going on a horseback riding trip through the mountains. We could only take one small backpack each. What would I need? I knew a first aid kit would be important. I also needed plenty of water. After I finished packing, I picked up my sister and set off on our adventure. We arrived at the camp four hours later. It was freezing! I didn't anticipate how much colder it would be in the mountains. I wished I would have squeezed a sweater into my tightly-packed backpack. I was immediately introduced to my horse, Lucy, who seemed, by her kicking and panting, to be quite anxious.

How do you think that example sounded, with no errors read? Do you hear the difference? The accuracy is much better in the second example, so therefore the fluency and comprehension of the text should be better as well.

---

## Using Appropriate Strategies for Full Comprehension

A good reader knows that when they read something, it is supposed to make sense. When you lose meaning of what you are reading, you need to choose a strategy that will help you make better sense of the text.

Strategies are ways to make learning easier. You need to use strategies for better understanding before, during and after you read. Some reading strategies that will help you gain full comprehension of a text are:

1. Access prior knowledge—what do you already know about this topic?
2. Look at the title and/or illustrations—what do you predict will happen?
3. Do a picture walk—have you skimmed the pages of the book to get an idea of what it will be about?
4. Connect—as you read, do you make connections to other stories, to your own experiences, or to the world around you?
5. Question—as you read, do you ask questions?
6. Reflect—after you have read, do you reflect on the information or relate it to a special character or to other information?
7. Extend and/or investigate—did you take your learning a step further by creating something new to showcase your learning or by checking other resources about the same topic?

All of these strategies will help you gain full understanding of your reading material. It's up to you whether you choose to use some or all of these strategies when reading.

When you are reading a textbook or studying for a test, one of the above strategies that is very useful is asking questions. You think up questions about your reading to help you look for the right information.

## ASKING QUESTIONS

- As you read, break up the main sections into smaller sections.
- Ask yourself questions by using key words, headings and sub-headings, and topic sentences.

*Example*
Suppose in your science text you were reading about camouflage. As you read, look and see if you have phrases or words that you can turn into good questions, such as:

1. What is good camouflage?
2. How do animals/insects change their color?
3. In what other ways do animals/insects escape being noticed?
4. What are some of the quick changing creatures of the sea?
5. Which animals/insects use decoys?
6. Why would animals/insects use decoys?

## READ ALOUD WITH APPROPRIATE PACING

Reading is a skill. When you become a master reader, you will be able to read with **fluency**, **accuracy** and **expression**. All three of these elements can affect each other.

Fluency is reading with an appropriate pace to increase understanding. When you are reading, your **pace** can affect your fluency. In this lesson we will be focusing on using the appropriate **pace** in your reading.

Pace is the speed at which you read a text. It can be measured by the amount of words read per minute.

Reading with the appropriate pace does not mean you must read fast or you must read slowly. The pace at which you read will depend on the different texts that you are reading.

- If you are reading for pleasure, your pace is fluent and steady.
- If you are searching through a lot of information, then your pace is more rapid.

## PACE YOURSELF

Read the following passage. This passage should take you approximately a minimum of 2 minutes and 40 seconds to about 3 minutes to complete. If you are able to time yourself, you may find this helpful.

*Example*

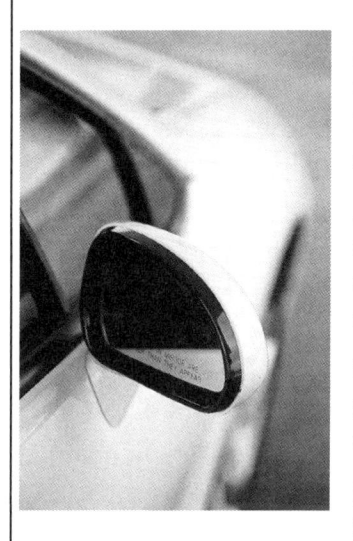

### An Invite from Uncle

Driving in Uncle's taxi was like entering another world, a crazy, mixed-up world where anything could and did happen. This world is my Uncle's home, not a taxi but a rolling chariot of dreams and tales and you as his special guest.

Just getting into Uncle's taxi, you knew this was something different. He would decorate the inside of his taxi with all kinds of frilly bits, a mix between kitsch and FOB, Christmas lights, pictures of Jesus, hanging tennis balls and even a disco ball.

Uncle also played a mix of Island and rock and roll music on his tape deck and you could be forgiven for thinking that you were riding in a rolling disco or even an evangelist tour bus. But this simply was Uncle, a part of him.

Uncle loved telling stories. He especially loved the one about the Elvis impersonator who jumped into his taxi and instead of paying for his fare plugged a microphone into Uncle's sound system and sang for the entire ride. Apparently, things got so carried away that when they stopped at the lights the impersonator jumped out and danced and sang on the street. Uncle turned up the sound and the whole street stopped to look and listen. It was a real traffic-stopper, Uncle would say.

Yep, Uncle had all the celebs in his taxi and it was funny how whoever was in the news at the time, Uncle just happened to have picked them up the night before: Mini-Me from *Austin Powers*, Mr. T from *The A-Team*, even Michael Jackson and his monkey. My Uncle had them all and with each there was a story, a fantastic story to be told.

Uncle's driving was a whole other experience too, a scary and nerve-racking one. He wouldn't drive as such but let his taxi drive while he sat and talked. Uncle would turn and look you straight in the eyes and have whole conversations, including hand gestures and self-applause, while the taxi swerved from side to side, over the median strip, towards parked and oncoming cars and back again. The whole time you would sit holding on for dear life, with a look of horror on your face as you screamed, "Look at the road!"

Then Uncle would drop you off, shaken and yet exhilarated. He would smile and say, "See you soon," and you would stand on the street dumbfounded at the very thought.

But you know what? Uncle never ever had an accident and driving with him was cheaper and more exciting than an amusement park or a show. So, if you're looking for an experience in the city, look for a taxi, the one with the flashing lights and a disco ball. There you'll find my Uncle. He'll invite you into his world, his home and an experience you won't soon forget.

—by Aaron Taouma

How did you do? How long did it take for you to read the above passage? If you completed the passage in less than 2 minutes and 40 seconds, you are probably reading at a very fast pace. This can affect your comprehension, fluency and accuracy in oral reading and you should try to slow down. If it took you longer than 3 minutes to read the above passage, then you may be taking too much time for pauses.

## READ ALOUD WITH APPROPRIATE INTONATION

Reading is a skill. When you become a master reader, you will be able to read with **fluency**, **accuracy** and **expression**. All three of these elements can affect each other.

When you are reading aloud, it is important to focus on the **intonation** of your voice to add interest to your expression. Intonation is the way you adjust the volume of your voice to place more emphasis on certain words or phrases.

- The intonation can change a statement into a question or vice versa, depending on where you use intonation within the sentence.
- Intonation can affect the meaning of a sentence. The word that you stress can change the meaning of the sentence.

Read the following examples to see how intonation can affect the expression and meaning as you read:

*Example*
**Mark** moved yesterday?

Mark **moved** yesterday?

Mark moved **yesterday**?

Intonation can also be affected by the situation the person is involved in. For example, the way that you would speak to your teacher may be very different from the way you would talk to a young child.

## YOUR TURN

Try reading the following sentences in a variety of different ways.

*Example*
Read the following sentence as if you were talking to your friend.

I've missed you.

---

*Example*
Read the following sentence as if you were talking to your favorite grandfather, who is very ill in the hospital.

I've missed you.

---

*Example*
Read the following sentence as if you were talking to a small child or baby.

I've missed you.

---

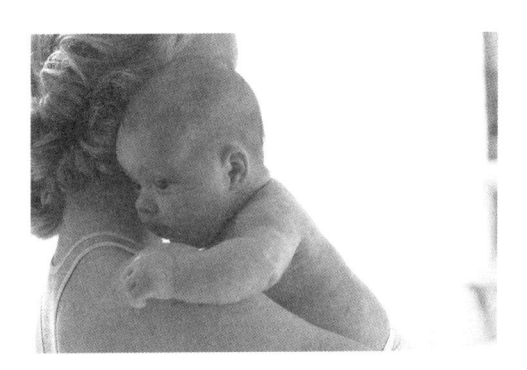

Notice how your voice changes depending on your audience. This is the intonation changing in your reading or speaking.

## READ ALOUD WITH APPROPRIATE EXPRESSION

Reading is a skill. When you become a master reader, you will be able to read with **fluency**, **accuracy** and **expression**. All three of these elements can affect each other.

In this lesson we are going to concentrate on reading with **expression**. Expression in reading can be described as "showing understanding of the text by using your voice as a way to produce emotions or interest." You must understand what you are reading to be able to use the appropriate expression. An expressive reader uses their voice in a variety of ways to make the text sound more interesting.

**Exclamation marks:** An exclamation mark will signal that you need to place more emphasis on what is being said. Your voice should go up in sound and in pitch.

**Question marks:** A question mark will signal that your voice should go up in pitch and volume towards the end of the sentence.

**Quotation marks:** Quotation marks signal that someone is speaking, so you must alter your voice to sound like the character.

## AN EXPRESSIVE READER

1. Pays attention to the punctuation marks and changes their voice accordingly
2. Varies their pace where necessary
3. Emphasizes dialogue differently for each character

Expression is not about reading loud enough. It is about reading that uses a controlled, enjoyable and understandable pace, volume and tone.

## TRY A MONOTONE

Look at the following passage. Read the paragraph out loud in a monotone voice. As you can see, there are no question marks, exclamation marks, or quotation marks to help signal you when to use more expression.

*Example*

Tracy was excited for her oldest and dearest friend to arrive from Newfoundland. She woke up Thursday morning and bounded out of her bed. The day had finally come. Her best friend would be arriving in only three short hours at the airport. There was so much to do before then.

Dad. We have to go to the mall right away. I forgot to pick up the last most important gift for Kayla's arrival.

Honey we just went yesterday. Do we really need to go again. The mall will be so busy and just finding parking will take up most of the time. We don't want to be late to pick Kayla up at the airport now do we. My dad said firmly.

I agreed sadly Ok. I guess it will have to wait.

How do you think that example sounded without any punctuation cues? Very bland, don't you think? Did it sound enjoyable to you? Do you think your audience might have a hard time understanding or being interested in what you are reading? Probably so.

## TRY IT WITH EXPRESSION

Now look at the next example to see where the proper punctuation cues are used to signal the use of expression while you read. Use the cues to read the passage again, this time using appropriate expression.

*Example*
Tracy was excited for her oldest and dearest friend to arrive from Newfoundland. She woke up Thursday morning and bounded out of her bed. The day had finally come! Her best friend would be arriving in only three short hours at the airport. There was so much to do before then.

"Dad! We have to go to the mall right away! I forgot to pick up the last, most important gift for Kayla's arrival!"

"Honey, we just went yesterday. Do we really need to go again? The mall will be so busy and just finding parking will take up most of the time. We don't want to be late to pick Kayla up at the airport now, do we?" my dad said firmly.

I agreed sadly, "Ok. I guess it will have to wait."

---

How do you think that example sounded with the punctuation cues to help with your expression? Do you hear the difference? The expression should be much better in the second example.

## USING THE RE-READ STRATEGY TO DETERMINE UNFAMILIAR WORDS

Sometimes when you are reading a text, you may come across a word that you do not understand. There are many different strategies you can try to figure out the unfamiliar word. One of those strategies is the re-read strategy.

When you come to the unfamiliar word, try going back and re-reading the sentence or even the paragraph, to review how the word is being used. This is called the **context**. Sometimes the context will trigger an idea that can help you determine the unknown word.

Re-reading has many benefits that help you with your comprehension of a text, and also help you determine those unfamiliar words.

## BENEFITS OF RE-READING

1. It can help you determine the hard words in the text.
2. It can help you find things you may not have realized before.
3. It can help you make sense of what is happening in the text.
4. It can help you find mistakes in your reading, if you possibly missed a word or a sentence.

*5L.1a  Demonstrate command of the conventions of standard English grammar and usage when writing or speaking. Explain the function of conjunctions, prepositions, and interjections in general and their function in particular sentences.*

## IDENTIFY COMMON CONJUNCTIONS

Conjunctions are a bit like bridges. Bridges join one side of a river to the other. Conjunctions join words, phrases, clauses, and sentences. They also show the relationship between the things that are joined. They show whether the things joined are equal or unequal.

Conjunctions connect both sentences and sentence parts.

## COORDINATING CONJUNCTIONS

**Coordinating** conjunctions like *and*, *so*, and *or* join equal parts.

*Example*
Sir Toby likes cakes *and* ale.

You must lead *or* follow.

Chopping firewood *and* painting the trim are next.

We went to the wedding *and* we went to the reception.

## CORRELATIVE CONJUNCTIONS

**Correlative** conjunctions like *either…or* and *neither…nor* join equal parts.

*Example*
Mark likes *neither* cakes *nor* ale.

You must *either* lead *or* follow.

*Either* you must chop firewood, *or* you must paint the trim.

## SUBORDINATING CONJUNCTIONS

**Subordinating** conjunctions like *whenever* and *however* join unequal parts.

*Example*
*Whenever* I hear that song, I want to laugh.

You must be careful *whenever* you cross the street.

*However* you arrange it, be sure that you are back by Thursday.

---

*5L.1e  Demonstrate command of the conventions of standard English grammar and usage when writing or speaking. Use correlative conjunctions.*

## USING CONJUNCTIONS IN YOUR WRITING

A conjunction connects words or groups of words.

Some common conjunctions are *and, but, or, nor, for, so, yet*.

*Example*
I love vanilla ice cream, **but** I love chocolate ice cream more.

---

In the above sentence, the word *but* is connecting two simple sentences.

*Example*
Mark watched a movie **and** wrote a reflection.

---

In the above sentence, the word *and* connects two phrases.

*Example*
Do you want to go swimming tonight **or** tomorrow night?

---

In the above sentence, the word *or* connects two words.

## OTHER CONJUNCTIONS

Other conjunctions will help you connect ideas in specific ways. Some of these conjunctions are *after, before, until, where, because, since, when, while*.

*Example*
I like to go golfing **when** it is hot.

She likes to eat her breakfast **before** she brushes her teeth.

In the above sentences the words *when* and *before* connect ideas in very specific ways.

---

## IT'S YOUR TURN

Can you fill in the following blanks using a conjunction to make complete sentences?

1. Would you like caramel sauce _____ hot fudge sauce on your ice cream sundae?
2. You cannot have an ice cream sundae _____ you are finished with your dinner.
3. Bobbie likes to jump rope _____ it is nice outside.
4. We are out of milk, _____ can you pick me up some at the store?

## HOW DID YOU DO?

Were you able to fill in the blanks with conjunctions? Look below for some possible solutions. Are they the same or different than yours?

1. Would you like caramel sauce **or** hot fudge sauce on your ice cream sundae?
2. You cannot have an ice cream sundae **until** you are finished with your dinner.
3. Bobbie likes to jump rope **when** it is nice outside.
4. We are out of milk, **so** can you pick me up some at the store?

## IDENTIFYING PREPOSITIONS

A *preposition* is a word that helps give a clearer idea to a noun, pronoun, and/or a verb in a sentence. A preposition can tell you the time, space, location of the noun or pronoun, or can show where, when, how or why action is happening. A preposition begins a phrase (small group of words) that can serve as an adjective or an adverb. The phrase would be called a **prepositional adjective phrase** or a **prepositional adverb phrase**.

Below is a list of commonly used prepositions.

- about, above, across, after, against, along, among, around, at
- before, behind, below, beneath, beside, between, beyond, by
- despite, down, during
- except
- for, from
- in, inside, into
- near
- of, off, on, onto, outside, over
- past
- through, to
- under, until, up
- with, without

In the sentences below, the prepositions are highlighted.

Joey ran **under** the shed as it started to rain.

Martha ran **up** the stairs and jumped **onto** her bed.

**During** the basketball game, the star basketball player hurt his foot by diving **off** the court **behind** the benches.

*Example*
Now it's your turn. Can you identify the prepositions in the sentences below?

The lamp is beside the sofa.

The lady climbed the wall without any fear.

The monkey climbed across the tree.

Do you think you were able to identify the prepositions in the above sentences? Check your answers below. The prepositions are highlighted for you.

The lamp is **beside** the sofa.

The lady climbed the wall **without** any fear.

The monkey climbed **across** the tree.

---

## Using Prepositions In Your Writing

Using prepositions in your writing can be very beneficial. Prepositions begin phrases which can act as adjectives or adverbs that add to your writing to make things clearer for the reader.

For example: Mary sat.

Many questions can still arise from this simple sentence, such as where Mary is sitting or with whom she is sitting.

If we were to add to this sentence using a preposition, we might say: Mary is sitting **beside** her brother **on** the park bench.

The words **beside** and **on** are both prepositions and they both give us a better idea of where Mary is sitting. Therefore they help the reader visualize a picture much more easily.

## Commonly Used Prepositions

- above, across, after, against, about, along, among, around, at
- before, behind, below, beneath, beside, between, beyond, by
- despite, down, during
- except
- for, from
- in, inside, into
- near
- of, off, on, outside, over
- past
- through, to
- under, until, up
- with, without

*Example*
Let's look at some more examples together.

1. Millie watched a video game. (Where did Millie watch the video game and what was it about?)Millie watched the video game **at** home, **on** her sofa, **about** catching falling objects.
2. Tonya ran. (Where did Tonya run?)Tonya ran **across** the yard **into** her home.

Now it's your turn. Can you add one or more prepositions to the following simple sentences in order to give them more details?

1. Molly cried.
2. Chris walked.
3. Nicole drove.

How do you think you did? Make sure you used a preposition to add to the sentence. If you think you've got it, check some of the possible solutions below.

1. Molly cried **about** her pet bird, Polly, because she was now going to have to live **without** her.
2. Chris walked **over** the bridge and **around** the parking lot.
3. Nicole drove **through** the Grand Canyon.

---

5L.1c  *Demonstrate command of the conventions of standard English grammar and usage when writing or speaking. Use verb tense to convey various times, sequences, states, and conditions.*

5L.1b  *Demonstrate command of the conventions of standard English grammar and usage when writing or speaking. Form and use the perfect verb tenses.*

## WHAT ARE VERB TENSES?

The tense of a verb will tell when an action takes place. The verb tense is usually shown by the ending letters (play**s**, play**ed**) and by helping verbs (**will** play, **has** played)

There are three main types of verb tenses: *present* tense, *past* tense and *future* tense.

**Present tense** means that the action is happening now or that it happens all the time.

*Example*
David **plays** on our basketball team.

Our coach **helps** us a lot.

---

**Past tense** means the action happened before, or in the past.

*Example*
David **played** on our basketball team.

Our coach **helped** us a lot.

---

**Future tense** means the action will take place at a later time or in the future.

*Example*
Tomorrow, David **will play** on our basketball team.

We **will see** a basketball video tomorrow at practice.

## It's Your Turn

Can you pick out which verb tense is being used in the sentences below?

1. Martha is baking a cake.
2. Philip crashed his bike into a tree.
3. Chloe will be going to a birthday party tomorrow afternoon.

## How Did You Do?

Do you think you identified all the verb tenses of each sentence correctly? Check your answers below to find out!

1. Martha **is baking** a cake. (**Present tense** - she IS baking the cake right now)
2. Philip **crashed** his bike into a tree. (**Past tense** - he CRASHED his bike into the tree - the crash has already happened)
3. Chloe **will be going** to a birthday party tomorrow afternoon. (**Future tense** - she WILL BE GOING to the birthday party - it will happen tomorrow)

## Using Appropriate Verb Tenses in your Writing

The tense of a verb will tell when an action takes place. The tense of a verb is usually shown by the ending letters (play**s**, play**ed**) and by helping verbs (**will** play, **has** played)

There are three main types of verb tenses: *present* tense, *past* tense and *future* tense.

**Present tense** means that the action is happening now or that it happens all the time.

*Example*
Misha **plays** on our soccer team.

**Past tense** means that the action happened before or in the past.

*Example*
Misha **played** on our soccer team.

---

**Future tense** means that the action will take place at a later time or in the future.

*Example*
Tomorrow, Misha **will play** on our soccer team.

---

## It's Your Turn

Can you change the verb tense in the following sentences according to the instructions?

1. Here is the sentence in the present tense: **Beyonce sings in a band.**
   Can you change the verb tense so it is in the past tense?
2. Here is the sentence in the present tense: **Michelle is coloring at school.**
   Can you change the verb tense so it is in the future tense?
3. Here is the sentence in past tense: **Ruby walked her dog, Bingo, around the block.**
   Can you change the verb tense to present tense?

## How Did You Do?

How do you think you did? Check your answers below for possible solutions.

1. Here is a suggestion for the sentence to be in past tense: Beyonce **sang** in a band.
2. Here is a suggestion for the sentence to be in the future tense: Michelle **will be coloring** at school tomorrow.
3. Here is a suggestion for the third sentence to be in the present tense: **Ruby is walking her dog, Bingo, around the block.**

# WHAT IS A VERB?

What is a verb?

A verb is a word that shows an action or links ideas in a sentence.

An **action verb** explains what the subject is doing.

Some examples of actions verbs are: jumping, skipping, smiling, singing, meowing, calling, fighting.

- The squirrel **jumps** from branch-to-branch.
  The verb in this sentence is "jumps". It explains the movement of the squirrel.
- The woman **watched** the birds from her porch step.
  The verb in this sentence is "watched". It tells what type of action the woman is doing.

A **linking verb** will link the subject to the action word that the subject is doing.

Some examples of linking verbs are: is, are, was, were, am, be, been.

- Marion **is** helpful.
  The subject is Marion, and the linking verb is the word "is".

- My friends **are** happy on the playground.
  The subject is friends and the linking verb is the word "are".

**Helping verbs** support the main verb. Some examples of helping verbs are: has, have, had, will, could, should, would, did, may, can.

- Mary **has** called three times.
  The helper verb "has" helps the main verb "called".
- Mary **will** visit you again.
  The helper verb "will" helps the main verb "visit".

# IT'S YOUR TURN!

Can you find the verbs in the following sentences?

There may be an action verb, a linking verb or a helping verb.

1. Natalie flew over the ocean in her private jet.
   The verb in this sentence is an **action** verb.
2. Matt should have gone to school.
   The verb in this sentence is a **helping** verb.
3. The dogs are excited to be at the dog park.
   The verb in this sentence is a **linking** verb.

## CHECK!

Think you have identified them correctly? The correct verbs are highlighted in each sentence.

1. Natalie **flew** over the ocean in her private jet.
2. Matt **should** have gone to school.
3. The dogs **are** excited to be at the dog park.

## How Do I Use a Verb Properly in my Writing?

A verb is a word that shows an action or links two ideas in a sentence.
Here are some examples of how a verb is used to show an action in a sentence.

*Example*
- The squirrel **climbed** across the tree branch.
- The car **raced** down the road.
- The baby **shook** the rattle.

---

## It's Your Turn!

What verbs would work in these sentences?
Fill in the blank with a verb.

1. The little girl _____ at the children in the playground.
2. The mouse _____ from the black cat.
3. The tree _____ in the backyard.

Did you think of a verb to fill in the blanks? If not, here are some helpful suggestions.

1. smiled, waved, giggled
2. ran, scurried, hid
3. swayed, grew, fell

## Linking Verbs

Here are some examples of how a verb is used to link two ideas in a sentence.

*Example*
- The plane **is** over the lake.

- I have **been** here before.
- My dad **was** helpful.

## It's Your Turn!

What verb would fit in these sentences in order to properly link two ideas together?

1. I _____ happy to see you today.
2. The children _____ late coming to school today.
3. Sam _____ wondering when dinner would be.

1. am, was
2. were, are
3. was

## Identify Correct Subject-Verb Agreement

When you are writing, it is important to check that all your verbs agree in number (singular and plural) with the verb in the sentence. Agreement can sometimes be confusing, so take care when you are editing your writing.

If the subject is singular, the verb must be singular.

*Example*

The <u>box</u> full of Christmas decorations *is* already open.

Subject: box - singular
Verb: is - singular

---

When using *either/or* or *neither/nor*, the verb should agree with the subject nearest to *or* or *nor*. If one subject is plural and one is singular, put the plural subject nearest the verb and make the verb plural.

*Example*

Neither the father nor his boys *were* able to attend the last game.

Make sure the verb agrees with the actual subject, not just the nearest noun.

*Example*
- One of the boys *was* (not *were*) late for the practice.
- Mother with her roses *is* (not *are*) always a hit at the flower show.

## Use Correct Subject-Verb Agreement

When you are writing, it is important to check that all your verbs agree. Agreement can sometimes be confusing, so take care when you are editing your writing.

*Example*
If the subject is singular, the verb must be singular.

The **box** full of Christmas decorations **is** already open.

**Box** is singular; therefore the singular form of the verb "to be" must be used.

Most of the difficulties in subject-verb agreement are caused by difficulties in recognizing singular and plural subjects.

When subjects are joined by *or* or *nor*, the verb agrees with the nearest subject.

*Example*
Either Miller *or* Smith *is* guilty.

Neither Miller *nor* Smith *wants* to confess.

Neither the speaker *nor* the *listeners* are aware of the irony.

---

When one part of the verb is singular, and the other plural, write the sentence so that the plural part is nearest the verb.

*Example*
Neither *band members* nor the *conductor* **is** satisfied. WEAK

Neither the *conductor* nor the *band members* **are** satisfied. BETTER

---

Nothing that comes between a singular subject and its verb can make that subject plural.

You should **not** make the verb agree with the nearest noun.

*Example*
Our school basketball team, the Gerbils, is victorious again. CORRECT

Our school basketball team, the Gerbils, are victorious again. INCORRECT

The contestant with the most votes is now on stage. CORRECT

The contestant with the most votes are now on stage. INCORRECT

---

## WHAT IS AN IRREGULAR VERB?

An irregular verb is a verb that does **NOT** end in 'ed' when you are writing in the past tense. For most irregular verbs, the letters in the word change.

Some examples of irregular verbs are shown below:

*Example*

| Present Tense | Past Tense |
| --- | --- |
| rise | rose |
| throw | threw |
| steal | stole |
| come | came |

## It's Your Turn!

Can you identify which verbs are **irregular** in the following sentences?

1. We go to take the dog for a walk every morning.
2. Did he blow out the candles on his birthday cake?
3. Will you swim with me in the lake?

4. The children will play outside today.

## Check!

Were you able to identify which verbs are irregular? Check your answers below.

1. We **go** to take the dog for a walk every morning.
   If the word **go** was written in the past tense it would become **went**. The verb **go** is an **irregular verb**.
2. Did he **blow** out the candles on his birthday cake?
   If the word **blow** was written in the past tense it would change to **blew**. The verb **blow** is an **irregular verb**.
3. Will you **swim** with me in the lake?
   If the word **swim** was written in the past tense it would change to **swam**. The verb **swim** is an **irregular verb**.
4. The children will **play** outside today.
   If the word **play** was written in the past tense it would become **played**. The verb **play** is a **regular verb**.

## Using Irregular Verbs in Your Writing

An **irregular verb does not end in 'ed'** when it is written in the past tense. For most irregular verbs, the letters in the word change.

*Example*

| Present Tense | I ride my bike in the summer. |
| --- | --- |
| Past Tense | I rode my bike in the summer. |

If the tense changes from present to past, the verb **ride** is **not** changed to **rided**. The verb **ride** is irregular.

Class Focus — Castle Rock Research

Not for Reproduction

## It's your turn!

1. I love to (**eat/ate**) ice cream with chocolate sauce.
2. My friend always likes to ask what I am going to (**wear/wore**).
3. My mom (**write/wrote**) me a long email today.
4. Yesterday we all (**drive/drove**) to my grandma's house.

## Check!

Check to see if you selected the correct irregular verb.

1. I love to **eat** ice cream with hot fudge sauce.
2. My friend always likes to ask what I am going to **wear**.
3. My mom **wrote** me a long email today.
4. Yesterday we all **drove** to my grandma's house.

## Correctly Use Verbs (lie/lay;sit/set)

The verbs **lie/lay** can be tricky and are often misused when spoken and written. Let's begin by looking at the definition of each word.

*Lay* means to physically put something down. **Note:** An object will always follow this word in a sentence.

*Example*
You should **lay** that glass vase down before it gets broken.

*Lie* means to take a rest. **Note:** An object won't follow this word in a sentence.

*Example*
If I **lie** down for an hour my headache might go away.

*Try This!*
Read the sentences below and choose the answer that you think fits the sentence correctly. Is it **lie** or **lay**?

1. Every night, I _____ in my bed with my dog.
2. I want you to _____ down and take a break because you've been working too hard.
3. Mrs. Flynn will _____ her coffee on her desk each morning.
4. I like to _____ down for an hour after I eat dinner to let my food settle.

How do you think you did? Check your answers below.

1. Every night, I **lie** in my bed with my dog.
2. I want you to **lie** down and take a break because you've been working too hard.
3. Mrs. Flynn will **lay** her coffee on her desk each morning.
4. I like to **lie** down for an hour after I eat dinner to let my food settle.

---

Let's take a look at the verbs, **sit** and **set**. They too can be tricky and are often misused.

Let's look at what exactly each of these words means.

*Set* means to place something down. **Note:** An object will always follow this word in a sentence.

*Example*
Could you **set** those flowers down on the table please?

---

*Sit* means to be seated. **Note:** An object will not directly follow this action.

*Example*
You can **sit** in the rocking chair with your baby.

---

*Try This!*

Read the sentences below and choose the answer that you think fits the sentence correctly. Is it **sit** or **set?**

1. Please _____ the dishes on the table for dinner.
2. Mom _____ the present down on my lap.
3. I want everyone to move into the dining room and find a chair to _____ in.
4. Everyone needs to _____ and listen to the story.

How do you think you did? Check your answers below.

1. Please **set** the dishes on the table for dinner.
2. Mom **set** the present down on my lap.
3. I want everyone to move into the dining room and find a chair to **sit** in.
4. Everyone needs to **sit** and listen to the story.

---

*5L.1d   Demonstrate command of the conventions of standard English grammar and usage when writing or speaking. Recognize and correct inappropriate shifts in verb tense.*

## EDITING YOUR WORK FOR THE PROPER VERB TENSES

As a writer, you must always edit your work. One area that needs careful editing is the correct use of verb tenses. If you are writing about something that has happened in the past, it is important that you are consistent with your verbs, making sure they are in the past tense. You may choose to write in the present tense. Either way, you should be consistent for the story or your writing piece to make sense.

It is usually very helpful when you are editing your work to read the sentences out loud. As you are reading, ask yourself, "Does this make sense?". If it doesn't, you are probably using the wrong verb tense, or are switching back and forth between two tenses.

The tense of a verb tells you whether something happened in the past, is happening in the present (now), or will happen in the future. Often, the spelling of a verb changes when its tense changes.

Most English verbs are **regular**; their words in the past tense end in *–ed*. Below are a couple of examples of some regular verbs, and the patterns they follow when their tenses change.

| Past | Present | Future |
|---|---|---|
| I **jogged** to school today. | I am **jogging** to school. | I will **jog** to school. |
| The cat **hopped** over the car. | The cat is **hopping** over the car. | The cat will **hop** over the car. |
| My dad **walked** to work. | My dad is **walking** to work. | My dad will **walk** to work. |

There are about three hundred **irregular** verbs. Below are a few examples of irregular verbs and their own "rules" that they follow when their tenses change.

| Past | Present | Future |
|---|---|---|
| I **ate** the banana bread yesterday. | I am **eating** the banana bread, I **eat** the banana bread. | I will **eat** the banana bread. |
| I **ran** to school. | I am **running** to school. | I will **run** to school. |
| I **wrote** a letter to my friend. | I am **writing** a letter to my friend. | I will **write** a letter to my friend. |

As you become more and more aware of the different verbs and their different tenses, it will become more natural to know what the tenses should be for regular and irregular verbs. Some helpful hints to have when writing and/or editing for the proper spelling of the different verb tenses are as follows:

1. When there is an "s" inflection at the end of a verb it signals that it is in the present tense.
   **imagines**: Kristin **imagines** a world where no one litters.
2. When there is an "ed" inflection at the end of a verb, it signals that it has happened in the past. The verb is in the past tense.
   **talked**: Jim **talked** to his dad on the phone.
3. When there is an "ing" inflection added to the end of a verb it usually signals that it is in a present progressing or progressive tense.
   **adding**: Pat is **adding** meat to his sandwich.

*Example*
Now it's your turn to try editing the following sentences for the proper verb tenses. Remember to read the sentences out loud so you can hear if they sound incorrect to you. Once you think you have gotten all the sentences changed to the proper verb tenses, check your answers below. The verb is highlighted for you in each sentence.

1. Joshua **chase** the cows through the field yesterday.
2. I **ate** the cookie tomorrow.
3. Bianca **kick** the soccer ball really hard.

How do you think you did? If you think you have correctly edited each question for the proper verb tenses, then check your answers below. The highlighted word has been changed to the proper verb tense to fit each sentence.

1. Joshua **chased** the cows through the field yesterday.

The word "yesterday" also helps hint to us that the verb needs to be in the past tense, because it indeed happened in the past (yesterday).

Eat is an irregular verb. The word "tomorrow" also helps hint to us that the verb needs to be in the future tense, because it is stating it will happen tomorrow (the future).

2. I **will eat** the cookie tomorrow.

3. Bianca **kicks** the soccer ball really hard.

---

## Editing Your Non-Fiction Work for the Appropriate Verb Tenses

As a writer, you must always edit your work. One area that needs careful editing is the correct use of verb tenses. If you are writing about something that has happened in the past, it is important that you are consistent with your verbs, making sure they are in the past tense. You may choose to write in the present tense. Either way, you should be consistent for your non-fiction writing piece to make sense.

Some non-fiction pieces where the verb tenses might get confusing, could be when writing a journal entry, a newspaper article or a biography about events that have happened in the past. It is important to be aware of these tenses, when you are writing from your present perspective.

It is usually helpful when you are editing your work to read the sentences out loud. As you are reading, ask yourself, "Does this make sense?". If it doesn't, you are probably using the wrong verb tense, or are switching back and forth between two tenses.

The tense of a verb tells you whether something happened in the past, is happening in the present (now), or will happen in the future. Often, the spelling of a verb changes when its tense changes.

Most English verbs are regular; their words in the past tense end in –ed. Below are a couple of examples of some regular verbs, and the patterns they follow when their tenses change.

| Past | Present | Future |
|---|---|---|
| I **walked** to school today. | I am **walking** to school today. | I will **walk** to school. |

There are about three hundred irregular verbs. Below are a few examples of irregular verbs and their own "rules" that they follow when their tenses change.

| Past | Present | Future |
|---|---|---|
| I **ate** the banana bread yesterday. | I am **eating** the banana bread.<br>I **eat** the banana bread. | I will **eat** the banana bread. |

When there is an "s" inflection at the end of a verb it signals that it is in the present tense.

*Example*
**imagines**

Kristin **imagines** a world where no one litters.

---

When there is an "ed" inflection at the end of a verb, it signals that it has happened in the past. The verb is in the past tense.

*Example*
**locked**

Brian **locked** the door to his house.

---

When there is an "ing" inflection added to the end of a verb it usually signals that it is in a present progressing or progressive tense.

*Example*
**adding**

Pat is **adding** meat to his sandwich.

---

Now it's your turn. Can you correct the following sentences to have the proper verb tenses to help them make sense? Once you think you've got them all corrected, check your answers below.

1. Michelle's team was amazing. They **play** 3 games yesterday and won all three.
2. Michael Jordan was known for being the greatest basketball player of all time. He could never have **knowed** he would be so successful.
3. David Beckham **kick** the soccer ball very hard when he plays in a soccer game.

**Answers**

1. Michelle's team was amazing. They **played** 3 games yesterday and won all three.

The word "yesterday" also helps hint to us that the verb needs to be in the past tense, because it indeed happened in the past (yesterday). Therefore, **play** must be turned into **played** because it happened in the past.

2. Michael Jordan is known for being the greatest basketball player of all time. He could never have **known** he would be so successful.

Known/Knew are irregular verbs. The word "**knowed**" does not make sense, nor does it sound correct in the sentence, so it became **known**.

3. David Beckham **kicks** the soccer ball very hard when he plays in a soccer game.

There are two ways you could have fixed this sentence to have the proper verb tenses.

In the first answer above, the word "**kick**" is changed to "**kicks**" as it could be in the present tense.

If you chose to add the word "**will**" in front of the word "**kick**" then that would also make sense.

3. David **will kick** the soccer ball very hard when he plays in a soccer game. (This makes it sounds like it is in the future tense - it is going to happen)

*5L.2a   Demonstrate command of the conventions of standard English capitalization, punctuation, and spelling when writing. Use punctuation to separate items in a series.*

## USE COMMAS IN A LIST

When writing a list of three or more things in a sentence, place a comma between each item to separate the items. The last comma before the "and" is optional.

*Example*
Jeremy likes running, jogging, hiking, and camping.

*Example*
Kelly went to the store to buy bread, milk, eggs, bananas and flour. (Optional comma left out)

## USING A COLON TO INTRODUCE A LIST

A colon (:) is used in a sentence in order to introduce a list.

*Example*
I love vegetables! Some of my favorites are these ones: cucumbers, spinach, snap peas, and carrots.

## IT'S YOUR TURN!

Can you correctly place the colon in the following sentences?

1. My sister plays many sports, for example basketball, volleyball, soccer, and tennis.

2. Grandma loves to bake, and some of her specialties are these apple pie, chocolate chip cookies, brownies, and marble cake.
3. Toronto is a great city for many reasons they have the CN tower, many professional sports teams (basketball, baseball, hockey, and lacrosse), fabulous shopping, and it's located on the shore of Lake Ontario.
4. Mom sent me to the store to pick up a few things for her apples, juice, milk, and bread.

## CHECK!

Were you able to correctly place the colon in the above sentences? Check your work below.

1. My sister plays many sports, for example: basketball, volleyball, soccer, and tennis. The colon is used to introduce the list of the sports played by her sister.
2. Grandma loves to bake, and some of her specialties are these: apple pie, chocolate chip cookies, brownies, and marble cake. The colon is used to introduce the list of Grandma's specialties.
3. Toronto is a great city for many reasons: they have the CN tower, many professional sports teams (basketball, baseball, hockey, and lacrosse), fabulous shopping, and it's located on the shore of Lake Ontario. The colon is used to introduce the list of why Toronto is a great city.
4. Mom sent me to the store to pick up a few items for her: apples, juice, milk, and bread. The colon is used to introduce the list of items to be picked up at the store.

*5L.2c  Demonstrate command of the conventions of standard English capitalization, punctuation, and spelling when writing. Use a comma to set off the words yes and no, to set off a tag question from the rest of the sentence, and to indicate direct address.*

## IDENTIFY COMMAS FOLLOWING INTRODUCTORY WORDS

Use commas to set off introductory words or expressions that begin a sentence. Examples of introductory words are: **well**, **however**, **in fact**, **of course**, **I believe**, **in my opinion**.

*Example*

In fact, it is Harry Potter who finally defeats the evil Voldemort.

However, I will start my new job tomorrow so I have nothing to be sad about.

*5L.2b* *Demonstrate command of the conventions of standard English capitalization, punctuation, and spelling when writing. Use a comma to separate an introductory element from the rest of the sentence.*

## Use Commas in Introductory Words

If a sentence begins with an introduction telling you about when, where, why, or how, then you must place a comma after the phrase to separate the introduction from the rest of the sentence.

Introductory words are words such as if, after, before, although, since, etc.

*Example*

If you want to stay healthy, you must exercise regularly and eat your veggies.

After the birthday party, we are going swimming.

Generally, we eat supper and then go to bed.

Before I left the dinner table, I complemented the chef.

Since it was a rainy day, we all slept in until noon.

Each of the sentences below need a comma placed after the introductory phrase. Can you find where the comma belongs?

1. During the rainy season we move to higher ground to avoid floods.
2. To get my report card I had to send a letter to my old high school along with my identification.
3. If the bus comes on time I will be able to go.
4. Because we are still dating you have to hold me hand.

How did you do? Look below to see the solution.

1. During the rainy season, we move to higher ground to avoid floods.
2. To get my report card, I had to send a letter to my old high school along with my identification.
3. If the bus comes on time, I will be able to go.
4. Because we are still dating, you have to hold my hand.

## IDENTIFY COMMAS BETWEEN DESCRIBING WORDS

Use a comma to separate two or more describing words (adjectives) before a noun in a sentence.

*Example*
The wet, hairy dog jumped up on me.

He is a handsome, caring, considerate man.

My youthful, adventurous grandmother adopts stray animals.

## USE COMMAS BETWEEN DESCRIBING WORDS

Use a comma to separate two or more describing words (adjectives) before a noun in a sentence.

*Example*

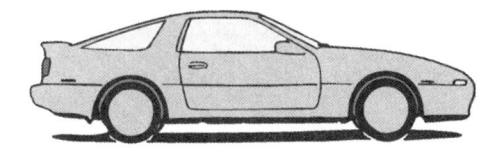

His new car was yellow, shiny, fast, and expensive.

## IT'S YOUR TURN

See if you can place the commas between each adjective in the sentences below.

1. My friend has a big hairy black dog.
2. The sweet amber sticky honey oozed out of the golden humming bee hive.

Check your answers below.

1. My friend has a big, hairy, black dog.
2. The sweet, amber, sticky honey oozed out of the golden, humming bee hive.

## USING COMMAS IN DIRECT QUOTATIONS

When using direct quotations in your writing, it is important that you punctuate them properly. One of the main things you need to remember is to use the **comma** when quoting someone. The comma must always follow the word or phrase that names the speaker, and be placed before the quotation marks.

*Example*
Jill yelled, "Step away from the cookie jar!"

Notice where the highlighted comma is placed? It is right after the exclamatory word (yelled) and right before the beginning of the quotation, which is indicated by quotation marks.

---

*Example*
As Jonathan and Sarah looked up, they saw a kitten crossing out to the middle of the road where a car was coming. Sally turned to Jonathan and said, "If that cat doesn't get going, it's gonna get hit!"

Notice once again where the comma was placed: right after the word "said". It also falls right before the beginning of the quotation, before the quotation marks.

---

*Example*
When the speaker is named after the quotation, you still need a comma after the quotation.

"I sure hope that kitten has a home," remarked Sarah after the kitten made it safely across the road.

Notice that the comma goes **inside** the second set of quotation marks.

---

*Example*
If the naming of the speaker divides the sentence into two parts, you will need to use two commas.

Jonathan looked thoughtful. "Maybe," he suggested, "Mom will let us get a kitten from the animal shelter."

## Now It's Your Turn

Can you find the appropriate spot to place the comma for the direct quotes in the sentences below?

1. The teacher responded "Tomorrow's test will be easy because you all know the material so well. You all can do it." The students all took a sigh of relief.
2. Marcus was stunned as he turned to his friend and said "How could that movie have ended so badly?"
3. Beth and Hillary were on their way to the fair. Beth squealed "I can't wait to ride the roller coaster. We are going to have so much fun!"
4. "Carlos can help us move the blocks" offered Sam.
5. "In a perfect world" Mother complained "my kids would do their homework without any nagging!"

## How Did You Do?

Do you think you were able to place commas in the proper spots? If you think you've got it, check out your answers below.

1. The teacher responded, "Tomorrow's test will be easy because you all know the material so well. You all can do it." The students all took a sigh of relief.
2. Marcus was stunned as he turned to his friend and said, "How could that movie have ended so badly?"
3. Beth and Hillary were on their way to the fair. Beth squealed, "I can't wait to ride the roller coaster. We are going to have so much fun!"

4. "Carlos can help us move the blocks," offered Sam.
5. "In a perfect world," Mother complained, "my kids would do their homework without any nagging!"

*5L.2d  Demonstrate command of the conventions of standard English capitalization, punctuation, and spelling when writing. Use underlining, quotation marks, or italics to indicate titles of works.*

## QUOTATION MARKS TO SHOW A TITLE IN WRITING

Quotation marks are used to punctuate titles of songs, poems, chapters of books, short stories, and articles found in magazines and newspapers.

*Example*
Before the hockey game, Canada's national anthem, "O Canada," was sung.

Miss Morris read us a poem titled "Whiskers" today.

In the book of short stories, Daniel's favorite was a story called "Friends Forever."

---

## IT'S YOUR TURN!

Can you identify which sentences have the correctly punctuated title?

1. My favorite chapter of the whole book was "Out in the Wild." OR
   My favorite "chapter" of the whole book was Out in the Wild.
2. We sang A Whole New World in music class today. OR
   We sang "A Whole New World" in music class today.
3. "Red, Yellow, Blue was the name of the poem" Mary wrote. OR
   "Red, Yellow, Blue" was the name of the poem Mary wrote.
4. Mom read "Too Much Snow" to me last night before bed. OR
   Mom "read Too Much Snow" to me last night before bed.

## CHECK!

How did you do? Check your answers below.

1. My favorite chapter of the whole book was "Out in the Wild." (The chapter title is "Out in the Wild.")
2. We sang "A Whole New World" in music class today. (The song title is "A Whole New World.")
3. "Red, Yellow, Blue" was the name of the poem Mary wrote. (The poem title is "Red, Yellow, Blue.")
4. Mom read "Too Much Snow" to me last night before bed. (The book title is "Too Much Snow.")

## USE QUOTATION MARKS TO SHOW A TITLE IN WRITING

Quotation marks are used to punctuate titles of songs, poems, chapters of books, short stories, and articles found in magazines and newspapers.

*Example*

We sang "It's a Small World" at the beginning of our cultural assembly.

Mother told me that "Someone Came Knocking" was her favorite poem when she was a child.

While Carlos was at the doctor's office, he read a magazine chapter called "Helicopter Rescues."

## IT'S YOUR TURN!

Can you correctly punctuate the titles in the following sentences?

1. Before bed last night, I read two chapters: Looking, Looking, Lost and Who Knew.
2. Changes Ahead was the title of the article on the front page of the newspaper.
3. Samantha writes amazing poems. Did you read her last one titled Floating in the Wind?
4. As Joey walked into the room, we all began singing Happy Birthday!

## CHECK!

How did you do? Check your answers below.

1. Before bed last night, I read two chapters: "Looking, Looking, Lost" and "Who Knew." (The chapter titles are "Looking, Looking, Lost" and "Who Knew.")
2. "Changes Ahead" was the title of the article on the front page of the newspaper. (The article title is "Changes Ahead.")
3. Samantha writes amazing poems. Did you read her last one titled "Floating in the Wind"? (The poem title is "Floating in the Wind.")
4. As Joey walked into the room, we all began singing "Happy Birthday!" (The song title is "Happy Birthday.")

# Using Underlining to Identify Titles of Documents

When you are writing a piece, and you would like to write about another document, whether it be a book, movie, magazine, play, etc., you must underline or italicize the title of that document. In this lesson we are just going to focus on underlining the title within your writing.

*Example*
As I sat there on the park bench reading <u>A Tale of Two Cities</u>, I knew that I was finally taking the time to relax.

---

Notice how the title of the book, *A Tale of Two Cities* was underlined? That is because it is a published piece that needs to be highlighted within the text. Let's look at another example.

*Example*
My family and I went to see the play, <u>The Fiddler on the Roof</u>, on Saturday night, and we had such a wonderful time together.

---

The name of the published play is "The Fiddler on the Roof", and therefore it needed to be underlined within the sentence.

*Try This!*
Now it's your turn. Can you identify what part of the following sentences should be underlined? Once you think you have identified them all correctly, check your answers below.

1. Mom and Dad decided to let me stay home and watch the movie Revenge of the Toys. It was a great movie.
2. When Jacob woke up from his nap, we decided to read his favorite magazine, Cars-R-Us. He just loves looking at all the different cars and I love learning about them too.
3. Aiden is interested in trying out for a play called, Night on Broadway. I think they should definitely give him a part because he is such a good actor.

How do you think you did? Check your answers below to see if you underlined the correct words.

1. Mom and Dad decided to let me stay home and watch the movie <u>Revenge of the Toys</u>. It was a great movie.

2. When Jacob woke up from his nap, we decided to read his favorite magazine, <u>Cars-R-Us</u>. He just loves looking at all the different cars and I love learning about them too.
3. Aiden is interested in trying out for a play called, <u>Night on Broadway</u>. I think they should definitely give him a part because he is such a good actor.

## USING ITALICS TO IDENTIFY TITLES OF DOCUMENTS IN YOUR WRITING

When you are writing a piece, and you would like to write about another document, whether it be another book, a movie, a magazine article, a play etc. you must underline or italicize the title of that document. In this lesson we are going to focus on **italicizing** the title within your writing.

As I sat there on the park bench reading *My Friendly Neighbor*, I knew that I was finally taking the time to relax.

Notice how the title of the book, "My Friendly Neighbor" was italicized? That is because it is a published piece that needs to be highlighted within the rest of the text. Let's look at another example.

*Example*

My family and I went to see the play, *Drama on Broadway*, on Saturday night and we had such a wonderful time together.

The name of the published play is called "Drama on Broadway" and therefore it needed to be italicized within the sentence.

*Try This!*

Now it's your turn. Can you identify which parts in the following sentences need to be italicized because they are titles? When you think you've got it, check your answers below.

1. My babysitter let me stay up with her to watch the movie, Rufus the Dog. It was a great movie.

2. Macy and I love reading about horses in our favorite magazine, Horses - R - Us.
3. I think I am a talented actress and I plan on trying out for the musical, Show Stoppers. I hope I get a part.

How do you think you did? If you think you have correctly identified the titles in each sentence that need to be italicized, check your answers below.

1. My babysitter let me stay up with her to watch the movie, *Rufus the Dog*. It was a great movie.
2. Macy and I love reading about horses in our favorite magazine, *Horses - R - Us*.
3. I think I am a talented actress and I plan on trying out for the musical, *Show Stoppers*. I hope I get a part.

---

*5L.2e   Demonstrate command of the conventions of standard English capitalization, punctuation, and spelling when writing. Spell grade-appropriate words correctly, consulting references as needed.*

## SPELL CORRECTLY ONE-SYLLABLE WORDS THAT HAVE BLENDS

Blends refers to combinations of vowels and consonants that together make their own sound.

## VOWEL BLENDS

There are many vowel blends, such as:

- ai, au
- ee, ei, ea
- ie

Let's look at some beginning with the letter o: **oi** and **oy**, **ou** and **ow**, **oo** and **ew**

Many words have similar sounds, but are written in different ways. This makes remembering how to spell them difficult. Some letter combinations that have similar sounds are **oi** and **oy**, **ou** and **ow**, and **oo** and **ew**.

Here is a hint to help you spell words with these similar sounds. Usually the vowel combinations **oi**, **ou**, and **oo** are found in the middle of a word, while the **oy**, **ow**, and **ew** combinations are found at the end of a word.

*Example*

*oi* words - n**oi**se, b**oi**l

*oy* words - b**oy**, pl**oy**

*ou* words - h**ou**r, cl**ou**d

*ow* words - all**ow**, pl**ow**

*oo* words - t**oo**l, h**oo**ves

*ew* words - bl**ew**, f**ew**

## CONSONANT BLENDS

There are many consonant blends to spell correctly, as well. As your vocabulary grows, you are becoming quite familiar with the sounds of the blends and the spelling of words containing the blends.

- school
- shock
- chick
- chill
- flip
- clop
- stone

## SPELL CORRECTLY ONE-SYLLABLE WORDS THAT HAVE CONTRACTIONS

A contraction is when two words are made into one word by leaving out letters. An apostrophe is used to replace the missing letter or letters. Most contractions are one-syllable words.

*Example*
Two words:

- we have
- you will
- it is
- she is
- there is

Here are the same words but using a contraction. Notice that the contraction forms a single syllable word because of the missing vowel sound from the second word.

- we've
- you'll
- it's
- she's
- there's

## SOMETHING IMPORTANT TO REMEMBER

**It's** got **its** own rule:
The dog ate its supper. (its = belonging to it)
It's a hot day outside. (it's = it is)

## SPELL TWO-SYLLABLE COMPOUND WORDS CORRECTLY

In order to spell two-syllable compound words correctly, it is best to use the following guideline:

Divide a compound word **between** the joined words:

*Example*
Look at the example list below to see how this guideline works with two syllable compound words.

- dog/sled
- play/ground
- pin/wheel
- home/work
- card/board

*Dogsled is a two syllable compound word.*

Since you probably know how to spell each small word that makes up the compound word, just put the two words together. Now you have correctly spelled the compound word! Just for practice, try the short exercise below, then look at the solution. See how easy it is to divide compound words into syllables for correct spelling?

*Try This!*

Which of the following sets of words contains compound words that are correctly divided?

*Solution*

The correctly divided set of words is hunch/back, green/house, port/hole, back/pack. Each compound word has been divided between the joined words.

## SPELL CORRECTLY ONE-SYLLABLE WORDS WITH ORTHOGRAPHIC PATTERNS

The English language contains many predictable spelling patterns that show up over and over in words. You have learned some of these to help with spelling old words and learning new words. A fancy name for predictable spelling patterns is *orthographic patterns*.

*Example*
- *i* before *e* except after *c* (bel*ie*ve but rec*ei*ve)
- *qu* (nearly always *q* must be followed by *u*) *qu*ack, *qu*ake, (exception "*q*at")
- double consonants after a short vowel (batted, stall)
- *y* changes to *ies* after a consonant (fair*y*=fair*ies*)

Examples of the above patterns which are single syllable words are *chief, quack, quake, stall,* and *ball*. Below are some other examples of orthographic patterns found in single syllable words:

*Example*
- closed pattern (lot) - vowel closed in by consonants makes a short sound
- open pattern (go) - word ends in vowel, makes a long sound
- silent *e* (kite) - word ends with silent *e*, vowel in middle makes a long sound
- vowel combinations - nail, real, out

## Spell Correctly One-Syllable words that are Common Homophones

Homophones are words that sound the same but are not spelled the same. The words have different meanings.

Here are some examples of one-syllable words that are homophones:

*Example*
1. *to* - toward
   *too* - also, as well
   *two* - the number 2
2. *threw* - did throw
   *through* - go in one side and out the other
3. *way* - direction or method
   *weigh* - to measure how heavy
4. *our* - belongs to us
   *hour* - a unit of time sixty minutes long
5. *their* - belongs to them  *there* - place or location
   *they're* - contraction of "they are"
6. *flu* - sickness
   *flew* - did fly

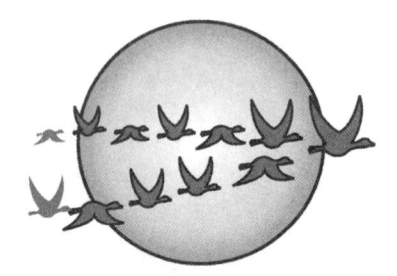

---

You must hear the word used in a sentence (context) to be able to spell it correctly.

## Spell Root Words Correctly

English words can be made up of three parts: the root, the prefix, and the suffix. The root word carries the basic meaning. Prefixes and suffixes are groups of letters that can be added to some root words. When a prefix or suffix is added, the meaning of the root word changes. Another name for prefixes and suffixes is *affixes*, which means "parts added on" to a root word. This lesson shows how to think about the root words and their affixes in order to spell longer words correctly.

A prefix is attached to the beginning of a root word.
Prefix *re* + root word *write* = rewrite

A suffix is added to the end of a root word.
Root word *jump* + suffix *-ed* = jumped

It is important to know whether a suffix begins with a consonant or a vowel because unlike with prefixes, when a suffix is added, the spelling of the root word sometimes changes.
The *t* is doubled: Root word *put* + suffix *-ing* = putting
The *n* is doubled: Root word *ban* + suffix *-ed* = banned

Letters are sometimes doubled when a suffix is added so that the vowel remains a short vowel. If the letter were not doubled, the vowel would be pronounced incorrectly as a long vowel.

- hop—The bunny can hop (rhymes with "stop").
- hopped—The bunny hopped over the carrot (rhymes with "stopped").
- hoped—The boy hoped his friend would come to play (rhymes with "soaped").

When the suffix -*ing* is added to words that end in *e*, the spelling of the root word undergoes a change. The *e* at the end of the word is dropped, and then -*ing* is added.
The *e* is dropped: Root word *choose* + suffix -*ing* = choosing

Words are made up of smaller parts called *syllables*. Each syllable contains one vowel sound.

*Example*
The word "goat" contains 2 vowels but only one vowel sound: long *o*. Therefore, it is one syllable.
The word "goatee" contains 4 vowels, but only 2 vowel sounds: long o and long *e*. Therefore, it has two syllables.

---

Dividing words into syllables helps you:

- spell correctly
- say or pronounce words correctly
- figure out word meanings

Here are some simple rules for syllables:

1. Count the number of vowel sounds.
   - eager - 2 vowel sounds –2 syllables – ea/ger
   - difficult - 3 vowel sounds –3 syllables – dif/fi/cult
   - unhappiness - 4 vowel sounds –4 syllables – un/hap/pi/ness
2. Divide the word.
   - after a prefix:
     pre/pare, re/turn
   - before a suffix:
     still/ness, play/ing
3. Divide a compound word between joined words:
   - play/ground
   - pin/wheel
4. Usually divide between double consonants:
   - put/ting
   - hap/pen
5. **Remember** when double consonants are part of the root word, do not divide.
   - tall/est
   - dress/ing
     Note: You are actually following rule 2 here.
6. Divide between two vowels or two consonants when they are pronounced separately.
   - re/act
   - li/on
   - bur/ger
   - mon/key

## SPELLING INFLECTIONS CORRECTLY

What are inflections?

*Inflections* are the grammatical changes that happen to a word when you change the tense of a verb (the past tense of the present word *play* would become *played or playing*) or it can also be the grammatical changes that happen to a noun when it changes from singular to plural (The singular word *cat* becomes a plural *cats* by adding an "s").

In the English language, there are many types of inflections that can be used. It is important to know the proper inflections to use in your writing and how to spell and use them correctly.

Let's focus on the different inflections that are used with nouns and verbs.

## NOUN INFLECTIONS

When changing a noun from a singular noun to a plural noun, the most general rule is to add an "s" to the end of the word.

*Example*
dog becomes dog**s**

snake becomes snake**s**

bag becomes bag**s**

With singular nouns that end with "ch", "sh", "x", "o", or "s" then you must add an "es" to the end of the word to make it a plural.

*Example*
hitch becomes hitch**es**

bush becomes bush**es**

fox becomes fox**es**

potato becomes potato**es**

miss become miss**es**

---

Singular nouns that end with the letter "y" following a consonant must have the letter "y" changed to an "i" and then have "es" added to the word to make the noun plural.

*Example*

baby becomes bab**ies**

candy becomes cand**ies**

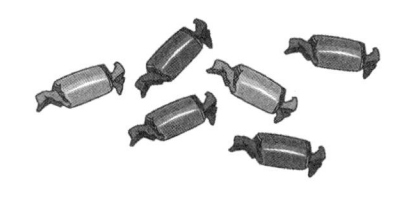

---

## VERB INFLECTIONS

When there is an "s" inflection at the end of a verb it signals that it is in the present tense.

*Example*

**sings**

**walks**

Mark walk**s** to school.

Mary sing**s** in the choir.

---

When there is an "ed" inflection at the end of a verb, it signals that it has happened in the past. The verb is in the past tense.

*Example*

**walked**

**jumped**

Mary walk**ed** to school.

Bob jump**ed** off his bed.

---

When there is an "ing" inflection added to the end of a verb it usually signals that it is in a present progressive tense. That means the action is happening right now or in the present.

*Example*

**drinking**

**jumping**

I am drink**ing** fresh orange juice.

Robert is jump**ing** into the pool and giant waves.

# Spell Suffixes Correctly

Suffixes are word endings that are added on to change the "form" or use of a word. The rules in this lesson will help you to spell most suffixes correctly.

## Drop the "e"

*Example*
imagine = imaginable
excite = exciting

## Keep the "e"

*Example*
excite = excitement
notice = noticeable

## Double Final Consonant

This rule usually works when the consonant is preceded by a short vowel

*Example*
admit = admitted
sag = sagged

## Do not Double Final Consonant

*Example*
defeat = defeated
regret = regretful
invert = inverting

## Change the "y" to "i"

Use this rule when there is a consonant in front of the "y".

*Example*
friendly = friendliness
carry = carried

## Do not change the "y" to "i"

Use this rule when there is a vowel in front of the "y", and for words like *dry, cry, fry*, etc.

*Example*
enjoy = enjoying
cry = crying

## Spell Prefixes Correctly

Sometimes it is hard to know which prefix to use in order to spell a word correctly. For example, *un, in, im*, and *il* all mean the same thing: *not*. Which one to use is easier to decide if you remember a few general rules:

1. The prefix *un* works in a lot of cases: unpopular, unafraid, unwilling.
2. The prefix *in* is also commonly used: inappropriate, insensitive.
3. The prefix *in* often changes to *im* for words beginning with *m* or *p*: immovable, impossible.
4. The prefix *in* often changes to *il* for words beginning with *l*: illegitimate, illogical.

## YOUR TURN

Test yourself on the correct spelling of prefixes by trying the questions below. A few suffixes have been included as well. The correct answers are there for you too!

1. Prefixes (im, un, re) and suffixes (ful, less) have been added to root words below. Which of the following lists has all the words spelled correctly?
   A. Immobile, reestart, unlikely
   B. Helpful, meaningless, likable
   C. Improper, regain, unimportant
   
   **Answer**
   The correct answer is C. The prefixes *im-*, *re-*, and *un-* are all used properly. In answer A, the prefixes *im-* and *un-* are used properly, but an extra *e* is added incorrectly before the word "start." In answer B, the suffixes -ful and *-less* were correctly added, but the *e* should have been left after the word "like" to form the word "likeable."

2. Which of the following lists has the correct prefixes and suffixes?
   A. Lifeless, reborn, pityful
   B. Impatient, joyful, untold
   C. Bendable, un glued, retold
   
   **Answer**
   The correct answer is B because the prefixes and suffixes are correctly added to the root words. In answer A, the *y* in "pity" should be changed to *i* before the suffix *-ful* is added. In answer C, the prefix *un-* should be joined to the word "glued."

## CORRECTLY SPELL SYLLABLE CONSTRUCTIONS

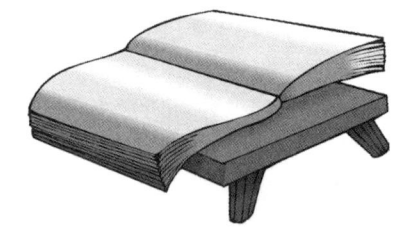

Words are made up of smaller parts called *syllables*. Each syllable contains **one** vowel sound.

- *goat* contains two vowels, but only one vowel sound—a long ō—so the word contains one syllable
- *goatee* contains four vowels, but only two vowel sounds—a long ō and a long ē—so the word contains two syllables

Dividing a word into syllables can help you:

- spell it correctly
- say or pronounce it correctly
- figure out its meaning

## Rules for Syllables

1. Count the number of vowel sounds in words: two vowel sounds – two syllables, three vowel sounds - three, etc.
   - eager - ea/ger
   - difficult - dif/fi/cult
   - unhappiness - un/hap/pi/ness
2. Divide words after a prefix:
   - pre/pare
   - re/turn
3. Divide words before a suffix:
   - still/ness
   - play/ing
4. Divide compound words between the joined words:
   - play/ground
   - pin/wheel
5. Usually divide words between double consonants:
   - put/ting
   - hap/pen
   - **Exception:** When double consonants are part of the root word do not divide them (tall/est, dress/ing)
6. Divide words between two vowels or two consonants when they are pronounced separately:
   - re/act
   - bur/ger
   - li/on
   - mon/key

## Syllable Rules Help You Spell

When you carefully sound out the natural parts, or syllables, of a word, you are more likely to spell the word correctly.

*Example*
mountain = mount-ain, NOT mount-i-an

---

## How to Use a Dictionary

A **dictionary** is a tool that helps you find information about words. You can learn

- how to spell words
- their definitions
- their function or parts of speech
- where the word was first used
- how to pronounce words

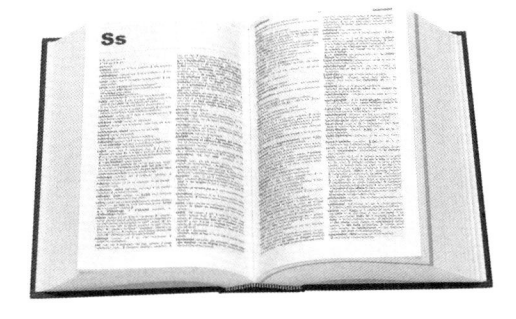

## A Dictionary Entry

When you look up a word, you will be reading a dictionary entry for the word that looks something like this illustration. This is where you will find the above information, and you can select the information you need. For example, you may only need to look at the pronunciation of the word.

> **rev•o•lu•tion** (rev'ə loō'shən), n.
> 1. the overthrow and replacement of an established government or political system by the people governed.
> 2. a sudden, complete, or radical change.
> 3. rotation on or as if on an axis.
> 4. the orbiting of one heavenly body around another.
> 5. a single cycle in a rotation or orbit.
> **—rev'o•lu'•tion•ary,**
>
> *adj*., **n**., *pl*–ies. – rev'o•lu'•tion•ist,**n**.

## How to Spell Words

Think of a word to look up. Open the dictionary, and look at the top corner of any page. You will see two words separated by a forward slash[/]. These words are the first and last words on the page. Next, you will need to decide whether you need to flip forwards or backwards to find the section your word is in. Don't forget that the words in a dictionary are found in alphabetical order.

**Note**: if you are unable to find the word that you are looking up, it might be because the word ends in "ed", "ing", or "s". You will need to find the root word. There, you will find its different endings.

*Example*

Think of a word: **fame**.

Open the dictionary: Suppose that you flipped to the page where it says **leap/leaves**.

As you can see these words start with the letter "L". We need to find the section that starts with the letter "F". That means we will have to flip back to the "F" section of the dictionary.

Keep on turning the pages until you get to the "F" section. Once you are in this section, look at the second letter of your word and repeat the first step. Since the second letter of **fame** is an "a" you will need to flip all the way back to the beginning of the "F" section since "a" is the first letter of the alphabet. You will need to repeat this process with each of the following letters of your word. Remember to check the bold words at the top of each page to see the range of words on the page.

## Definitions

Once you find the word you are looking up, you will you will notice the part of speech it is. In this case, the letter "n." is representing the word "noun". Next, you will find one or more definitions of your word. You will have to read each definition to know which one best fits the way that your word is used in a sentence.

*Example*
**fame.** n

1. Great renown: a concert violinist of international fame.
2. Public estimation; reputation:a politician of ill fame.
3. Rumor. To make renowned or famous.
4. To report to be.

---

## Function or Part of Speech

The first thing you need to know is that function is the same as part of speech. In the example that we have used (fame) you will notice that there is the letter "n." in front of the definition. This lets you know that "fame" is a noun. Other abbreviations you may find are: adj.- adjective, adv.- adverb, v.- verb, ANT.- antonym and SYN.- synonym.

## First Used

Along with definition you will also notice a country of origin. This is the country where the word was first used.

## How Pronounced

Before the definition of the word is given, you will notice brackets around how to say the word. The word will be spelled the way it sounds (phonetically), for example, fame (feym).

## How to Use a Thesaurus

Synonyms are words that have the same or similar meanings. Antonyms are words that have opposite meanings. A *thesaurus* lists words with their synonyms and, usually, their antonyms.

The words in a thesaurus are arranged in alphabetical order. Here is an example of an entry for the word "bright."

| *bright*-adj | (adjectives/ synonyms) | 1. fair, mild, balmy, brilliant, vivid, resplendent<br>2. brilliant, clever, gifted, talented, sharp, keen |
|---|---|---|
|  | (antonyms) | 1. flat, cloudy, dim, dingy, faded, leaden, pale, weak<br>2. bland, desensitized, dim, slow, thick-headed |

How can a thesaurus help you? Here is a paragraph written by a student. Notice the emphasized words.

It was a *warm* spring day. Mother had asked me to *come* straight home because she had a *bright* idea. Out of the wood and chicken wire she had recently *bought*, we could *make* a *home* for our two bunnies, Springbank and Colchester. As a *good* carpenter, Mother would make a *great* assistant for the project.

Here is the same paragraph after the student used a thesaurus to find more interesting words to replace the emphasized ones.

It was a *balmy* spring day. Mother had asked me to *scurry* straight home because she had a *brilliant* idea. Out of the wood and chicken wire she had recently *purchased*, we could *construct* a *hutch* for our two bunnies, Springbank and Colchester. As a *gifted* carpenter, Mother would make a *superb* assistant for the project.

*5L.3a   Use knowledge of language and its conventions when writing, speaking, reading, or listening. Expand, combine, and reduce sentences for meaning, reader/listener interest, and style.*

## USE A VARIETY OF SENTENCE BEGINNINGS

If too many of your sentences begin with the same word or phrase, the reader could become bored or disinterested. To make a sentence more interesting, you may want to begin with different words or phrases.

*Example*

The most shocking coincidence this weekend happened when we saw that Mike and Jesse had set up a campsite right next to ours.

Look below to see other possible ways to write this sentence.

- What an amazing coincidence, that Mike and Jesse would set up a campsite right next to ours.
- Coincidentally, Mike and Jesse set up a campsite right next to ours.
- Setting up a campsite next to Mike and Jesse was an amazing coincidence.
- When I set up camp and realized, by coincidence, Mike and Jesse had set up their campsite right next to us, I was shocked!
- Without any idea, we ended up setting up our campsite right next to Mike and Jesse.
- Could it be any more of a coincidence that Mike and Jesse set up a campsite next to ours?
- The most amazing coincidence that happened that weekend was that Jesse and Mike were in the campsite right next to ours.

## It's Your Turn

It's easy to "spice up" a sentence by rewording it to make it sound more interesting to the reader. Change the sentence below into a variety of different sentence beginnings.

Peter received 22 medals for his courageous acts of bravery as a firefighter.

## Explore the Possibilities

Below are a variety of sentence beginnings you could have used. There are many other answers that would work as well.

- For his courageous acts of bravery as a firefighter, Peter received 22 medals.
- Firefighter Peter received 22 medals for his courageous acts of bravery.
- The 22 medals that Peter received are for his courageous acts of bravery as a firefighter.
- Receiving 22 medals for his courageous acts of bravery was what a firefighter like Peter deserved.
- Peter, the firefighter, received 22 medals for his courageous acts of bravery.
- Bravery and courage are two reasons why Firefighter Peter received 22 medals.
- Could anyone be more courageous than Firefighter Peter, who won 22 medals for his acts of bravery?

## Use a Variety of Sentence Lengths in your Writing

Adding a variety of sentences to your writing will make it more enjoyable to the reader. Longer sentences allow you to add more detail or information to your sentences. Shorter sentences often highlight important points.

Below is a paragraph using only simple, short sentences.

*Example*

A dog sled is pulled by dogs. They are used to travel over ice and snow. It was a main method of transportation in the Arctic long ago. They were important to humans long ago. They would transport food and medicine. There are different types of dog sleds. To make a team you need dogs. You need to choose a leader dog. You need point dogs. You need swing dogs. You need wheel dogs. The lead dog is most important. Team dogs are the dogs in the middle. Point dogs are optional. Siberian Huskies or Alaskan Malamutes are the best dogs for dog sledding.

Now let's see what this paragraph would sound like if it were made up of different sentence lengths.

*Example*

A dog sled is a sled that is pulled by a team of dogs and is used to travel over ice and snow. Dog sledding was once the main method of transportation for humans in the Arctic regions before the invention of snowmobiles and airplanes. Hundreds of years ago, dog sleds were used to transport people and goods through the deep snow and over slippery ice. People used dog sleds to transport everything from food to medicine. Assembling a dog sled involves choosing the leader dogs, point dogs, swing dogs, and wheel dogs. Mushers, the sled drivers, take particular care of the lead dogs, as these dogs are the most important dogs in the team. Point dogs are optional and are located behind the leader dogs.

Did you notice how much more interesting the second paragraph was? The second paragraph contained a variety of longer and shorter sentences. This keeps the reader more interested.

## Now It's Your Turn

Below is a short paragraph about African elephants. Your job is to turn the paragraph into a more interesting one by creating different sentence lengths.

African elephants are large animals. They are the largest land mammals on earth. They are bigger than Asian elephants. The African elephant has large, distinct ears. Their ears somewhat resemble the shape of the continent of Africa. It can get very hot in Africa. African elephants cool off with water. To cool off, they suck water into their trunks. Then, they spray it all over themselves. Elephants don't sleep much. They walk great distances looking for food.

## A Possible Revision

One of many possible revisions is below. If your revision contains shorter and longer sentences, then you have successfully revised the paragraph.

African elephants are the largest land mammals on earth. They are bigger than Asian elephants and have distinctly large ears that somewhat resemble the shape of the continent of Africa. It can get very hot in Africa! To cool off, the elephants suck water into their trunks and spray it all over themselves. Elephants don't sleep much and spend most of their time walking great distances in search of food.

## Combining Short Related Sentences With Appositives

What is an **appositive**?

An **appositive** is a noun or a noun phrase that re-describes itself, directly after stating the original noun.

When writing an appositive, you must separate the appositive from the rest of the sentence with commas.

*Example*
The **insect**, a large black and yellow bee, was finding its way through all of our fruit at the picnic.

---

Notice in the first example how the **appositive,** "the large black and yellow bee" is separated from the **original noun** "insect" with a comma before and after the appositive. This is generally how you are to correctly write an appositive in your own writing.

*Example*

During dinner with the Queen of England, **Max,** <u>the sloppiest eater at the table</u>, spilled gravy all over the queen's dress!

Notice in the second example how the **appositive,** "the sloppiest eater at the table" is separated from the **original noun,** "Max" with a comma before. Then, there is a comma after the **appositive** "the sloppiest eater at the table" as well, to differentiate it from the rest of the sentence.

*Example*

An ill-mannered player, <u>Ryan</u>, was in big trouble for breaking a bat over the fence when he was upset.

In the third example the **appositive,** "Ryan", is separated from the rest of the sentence with commas.

## It's Your Turn

Now it's your turn to try creating complete sentences using appositives! In each question below, you will be given a noun, an appositive, and a context for you to write the sentence about. See if you can create a complete sentence, using all three parts.

*Example*

For example, if you are given the following three things:

- Noun: Blake
- Appositive: a friendly little boy
- Context: playground

The sentence you could create might look something like this:

Blake, a friendly little boy, could not wait to get to the playground with his friends.

OR

A friendly little boy, Blake, was swinging on the swings at the playground.

Remember when you are writing your sentences, to use commas to separate the noun from its appositive!

## Try Writing Appositives

Now give it a try. You may want to get out a piece of paper and a pencil to write out each of the sentences.

1. **Noun:** Janet **Appositive:** the cranky old lady from across the street **Context:** picking flowers
2. **Noun:** Michael **Appositive:** my sister's mean boss **Context:** getting a raise
3. **Noun:** Miss Kober **Appositive:** one of the nicest people on the planet **Context:** school

Do you think you have created complete sentences using the noun and appositives correctly? Check your answers below for some examples you might have tried. Remember you were to make sure to use a comma to separate the noun from the appositive and the rest of the sentence. See how you did!

## Possible Answers for Question Number 1:

Janet, the cranky old lady from across the street, was picking flowers in her yard when I looked out my window.

or maybe you decided to write it like this:

The cranky old lady from across the street, Janet, was picking flowers all day long.

### Possible Answers for Question Number 2:

Michael, my sister's mean boss, is finally thinking about giving her a raise.

or maybe you decided to write it like this:

My sister's mean boss, Michael, is talking about giving my sister a raise.

### Possible Answers for Question Number 3:

Miss Kober, one of the nicest people on the planet, is coming to teach at our school.

or maybe you decided to write it like this:

One of the nicest people in the planet, Miss Kober, is teaching me how to draw portraits at school.

*5W.1c   Write opinion pieces on topics or texts, supporting a point of view with reasons and information. Link opinion and reasons using words, phrases, and clauses.*

*5W.2c   Write informative/explanatory texts to examine a topic and convey ideas and information clearly. Link ideas within and across categories of information using words, phrases, and clauses.*

## Combining Sentences Using Participial Phrases

As you grow as a writer, use varying lengths and types of sentences in your writing. Sometimes when you are writing, it is important to combine some of your shorter sentences, so your writing does not sound so choppy.

One way to combine short choppy sentences into one is by using **participial phrases** to combine them.

What is a participial phrase?
A *participial phrase* is a group of words that serve as an adjective in a sentence to help modify or describe something more clearly.

## How It Can Be Done

*Example*

The bus slides across the icy road. The bus is moving uncontrollably. It will likely hit the street sign.

This sounds choppy. We may choose to make the sentence like this instead:
The bus, **sliding uncontrollably** across the icy road, will likely hit the street sign.

In the above sentence, the word **sliding** is the participle and the word **uncontrollably** directly follows the participle to create a participial phrase. This sentence flows much more smoothly than the original three choppy sentences.

---

*Example*

Mary went jogging through the forest. Mary went quickly.

Mary went **jogging quickly** through the forest.

In the above sentence, the word **jogging** is the participle and the word **quickly** is the adverb that directly follows the participle, creating the participial phrase.

---

## YOUR TURN

Combine the following sentences into one sentence using a participial phrase.

1. Michael saw the bunny jumping. The bunny was anxious. It was running through the back yard from the fox.
2. Kate loves the waffles and pancakes her mom makes for her. She like eating them furiously.
3. The wind blows through our small town. The wind is careless.

## HOW DID YOU DO?

Your answers should flow smoothly like the combined sentences below. Each answer contains a participial phrase.

1. Michael saw the bunny **jumping anxiously** through the back yard away from the fox.
2. **Eating furiously,** Kate loves the waffles and pancakes her mom makes for her.
3. The **carelessly blowing** wind sweeps through our small town.

# Combining Sentences With Adjectives

It is important as you grow as a writer to use varying lengths and types of sentences in your writing. Sometimes when you are writing, it is important to shorten and combine your sentences, so your writing does not sound so choppy.

One way to improve your sentences is to combine short choppy sentences into one by using **adjectives** to combine them.

*Example*

Someone might have a story that sounds something like this:

Mark had a beard. The beard was gray. The beard was very thick.

This sounds very choppy.

Another way to write these sentences is to combine them in one flowing sentence using the adjectives:

"Mark had a very thick, gray beard." or "Mark had a beard that was gray and very thick."

Doesn´t the combined sentence sound smoother?

---

*Example*

The young child gave me a flower. The flower was yellow. The flower was droopy.

The above sentences sound quite choppy.

It might flow better if it was written as follows instead:

"The young child gave me a droopy, yellow flower". or "The young child gave me a flower that was yellow and droopy."

---

*Try This!*

Now it's your turn to try. In each question, try to combine the short choppy sentences, into one smooth, clear sentence. When you think you have got it, check your answers below for some possible solutions.

1. My mom is the greatest. She is the best cook. She is giving.
2. Misty is a great dog. She is smart. She is funny.
3. The house was so old. It was run down. It was brown.

How do you think you did? Were you able to combine the sentences into one clear sentence? Check below for some possible solutions.

1. "My mom is the greatest because she is giving and the best cook." or "My giving mom is the greatest and the best cook."
2. "Misty is a great dog because she is smart and funny." or "Misty is a smart, funny, great dog."
3. "The old brown house was run down." or "The brown house was old and run down." or "The house was old, run down and brown."

## COMBINING SENTENCES WITH ADVERBS

It is important as you grow as a writer to use varying lengths and types of sentences in your writing. You can combine some of your shorter sentences, so that your writing does not sound so choppy.

One way to improve your sentences is to combine short choppy sentences into one by using **adverbs**. Look at some examples below to see how adverbs can be used to combine sentences. The adverbs are highlighted.

*Example*

For example, a story might sound something like this:

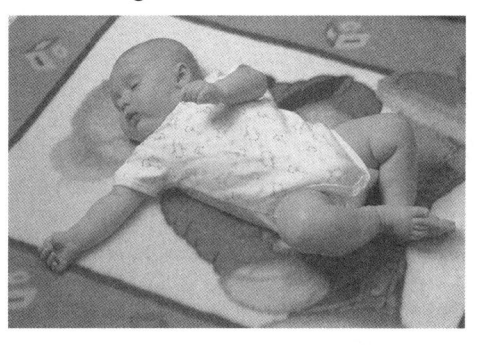

Mary handed the baby a rattle. She did this silently. The baby crawled towards the rattle. The baby did this quickly.

This version of the story sounds quite choppy. To combine these sentences using the adverbs, it might look something like this:

Mary **silently** handed the baby a rattle as the baby crawled **quickly** towards it.

Read the first version of the story out loud and then read the second, revised version. Which one sounds like it flows better when reading? Do you agree it's the second one?

Let's try combining a few more short, choppy sentences by using adverbs.

*Example*

I opened up a photograph book. The memories from my childhood came back instantly. I flipped through the pages. I did this eagerly.

Instead of using the four choppy sentences, you might try to combine them using the adverbs. It could sound like this:

**Instantly**, the memories of my childhood came back as I opened up the photograph book and **eagerly** flipped through the pages.

---

*Example*

John raced toward first base. He did this quickly. The crowd cheered for him. They cheered loudly.

How could we make these four sentences into one smooth sentence?

It could sound something like this:

John raced **quickly** towards first base and the crowd cheered **loudly** for him.

---

## Now it's Your Turn

Can you combine the following sentences using the adverbs provided?

1. Mark yelled at his mom. He yelled very angrily. He stormed out his front door. He left loudly.
2. Sophie was stressed about moving. She wanted people to move her things carefully. She needed to move quickly. She had a lot of things to move.
3. Ryan worked on his paper. He worked nervously. He wanted good grades. He worked diligently.

Do you think you have combined the sentences correctly? If you think you have, check some of the suggestions below for possible ways to combine the sentences.

1. Mark **angrily** yelled at his mom and **loudly** stormed out his front door.
2. Sophie was stressed about moving because she had a lot of things for people to move **quickly** and **carefully**.
3. Ryan worked **nervously** and **diligently** on his paper because he wanted good grades.

## Combining Sentences with Prepositional Phrases

It is important as you grow as a writer to use varying lengths and types of sentences in your writing. Sometimes when you are writing, it is important to shorten and combine your sentences, so your writing does not sound so choppy.

One way to improve your sentences is to combine short choppy sentences into one by using **prepositional phrases**.

Prepositional phrases are short groups of words that begin with a preposition. They add detail, or modify nouns or verbs.

*Example*
- above the tower
- before the game
- beyond the lane

---

Class Focus  Castle Rock Research

## COMMONLY USED PREPOSITIONS

- about, above, across, after, against, along, among, around, at
- before, behind, below, beneath, beside, between, beyond, by
- despite, down, during
- except
- for, from
- in, inside, into
- near
- of, off, on, outside, over
- past
- through, to, toward
- under, until, up
- with, without

You may use some of the above prepositions in your writing to combine short, choppy sentences into longer, flowing sentences.

Let's look at some examples together.

*Example*
A story might sound something like this.

The dog was on the sofa. The dog jumped down. He hurt himself. He banged his head. He kept playing.

Below is another version of the above story that uses prepositional phrases to combine the sentences.

The dog was **on the sofa** and he jumped **to the hardwood floor**. **Despite hurting his head**, he kept playing.

---

Now let's try another example of combining some ideas by using prepositional phrases.

*Example*
A sentence could look something like this.

Tonya sat.

This is a very short, simple sentence. One might ask where is she sitting? Whom is she sitting with? By answering these questions and adding to your sentence, you may need to use some prepositional phrases. Let try adding to it together.

Tonya sat **with her friend Mary on a park bench**.

Which sentence helped paint a better picture? The second one of course! By using prepositional phrases, you can really improve your sentences in your writing.

Let's try this again. Can we try to combine the following sentences using some more prepositional phrases?

*Example*

The teacher spoke. She taught about bugs. The class listened. It was boring.

We could combine the above four choppy sentences into one flowing sentence by using prepositional phrases.

The teacher spoke **about bugs** and the class listened **despite their boredom**.

---

## Now It's Your Turn

Can you combine the following sentences using one or more prepositional phrases? Give it a try and when you think you've got it, check your answers below.

1. A man fell off his bike. The students laughed.
2. My cousins visited. They live in California.
3. Tori hid her candy bar. She put it under the pillow.

How did you do? Do you think you were able to combine the sentences using some prepositional phrases? Below are some suggestions you may have used.

1. The students laughed **at the man** when he fell **off his bike**.
2. My cousins visited **from California**.
3. Tori hid the candy bar **under the pillow**.

## Let's Try One More Activity

To help us learn about adding prepositional phrases to help combine or improve our sentence writing. First there will be a simple sentence. In brackets there is a question prompt. Try to add to the sentence by answering the questions using prepositional phrases.

1. I watched a movie. (Where did you watch the movie and what was it about?)
2. The man tripped. (Where did the man trip?)
3. Charlie sat. (Where did Charlie sit?)

How do you think you did? Make sure you used prepositional phrases to add to the sentences. If you think you've got it, check some of the possible solutions below.

1. I watched a movie **about a dying dog**, **at home**, **on my sofa**.
2. The man tripped **off the sidewalk**.
3. Charlie sat **against the wall**.

*5L.4b   Determine or clarify the meaning of unknown and multiple-meaning words and phrases based on grade 5 reading and content, choosing flexibly from a range of strategies. Use common, grade-appropriate Greek and Latin affixes and roots as clues to the...*

## WHAT ARE WORD ORIGINS?

Word origin refers to the original meaning of a word. **Etymology** is the study of the origins of words. Etymologists study how a word came to be.

*Example*

Let's take the word *telephone*:

- *tele* means long distance
- *phone* means speak

So you can see how the word *telephone* originated.

## DEFINE UNFAMILIAR WORDS USING WORD ORIGINS

Knowing word origins can be helpful in spelling unfamiliar words. The chart below shows the main 'ancestors' of our English language. You can see, for instance, that Latin and Greek were both ancestors. That means that many of our English words once started out as Latin or Greek words.

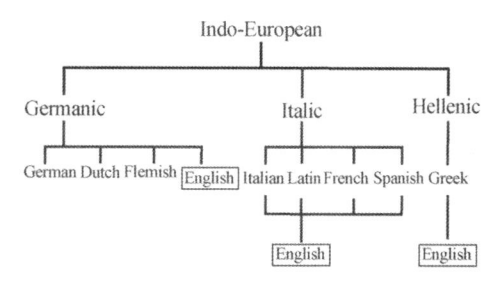

```
                    Indo-European
         ┌──────────────┼──────────────┐
      Germanic         Italic        Hellenic
   ┌─────┼─────┬─────┐  ┌────┬────┬────┐   │
German Dutch Flemish English Italian Latin French Spanish Greek
                              └────┬────┘       │
                                English      English
```

*Example*

In Latin, the word *ego* means "I." If you know this, then it will help you to define other words that contain the word *ego*, such as *egocentric* and *egotistical*.

The word *anti* has a Greek origin and means "against," so if you discover a word that contains *anti*, it will help you better understand the meaning of the word.

The same goes for the Latin word *sub*, which means "beneath" such as *submarine* (beneath or below water) and *subdue* (to bring down).

## Your Turn

In Latin, *oper* means "to work." Read the sentences below, and try to figure out the meaning of the highlighted words.

1. Kelly's leg did not heal properly so she is scheduled to have an **operation** in the morning.
2. If we all **cooperate**, then we will get the job done quickly.

Let's see how you did.

*Operation* means "to work on, fix or improve a part of the body."

*Cooperate* means "to work together for a common goal."

*5L.4c   Determine or clarify the meaning of unknown and multiple-meaning words and phrases based on grade 5 reading and content, choosing flexibly from a range of strategies. Consult reference materials, both print and digital, to find the...*

## USING A THESAURUS TO DETERMINE THE MEANING OF AN UNFAMILIAR WORD

Words can have different implied meanings, so when you come across a word you're not familiar with, you may want to use a thesaurus to compare your unknown word to those in the thesaurus to help you see a variety of other words that have a similar meaning.

*Example*

**bright**– ADJS (adjectives/synonyms) 1. sunny, fair, mild, balmy; brilliant, vivid, resplendent 2. smart, brainy, brilliant, clever, gifted, talented, sharp keen
– (antonyms) 1. dull, flat, dingy, cloudy, faded, leaden, dim, pale, weak, faint 2. slow-witted, dim, slow, thick-headed, bland, desensitized

---

A thesaurus is a list of synonyms (words that have similar meanings) and antonyms (words that have opposite meanings). It usually comes in one of two forms. One way is in a dictionary like form, where the words are in alphabetical order. If you are looking for a similar word for *happy*, you would look under the letter **H**.

The second way is in an index form. In an index type thesaurus, there is an index at the back, with the words listed in alphabetical order. If you were to look up the word "happy", in the index type thesaurus, you would look at the back index page under H and it might send you to several pages where "happy" would have synonyms. You might find "happy" listed under several other words within the thesaurus like "ecstatic" or "overjoyed" The index would guide you to the page or pages where "happy" appears.

A thesaurus is a valuable tool to help determine an unfamiliar word by locating words with similar meanings.

*Example*

Let's use the words "slender" and "skinny" for example. Both words are found under the heading **thin** in the thesaurus, but "slender" can have a more positive tone, while "skinny" may not.

"The slender man walked down the street." and "The skinny man walked down the street."

Both words may have two different images or create two different images, even though the words are similar.

## It's Your Turn!

If you were reading a novel and read the following sentence, "He was aware of the **precarious** lifestyle of an undersea diver but he insisted that he still begin his training." **Precarious** might be an unfamilar word. You might want to look in the thesaurus alphabetically under the "P" words. Look in a thesaurus to locate the word PRECARIOUS. Some of the synonyms you could replace with the unknown word would be *hazardous, dangerous* or *tricky*.

Replacing the unknown word in context may help you understand the meaning of the word and help you to make sense of the text you are reading. Try out the different meanings for the word by substituting them below:

1. He was aware of the **hazardous** lifestyle of an undersea diver.
2. He was aware of the **dangerous** lifestyle of an undersea diver.
3. He was aware of the **tricky** lifestyle of an undersea diver.

What did you conclude? Because there are hazards, or dangers, the diver will need the training to be prepared. The meaning of **precarious** in this context probably doesn't mean tricky, because the diver is beginning his training. Precarious means that the diver could be in danger because of the risks of being underwater. That is why he needs to be well trained and prepared.

## Using a Dictionary to Determine Unfamiliar Words

Sometimes when you are reading and you come across a word you are unsure of, the best solution to determine its meaning is to look in a **dictionary**. A **dictionary** is an alphabetical list of words and their meanings. Some words may have multiple meanings. Typically, dictionaries will list the most commonly used meanings first. If the dictionary does give multiple meanings for the unknown word, you will have to see what definition would make sense in the context of the text you are reading.

Each word that is explained in the dictionary is usually in bold type.

After the bold word, it may also show the word divided into syllables. (For example: cal-am-i-ty)

## LET'S TRY THIS TOGETHER

Let's use the sentence below as our context to figure out what *sarcasm* means by using a dictionary.

*Example*

"How unselfish you are!" Mary said with **sarcasm**, as her brother took the biggest piece of cake from the plate.

When locating a word in a dictionary, you must look for it alphabetically. Using **sarcasm** as our example, and using the dictionary meanings below, let's determine which definition would be suitable for this context.

Sar*casm

- sharp or bitter irony
- sneering or cutting remark

Both definitions would make sense within this context, as we understand the girl is probably saying the opposite of what she is really thinking.

## USING A PICTURE DICTIONARY TO DETERMINE AN UNFAMILIAR WORD

When reading, you may come across a word that you do not recognize or know the meaning of. If available, one resource you can use to help you is a **picture dictionary**. A picture dictionary is always listed in alphabetical order and will have a picture of the word along with the word being described. Usually the picture can give you hints about what the word means.

*Example*

*island* (i/lend), *n.* 1. a piece of land surrounded on all sides by water but too small for a continent. 2. something isolated and apart like an island.

---

If you were to look at the above example, after looking at the picture of the _____, you might assume _____ means _____.

**Answer**: After looking at the picture of the *island*, you might assume that *island* means a fairly small piece of land completely surrounded by water.

## USING A GLOSSARY TO DETERMINE AN UNFAMILIAR WORD

If you are reading a textbook and come across a word that is **bolded**, you can usually find the definition of the word in a section in the back of the book, called the *glossary.*

A *glossary* is an alphabetical list of individual terms and their meanings that a reader may be unfamiliar with.

**air pump**   a device for pumping air into or out of a vessel, a room, etc.

**decompression**   a gradual lowering of pressure on a person who has been on an underwater dive

**diving bell**   an open-bottomed box or bell, supplied with air, in which a person can be lowered into deep water

**SCUBA**   Self Contained Underwater Breathing Apparatus

**submarine**   a vessel able to operate under water

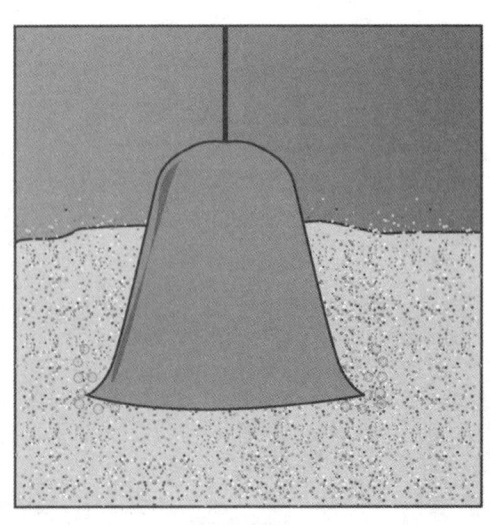

Class Focus — Castle Rock Research

It is a great tool to use when you come across a word you are unfamiliar with in a text.

When you are reading, and the bold word does not make sense to you in the context, sometimes looking up the meaning of the word in the glossary can help it make more sense to you. Usually the bold words in a text are important words to know about, and that is why they are bolded.

*5L.5a   Demonstrate understanding of figurative language, word relationships, and nuances in word meanings. Interpret figurative language, including similes and metaphors, in context.*

## UNDERSTAND FIGURATIVE USE OF WORDS IN CONTEXT

Figurative is when you describe something by comparing it with something else. Figurative means something other than what it says.

*Example*

You are a shining star.

It's raining cats and dogs.

---

When you read the above example, common sense tells you that it can't possibly be raining cats and dogs. You also know that you are not really a star that shines. However, these words, "shining star" and "cats and dogs" do mean something within the sentence. When you come across a word like the ones above, know that the author is doing it to achieve some kind of special effect to make the reading more interesting. That's what figurative language does.

Look closely at the sentences below. What word or words in the sentence do you think are figurative? What do they really mean?

1. I'm so nervous that I have butterflies in my stomach.
2. Break a leg!
3. She was as light as a feather.
4. I'm falling in love with you.

Let's see how you did. Check for the correct answers below.

1. The expression "butterflies in my stomach" is figurative and means that I'm feeling nervous.
2. "Break a leg" is figurative and means good luck.
3. The phrase "light as a feather" is figurative and means she is very light.
4. "I'm falling in love" is figurative and means you are beginning to feel that you are in love with someone.

When you see the word butterfly, you think of a beautiful insect flying through the air, not in a person's stomach. In the case of "I have butterflies in my stomach" we know that it must be figurative because butterflies don't really live in a person's stomach.

## EXPLAIN FIGURATIVE USE OF WORDS IN CONTEXT

Often, you can understand the meaning of a word by reading it in context. When we refer to a word's **context**, we mean the words around the word help you understand it. This strategy also works when words are used figuratively. This means that words are being used in special ways intended to present you with a mental image or picture. "Dad is a real bear until he gets his first cup of coffee in the morning" is a metaphorical or figurative use of words in context. Of course, your dad is not an actual bear!
You understand from the sentence that he just acts grouchy until he gets some coffee in the morning.

Authors and poets often use **figurative language** to make ideas and thoughts clearer to readers. Figurative language can help to describe the setting of a story and the feelings of the characters. There are many different types of figurative language. A few of the most common types are included below, because you will frequently come across examples of these types of figurative language in stories you read.

**Alliteration**– the repeated use of the first letter or sound in two or more words set closely together.

*Example*
Sally sells seashells by the seashore.

---

**Onomatopoeia**– the use of a word that imitates the sound it describes

*Example*
The bird *squawked* endlessly.
The sound of the drums *boomed* in my head.

---

**Metaphor**–a comparison of two unlike things made without using the words "like" or "as"

*Example*

The stars were diamonds in the sky.

---

**Simile**–a comparison of two unlike things that is made by using the words "like" or "as"

*Example*
The kite flew *like* a bird.
She was *as* quiet *as* a mouse.

---

## Evaluate Influence of Figurative Language on Readers

Writers and poets will often use special ways of writing called figurative language. When you compare something with something else to describe it more clearly or use words that are not meant literally, you are using figurative language. Figurative language is a tool for clear communication. Writers will often use figurative language to describe the setting of a story and the feelings of the characters.

Authors often use figurative language to make their writing more descriptive and interesting, and to show meaning in different ways. It can also be used to set the mood in a piece of writing.

Sometimes, figurative language is also called imagery. Imagery is language that appeals to the senses of taste, touch, sight, smell, or hearing. Writers often "show" us as well as tell us, by using images that readers will understand. The language of imagery allows readers to "see" more vivid word pictures, and to understand exactly what the writer is trying to express.

## LITERAL AND FIGURATIVE MEANING

What does it mean when we say that words can have both a literal and a figurative meaning? When a word has a literal meaning, it is used in a factual manner. If you use a word figuratively, it conveys more than just facts. It requires that the readers or listeners use their imagination.

*Example*

Beth froze at the sound of that voice, fear turning her feet to stone.

---

Of course this does not mean that Beth is cold, or even frozen, or that her feet transformed into rock. This statement uses *figurative language* – in this case, metaphors. By saying that Beth "froze" and that her feet turned "to stone," it suggests that she is very frightened. If we wanted to be *literal*, we might say, "Beth was so terrified, she could hardly move. "Beth froze" is far more interesting and it encourages the reader to use imagination to form an image.

We can tell that someone is using figurative language, if the literal meaning does not make sense. We know then, that the words require our imagination. Using our imagination, we can see what the writer meant.

## KINDS OF FIGURATIVE LANGUAGE

There are many different types of figurative language, but the main ones that you should understand right now are shown here.

1. *Simile*: This figure of speech draws a comparison between two things that are not alike, to show that they are alike in an important way, usually using the word, "as" or "like." By mentioning the likeness between one thing and another, the writer helps the reader to imagine the image more clearly: "The stars sparkled like diamonds."
2. *Metaphor*: This figure of speech makes an implied comparison of two things that are not alike, in order to emphasize a certain quality. It does not use the words, "as" or "like" as a simile does: "The mountain was a dark fortress against the far horizon."
3. *Alliteration*: Alliteration is the repetition of similar consonant sounds at the beginning of words or within words. This emphasizes the phrase, calling the reader's attention to it: "babbling, bubbling brook".
4. *Personification:* This is the giving of human characteristics to an object or an idea: "The mountain, hunched and sulking, towered in the distance."

## EVALUATING THE INFLUENCE

The following poem, "Stars", contains many examples of effective word use. Word choice and figurative language work together to produce a feeling about night: a calming experience of peace, beauty, and unending time, with which readers can identify.

---

**Stars**

Now in the West the slender moon lies low,

And now Orion[1] glimmers through the trees,
Clearing the earth with even pace and slow,
And now the stately-moving Pleiades[2],
In that soft infinite darkness overhead
Hang jewel-wise upon a silver thread.

And all the lonelier stars that have their place,
Calm lamps within the distant southern sky,
And planet-dust upon the edge of space,
Look down upon the fretful world, and I
Look up to outer vastness unafraid
And see the stars which sang when earth was made.

—*by* Marjorie Pickthall

[1] Orion: constellation, taking the form of a hunter with a belt and a sword.
[2] Pleiades: the seven daughters of Atlas in Greek myth; and, a group of stars in the constellation Taurus, not far from Orion

---

*Example*
- Orion is pictured as a hunter, "Clearing the earth with even pace and slow". (personification)
- Pleiades is beautifully portrayed as the seven daughters of Atlas "stately-moving" across the heavens (personification) or hanging "jewel-wise upon a silver thread" (simile).
- The "lonelier stars" (personification) are described as "Calm lamps within the distant southern sky" (metaphor)

This imagery is as moving as it is beautiful. The figurative language helps you to connect with the poet's awe as she gazed up at the star-studded heavens.

*5L.5b Demonstrate understanding of figurative language, word relationships, and nuances in word meanings. Recognize and explain the meaning of common idioms, adages, and proverbs.*

## WHAT ARE IDIOMS?

An idiom is a type of language that is used by a person or a group of people and is only used by them. When you are around your friends are there certain words that you only use around them? These words that you use around your friends are called idioms. If you use these words or phrases around other people, the words are often difficult for them to understand or may have a completely different meaning. Idioms can also be acronyms for a word or phrase. An acronym is a word that is formed from the beginning letters of several words. For example, "Bald eagles eat mice" would form the acronym BEEM.

*Example*
When people refer to the bathroom as a "loo," you will know that these people are originally from England and the word "loo" is unique to them.

*Example*
Another famous idiom is when someone says that "they are feeling under the weather." In this example, they do not actually mean they are under a cloud and the sun; what they mean is that they do not feel well or they feel sick.

Today, the meaning of the word *idiom* has changed to include acronyms that are often used in technology terminology by people who are referred to as the net generation. Some of the more famous acronyms are listed as follows:

| Acronym | Meaning |
|---|---|
| LOL | Laughing Out Loud |
| BTW | By The Way |
| AKA | Also Known As |
| ETA | Estimated Time of Arrival |
| ROFL | Rolling On The Floor Laughing |

## Demonstrate Knowledge of Idioms

**Idioms** are expressions with meanings that are different from their literal, or dictionary, meanings.

*Example*

She really <u>saved my bacon</u> by having an extra pair of keys in her purse when I locked myself out of the house.

Obviously, the person with the extra keys did not really save the bacon of the person who was locked out, but rather prevented something from becoming a big problem.

Idioms are expressions that cannot be understood literally. They have figurative meanings, or how you should understand the phrase in today's usage. Some idioms have interesting origins that show how the expression came into existence. Here are three examples with their original, literal, and figurative meanings.

| Idiom | Original Meaning | Literal Meaning | Figurative Meaning |
|---|---|---|---|
| Don't throw the baby out with the bath water. | In medieval times when water was heated on open fires, families shared the bath water. The men of the family went first, then the women, then children, and last of all, the baby in the family. The water was thrown away after everyone had bathed. This was a warning to take the baby out of the bath before throwing it away. | Do not throw the baby out when you throw out the water. | When you are getting rid of something, do not also throw away something worth keeping. |
| It's raining cats and dogs. | In early times, houses in England had thatched roofs where cats, mice, and other small animals made their home. When it rained, the wooden base for the thatch became slippery and these small animals would slide off the roof structure into the street. | Cats and dogs are falling from the sky like rain. | It is raining very heavily. |

| Idiom | Original Meaning | Literal Meaning | Figurative Meaning |
|---|---|---|---|
| Chow down. | This expression originates from the belief that the Chinese used to eat dogs (Chows are dogs that originated in China). This practice was considered horrible by westerners who kept dogs as pets. Over time the word "chow" became slang for food, and so the idiom "Chow down" was born. | A Chow dog is down. | Start eating. |

## WHAT ARE HOMOGRAPH WORDS?

Homograph words are also called multiple-meaning words. These words are spelled the same but can have different meanings. The meaning depends on how the words are used. The meanings can be quite different, as in coffee break, break the eggs, break the news, or the expression, "Give me a break!"

*Example*
well (noun) - a hole drilled into the earth
well (adverb) - in good health
I was feeling *well* enough to help my father drill a new *well*.

Sometimes the words are pronounced differently, although the spelling stays the same. You may *read* a book today in class, but return a book you *read* last week to the school library.

The context (words, phrases, and sentences used near a word) often will provide clues to the correct dictionary definition for that use of the word. Consider the following uses of the word *cool*, and then choose the most accurate meaning from the dictionary entry below.

1. We weeded the garden in the early morning while it was cool.
2. The campers lit a bonfire after sundown because it was cool.

3. My friend was cool to me over the phone because I had insulted her in the lunchroom.

**cool** (kōōl), *adj.* –er, –est, *n.*, *v.* –*adj.*1. moderately cold. 2. permitting relief from heat; *a cool dress.* 3. not excited; calm. 4. lacking in cordiality. 5. calmly audacious. 6. unresponsive; indifferent. 7. *Slang.* a. great; excellent. b. socially adept. –*n.*8. a cool part, place, or time: *the cool of the evening.* 9. calmness; composure. –*v. i., v. t.* 10. To become or make cool.

In sentence 1, the context implies that the word refers to the cool part of the day (definition 8). If it were definition 2, the context would probably involve an item of clothing.

In sentence 2, the context refers to definition 1 (moderately cold).

The context in sentence 3 suggests that the friend is still upset, which is closest to definition 4 or 6.

*5L.5c    Demonstrate understanding of figurative language, word relationships, and nuances in word meanings. Use the relationship between particular words to better understand each of the words.*

## DEMONSTRATE KNOWLEDGE OF HOMOGRAPH WORDS

A *homograph* is the name given to a word that has the same spelling as another word, but a different meanings and sometimes a different pronunciation, such as **bat**, **fair**, **bear** and **wind**.

*Example*

The boys took the **bat** to the field.

In this example the boys may have taken a "bat" that you swing to play **baseball** or perhaps they caught the **flying creature** and have decided to release it. In this example, it is difficult to figure out the intended meaning of the word.

*Example*

The **fair** lady went to the market to buy some goods for her home.

In this sentence the word "fair" is talking about the lady, saying that she is fair means that she is a **good looking person** or has **good personal qualities**. The word "fair" could also be referring to the **market as a fair**. However, this is not the case, since the word **market** is used in the sentence.

*Example*

It was difficult for the family to **bear** the loss of their loved one.

In this sentence the word "bear" is talking about the family's ability to **handle the loss of their loved one**. The word "bear" can also refer to the **animal that is found in the wild**. Again, based on the sentence and its context we have to assume the first meaning.

*Example*

After a long day at school my friends and I like to **wind** down and have a glass of milk and cookies.

In this sentence the word "wind" is talking about my friends and how we like to **relax** after school by having a glass of milk and cookies. The word "wind" can also refer to the **air movement cycle** that takes place in atmosphere. However, based on the context of the sentence we have to assume that I am relaxing with my friends and not going flying in the atmosphere.

## WHAT ARE SYNONYM WORDS?

A *synonym* is word that has the same or almost the same meaning as another word. Synonyms are two words that can be interchanged (swapped) in a sentence, leaving the sentence with the same meaning.

*Example*

After the bears went **walking** in the trees, they made their way back to their **home**.

In the sentence above there are two words that are highlighted "walking" and "home". We will be replacing these words with synonyms that will add more meaning and flavor to our sentence. To do this, we have to think of other words that have the **same meaning** as "walking" and "home" but will add better expression to our sentence.

You need to be careful when you are replacing words, making sure not to change the meaning of the sentence!

Instead of the word "walking" what else can we use? We can use **strolling**, **pacing**, **toddling** or **sauntering**. After you have brainstormed for other words that mean the same as "walking", you will need to choose one that you think would fit best into your sentence. For this example, you could choose the word "strolling".

Now we will have to do the same steps again with the word "home". We will need to think of other words that mean "home" **and will add more descriptive expression to our sentence**.

Instead of the word "home" what else can we use? We can use **residence**, **shelter**, **dwelling** or **habitat**. After you have brainstormed for other words that mean the same as home, you need to choose one that you think would **fit best into your sentence**. For this example, you might choose the word "shelter".

Rewriting the original sentence with our changes we get: "After the bears went **strolling** in the trees, they made their way back to their **shelter**."

*Example*

Some examples of synonyms are:

| Original Word | Synonyms |
|---|---|
| home | shelter, residence, dwelling, habitat |
| see | watch, view, observe, witness, notice |
| fall | drop, collapse, plunge, plummet |

## DEMONSTRATE KNOWLEDGE OF SYNONYM WORDS

A *synonym* is word that has the same or almost the same meaning as another word. Synonyms are two words that can be interchanged (swapped) in a sentence, leaving the sentence with the same meaning.

Can you identify the appropriate synonym from the lists?

## DEMONSTRATING YOUR KNOWLEDGE OF SYNONYMS #1

In the sentence below can you identify the appropriate synonym for the highlighted word?

The boys **ran** after the soccer ball hoping to get the first goal of the game.

1. scattered
2. strolled
3. crawled
4. lazily

## DEMONSTRATING YOUR KNOWLEDGE OF SYNONYMS #2

In the sentence below can you identify the appropriate synonym for the highlighted word?

The girls were **mad** when they were told that there was no more ice-cream left!

1. sorry
2. content
3. blissful
4. irritated

## Demonstrating Your Knowledge of Synonyms #3

In the sentence below can you identify the appropriate synonym for the highlighted word?

As the mouse looked at the **piece** of cheese its mouth began to plan its attack.

1. nil
2. morsel
3. naught
4. member

## Solutions

In the examples above the best responses are: scattered, irritated, morsel.

## What are Antonym Words?

An *antonym* is a word that has the opposite meaning of another word. If a word in a sentence is replaced by its antonym, the sentence will have the opposite meaning.

## Using Antonyms in a Sentence

*Example*

In this example please pay attention to the highlighted word:

The boys went to the water park and had the **greatest** day of their lives. (Original sentence)

The boys went to the water park and had the **worst** day of their lives. (Antonym sentence)

---

Please notice that in the first sentence the word **greatest** is highlighted. By replacing this word with its antonym you have to think of a word that has the **opposite meaning**. The antonym word **should fit the flow of the sentence** while changing its meaning.

In the second example the word **greatest** was replaced with **worst** making the boys' day a very bad one.

## TRY USING ANTONYM WORDS

*Try This!*

Now it's your turn. In the sentences below try replacing the highlighted words with appropriate antonyms.

One **sunny morning** a **small** group of friends got on their bikes and decided to go for a picnic at the park. When they got there, they decided to play a game of soccer. They had such a **wonderful** time kicking the ball around. After a few hours they started to get really hungry, so they sat down and started eating their **perfectly organized** lunch.

*Reflection*

Your thinking process should be something along these lines:

"What words can I use that have the opposite meaning for the words: **sunny morning, small, wonderful** and **perfectly organized**?"

| Original words | Antonyms |
| --- | --- |
| sunny morning | depressing, cheerless, uncheerful, dreary |
| small | gigantic, colossal, massive, enormous |
| wonderful | ordinary, horrible, terrible, gross |
| perfectly organized | disorganized, messed up, destroyed, mangled |

Now that you have a set of words to choose from you can start picking which words would fit best into the sentence, giving it the opposite meaning.

One **dreary afternoon** a **massive** group of friends got on their bikes and decided to go for a picnic at the park. When they got there, they decided to play a game of soccer. They had such a **horrible** time kicking the ball around. After a few hours they started to get really hungry, so they sat down and started eating their **mangled** lunch.

As you can see from the example above, the meaning of the first sentence has completely changed when you replaced the four highlighted words.

## DEMONSTRATE KNOWLEDGE OF ANTONYM WORDS

An *antonym* is word that has the opposite meaning of another word. If antonyms are interchanged (swapped) in a sentence, the sentence takes on the opposite meaning.

## Demonstrate your Knowledge of Antonyms #1

*Try This!*

In the sentence below can you choose the best antonym for the highlighted word?

Students in Mr. Smith's science class are always **excited** to see what they are going to learn next.

A. enthralled
B. captivated
C. unenthusiastic
D. disrespectful

## Demonstrate your Knowledge of Antonyms #2

*Try This!*

Over the summer children **adore** playing sports, watching television and eating junk food all day.

In the sentence below can you choose the best antonym for the highlighted word?

A. detest
B. dread
C. enjoy
D. like

## Demonstrate your Knowledge of Antonyms #3

*Try This!*

In the sentence below can you choose the best antonym for the highlighted word?

Some people think that recycling is a **waste** of time and should not be done.

A. valuable use
B. misuse
C. stretching
D. misguided use

*5SL.1a Engage effectively in a range of collaborative discussions (one-on-one, in groups, and teacherled) with diverse partners on grade 5 topics and texts, building on others' ideas and expressing their own clearly. Come to discussions prepared...*

## WORKING IN A GROUP: ADDING YOUR PART TO A DISCUSSION

Working with a group can be both fun and interesting. More people means more ideas and different points of view. On the other hand, more people might mean more confusion and more noise! This is why it is a good idea to have some rules about how your group will behave in a discussion. Helpful rules may include the following:

- Everyone gets a turn to speak.
- Speak in a strong, clear voice.
- Stay on topic.
- Only use respectful words.
- Raise your hand to ask a question.
- Ask questions if you do not understand.
- Pay attention to whoever is speaking.

## MAKING A CLASS PLAN TO GET INFORMATION

One of the great things about working with a group is that everyone has different ideas and knowledge to add. This is true whether you are working in a small group on a project, your whole class has a problem to solve, or the class has a celebration to plan. In all these situations, it is important that you add your ideas, even if you are not sure they will be the best ideas. Sometimes when one person shares an idea, it gives another person a chance to think of something new. As the scientist Linus Paul once said, "The best way to have good ideas, is to have lots of ideas." In other words, one idea can lead to another bigger and better idea.

Let's say that someone in your class has noticed that there is a lot of litter in the school field. You and your classmates want to do something about this problem, so you have a meeting to come up with ideas. There are a few different ways you could do this.

1. Everyone could raise hands to share ideas and the meeting leader or teacher would write them down. The person who shares an idea may explain why she thinks her idea could help solve the problem. The leader might let others ask questions or make comments about each idea. This is not always the best way to share ideas because some people may feel shy or nervous. They may worry "What happens if my friends don't like my idea?" or "Am I going to be embarrassed?"
2. You could brainstorm. In brainstorming, everyone can shout out ideas and someone writes them all down. The ideas can be sensible or silly - just whatever comes to your mind. No one can talk about the ideas until the brainstorming is finished. This is often a good way to come up with creative answers to problems because sometimes an idea that seems silly at first can lead to a good idea no one else has thought of yet. Brainstorming can be fun and no one needs to worry about feeling nervous or embarrassed.
3. You can ask for secret suggestions. Everyone writes down an idea on a card or suggestion slip. The leader collects the ideas and writes them down before the meeting. Then the class reads and discusses them together. No one needs to know who came up with each idea.

Now that everyone has shared their first ideas, you will need more information to come up with a plan that works to reduce the litter. You need an information-gathering plan. Again, you could contribute ideas for collecting information. The teacher or a classmate could be the recorder. Your list might look something like the list below.

## GATHERING INFORMATION FOR LITTER PROJECT

1. Your teacher will ask the principal about the possibility of placing extra recycling bins in the schoolyard.
2. Three students will go online to see if they can find stories of other schools that worked together to clean up their school environment.
3. Three students will plan to gather more information about some of the good ideas that the class discussed earlier.
4. Four students will go in pairs to interview the two school caretakers (at a time they agree to during the school day) to get suggestions from them about cleaning up the litter.
5. All students will ask their parents to donate litter collection bags for the project and get information about parents who can donate their time as volunteers to help supervise the project outside.
6. Two students will phone the community recycling center to find out how the litter needs to be sorted before it is brought to the center.
7. Two students will visit the office to ask the vice-principal about the possibility of putting posters up around the school about not littering.
8. Five students who like working with online graphics can use the computer lab to gather pictures or graphics that they can use in creating posters.

*5SL.1b Engage effectively in a range of collaborative discussions (one-on-one, in groups, and teacher-led) with diverse partners on grade 5 topics and texts, building on others' ideas and expressing their own clearly. Follow agreed-upon rules...*

## USE QUESTIONING FOR COMMUNICATING

We all ask questions many times a day. They are an important part of communicating with others and finding out about the world around us. Consider some of the following examples of types of questions.

*Example*

| Type of Question | Examples |
|---|---|
| To find out a quick fact | "What time is it?" or "Where is Jacob today?" |
| To ask for permission | "May I have another cookie?" |
| To get an opinion | "Which do you like better, the red one or the blue one?" or "What do you think we should do to celebrate?" |
| To clarify meaning | "I'm not sure I understood that. Would you please explain a bit more?" or "Did you mean that you are the best artist in the class or that art is your best subject?" |
| To encourage other people to share their ideas | "What do you like about dragons?" or "Can you think of anything else we could add to this project?" |
| To show people we care about them | "How are you today?" or "Did you have a fun weekend?" |
| To learn new things | "Why do dogs sniff each other's pee?" or "Why do geese always fly in a V?" |
| To solve a problem | "If there are 12 cupcakes in a package, how many packages will I need to buy for a class with 24 students?" or "If it takes 1/2 an hour to get to Jonah's house, what time do I need to leave to get to his party at 3:00?" |

When you work in a group, questions are important tools for getting work done. All the above types of questions can be used in group work. When you ask people questions, it shows that you care about them, their feelings and their thoughts. If you notice that someone in your group is very quiet or is not joining in discussions, questions may help them to participate more. Below, see how the same question types are used in a group discussion. The group is creating a display about how to create a school garden.

Notice how the questions work better than the statements to make everyone in the group feel important.

*Example*

| Type of Question | Useful Examples | Instead of These Statements |
|---|---|---|
| To find out a quick fact | "Amir, do you know who else is in our group?" | "I don't know who else is in my group." |
| To ask for permission | "Jake, may I please borrow a pencil?" | "Someone needs to lend me a pencil!" |
| To get an opinion | "What does everyone think - should we talk about just flower gardens or vegetable gardens too?" | "We should definitely talk about flower gardens and vegetable gardens." |
| To clarify meaning | "Did you mean that I should type one of the text boxes on my computer to test out which fonts and titles we want to use?" | "You've got to be kidding! I'm not going to type up all the words. You make me do all the boring work!" |
| To encourage others to share their ideas | "Mikkel, what do think we should add to the poster?" | "Mikkel, you never say anything or help us come up with ideas." |
| To show people we care about them | "How are you feeling today?" | "You don't have much to say today." |
| To learn new things | "Are there any other schools nearby that have started gardens? Who would like to find out?" | "You should find out if any other schools have started gardens." |
| To solve problems | "If we have to hand this in next Friday, how many days do we have left to work on this?" | "We have only 6 days to work on this, so you had better get busy!" |

## CLARIFYING MEANING IN A GROUP DISCUSSION

When you work in a group, it is very important to make sure you are communicating clearly, and also that you clearly understand other people in your group.

Sometimes when you tell people something, it seems really clear to you, but you look around and realize that perhaps other people did not quite understand you. Perhaps they completely misunderstood you, or perhaps they just look a bit unsure. If you go back and explain your meaning in a different way to make sure everyone understands, this is called clarifying.

Sometimes you need to help clarify what another person says. If you are not sure you understand his meaning or if you see that other people in your group look a bit unsure, clarification may be needed.

One way to do this is to say "I just want to make sure I understand what you just said," and say it again in your own words. Then say "Is this what you meant?" and give them a chance to explain further.

*Example*

Anna: "I think I should be the illustrator for our book because I am the best at that."

Grace: (notices that some kids look offended) "I just want to make sure I understand what you just said. You think you should be the illustrator because you think you are better at drawing than writing?"

Anna: "Yes, that's what I just said!"

In this example, Anna thought she was being very clear, but Grace noticed that some people thought Anna meant that she was better at drawing than the other group members. By stopping and clarifying Anna's meaning, Grace may have stopped an argument from breaking out and prevented feelings from being hurt.

---

Another way to get clarification is to say "I'm not sure if I understood you. Would you please explain that a little bit?"

What you **do not** want to do is say anything that might hurt another person's feelings. It is easy to get frustrated when people do not understand each other, but letting frustration show will probably not help to clarify things.

*Example*

Anna: "I think I should be the illustrator for our book because I am the best at that."

Orion: "You think you are the best artist? Thanks a lot! Maybe I wanted to be the illustrator!"

Anna: "That's not what I meant. I meant that I'm better at drawing than writing. I never know what to say! I guess you think I'm not good at anything!"

You see how, in this example, things got out of hand very quickly because Orion misunderstood Anna's meaning. He did not try to clarify it before he let his frustration show and they both ended up with hurt feelings.

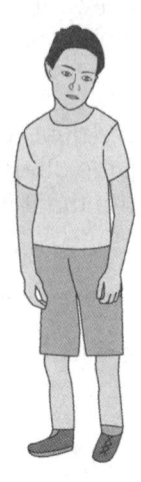

## WORKING WITH OTHERS BY NEGOTIATING

Being part of a group, a family, a team, or a friendship is about helping each other, enjoying time together, encouraging each other, and learning from each other. Sometimes you agree on things and it is easy to work or play together, but sometimes you will disagree or have different wants and needs. Sometimes you can make a deal or an agreement to help get what you want. This is called negotiating.

*Example*

Alycia's teacher gives the class homework to do that evening. Alycia knows that she will not have time to work on it at home because it is her great-grandmother's birthday and Alycia is helping with a party for her that evening. Alycia explains this to the teacher and asks if she may work on the homework during library period. The teacher knows that Alycia uses the library and reads on her own, so he agrees that this is a good solution for this one special situation.

Jonathan is working at the computer, but Samara wants to quickly change a spelling mistake and reprint her story. Jonathan does not want to be interrupted, so he asks Samara to wait until he is finished. Samara does not want to wait because she has to go to choir practice. Samara offers to let Jonathan look at her Guinness Book of World Records while he waits for her. Jonathan agrees that this is a good trade and lets her have five minutes on the computer.

Negotiating may involve the following things:

- listening to different points of view
- finding something you can agree on
- making a deal
- offering help
- trading
- sharing
- taking turns
- compromising or giving up a bit of what you want

## WORKING WITH OTHERS: COMPROMISING

Working with friends can be interesting and fun. The more people there are, the more ideas there are to share. Sometimes, however, people in a group disagree with each other. When this happens, they still need to be able to work together, so they need to find something they can agree on.

If two people each change a little so that they can agree on something, this is called compromising. When they compromise, both people get something they want, but they also each have to give up a little bit. Here are some examples of compromising to resolve disagreements:

*Example*

| Disagreement | Compromise |
|---|---|
| Stefan and Andrea both want to be the group presenter. | Stefan and Andrea decide that each will do a part of the presenting. They each had to give up part of the presenting, but the ending up with something that they both will enjoy doing. |
| Kylie thinks her group should perform a play for their presentation about Mexican folktales, but Andrew does not like plays because he is nervous about acting. | Kylie changes the play so that only half the group members have acting parts. Andrew agrees to be in charge of sets, music, and sound effects and he does not have to be an actor. |
| Allyssa and Jagdeep are partners for a project. Allyssa loves all kinds of creepy-crawlies, so she wants to do a project about spiders. Jagdeep is very scared of spiders and would like the project to be about puppies. | Allyssa suggests that they do a project on an insect that does not scare Jagdeep. They agree to make their project about ladybugs and how useful they are to gardeners. They have each give up their first choice of topic, but they found something else that they both agreed on. |

## WORKING IN A GROUP: THE PRESENTER ROLE

Usually when you work in a group, it is a good idea to decide which job or role each group member will work on. One of the jobs that groups often use is that of presenter. Not every project ends with a presentation, but if there is one, the presenter's job will include:

- Introducing the project to the audience, including the topic or title and why the group chose it
- Introducing the group members to the audience
- Speaking in a clear, strong voice
- Describing the project, or reading it aloud, if it is a story or report
- Answering any questions from the audience

The presenter may also:

- Explain what the group learned from the project
- Describe any difficulties the group had and how they resolved them

## MAKE AND SHARE CONNECTIONS WHEN INTERACTING WITH OTHERS

When we interact and have conversations with others, it allows us to share and compare ideas. We are then able to open our minds to opinions and ideas from other people. Discussing ideas can also allow us to look at something in a different way.

Sharing connections can help bring more understanding into a discussion.

*Example*

If we were discussing the impact that global warming is having on polar bears, and I did a research project on a similar topic a year ago, then I would bring some important ideas into the discussion. Perhaps my partner had watched a documentary on polar bears. This would enable us to have an in-depth discussion on the topic.

We share our connections with others to help us make more sense of things. We learn a lot about ourselves and our world by taking part in discussions with others.

*5SL.1d Engage effectively in a range of collaborative discussions (one-on-one, in groups, and teacherled) with diverse partners on grade 5 topics and texts, building on others' ideas and expressing their own clearly. Review the key ideas...*

## WORKING IN A GROUP: REFLECTING

When you talk with a group, people can share ideas, feelings, facts, questions, and plans. Sometimes it can be hard to remember all the things that were discussed by the time you have your next group meeting. As well, you may find it hard to understand everything that is happening during the meeting. Perhaps things went too quickly, or someone started talking about a new topic while you were stilling thinking about the first one. One thing that can help you to sort out your thoughts and remember important things is called reflecting. When your face is reflected in a mirror, your face looks back at you. This kind of reflecting is like the mirror except that it is your mind that looks or remembers back to what you talked about in the group discussion.

Reflecting is more than just remembering, however. It is more like remembering, sorting, learning, and planning all rolled up together. As you think back to your group discussion, you might ask yourself the following questions to help your reflecting:

- Was there anything you did not understand? If so, what could you do to understand better? (e.g. talk to another person in your group, ask another friend or grown-up, read a book, etc.)
- What surprised you? Why? (e.g. Were you surprised that someone really like your idea? Why did that surprise you? Were you surprised to find out that Olivia is really good at spelling? How could this help your group?)
- What did you think was interesting? Do you want to find out more about that? How could you find out more? (e.g. Maya said that elephants are actually quiet when they walk. So why do people say that noisy kids sound like a herd of elephants?)
- Did you add your thoughts or ideas to the discussion? If not, what stopped you? What could change that for next time?
- Who spoke clearly in the group? Do you think that you spoke clearly when it was your turn?

You might write down the answers to these questions, or you might just keep them in your head. Some people keep a journal or reflection book so that they can remember better.

## STATE A POSITION IN SUPPORT OF A PROPOSAL

Look at some examples of proposals (viewpoints) that you could argue or debate:

- Cell phones should be banned from schools.
- Students at middle schools should wear uniforms.
- We should adopt a four day school week.
- Hot school lunches should be free for students.
- All parents should be required by law to take a parenting course.

In order to write about a proposal, you need to take a position. You do not have to agree with the proposal. You might begin your piece of writing by stating, "Cell phones should not be banned from schools" or "It would be unwise to adopt a four day school week". Once you have written a clear, strong statement of your position on a proposal, you must find evidence to prove that statement to be truthful, or at least the strongest position. Your own real life experiences might be relevant evidence. You can also use proven facts and statistics to support your position.

To clarify and defend your position, use precise and relevant evidence, including:

- facts
- expert opinions
- quotations
- expressions of commonly accepted beliefs
- logical reasoning

Keeping animals in zoos is a very controversial topic. People often feel strongly in support of it or not in support of it. Below is an example of a person who has provided evidence for their strong position against animals being kept in zoos.

*Example*
**My Position**
Wild animals should not be kept in zoos.

**Evidence to Support my Position**

- I've seen animals in the wild and they don't act the same in a zoo. It isn't natural. (personal experience)
- Killer whales often suffer from skin and eye problems due to the chlorine in their tanks, and their dorsal fin can collapse because they aren't diving to their natural depths in the ocean. (fact)
- Some animals in zoos have anywhere between 100 to 1,000 times less space to live in than they would if they lived in their natural habitat in the wild. (statistic)

---

Once you have presented all your evidence, your audience should fully understand your position.

Your evidence might involve acknowledging the opposing position, then providing evidence to refute it. Suppose your opposition says, "I agree with you that it would be better for animals to live in their natural habitat, which is much larger than their space at the zoo. However, if the animals belong to an endangered species, and their habitat is in a country where illegal hunting or poaching is a problem, then they have a better chance of surviving in the protected environment of a zoo." To this, you might answer, "That indeed has been a problem in the past, but according to my recent copy of the *National Geographic*, that is changing in many countries. These countries are taking dramatic steps to reduce poaching and illegal hunting in endangered animal habitats."

## SUPPORT A POSITION WITH RELEVANT EVIDENCE

Once you have provided a clear, strong statement of your position on a topic you must find evidence to prove that statement to be truthful. Your own real life experiences might be relevant evidence. You can also use proven facts and statistics to support your position.

Keeping animals in zoos is a very controversial topic and people often feel strongly in support of them or not in support of them. Below is an example of a person who has provided evidence as to their strong position against animals being kept in zoos.

*Example*

**My Position**
Wild animals should not be kept in zoos.

**Evidence to support my position**

1. Some animals that have been taken away from their pack or pride will not reproduce. (Fact)
2. I've seen animals in the wild and they don't act the same in a zoo. It isn't natural. (Personal experience)
3. Killer whales often suffer from skin and eye problems due to the chlorine in their tanks and their dorsal fin can collapse because they aren't diving to their natural depths in the ocean. (Fact)
4. Some animals in zoos have anywhere between 100 to 1,000 times less space to live in than they would if they lived in their natural habitat in the wild. (Statistic)

Once you have presented all your evidence, your audience should fully understand your position.

Your evidence might involve acknowledging the opposing position.

*5SL.5  Include multimedia components and visual displays in presentations when appropriate to enhance the development of main ideas or themes.*

## USE VISUALS TO ENGAGE AN AUDIENCE

People like to see things. Looking at objects helps us to understand what we are learning about and also helps keep us interested. We remember more information if we can look at an object or a picture while we hear someone speak about a subject.

When you are giving a presentation to an audience (a group of people) you can help them pay attention by using visuals. Visuals are any objects that stand for what you are talking about. Photographs, maps, charts, books, models, and drawings are all examples of visuals.

Let's imagine you are giving a presentation on eagles. There are a number of visuals you could use that would help keep your audience interested in what you are saying.

- An eagle's egg
- An eagle's nest
- A photograph of an eagle
- A map of North America showing where eagles live

Almost any presentation you do will have visuals that you could use. Use your imagination to come up with ideas. Try asking your parents, your teacher, and your friends for suggestions. Or imagine you are someone in the audience. Ask yourself what you would like to see!

## USE VISUALS TO SUSTAIN AN AUDIENCE THROUGHOUT A PRESENTATION

People like to see things. Looking at objects helps us to understand what we are learning about and also helps keep us interested. We remember more information if we can look at an object while we hear someone speak about it.

When you are giving a presentation to an audience (a group of people) you can help them pay attention by using visuals. Visuals are any objects that stand for what you are talking about. Photographs, maps, charts, books, models, and drawings are all examples of visuals.

Let's imagine you are giving a presentation on robins. There are a number of visuals you could use that would help keep your audience interested in what you are saying.

- A robin's egg
- A robin's nest
- A photograph of a robin
- A map of the USA so that you could show where robins live throughout the year

You can also plan ahead for when you are going to use your visuals in your presentation. Rather than showing the audience all of your visuals at once, you may want to bring the objects out one at a time.

Let's think about the robin presentation. Perhaps you start the presentation with the photograph of the robin to be sure everyone knows what one looks like. Further on in your presentation, when you talk about the robin's habitat, you could bring out your map that shows where robins live. Finally, when you are talking about the robin's nesting habits, you could bring out the nest and the egg.

Spacing out when you show your visuals will help keep audience members interested for your whole presentation. They will be curious to know what you are going to show them next.

## Use Visuals to Engage an Audience at the End of a Presentation

People like to see things. Looking at objects helps us to understand what we are learning about and also helps keep us interested. We remember more information if we can look at an object while we hear someone speak about it.

Often by the end of a presentation, audience members are getting tired and their attention wanders. What could you do to keep them focused on what you are saying? One of the best ways is to give them something to look at.

Imagine you are doing a presentation on volcanoes. It would be impossible to bring an actual volcano into the classroom, but there are several things you could do instead. At the end of your presentation you could do the following:

- Show a short Internet-based video clip of an active volcano.
- Bring out a model of a volcano that you built (maybe even one that erupts when you combine baking powder and vinegar).
- Present a short slide show with photos of volcanoes from around the world.

Giving your audience members something to see at the end of your presentation will help to keep their interest and also help them to remember what you told them.

## Use Audio to Engage an Audience

What is audio? Audio is anything to do with sound. Just by speaking to an audience you are using audio, your voice! To make things more interesting for your audience and to keep their attention, you might consider adding other forms of audio. Here are some examples of how you could add audio to a presentation to keep your audience's interest:

## Sound

Does your topic have a sound that represents it? If your presentation is on an animal, you could play a clip of the sound that animal makes: the call of a loon, the trumpet of an elephant, the clicking of dolphins.

## Language

Perhaps you are presenting on a particular country or group of people. Do they speak a language other than English? Play a clip of someone speaking that language.

## Music

Music can be an excellent way to set the mood for a presentation.

If there is a piece of music that you feel represents your topic, you could play it for your audience. If your presentation is on a particular country or group of people, you could play music from that country or culture. If your presentation is on a composer or instrument, you could play music written by the composer or a piece featuring that instrument.

*5SL.6 Adapt speech to a variety of contexts and tasks, using formal English when appropriate to task and situation.*

## Demonstrate Voice Through Word Choice

What is a writer's voice? A writer's voice means how the writing sounds, or its effect on the writer's audience. The writer's voice includes careful word choices that express what the writer means, as well as the writer's attitude toward their topic. You might choose a serious voice to write a report, or a joking voice to write a story about your trials with a younger brother who steals your stuff without asking. Even punctuation plays a part. You will discover that you will use a changing writer's voice in different writing assignments. Try to make your voice fit the kind of assignment. Also make sure that it is right for your audience. Are you writing for classmates? Parents? A celebrity hero? The principal?

## Whom Are You Writing For?

The word *diction* refers to word choice. You do not want to use big words just to impress your audience, if they will not be able to understand your ideas. Instead, try to choose accurate and precise words. Only turn to special terms when more commonly used words are not available. Diction is closely related to voice. The words you choose give readers an impression. If your writing contains many unusual or long words, some readers may feel annoyed and stop paying attention to what you have to say. Don't distract them with big words. Instead, impress them with clear ones that make sense to them.

## Formal or Informal

Formal word choice is the way you would speak to an adult, especially a professional person like your teacher or family doctor. Informal word choice is the way you would talk to a friend or family member.

*Example*

A young girl peers into the microwave and sees that the pizza is overdone, burned, in fact. The examples below show how she might express her thoughts to a teacher, or, on the other hand, to a friend.

1. To her teacher: "Oh, Miss Allers! I am so sorry that I burned your pizza! I think I must have pushed the wrong numbers on this microwave. It looks like I hit 20 min instead of 2 min. I will get you a piece of mine right now!"
2. To her friend: "Alecia! Get over here! You burnt my pizza, you dummy! I'm takin' one of yours right now, dude!"

---

You should suit the level of formality in your writing to your audience. Your readers could be adults, peers, or children. If you have to use some technical language in a report, make sure you explain what it means. Do not expect your audience to be experts in your topic.

# Understand Language Appropriate for Variety of Contexts

When you are creating a project, whether it a written piece or an oral presentation, it is important to use the appropriate language for your intended audience. It is also important to understand the language that is appropriate for different situations, so that you feel comfortable and able to respond in a manner that fits the occasion.

*Example*
Here are a few situations when you would need to understand the kind of language that is appropriate:

- When you are riding a public bus with your friends, you are expected to watch your language and not use words that might be offensive to your fellow passengers, especially the adults.
- When you are picking up a few things for your mother at the grocery store, you would be expected to understand and use appropriate, courteous language.
- When you are presenting a research report to the class, you are expected to use correct English and fairly formal language.
- When you are babysitting your three year old brother, you are expected not to use "baby talk", but to use simple vocabulary that he will understand.

---

When writing a report for your peers, you will want to use words that are appropriate for your age or grade level. The following example would **not** be realistic wording for a Grade 5 class report on cougars:

*Example*
The puma concolor terrestrial mammal is a division of the Felidae family. Their primary provision sources are ungulates.

---

Instead, the following example is much more appropriate language to use for a Grade 5 class report on cougars:

*Example*
The cougar is a part of the feline, or cat family. The main foods cougars eat to survive are animals like deer, elk, and moose.

---

As you can see in the second example, the wording is much more child-friendly.

The same type of attention should be paid to the wording in an oral presentation. If you are presenting to your peers, you may want to include humor or relevant pop culture items that would be interesting and informative to your peers, but that still support your presentation.

If you are presenting to your teacher, you may want to be more professional and stick to the assigned guidelines. You can always talk to your teacher about what language would be appropriate to use within your presentation.

*5W.1b  Write opinion pieces on topics or texts, supporting a point of view with reasons and information. Provide logically ordered reasons that are supported by facts and details.*

*5W.1d  Write opinion pieces on topics or texts, supporting a point of view with reasons and information. Provide a concluding statement or section related to the opinion presented.*

## CREATE A WRITTEN PIECE TO CONVINCE

There are at least three different ways to create a convincing or a persuading argument. We say that you need to appeal to an individual in order to convince them of an argument or a point of view. Three kinds of appeals are as follows:

1. Appeal to character
2. Appeal to reason
3. Appeal to emotion

**Appeal to Character**: The arguments involve people of high distinction in a particular field who provide their support.

*Example*

Doctors are always telling people to eat healthy and to stop smoking.

This statement is using appeal to character, because doctors are professionals that people trust when it comes to their health. Therefore, a person reading this sentence will be more willing to listen and incorporate the information into their life.

**Appeal to Reason**: This type of persuasion uses many different examples of factual information to help make a convincing argument.

*Example*

Going back to the example above about smoking, if you are trying to use appeal to reason, you would need to present factual arguments that are supporting your argument.

5.4 million people each year lose their lives due to smoking. According to the World Heath Organization, every 6.5 seconds, another smoker loses the battle with cigarettes. Smokers on average die 15 years sooner than non-smokers as recorded by the World Health Organization.

---

**Appeal to Emotion**: Using this type of persuasion, you will need to present arguments that evoke the readers' emotions. You want the readers to feel for your cause, making them want to support your point of view.

*Example*

Once again, using the example of smoking, you must think of the different ways to state your arguments so that people's emotions are supporting your cause.

Every year there are millions of children who will lose their parents to cigarette smoking. Smoking not only affects the smoker but the loved ones that are around them. Children are often addicted to smoking by the age of five, simply by inhaling second-hand smoke from their parents. People may get lung cancer from third-hand smoke; often this is from furniture where smokers may have sat, such as a movie theater chair.

---

The final thing that you will need to remember is that even though there are three different types of convincing arguments, the best argument that you can make will need to use all three. In other words, you will need to write a persuasive piece that uses appeal to character, reason, and emotion to create the best argument.

*5W.1a  Write opinion pieces on topics or texts, supporting a point of view with reasons and information. Introduce a topic or text clearly, state an opinion, and create an organizational structure in which ideas are logically grouped to support the...*

## CREATE AN INTRODUCTORY PARAGRAPH

The purpose of the introductory paragraph is to tell your audience what they will be reading and learning about in the text.

The introductory paragraph should state the main idea of the writing piece and what main topics it will cover.

Your first sentence should introduce the main idea of the writing piece. The next sentences should state the main details that support the main idea, and about which the reader can expect to learn. The number of sentences usually varies depending on the length of the writing piece. The last sentence of the introductory paragraph will wrap up or summarize again the main idea or topic.

*Example*
Below is an example of an opening paragraph for a writing piece about how dogs are wonderful additions to our planet.

Dogs are wonderful animals and a great addition to our world. Dogs are known as very intelligent animals that can perform many different acts. Most dogs are great pets for humans. Dogs can also be helpful to people with disabilities or who have severe injuries. Dogs are amazing, helpful animals.

---

The above paragraph is an example of a beginning paragraph that supports the central idea of what the writing piece is about. It states the main idea - that dogs are extremely beneficial animals to have in our world. Then the paragraph gives some of the specific topics that you might learn about when reading the written passage about dogs. You will learn different acts that dogs can perform. You will learn about the different reasons why dogs make great pets. Then you will learn more about the ways that dogs help people with disabilities or injuries.

## USE SIMILARITIES AND DIFFERENCES TO CONVEY INFORMATION

Using similarities and differences to convey information is sometimes known as comparing and contrasting.

To compare two or more things means to look for the **similarities** between them. To contrast two or more things means to look for the **differences** between them. For example, the following paragraph compares and contrasts millipedes and centipedes.

Millipedes and centipedes look similar but have different ecologies. Both look like worms with lots of legs. Millipedes are round in cross-section and have two pairs of legs on each body segment. Centipedes are flattened, and only have one pair of legs per segment. Millipedes are slow moving, often burrow, and eat dead leaves, detritus, and fungi. If threatened, they often curl up, and some exude bad-tasting chemicals. Centipedes are quick-moving predators, eating any small animals they can catch. They have a venomous bite, but no Michigan species are dangerous to people. Both centipedes and millipedes need a damp environment to survive and mostly stay on or under the ground.

To help you understand the differences and similarities between millipedes and centipedes, you can put all of the facts given in the paragraph into a Venn diagram. Draw two circles that overlap in the middle. Write the things that are true only about millipedes in one circle, and the things that are true only about centipedes in the other. In the area where the circles overlap, write the similarities that the two share.

Here is how it might look:

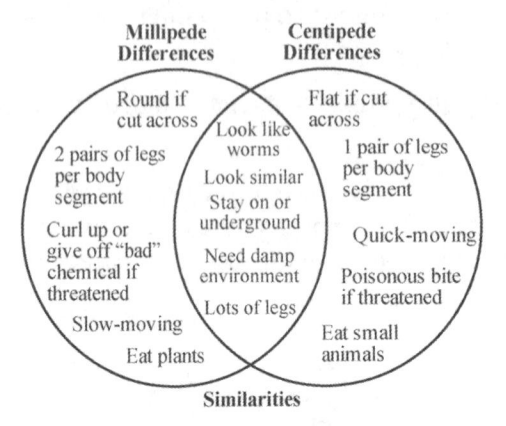

**Millipede Differences**
- Round if cut across
- 2 pairs of legs per body segment
- Curl up or give off "bad" chemical if threatened
- Slow-moving
- Eat plants

**Similarities**
- Look like worms
- Look similar
- Stay on or underground
- Need damp environment
- Lots of legs

**Centipede Differences**
- Flat if cut across
- 1 pair of legs per body segment
- Quick-moving
- Poisonous bite if threatened
- Eat small animals

*Try This!*
What can you learn about the similarities and differences between plasma and LCD televisions, by looking at the Venn Diagram below?

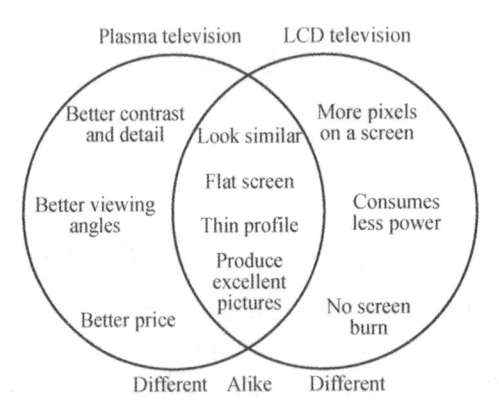

**Plasma television (Different)**
- Better contrast and detail
- Better viewing angles
- Better price

**Alike**
- Look similar
- Flat screen
- Thin profile
- Produce excellent pictures

**LCD television (Different)**
- More pixels on a screen
- Consumes less power
- No screen burn

---

When you are conveying information by looking at similarities and differences, the information will be more clear and easy to understand if you put it on a comparison chart or a Venn Diagram like the above.

## CREATE SUPPORT PARAGRAPHS WITH FACTS, DETAILS, AND EXPLANATIONS

Once you have decided on your topic, you need to collect ideas and information about your topic. This is called shaping your ideas.

Here are some examples of what to have in your support paragraphs:

**Facts and Statistics**: Facts are objective pieces of information; statistics are collections of facts that are organized into numerical data. When using facts or statistics in your writing, remember to give the source from which you took them.

**Contrast and Compare**: The purpose of contrasting and comparing objects or ideas is not necessarily to show the superiority of one over the other; it may be to show their relationship to each other. By comparing a familiar object with one that is unfamiliar, a writer can introduce a reader to an unknown object within a known context or background.

**Cause and Effect**: The cause and effect writing strategy shows the relationship between events and their result. The paragraph does not need to begin with the first cause and work its way chronologically to the final effect. However, that is probably the easiest way for you to organize the paragraph.

## USE CONNECTING WORDS TO LINK IDEAS IN SENTENCES

Connecting words help link ideas in sentences. Ideas are often linked by the words such as *and*, *or*, *but*, and *so*. Below are some examples of how you can take two short sentences and link them together, using a connecting word to make a longer sentence.

*Example*
1. I am going to dinner. Then we plan to see a movie.
   I am going to dinner **and** then we plan to see a movie.
2. You can send me a letter. You can write me an e-mail.
   You can send me a letter in the mail **or** just write me an e-mail.
3. I would love to join you for dinner. I have a guitar lesson.
   I would love to join you for dinner **but** I have a guitar lesson.
4. I returned the dress. It didn't fit.
   The dress didn't fit **so** I returned it.

## IT'S YOUR TURN

There are many other words you can use to link your ideas together. Try linking the sentences below together with one or more of the following words: **however**, **but**, **although**

1. She broke her foot. She ran the race with crutches.
2. She never ate healthy. She lived to be 99 years old.
3. Hunter had a high fever. He still went to school.

The following are some possible solutions:

1. **Although** she broke her foot, she ran the race with crutches.
   She broke her foot; **however**, she ran the race with crutches.
   She broke her foot, **but** she ran the race with crutches.
2. **Although** she never ate healthy, she lived to be 99 years old.
   She never ate healthy; **however**, she lived to be 99 years old.
   She never ate healthy, **but** she lived to be 99 years old.
3. Hunter had a high fever; **however**, he still went to school.
   Hunter had a high fever, **but** he still went to school.
   **Although** Hunter had a high fever, he still went to school.

## OTHER WORDS THAT LINK IDEAS

The following sentences illustrate some other words you could use to link ideas:

- She stayed out past her curfew; <u>therefore</u> she got grounded.
- He had to hurry <u>if</u> we were going to make the movie on time.
- Spread the sunblock on thick <u>because</u> you don't want to burn.
- I like to run <u>before</u> I eat breakfast.
- It was definitely at the park <u>that</u> I lost my purse.
- We swim <u>whenever</u> the weather is hot.

## DEVELOP SENTENCE FLUENCY

**Sentence fluency** is the flow of language. Some sentences are long and some are short and snappy. Sentence fluency creates rhythm in your writing. Developing sentence fluency shows growth in your writing. It is achieved through:

- varying your sentence structure
- beginning sentences differently
- using joining words (e.g., *and*, *or*, *but*) to combine simple sentences

Always reread a sentence to make sure that the words flow together easily.

It is important to use a variety of sentences in your writing. It is more interesting to read writing that contains simple sentences, compound sentences, and complex sentences. Take a look at the next piece of writing. It is formed only using simple sentences.

*Example*
**My Summer Vacation**

My summer vacation was fun. I went to summer camp. I made many friends there. Then my family went to the state of Hawaii. Hawaii is beautiful. I learned how to snorkel. Snorkeling is awesome. I also relaxed a lot this summer. I saw some movies. I also rode my bike. I had so much fun. I think summer vacation should last all year.

---

The passage tells you all of the information the writer wanted to tell, but too many simple sentences in a row make the information sound less interesting. People do not usually speak using one kind of sentence, so it sounds strange to read something that is written in that way. Now, take a look at the same information in a passage that uses a variety of sentence structures.

*Example*
**My Summer Vacation**

My summer vacation was fun. I went to summer camp, where I made many friends. Then my family went to the beautiful state of Hawaii. In Hawaii, I learned how to snorkel and found out how awesome snorkeling is. I also relaxed a lot this summer. I saw some movies and rode my bike. I had so much fun that I think summer vacation should last all year.

---

The second example is much smoother and easier to read. You can better hear the writer's voice in the second example. The second example has a good mix of simple, compound, and complex sentences. When you are writing, try using different types of sentences to keep your reader interested.

## Ways to Vary Sentences

Sentence variety can refer to any of the following:

- Sentence length. A series of short sentences can be used for strong effect after a series of longer sentences.
- Sentence type. Simple, compound, and compound-complex sentences can be used for variety or to control the development of ideas. Joining or transitional words (like *and*, *but*, *so*, *therefore*, *when*) can be useful for this purpose.
- Sentence order. The most important part of a sentence can be emphasized by putting it first.
  NASA might note that "A meteorite hit a man in Whitehorse," while the Whitehorse Star might report, "Local Man Hit by Meteorite."
- Word order is closely related to sentence order. For example, at first glance, "accused mass murderer Goneril Brocadie" appears to have the same meaning as "Goneril Brocadie, who is accused of mass murder". However, the first phrase suggests that Brocadie is actually guilty, not merely accused. The adjectives closest to the noun clearly imply or suggest the message: *mass-murderer-Brocadie.*

*5W.2e Write informative/explanatory texts to examine a topic and convey ideas and information clearly. Provide a concluding statement or section related to the information or explanation presented.*

## Create a Concluding Paragraph That Summarizes Main Points

The concluding paragraph summarizes the points brought forward in the introduction, although you should *never restate* the introduction. The conclusion is your last chance to say something important to your reader; perhaps you want to motivate them to take action, to understand a topic differently, or to consider future inquiry or investigation of the topic.

In your concluding paragraph, you should always

- begin with a transition and let your reader know that you are summarizing the main points of your essay
- recall your major points
- explain the significance of your findings
- end with a strong sense of closure

Be sure to stay focused on your controlling or main idea right through to the concluding sentence of your essay.

*Example*
To sum it up, then, plastic packaging has allowed us to see what we are buying, which seemed like a benefit, at first. Now, however, the problems outweigh the benefits. Not only does plastic create a major trash overload for the world, but it is manufactured from two resources that are needed for other products: oil and petroleum. Plastic packaging is a luxury that the world must give up, or face the consequences.

Never introduce new ideas or material in your conclusion.

**5W.5** *With guidance and support from peers and adults, develop and strengthen writing as needed by planning, revising, editing, rewriting, or trying a new approach.*

## REVISING YOUR NON-FICTION WRITING PIECE TO PROVIDE FOCUS

The purpose of non-fiction writing is to communicate and provide accurate and concrete information to an audience searching for information on a wide variety of different topics. The topics can range from different people, to different places, to different ideas, concepts, theories, events and even things. As long as the information is completely true, it is considered non-fiction.

It is important when you are writing a non-fiction piece, that you stay close to the topic you are writing about and the point or idea that you want to get across.

If you choose to write about sharks and where they live, you would not want to go off topic by talking about what they eat.

The best way to revise your writing is to read through each paragraph of your piece and make sure each paragraph is about the subtopic you are writing about. That subtopic should contribute to the entire piece. If you get to a paragraph or part of a paragraph that does not add to the topic, then it may be best to edit it out.

It is important to make sure each sentence and each paragraph stays focused on your topic. When you have pieces that do not add to the main focus, those pieces become distractions, instead of helping add to the topic.

Let's look at a paragraph together that is about turtles and the color of their shells. Is there any line in the paragraph below that does not fit in with this paragraph about the color of a turtle's shell?

*Example*

Turtles are amazing reptiles that have extraordinary shells. The shells can range in all types of colors, depending on the type of turtle it is. A turtle's shell is usually either a black, brown or olive green color. Some species of turtles may even have red, orange, yellow and gray colored spots and blotches on their shells. The tortoise, the turtle that lives on land has a very heavy shell. The eastern painted turtle is one of the most colorful turtles in the world, with its yellow and black or olive green shell and red markings around the outside of the shell.

The line, "**The tortoise, the turtle that lives on land has a very heavy shell.**" does not belong in the above paragraph. Yes, even though it is talking about the turtle's shell, it is not talking about the **colors** of a turtle's shell, which is what the rest of the paragraph is talking about.

---

## It's Your Turn

Can you find any of the sentences that do not belong in the following paragraph about honeybees and their appearances?

Honeybees are beautiful insects, with yellow and black stripes. Bees have three body parts. The thorax, which is the middle section of the bee, a head and an abdomen, which is the end section of a bee. The thorax has the bee's six legs and two wings attached to it. The honeybee has a stinger, or poison gland that sticks out of the abdomen. But don't worry, a bee will only sting you if you are mean to it. Honeybees are hairy.

There is **one** sentence that does not belong in the above paragraph.

## How Did You Do?

Were you able to identify which line does not belong in the paragraph? Check your answer below.

Honeybees are beautiful insects, with yellow and black stripes. Bees have three body parts. The thorax, which is the middle section of the bee, a head and an abdomen, which is the end section of a bee. The thorax has the bee's six legs and two wings attached to it. The honeybee has a stinger, or poison gland that sticks out of the abdomen. **But don't worry, a bee will only sting you if you are mean to it.** Honeybees are hairy.

The highlighted sentence does not belong in this paragraph because it is only telling an outside idea about the bee's stinger, and it is not about the bee's appearance. It does not belong in this paragraph.

*5W.2d Write informative/explanatory texts to examine a topic and convey ideas and information clearly. Use precise language and domain-specific vocabulary to inform about or explain the topic.*

*5W.2b Write informative/explanatory texts to examine a topic and convey ideas and information clearly. Develop the topic with facts, definitions, concrete details, quotations, or other information and examples related to the topic.*

## CREATE A WRITTEN PIECE TO INFORM

The main purposes an author has for writing are as follows:

- To inform
- To explain
- To entertain
- To impress
- To convince

As you review the different forms of writing, think about what a writer's purpose might be for using each of the forms. Always remember that the purpose comes first, and that the writer chooses the form that best suits that purpose.

The purpose of writing to inform is to give the reader specific information. School texts give information about specific subjects; newspapers inform the public about news events, and "how to" articles inform interested people how to make, draw, play, or do something. Dictionaries, encyclopedias, reference books, and Internet sites are all sources of information.

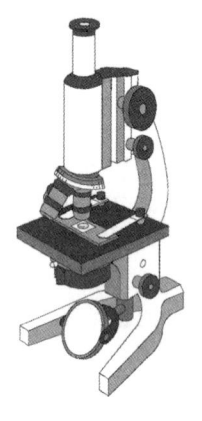

*Example*

The purpose of this paragraph is to inform you about how a microscope works.

A microscope is made up of a series of lenses (the eyepiece lens, the low power and the high power objective lenses) that magnify objects. Light is reflected by a mirror up through the hole on the stage and onto the object to be magnified, which lies directly over the hole. The objective lenses now magnify the object and send the image up to the eyepiece lens, which further magnifies the image before sending it to the eye.

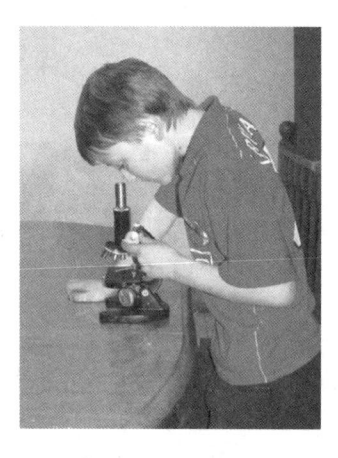

As you can see from this example, *inform* can be very close to *explain* when it comes to purpose. The back of a medicine bottle is a better example of text that informs, because it provides information about the product and how to use it safely.

## CREATE A WRITTEN PIECE TO EXPLAIN

The main purposes an author has for writing are as follows:

- To inform
- To explain
- To entertain
- To impress
- To convince

As you review the different forms of writing, think about what a writer's purpose might be for using each of the forms. Always remember that the purpose comes first, and that the writer chooses the form that best suits that purpose.

When the writer's purpose is to explain, he or she wants to give the reader the **why** or **how** of a situation. This is also known as explanatory writing because readers are given an explanation, not just told the facts of an event.

*Example*

Because he was afraid of the monster behind him, the dog ran as fast as he could through the neighbor's house. Unfortunately, he tracked mud all over the rug as he went.

When you are writing to explain, remember to use words like *how*, *why*, and *because*. Here are some topic ideas that would require you to explain something:

- How to make a creative pizza?
- Why you were late to your music lesson?
- How to take care of a pet?
- Why you want to take babysitter training?

## INCLUDING DETAILS

Details have the power to bring writing to life for the reader and to make a story compelling and believable. Details should be included in all elements of a story—characters, setting, and plot—but the trick is to decide how many details to include at any given place in your writing.

Details should always have a purpose. Too many details can take away from the text and frustrate the reader. Think about a story you like. How does the writer introduce the main character? Which physical details are described? Describing hair color, eye color, complexion, clothing, and accessories is too much. Only the details that grab the reader's interest and are important for the role that the character plays in the story should be described.

In the following passage, the main character is introduced without a physical description. The author does not refer to his age or looks. He is described purely through his nervousness about his first musical performance and how important it is to him. Luke's fear and nervousness about performing are far more important to the plot than what he looks like, so the writer focuses the details on these things.

*Example*

Luke knew that he couldn't be more nervous. It felt like a hyper group of mice were running around in his stomach, alternately tickling him with their whiskers and tails and poking him with their sharp little nails. Soon he would go on stage to perform his first guitar solo, and he was quite convinced that his precious guitar would slip from his hands, which were coated in a greasy, cold sweat. When he tried to visualize himself walking out onto the stage, he shivered as if the outside winter cold had surrounded him, even while he could feel the perspiration forming under his arms and in between his shoulder blades like he was somewhere overly warm. Just now, he had a moment of such light-headed dizziness that it reminded him of the time right before he was put to sleep when he'd had his tonsils out.

In the following excerpt, Billy is entering a shabby sitting room. It is easy to picture Billy wishing that the room could be more inviting.

*Example*

Billy entered the room. Sunlight ran in through the windows like it was finally home, casting a light that warmed and renewed the shabby old sitting room. The musty smell, dust, and cobwebs had been driven back just like time, pushed back like the schoolyard bully who is all bluster and no blow. It was too short, the sweet moment of past glory, because a cloud oozed in front of the sun and the dingy reality came pushing back like the bully with renewed vigor.

## USE CONTENT-SPECIFIC VOCABULARY IN YOUR WRITING

*Diction* is word choice. It is important that your ideas are expressed simply and accurately so that your reader can easily understand them. When you are speaking, your tone can be more readily attained from your body language, facial expressions, and intonation. However, when you are writing, your choice of words (your diction) indicates your tone or attitude.

Sometimes, identifying appropriate language is as simple as being sensitive to situations. For example, when you leave your locker and walk through the doorway of your English classroom, you will probably temporarily abandon the casual and slangy exchanges you were enjoying with your friends before class. You will instead adopt a more formal manner of expression for the duration of the class, particularly if the teacher calls upon you for a commentary on the Shakespeare play the class is studying, or you are asked to express your views on a topic by writing an essay.

Appropriate language refers to language that suits the expressive format being used or the situation. It ranges from formal to informal, from vernacular to precise, and covers many specialized categories, such as jargon and subject-specific terminology.

Some words in the English language are specific and some are general. Specific words give you more detail, while general words are more vague.

Let's look at the following sentence to show the different levels of specificity among the words in the sentence.

An animal bit the young boy's leg.

The word *animal* is a broad term. Let's change the sentence to tell what kind of animal.

A dog bit the young boy's leg.

The word *dog* is more specific but still leaves us wondering what kind of dog. Let's change it again to be more specific.

A German Shepherd bit the young boy's leg.

The word *animal* wasn't giving us much information but *German Shepherd* gives us a clear picture of what bit the young boy's leg.

There are many different levels of specificity among words. *Animal* is a general term but can be made more specific by changing it to *dog* and even more specific by changing it to *German Shepherd*.

Revision literally means "to look over again". Revision allows you as a writer to craft and shape your final product. You can make revisions to improve the content, clarity, and interest of your written work by using several types of strategies. These strategies might involve using a contrasting color of pen to underline or cross out text that you want to revise or using arrows or sticky notes to identify text that needs to be moved or inserted.

For example, if a classmate noted a lack of inclusive language (language that includes both genders) in your writing, you could go through your text changing all references to "policeman" to "police officer."

Try to use more exact and specific words. *Sun-drenched* is more exact than *sunny*. The overused verb *said* can be changed to more specific verbs like *announced, argued, wailed, screeched*, which are stronger verbs because they are more specific.

Add words that make your descriptions more vivid or clear. For instance *birch* or *maple* can be added to *trees* so that the reader can picture a certain type of tree. A color like *yellow* or *blue* can be added to *paper* to create a clearer picture for the reader. The adjective *chocolate* makes the word *milkshake* more specific.

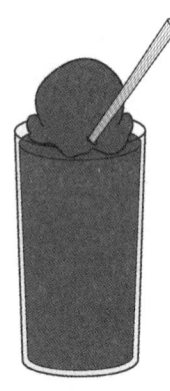

*Slang* words are expressions used by a certain group of people, such as teenagers. Slang differs from *jargon* in the sense that slang is regarded as very casual or playful language, whereas jargon is usually used by professionals to discuss something specific. Slang expressions tend to come and go.
For example, in the 1950's, a "hot rod" referred to a powerful car, while today the term is used very rarely and may not be used to refer to a car.

Jargon refers to a specialized set of words and phrases commonly understood by a group, such as members of a profession, hobby, or field of study. For example, imagine going to the dentist. If, after examining your teeth and X-rays, the dentist tells you that you have a "cary on your 1-3," you would not know what she is talking about. She is using jargon that is specific to dentists, and she would have to explain to you that she has found a cavity in one of your teeth.

Jargon is common among different professions and can be confusing or meaningless to someone who does not belong to the special group for whom the jargon has meaning.

Most students today are, for the most part, computer literate. The Internet is still a new technology, and Internet jargon continues to grow and change. A good example is the blog. Words that have to do with blogs, such as *blogosphere*, *flaming*, and *vlogs* (video blogs), are all Internet-specific jargon words that not everyone will understand unless they use a computer in their daily lives.

In all forms of online writing you will find frequent use of shorthand. *Leetspeak* is often used to indicate emotions or actions that would take a long time to type out conventionally.

For example, rather than saying "I'm laughing out loud" or trying to indicate laughter by typing "ha ha ha," many people online just type "lol." This makes online conversation faster and more similar to real-time conversation. Leetspeak has quickly become incorporated into online communication. It is also easily adapted to text messaging on cellphones.

It is strongly discouraged, however, in any formal writing for school or work.

*Subject-specific terminology* refers to the terms that are central to an area or unit of study. These terms are generally introduced at the beginning of a new unit or chapter. For instance, before beginning a poetry unit, an English teacher will first review common poetry terms, such as *sonnet*, *lyric*, *metaphor*, *onomatopoeia*, and so on, because these terms are often used with respect to poetry.

Subject-specific words that are important are often

- bolded in math, social studies, and science textbooks
- defined at the beginning of a new chapter
- defined at the bottom of the page or at the back of the textbook
- used by the teacher on the board, overhead, or for assignments

When new words appear in content areas, you will better understand and remember information, ideas, and concepts by adopting the new words into your vocabulary. Ensure that you know the spelling and meanings of the word, and try to use the word, when appropriate, in conversation and writing.

- Before plunging into a new text, learn any terms that will help you to better understand the information. If the term is not defined in the text, use the glossary.
- List the terms beside their meanings in your notes for quick reference.
- Since most subject-specific terminology is not language that you use every day, learn it as you need it.
- Refresh your memory occasionally, and the words you need will be relatively easy to review later when you need them.

Most of the time, identifying appropriate language becomes almost an automatic skill. Identifying and using appropriate language tends to be a matter of courtesy, necessity, expediency, or straightforward common sense. It is wise to adapt as the situation requires.

## CHOOSE PRECISE WORDS FOR WRITING TASKS

Precise means exact. Choosing precise words means that you are trying to choose the words that most exactly fit the:

- situation
- person who will be reading your assignment
- form you are using (letter, journal, story, note, etc.)
- idea or event you are trying to describe
- personality of the character who is speaking

The word **diction** refers specifically to word choice. You do not want to use words that will make understanding your ideas harder than is necessary. Instead, you should aim for accuracy and precision in your word choice. Only turn to special terms when more common words are not available to describe what you need to describe. Since diction is closely related to voice, the words you choose also give readers an impression of where you are placing yourself in relation to them. If your writing contains many unusual or long words, some readers may feel put off by your diction, and your time spent writing will be wasted. It is best to select common words so the reader's attention is not distracted from the ideas you are discussing.

Most of the time, identifying appropriate language becomes almost an automatic skill. Identifying and using appropriate language tends to be a matter of courtesy, necessity, or straightforward common sense. It is wise to adapt as the situation requires.

Sometimes, identifying appropriate language is as simple as being sensitive to situations. For example, when you leave your locker and walk through the doorway of your classroom, you will probably temporarily quit using the casual and slangy language you were enjoying with your friends before class. You will instead use more formal language, especially when the teacher is nearby! If you are asked to write something, you will try to use words that you are sure the teacher will like to read. However, even "appropriate" language can be exact and precise. Try to say exactly what you mean, even if you have to pause before you begin to write.

Writers choose their words carefully to fit the audience, text form, and purpose of their writing. For example, when writing a business letter, a writer should use a simple and more formal style than when writing a diary or blog entry. In the same way, a poet must choose his words very carefully to fit the form of the poem and capture the image or feeling he wants to express as precisely as possible. When writing a haiku, for example, a poet will choose very different words than when writing a limerick or a rhyming ballad on the same subject.

## CREATE A STORY WITH A LOGICAL SEQUENCE

When writing a story, you want to make sure it follows a logical sequence so that it makes sense to your audience. One way to make sure that your story follows a logical sequence is to write the events of the story in chronological order.

## LET'S TRY TOGETHER

Let's try writing a story together using a logical sequence. The easiest way to do this would be to list the events of the story in a timeline.

#### STEP ONE: STORY IDEA

The first step in writing any story is to come up with a good story idea. The best ideas come from the events in our own lives. How about writing a story about learning to ride a two-wheeled bike?

#### STEP TWO: DEVELOP YOUR CHARACTER

Next we need to create a character and a list of character traits. Sometimes it helps to think of a couple of people we know really well and create a character based on them.

#### STEP THREE: STORY PROBLEM

Your next step is to come up with a problem or struggle your character might have within your story idea. Our character's struggle is going to be learning how to ride a two-wheeled bike.

#### STEP FOUR: SETTING

Now we need to think about where our story should take place. Think about where you learned to ride a two-wheeled bike. Our story can take place on the quiet street where the main character lives.

#### STEP FIVE: TIMELINE

We can use a timeline to organize the events of our story. We want to place our events in chronological order. Each dot should include a character doing something somewhere.

- Dad and I are on the driveway taking the training wheels off my bike.
- I am nervous to ride with no training wheels and pretend my stomach hurts, but Dad doesn't believe me.
- I get on and Dad holds the back of my bike to steady my balance but I wobble and tell him not to let go.
- I begin to pedal and Dad holds on as I move forward. I lose my balance, tip over, and am mad at Dad.
- Dad helps me up. He tells me that I almost had it and tells me to try again.
- I climb back on, make Dad promise to hold on and I try again.
- I begin to pedal, to move faster down the sidewalk
- I begin to smile, then realize that Dad is no longer holding on. I am on my own.
- I stop my bike to turn and wave at Dad. He waves back with a big smile.

## Step Six: Write the Story

Our next step now is to write our story. We begin with the first dot, which is our first event in our story and begin to write. We can think of each dot as a new paragraph, since each dot is a new event within the story. Writing your story in this order will create a story that follows a logical sequence.

*Example*

---

### Losing the Wheels

"Dad, are you sure I am ready?" I questioned my Dad as I handed him the wrench.

"More than ready!" Dad responded as he turned the wrench loosening the bolt that attached my training wheels to my bike. I had been riding my bike all summer, up and down our quiet street, through the River Valley on Sundays with Dad and now at the end of summer we were finally taking off the training wheels that had supported my riding all summer.

My stomach began to fill with butterflies. I was so good a riding with those training wheels! I wondered if I would ever be able to ride the same way again without them. Dad finished removing that last training wheel and turned and looked at me and asked "Ready to give it a go, kiddo?"

A nervous smile came across my face as I said "Actually Dad, I am not feeling too great; my stomach is hurting again."

"Oh, kiddo you are just fine, you are just feeling a little nervous which is fair enough but you are ready, I know you are!"

---

In the above example, the first two dots of the timeline have been written into paragraphs. As you read, you can see how the story is following a logical sequence. The events of the story are being told in the order they would have actually happened.

## Your Turn!

Now try writing the rest of this story using the above timeline.

## Create a Story with Relationships between Characters and Plot

When you are writing a story, it is very important to know your characters well. When you know your characters well, your plot will develop from them. Writers spend a great deal of time getting to know their character so well that they would know what their character would do or say in any situation.

## Let's Try

### Step One: Developing A Character

Your first step is to develop your main character, to think about what this person is really like on the inside (personality traits) and the outside (physical appearance). When you are developing your character, it is also very important to think about how a character's inside is reflected on their outside. If you say your character loves to play sports and is always ready to drop anything and join in a game, would it make sense that this character always wears high heels? No, you would imagine your character dressed more casually. Also, to help you get started in developing your character, it is sometimes helpful to think of one or two people you know really, really well. Basing your character lightly on a real person will make the character more realistic for your readers. As well, sometimes it is helpful to organize your thoughts in a chart to keep beside you as you write.

In the chart below, begin getting to know your character by listing details about them. Use the following questions to help you get started:

- Are they male or female?
- How old are they?
- What color is their hair, eyes?
- How tall are they?
- What do they like to do in their spare time?
- What is their family like (brothers, sisters, mom or dad)?
- Do they have any pets?
- Do they have any hobbies or play any sports?
- Who are their friends?
- What makes them happy, sad, nervous, excited, mad?
- What is their favorite thing to eat?
- What type of clothes do they like to wear?
- What are they like in new situations (friendly, nervous, outgoing, shy)?
- What are they like (kind, thoughtful, generous, funny, easy going, stubborn)?

| Inside (personality traits) | Outside (physical appearance) |
| --- | --- |
|  |  |

*Step Two: What would your Character do?*

After you have completed your chart and feel like you know your character very well, it is time to begin imagining your character in different situations.

In each of the following situations imagine what your character might do:

- First day at a brand new school
- At an amusement park and in line for the biggest roller coaster
- Leaving for summer camp
- Trying out for the school soccer team
- Auditioning for the school musical
- Watching young sister eat the last piece of birthday cake

When you know your character really well, it becomes easy to imagine what your character would do in any situation.

*Step Three: Character and Plot*

Now that you know your character well and can imagine them in any situation, you can see how your story plot can develop from your character. When writing a story after you have established your story idea, character and setting, your next step is to imagine how this story might unfold for your character.

*Example*

Imagine your character as a girl in fifth grade who is fun, friendly, outgoing, loves playing sports, is on the basketball team, lives with her mom, dad, older brother, and two younger sisters, has lots of friends but three best friends, always wears her hair in a pony tail, dresses casually and usually in her older cousin's hand me downs.

Now let's say the story idea is that she sprains her ankle right before the final basketball game. Her struggle is not being able to play the last game of the season. Based on what we already know about our character, we can easily imagine the plot of this story. Since she loves basketball so much, we know she is going to be upset. We also know she has three best friends, so we can also imagine what they might do to cheer her up because she can not play.

---

Character and plot go together. You cannot have a plot without character, because the plot develops from the character's actions in the story.

*5W.3e Write narratives to develop real or imagined experiences or events using effective technique, descriptive details, and clear event sequences. Provide a conclusion that follows from the narrated experiences or events.*

## NARRATIVE-DESCRIPTIVE WRITING

Narrative writing tells a story. Usually, the story happens to characters that you imagine, but sometimes you are telling a personal story. You have had many experiences that could be turned into a great story. Whenever you write a story, you use narrative paragraphs. Organize these paragraphs in time-order, and add descriptive details to make your writing more interesting or exciting.

Here is an example of a narrative paragraph from the book *Jennie* by Paul Gallico, which is about a boy Peter, who takes care of a stray cat. In this narrative paragraph, Peter is giving the cat a bath.

*Example*

Peter found that after this recital he had need to wash himself energetically for a few moments, and then he went over to where Jennie was lying and washed her face too, giving her several caresses beneath her soft chin and along the side of her muzzle that conveyed more to her than words. She made a little soft, crooning sound in her throat, and her claws worked in and out, kneading the canvas hatch cover faster than ever.

---

Notice that the paragraph is also very descriptive:

- Telling how Peter washes himself "energetically"
- Describing "caresses" that show how much affection Peter already feels for the stray cat
- Using the moving claws of the cat to describe her contentment

## WRITE A STORY BEGINNING THAT HAS ACTION

When you are writing a story you want to have an interesting and exciting beginning, one that catches the attention of your audience so that they want to continue reading to find out what is going to happen next.

One way to to begin a story is to use **action**, beginning your story with your **character doing something**.

## USING ACTION

*Example*

Instead of "There was a black cat who wanted to catch a mouse."

Try "The black cat pounced quickly upon the little mouse that had just darted out from under the old sofa."

See and feel the difference? By using action in the second sentence, you make your audience want to know if the cat actually catches the mouse. Your audience will want to continue reading your story.

## YOUR TURN!

Let's say your story was going to begin with your main character leaving for school in the morning. Try writing three story beginnings that use action to show your character leaving.

## HOW DID YOU DO?

Below are three ways you could have begun your story with action:

- Mary ran down the stairs, quickly grabbed her coat and book bag from the front entrance, and rushed out the front door in an attempt to catch the school bus before it drove away.
- Mary chatted excitedly with her sisters as they walked out the front door of their home towards the bus stop.
- As Mary sat on the steps of her front porch, she looked at her watch again. Beth said she would be here by now. Mary thought to herself that if Beth didn't show up soon they would both be late for the first day of school.

The three above examples all have the main character Mary performing some type of action (doing something). These actions catch the attention of the audience and make them excited to hear more of the story.

## CREATE A STORY BEGINNING USING DIALOGUE

When you are writing a story, it is important to have a strong beginning that catches the attention of your audience. One way to do this is to begin your story with dialogue, having your character say something that hooks the attention of your audience.

## Using Dialogue

*Example*
Instead of:

The teacher asked the students to sit down on the bus.

"All of you need to sit down immediately. This bus isn't going anywhere until you are showing you are ready!"

The second beginning gets your attention! You can feel the teacher's frustration in the second beginning, while the first one just tells you what the teacher wants and shows no emotion. When writing, you want your audience to feel what your characters feel, so using dialogue is a good way to do this. Using dialogue at the beginning of a story will grab the attention of your audience.

---

## Let's Try Together!

Let's say your story idea is about a surprise birthday party for you. First, close your eyes and imagine how this story might begin. Where are you? What are you doing? What might you be thinking? What might you say?

Story tell aloud a couple of different ways this might begin, using dialogue (having your character say something).

*Example*
- "Hey, Susan!" It was my best friend Meg, who lives just around the corner from me. "Do you think your mom might let you come to a sleepover Friday night? Just you and me!"
- "Susan, would you be able to babysit Tommy for a few hours Friday evening?"
  I was about to answer, "No, it's my bir…" when my mom popped her head around the kitchen door. "Is that Mrs. McNally? Does she want you to babysit? I think you should go, dear! We can have your birthday cake on Saturday."

---

## Your Turn!

Choose one of your story ideas or the story idea of a surprise birthday party and try writing a couple of different beginnings that use dialogue to capture the audience's attention. Remember to appeal to emotion. You want your audience to feel what your character is feeling.

*5W.3d Write narratives to develop real or imagined experiences or events using effective technique, descriptive details, and clear event sequences. Use concrete words and phrases and sensory details to convey experiences and events precisely.*

## CREATE NARRATIVES TO RELATE IDEAS, OBSERVATIONS, RECOLLECTIONS

When you create narratives, you are telling real or fictional stories about real or imagined events. Sometimes your emphasis is on relating ideas or observations. Other times, your focus is on retelling a personal experience.

## RELATING IDEAS

"Jordan didn't know who to talk to. She thought her friend would laugh at her. She was sure her family would think she was crazy. She was pretty certain that her teachers would try to talk her out of it."

Relating Ideas is the focus of the above narrative paragraph. The girl wants to communicate the idea that she is afraid of what others may think of her in her situation.

## RELATING OBSERVATIONS

What a sight! The two dogs were rolling and tossing their black and white bodies as they play-wrestled with each other. The white carpet was spotted with tufts of hair. They went on for nearly an hour.

Relating Observations involves noticing and sharing descriptive details of an event. You write your narration from the point of view of a spectator.

## NARRATING RECOLLECTIONS

### from I Survived the Titanic

*Ruth Becker was 12 years old when she set sail on the R.M.S.* Titanic. *This is her true story.*

…An inspection of the ship revealed the worst. The iceberg had bashed the hull and water was gushing in. Six of sixteen compartments were flooding. The *Titanic* was doomed.

At 12:02 A.M. Captain Smith fired orders to the crew. Radio operators telegraphed nearby ships for help.

Stokers deep below deck continuously shoveled coal into giant boilers, supplying power to keep the pumps running and the lights lit. Stewards started knocking on cabin doors, alerting sleeping travelers of trouble.

Some passengers had been awakened by a slight jolt when the *Titanic* struck the iceberg. A curious few discovered tons of ice on one of the decks. Some men even began a playful ice fight.

Deep in the forward section a few people realized something was seriously wrong. Postal workers lugged bags of sopping wet mail to a higher deck. Water swirled on the floors of some third-class cabins.

"My mother had just gone to bed…when she was awakened by the engines stopping," described Ruth. "Then she heard a pounding noise." One steward reassured her it was nothing. Their own steward, however, told her to get up on deck—that the ship was sinking. "So she awakened me and we put on our clothes, stockings, and our coats over our nightclothes and went to the upper deck. It was almost like a dream—everything was very orderly and very quiet. We had to climb five flights of stairs to a room full of women. They were all weeping—in all states of dress and undress. Everyone was frightened—no one knew what would happen to them. But I was never scared. I was only excited. I never for one minute thought we would die."

Officers were lowering lifeboats. Orders were to load women and children first. But… there were too few lifeboats! They had space for only 1,178 of the 2,228 passengers and crew aboard. The only hope for the others was help from another ship…

On deck, the crew fired distress rockets. The orchestra played lively tunes to calm passengers. Mrs. Becker sent Ruth back to their cabin for blankets. Ruth returned to find officers loading women and children into a nearby lifeboat. "One officer grabbed my sister, another carried my brother into a lifeboat and yelled, 'All full!' My mother screamed…. They let mother on, but they left me behind.

"My mother yelled at me to take the next lifeboat, and before I knew it, an officer picked me up and dumped me into a boat." Seconds later, the crew lowered Ruth's lifeboat, #13, down 50 feet. As it neared the sea, jets of water spewed from the *Titanic*, pushing Ruth's boat directly beneath the next lifeboat, #15, being lowered. People shouted desperately for someone to stop lowering #15, but it kept coming. An instant before the lifeboats collided, a man cut #13's lines. Freed just in time, the boat swung away from the ship.

—*by* Jennifer A. Kirkpatrick

http://www.nationalgeographic.com/ngkids/9607/titanic.html

Part of this passage, in quotation marks, narrates the recollection of an old woman (Ruth Becker) who was a child when the Titanic went down in 1912. She was there, which allows you as a reader to see how dramatic and important personal recollections or memories can be to narration.

## CREATE NARRATIVES THAT USE CONCRETE SENSORY DETAILS

You need to include more details about the facts that you give in your narrative compositions or stories. It is important that your details and examples fit the topic and are interesting. Your details also help to make your writing come alive for your reader.

When you picture a rainy day, for instance, what do you think of or see in your imagination?

- slick streets?
- umbrellas?
- rain streaming down windows?
- driving rain pounding on pavement?
- windshield wipers?
- dark, boiling clouds?

You need to create details for your reader that will help them to picture in their minds the kind of rainy day you are describing. Look at the chart below to see how ordinary writing comes alive when concrete details are added. Concrete means that the details are realistic or can be easily imagined through your senses.

*Example*

| Without details | With details |
| --- | --- |
| It was raining. | The rain poured steadily down, drenching the fields and the children as they rushed home. |
| The food was good. | The fried chicken was well-browned and crisp, and the corn bread was so hot the butter melted straight off it. |
| The horse galloped by. | The steady, loud *clip-clop, clip-clop* of the horse's hooves drowned out all of the other night-time noises. |

## CREATE NARRATIVES TO PROVIDE INSIGHT ABOUT MEMORABLE EXPERIENCES

When you are creating a narrative it is important (and easier!) to choose to write on a topic that you know best - your personal experiences. When you write about your own experiences you can truly create authentic pieces. You are able to add more vivid details, because they are yours!

Have you ever had to write about "What I Did on my Summer Vacation", or "My Most Embarrassing Moment"? You may groan, "Not again!" when you see these wonderful topics, but the reason they are popular with teachers is that they invite you to write about what you know best, your life. Following are some topics that invite you to write about a memorable personal experience. Why don't you try developing one of these topics into a story or piece of narrative writing? Try to include something you learned, or how you grew more mature following the experience. That is what is meant by insight.

- The Day I Was a Hero to my Brother (or Sister)
- The Year my Best Friend Moved
- Starting Hockey
- Starting Over at a New School
- How I Remember My Grandma
- The Toughest Decision I Ever Made
- The Time I Did the Right Thing
- What I Remember about (fill in the name of a favorite pet)
- The Day I Went to Work with Dad
- The Best Birthday I Ever Had

Many authors use their most memorable experiences to create stories, whether they are detail for detail, or elaborated to create a more fictional story. Some of the best writing out there is based on the author's personal experience.

## Ending a Story with a Whole Story Reminder

The ending of your story is very important! You want to leave your audience satisfied with the resolution to the problem your character or characters were facing. One way to end your story is to use a **whole story reminder**, that takes your audience back through the events of the story and brings the problem to a conclusion with a lesson learned.

*Example*
**First Day at School**
As I hopped on the yellow school bus at the end of the first day of grade 3 my mind raced with the events of the day. I thought back to only seven hours earlier when I was boarding the bus this morning with worry, wondering if I would like my new school, my new teacher, and would I make any friends. The day had turned out even better than expected! I was excited to get home to tell Dad all about my fabulous new school, my fantastic new teacher and all the new friends I had made. I think I learned one of the most important lessons today at school and it had nothing to do with Math or Science or any other subject! I learned that although new can be scary it can also be so exciting! This was the best day of school ever!

In the above example the main character was struggling with the first day of school at a new school. As the character reflected at the end of the day, she learned that new can be scary but it can also be exciting.

## Create an Ending for a Multi-Paragraph Narrative Composition

The ending of a story is one of the most important parts. It is the place in the story where a problem is resolved, a struggle is overcome, and the audience's questions are answered. One way you can end a story is to use dialogue, not just "talking" between characters, but characters making important statements that bring the story to a close.

*Example*
And so, to sum it all up, the cat came back. As my dad said, once Cicero was back at his command post looking out the living room window, "Never underestimate the power of an animal to return to its castle, especially a cat! They like being warm, they like being well-fed, and they like being comfortable, in that order. I never yet met a cat that liked being a hobo!"

With the ending of your story, you want to leave your audience satisfied with the resolution to the problem your character or characters were facing. Another way to end your story is to use a **whole story reminder**, that takes your audience back through the events of the story and brings the problem to a conclusion with a lesson learned.

*Example*

Later that night as I lay in bed staring up at my ceiling fan, I thought back over the week. When Cicero disappeared during the thunderstorm on Monday, I thought I would never see him again. I remembered how Mom and I rode our bikes all over the neighborhood Tuesday and Wednesday, looking and looking, how we returned home with lots of muscle aches and no cat. I remembered walking home after school Thursday and staring into every living room window, just in case Cicero would pop up on a sofa. I can't believe he was there on the front step, Friday, calmly licking his paws as if he hadn't even left! My advice to cat-lovers everywhere is: If you see lightning and hear thunder, don't let your cat out!

# Use Chronological Order for Conveying Information

Chronological order means that the information is organized according to the order in which it occurs. Some stories do not follow chronological order, but dates and times are provided for readers to understand the time frame. Chronological order provides a clear sequence of information for the reader, and is a good way to organize writing that describes a sequence of steps or events.

*Example*

### The Story of Plasticine

Have you ever wondered how Plasticine was invented? It was actually invented by an art teacher who didn't like clay. He found it to be heavy and difficult for his students to shape.

The teacher, William Harbutt, began mixing batches of clay-like dough in his basement. One day in 1887, the mix was perfect—it was soft, light, and easy to shape. He called the mix Plasticine.

Mr. Harbutt's students loved the fake clay, and so did his own six children. It was obvious that Mr. Harbutt needed to make more Plasticine to sell to others. After Mr. Harbutt began to advertise his invention, he was so swamped with orders that he hired an ex-soldier to mix and prepare huge batches of Plasticine. The final change that was made to Plasticine was the addition of color to the gray mix. You can still buy Plasticine like this in stores today.

Following is the chronological order of "The Story of Plasticine."

1. An art teacher mixed a substance to replace clay.
2. By 1887, the mixture was perfect.
3. Mr. Harbutt named his mixture Plasticine.
4. The students loved Plasticine.
5. Mr. Harbutt's children loved Plasticine.
6. Mr. Harbutt advertised his product.
7. Orders poured in.
8. Mr. Harbutt hired an old soldier to mix large batches of Plasticine.
9. Color was added to the gray Plasticine.

From reading this passage, you can see that there is a definite order in which the events occur, and that one event is related to or leads to the next.

*Example*

### from Nim's Island

There were plants to prop up that had toppled over in the wind, weeds to pull, strawberries to nibble, and a huge bunch of bananas just green enough to pick.

Nim liked bananas, but what she liked even better was swinging Jack's machete. It was shiny and sharp and made her feel like a pirate.

"Aargh, me hearties!" she shouted, and chopped down the bunch.

She dragged them to the shed and hooked them to a rope looping over a beam in the roof.

"I'm swinging the bananas!" And she grabbed the rope just above her head. Fred jumped and clung to the end with his claws. Swinging hard and heavy, they hoisted the bananas up to the roof to ripen.

It would have been easier if Selkie had helped, but sea lions aren't much good at swinging on ropes.

Fred knew what she was thinking. He raced her up the path to the top of the waterfall.

Over thousands of years, the water trickling down the mountain had worn away the steep black rocks to make a curving slide. It was perfect for *whooshing* a girl and an iguana over bumps and dips and splashing them into the pool at the bottom.

Nim and Fred ran up and slid down until it was time for lunch. Then Nim picked up a tomato and an avocado that had fallen off in the wind and weeded quickly around the peas.

"They'll be ready tomorrow," she told Fred.

But Fred didn't like peas, and he was getting bored. He started chewing leaves and spitting them out.

"I won't bring you up to the garden again!" Nim said sternly. Fred spat out the last bit of pea leaf and crawled into the wagon for a wild ride down the hill.

—*by* Wendy Orr

Look below to see the chronological order of "Nim's Island".

- **First:** Nim chops down the bunch of bananas.
- **Then:** She drags them to the shed.
- **Then:** She hooks them to a rope looping over a beam.
- **Then:** She and Fred (the iguana) swing the rope to hoist the bananas to the roof to ripen.
- **Then:** Fred races Nim to the top of the waterfall.
- **Then:** Nim and Fred try the slide created by the trickling of water to the pool at the bottom.
- **Then:** Nim and Fred slide till lunchtime.
- **Then:** Nim picks a tomato and avocado from her garden and weeds the peas.
- **Last:** The two friends crawl into the wagon for a wild ride down the hill from the garden.

## Use Cause and Effect for Conveying Information

Authors often use a technique called cause and effect to develop a paragraph or story. This technique tells why events happened and why things are as they are. Cause-and-effect relationships are frequently used in writing that informs, explains, or persuades. The words *if* and *then* are used to show how one thing can lead to another. For example, if a person never practices writing, then that person will probably not become an author. Some other cause-and-effect words are *because*, *as a result*, *why*, *when*, *therefore*, *so*, and *for this reason*.

*Example*
The following passage by Farley Mowat, which is followed by a chart of cause-and-effect relationships.

There was a summerhouse in our back yard, and we kept about thirty gophers in it. We caught them out on the prairie, using snares made of heavy twine.

The way you do it is like this: You walk until you spot a gopher sitting up beside his hole. Gophers sit straight up, reaching their noses as high as they can, so they can see farther. When you begin to get too close, they flick their tails, give a little jump, and whisk down their holes. As soon as they do that, you take a piece of twine that has a noose tied in one end, and you spread the noose over the hole. Then you lie down in the grass holding the other end of the twine in your hand. You can hear the gopher all the while, whistling away to himself somewhere underground.

| Cause | Effect |
| --- | --- |
| Gophers sit straight up | They can see farther |
| People try to get close to gophers | They flick their tails |
|  | They give a jump |
|  | They whisk down their holes |

In science textbooks, you will often see cause/effect relationships, particularly with experiments. In social studies, cause/effect relationships are also evident, especially when you study the causes of a historical event, such as the Industrial Revolution or the California Gold Rush.

*5W.4  Produce clear and coherent writing in which the development and organization are appropriate to task, purpose, and audience.*

## SELECT A PARAGRAPH FOCUS BASED ON PURPOSE

Reading without a purpose is like setting off on a road trip without a map. You find yourself wasting a lot of time because you do not know where you are going, what is important (e.g., road signs, last gas station for 100 miles), and the whole experience becomes very frustrating. At some point, you find yourself way off course because you went too far and did not think to stop and ask for directions. If you do not set a purpose for reading you may find yourself in the same situation.

What you do before you start to read can make or break the reading experience. First of all, you have to determine what your reason for reading is. Is it to research information for an essay, answer questions for an assignment, get instructions for assembling a new bike, find out the highlights of the basketball game, or to escape into the latest bestseller book. Once you decide what your reason is, you have also decided your purpose for reading…now you know where you are going.

Though your teacher may often set your reading purpose, you might want to clarify your purpose by asking yourself the "five W's" before you read: Who? What? Where? When? Why? How? Asking your own questions will help you read better and gain more meaning from the reading process.

Good readers know that when you have a purpose for reading you can keep a closer eye on your progress and know when to stop and turn around when something is not quite right. Sometimes you need to revisit your purpose, and sometimes your purpose changes—as in the case of state tests, when you often have to read the same story or article for different purposes.

## PURPOSE-BASED PARAGRAPHS

Just as purpose is important to reading, it is important to writing. Look at the topic sentences below, to see how the purpose is set up in the first sentence of the paragraph.

1. If you follow three simple guidelines, it is possible to do well on a multiple-choice test. (Purpose of paragraph will be to explain)
2. My most embarrassing moment happened like this. (Purpose of paragraph will be to entertain)
3. If you read these instructions and examine the two diagrams, you will be able to tie a slip knot. (Purpose of paragraph will be to instruct)
4. Above all, never, never say, "I can't do that." (Purpose of paragraph will be to inspire or challenge)
5. Before us, spreading toward the horizon like a dream, lay the legendary Forgotten Valley. (Purpose of paragraph will be to describe)

*5W.10 Write routinely over extended time frames (time for research, reflection, and revision) and shorter time frames (a single sitting or a day or two) for a range of discipline-specific tasks, purposes, and audiences.*

## SELECT A PARAGRAPH FOCUS BASED ON AUDIENCE

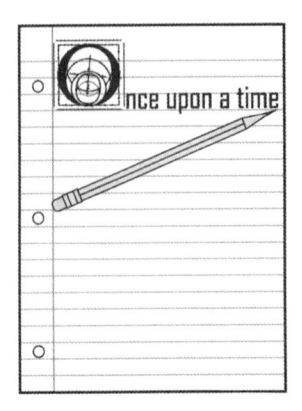

Your audience is the person who will read your writing. You must learn to write for a variety of audiences. Here are some examples of who you may be writing for:

- an adult, such as your parents, teacher, or principal
- classmates or other students
- younger children, for whom you are creating a folktale
- a friend, relative, or pen pal to whom you are writing a letter
- a guest speaker, such as the mayor of your town, political leaders, a sports star, a community helper like a fireman or policeman, or a famous person
- businesses in the community, such as the local newspaper, television, or radio station

Imagine you are going to share a story with your teacher. Would you use the same expressions and words with your teacher as you would with a friend? It is very likely that you would speak more formally with your teacher and use less formal words with your friends.

*Example*

| Less Formal Words | More Formal Words |
| --- | --- |
| kids | children |
| thanks | thank you |
| see you | goodbye |
| cool | stylish |

## PARAGRAPH FOCUS BASED ON FORMAT REQUIREMENTS

Have you ever been asked to write a Five Paragraph Essay Format? If so, then you know there are a few simple rules to follow to have a successful writing piece. For those who haven't done this before, it's an essay consisting of:

- an introductory paragraph
- three paragraphs which make up the body
- a concluding paragraph

With a Five Paragraph Essay format, you know you only have five paragraphs to work with so you are limited to what you can write about. This can be helpful to new writers, giving them some idea of how to organize an essay. Another way to understand how this format works is by thinking of a hamburger, with three main parts: the top bun, the burger, and the bottom bun.

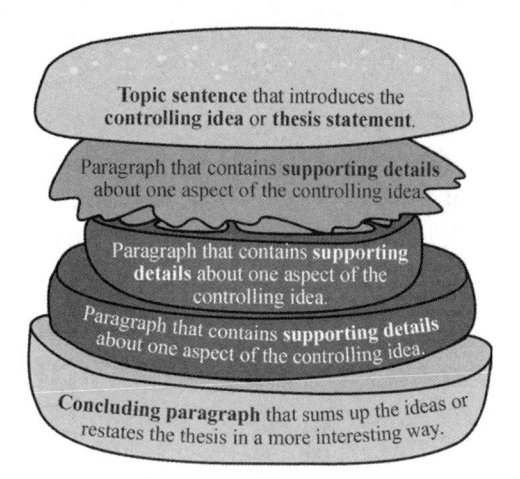

- **Topic sentence** that introduces the **controlling idea** or **thesis statement**.
- Paragraph that contains **supporting details** about one aspect of the controlling idea.
- Paragraph that contains **supporting details** about one aspect of the controlling idea.
- Paragraph that contains **supporting details** about one aspect of the controlling idea.
- **Concluding paragraph** that sums up the ideas or restates the thesis in a more interesting way.

Each of the paragraphs in your essay would need to contain facts to support your introductory sentence. Your paragraphs can be any length you want them to be, but make sure you are keeping one idea to one paragraph.

The next time you have to develop paragraphs according to a certain format, just think of a big juicy hamburger! You can also use this idea to organize the format for a single paragraph. Just adapt it as shown in the diagram below.

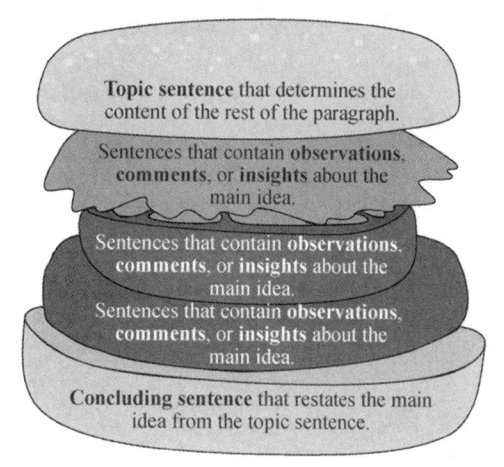

- **Topic sentence** that determines the content of the rest of the paragraph.
- Sentences that contain **observations**, **comments**, or **insights** about the main idea.
- Sentences that contain **observations**, **comments**, or **insights** about the main idea.
- Sentences that contain **observations**, **comments**, or **insights** about the main idea.
- **Concluding sentence** that restates the main idea from the topic sentence.

## SET A PURPOSE FOR WRITING

Every author writes for a specific reason or purpose. The main purposes for writing are to inform, explain, entertain, impress, and convince. Decide what your purpose is going to be before you begin to write. Stick to your purpose. If you are trying to write out the directions to your house, stay focused on explaining. Don't sidetrack into a joke about the time you got lost on the way home. If you stay focused, your reader will see your purpose immediately.

*Example*
The given map shows the most direct way to my (Jim's) house from the school. If you pass a church on your right, you will have gone too far. If you miss the turn and that happens, just continue down the highway to the hospital at the edge of town. You can turn right into the hospital driveway and get turned around.

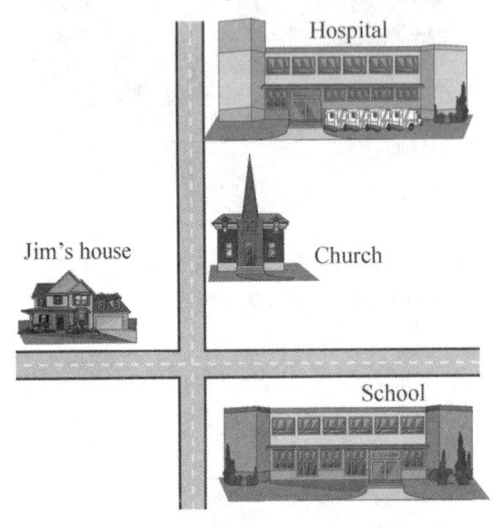

## TO INFORM

When your purpose is to inform, you want the reader to understand the facts.

## TO EXPLAIN

When your purpose is to explain, you want to give the reader the *why* or *how* of a situation. You are explaining something so that the reader will understand.

## To Entertain

When your purpose is to entertain, you are trying to amuse your readers, make them laugh, or allow them to escape the real word for a while.

*Example*
The dog tore past us through the kitchen, yelping in fright. He collided with a small table, knocking over a fish bowl and finally coming to a screeching halt against the wall in a soggy jumble of dog, fish, table legs and flowers. He looked back with as much dignity as he could muster with a goldfish bowl stuck over his nose. To his great surprise, he saw that the monster chasing him was nothing but a tiny mouse, who now giggled happily from the doorway.

## To Impress

When your purpose is to impress, you are trying to make readers feel strongly about something.

*Example*
Do you realize that here in our home country, where we make up 5% of the world's population, we create 30% of its garbage? Can we change that statistic? Of course we can, but everyone has to do their part.

## To Convince

When you write to convince, you are trying to change the reader's mind about something. You try to get the reader to agree with you. This reason for writing is also called persuading.

*Example*
It is extremely important that you lock your doors to keep out that horrible black beast. You may think he is a harmless cuddly pup. However, he destroyed my rug and smashed my best vase. If you are not careful, he will do the same or worse to your home.

## Mixed Purposes

It is always a good idea, most of the time, to stay focused on one purpose. That way, your readers don't get confused. Of course, you may experiment with writing for more than one purpose. For instance, you might write an entertaining story that also teaches the reader something while they are being amused.

## Thinking of a Story Topic

Your life is filled with so many small moments that you can write about! When you are thinking of a story topic, the best ideas come from your own life experiences! Three strategies you can use to help you think of a topic are to think of a person, place, or thing.

## THINK OF A PERSON

Think of a person that matters to you and then begin writing a list of small memories you have with that person.

*Example*
**My Sister**:

- The moment she placed my new kitty in my hands
- The moment she told me she was going away for school
- The day we had the water balloon fight
- The time when we were eating ice cream and her scoops fell off her cone and to the ground

## THINK OF A PLACE

Think of a place you have been that matters to you, and then begin writing a list of small memories you have had at that place.

*Example*
**The Cottage**:

- The day I learned to water ski
- The day the mouse ran into the bedroom and hid under my bed
- The time I ran through the screen door and broke it
- Playing kick the can with my cousins after dark
- Playing with my cousins on the raft and flipping it over in the water

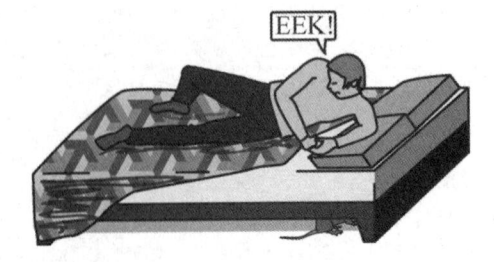

## THINK OF A THING

Think of a thing that matters to you and then begin writing a list of small memories you have about that thing.

*Example*
**My Bike**:

- Going to the bike store and picking my bike out
- Riding my bike for the first time up and down my street then falling off just in front of my house
- My friend Beth and I discovering we both had the same bike
- Riding my bike in a charity race for cancer

## USING AN IDEA FOR WRITING

After you have created a list of story topics, choose one that matters the most to you and begin the story writing process.

## USING A CHECKLIST TO EDIT YOUR STORY

An important step in the story writing process is editing your work. Some writers find it helpful to use a checklist as a guide. You can use the following checklist to help make your story an even stronger piece of writing.

## A HELPFUL REMINDER

When using an editing checklist you will be reading your story many times. Each time you read your story, you will be looking for something different. Many writers find it helpful when editing their work to read their writing aloud, slowly pointing to each word as they read it. This will help you read what you **actually** wrote rather than what you **thought** you wrote.

*Example*
The first item on your checklist is to correct all misspelled words, so you are going to read your story just looking for misspelled words and correcting them. The next item on your checklist is correct verb tenses, so this time you are just going to read, checking for correct verb tenses. The next item on your checklist is variety of sentence types, so on your third reading you will just be looking for sentence types. You will continue on like this for each item on your checklist. As you can see, you will be reading your story LOTS! But you know that after all of this reading and editing you will have a fantastic story to share!

# Editing Checklist

## General:

- I have corrected all misspelled words.
- All my verb tenses are correct.
- I have used a variety of sentence types.
- I have organized my writing into paragraphs.

## Capitalization:

*Hmm, where do I put the capitals again?*

- Each sentence begins with a capital letter.
- The names of people and places begin with a capital letter.
- The first letter of each word in the title begins with a capital letter.

## Punctuation:

- Each sentence ends with a period, question mark or exclamation mark.
- Commas are used where needed.
- Quotation marks are used to show where speech begins and ends.

## Description:

- I have used descriptive language.
- I have shown my readers what is happening not told them.
- My readers can "see" the location of the story.

## Character:

- My readers should be able to feel the emotions of the characters.
- The struggles of my character are clear.
- I have shown how my characters have grown and changed to overcome their struggles.

## Plot:

- My story follows a logical sequence of events.
- Each event has a character doing something somewhere.

## GENERATING IDEAS FOR A NON-FICTION TOPIC USING A WORD WEB

When you are going to begin writing a non-fiction piece, it is always important to begin with generating ideas of what you may want to focus on in your written piece. One way that many people try to brainstorm and organize their ideas is by using a **word web.**

Many times a word web is a starting point for you to begin brainstorming ideas about what you know of the topic at hand. It is usually very general information, but helpful, none the less. Let's look at how this might look.

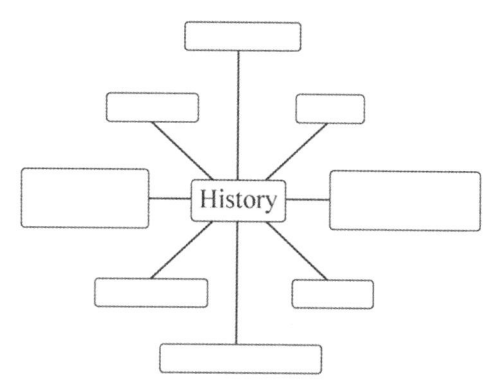

Let's say we were brainstorming about the word *history*.

What ideas might come to your mind, when you think of the word *history*?

When using a word web, you would place the word *history* in the center. Each word, idea, or topic that comes to your mind is then written down as an extension to the center word (in this case: History)

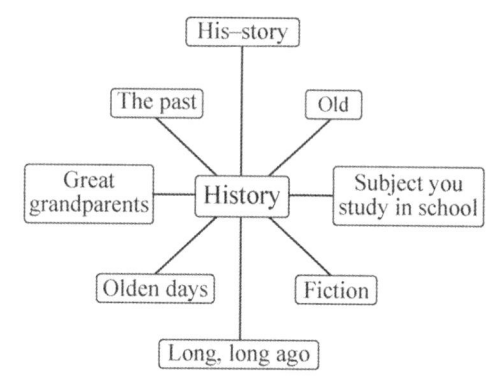

Some of the words that may come to your mind, may be: the past; old; great grandparents; olden days; his - story; fiction; long, long ago; subject you study in school.

These are all great starting points to get your mind thinking about the word history.

Depending on the area you are going to write about, by placing your ideas on the word web, you may be able to get an idea or a feel as to where you want your written piece to go.

A word web is just a great way to get your ideas flowing. Anything goes! So be brave and just start writing down anything that comes to your mind about your given topic.

Let's try this together.

If I said the word *baseball* what words might come to your mind?

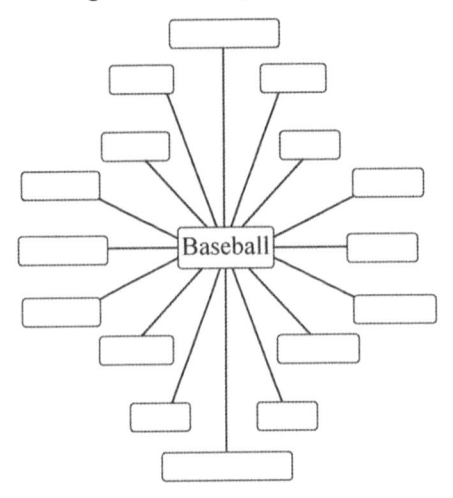

Brainstorm all the things that come to your mind. Write them down in a word web.

Baseball would be placed in the center of your word web.

Some of the extended pieces to your word web might be: innings, players, pitcher, hitter, back catcher, balls, bats, bases, home run, stadium, food, fans, crowds, boos, cheers, chants.

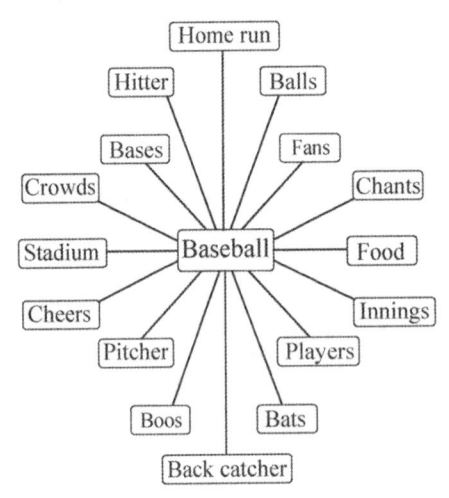

All of these words are ideas, or things you may think of when you think of baseball.

Generating ideas using a word web is an excellent idea when trying to figure out a non-fiction idea to write about because it helps you think about WHAT YOU KNOW. Writing about things that you know about and are interested in, is always a great start to your writing pieces.

Now it's your turn. Can you make a word web about the word *summer*? Once you think you have a great word web for the word *summer*, check out a possible word web example below.

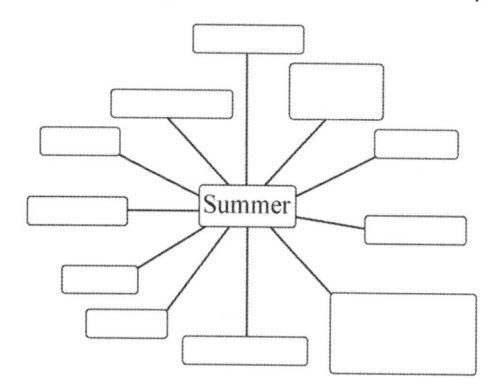

[Word web diagram with "Summer" in the center and empty boxes connected to it]

Remember to stick to what you know! What things, words, ideas, come to your mind when you think of summer? What do you do in the summer? What is the weather like in the summer? What do you wear in the summer? All these things are worth writing down for your word web about summer.

How do you think you did? If you have a word web about summer completed, look at the example below for more ideas or to compare your word web to.

Summer—vacations, hot, boating, waterskiing, kneeboarding, tubing, suntanning, sunscreen, music, towels, friends and family, hot weather.

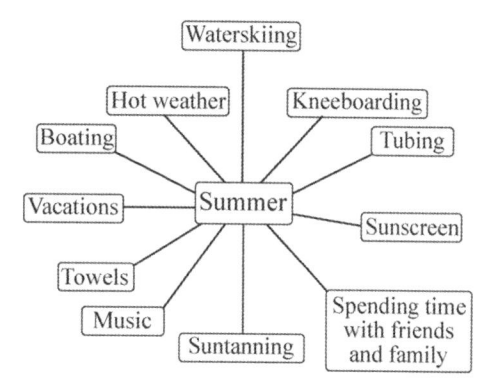

[Word web diagram with "Summer" in the center connected to: Waterskiing, Hot weather, Kneeboarding, Boating, Tubing, Vacations, Sunscreen, Towels, Music, Suntanning, Spending time with friends and family]

## GENERATING IDEAS FOR A NON-FICTION TOPIC USING THE KWL CHART

When you are going to begin writing a non-fiction piece, it is always important to begin with generating ideas of what you may want to focus on in your written piece. One way that many people try to brainstorm and organize their ideas is by using a **KWL Chart**.

What is a KWL Chart?

A KWL Chart is a way to organize your ideas and or thoughts about a given topic. The letter **K** stands for WHAT DO YOU ALREADY **KNOW** about the given topic? The letter **W** stands for WHAT DO YOU **WANT** TO KNOW about the given topic? And the letter **L** stands for WHAT HAVE I **LEARNED** about the given topic.

| What I Know | What I Want to Know | What I Learned |
|---|---|---|
| | | |

As you can see, the chart is split into three columns. One heading is the **K**—where you ask yourself and jot down everything you already **KNOW** on the given topic. The next column is the **W**, where you jot down all the things you **WANT** to know about the given topic and the next section is the **L**. It is this section that you come back to after the research has been done, or even the whole written piece and reflect upon what you have **LEARNED** through out the research process.

Let's look at one KWL chart together.

Let's say we are brainstorming about the topic BOATS. Under the "K" section (What we KNOW) some of the things we might jot down are: Titanic, must float, they can be big and small boats, canoes, ships, fishing boats, or kayaks.

Under the "W" section (What we WANT to know about) we might write something appealing to our interests like: "What is the biggest boat ever made?" "How do heavy boats actually stay floating?" "What is the fastest boat ever made?"

**Boats**

| What I Know | What I Want to Know | What I Learned |
|---|---|---|
| • Titanic<br>• Must float<br>• They can be big and small boats<br>• Canoes<br>• Ships<br>• Fishing boats<br>• Kayaks | • What is the biggest boat ever made?<br>• How do heavy boats actually stay floating?<br>• What is the fastest boat ever made? | |

These are all questions you may choose to research into and possible create a non-fiction writing piece on.

Once you have finished researching about the topic BOATS, you then would go back and fill in the last section "L" (What we LEARNED)

## GENERATING IDEAS FOR A NON-FICTION TOPIC USING MIND MAPPING

When you are going to begin writing a non-fiction piece, it is always important to begin with generating ideas of what you may want to focus on in your written piece. One way that many people try to brainstorm and organize their ideas is by using **mind mapping**.

Many times mind mapping can help as a starting point for you to begin brainstorming and organizing your ideas about the topic at hand. It can start off very general, and become more complex as you continue to brainstorm and add to the mind map. Let's look at how one might look.

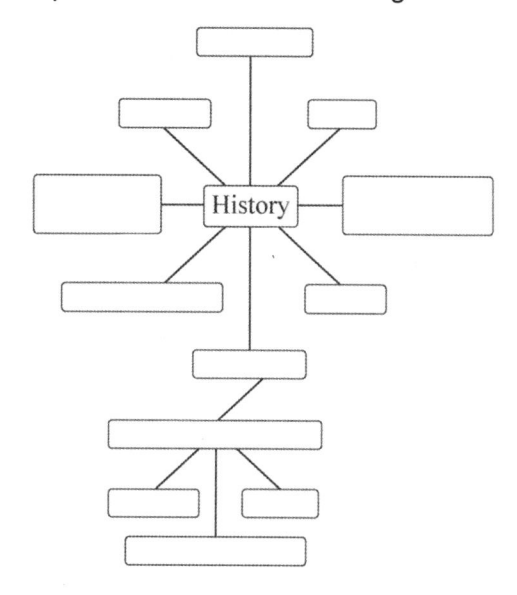

Let's say you were brainstorming about the word *history*.

What ideas might come to your mind, when you think of the word *history*?

When using a mind map, you would place the word *history* in the center. Each word, idea, or topic that comes to your mind is then written down as an extension to the center word (in this case: history).

Some of the words that may come to your mind may include: the past; old; great grandparents; olden days; his - story; fiction; long, long ago; subject you study in school.

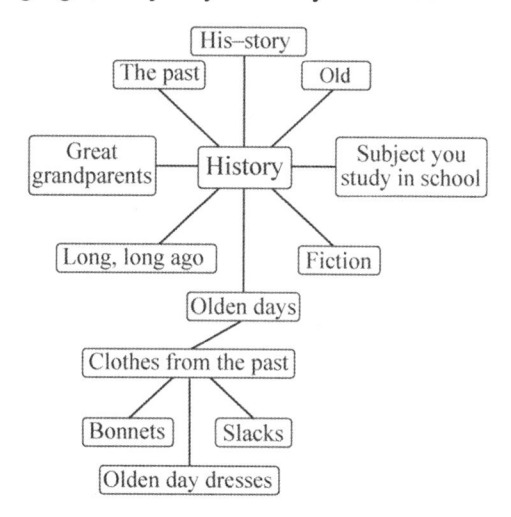

These are all great starting points to get your mind thinking about the word *history*.

Using mind maps is different from using a word web, as you can extend your ideas out even further into even smaller subsections and categories.

For example: from *History*, you may have written *olden days* and then attached to olden days you may have written *clothes from the past* and from there you may have an extended list of clothing like *bonnets, olden dresses, slacks*, etc.

A mind map is a great way to get your ideas organized into topics and subtopics.

## LET'S TRY THIS TOGETHER

If I said the word *baseball* what words might come to your mind? You may begin to brainstorm ideas about baseball. "Baseball" would be placed in the center of your mind map.

Some of the ideas that come to your mind about baseball might include the following: innings, players, pitcher, hitter, back catcher, balls, bats, bases, home run, stadium, food, fans, crowds, boo's, cheers, chants,

All of these words are ideas, or things you may think of when you think of baseball. When you use mind mapping, it can help you to organize your thoughts into categories or sub topics. In the middle of your mind map you would put the word *baseball*, then an extension of that might be BASEBALL EQUIPMENT, then attached to that might be the words *balls*, *bats*, *bases*. Another section attached to the word *baseball*, may be *fans*, and then attached to that might be the words *crowds*, *boo's*, *chants*, *cheers*.

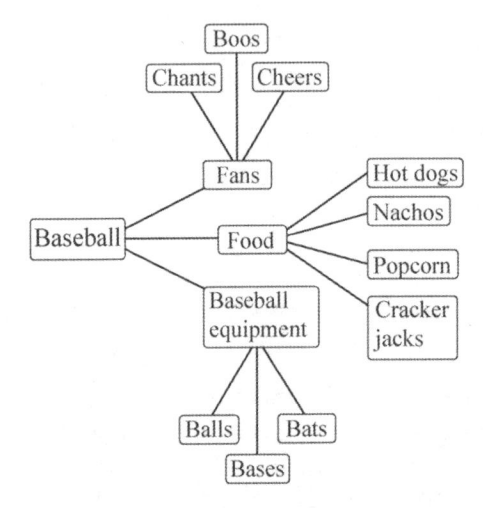

Maybe when you used the mind map to brainstorm things about baseball, you came up with the word *food*, and that sparked an idea to write about all the types of food you might eat if you were at a baseball game.

Do you see how the mind map can help you organize your thoughts?

Generating ideas using a mind map is an excellent idea when trying to figure out a non-fiction topic to write about, because it helps you think about WHAT YOU KNOW. Writing about things that you know about and are interested in, is always a great start to your writing pieces.

## IT'S YOUR TURN

Below are some things a person might brainstorm about SUMMER. Can you organize these ideas into a mind map, breaking the words down into subsections?

Summer: vacations, boating, waterskiing, kneeboarding, tubing, suntanning, sunscreen, music, towels, time spent with friends and family, hot weather, tornado weather, sunshine, rain, barbecues, get-togethers.

## How Did You Do?

Were you able to organize the brainstormed words into separate categories? Check a possible solution below.

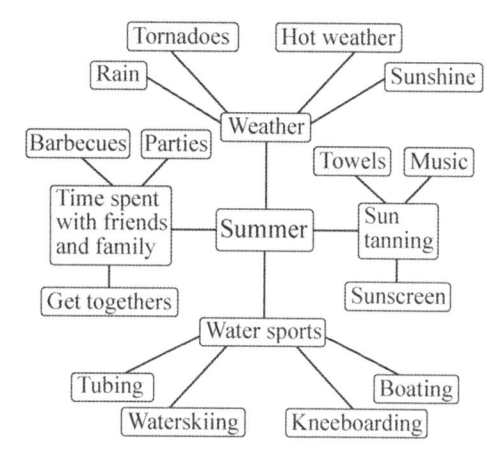

```
        Tornadoes    Hot weather
   Rain          \  /      Sunshine
         \    Weather    /
          \     |      /
 Barbecues  Parties    Towels   Music
        \  |           \  |
   Time spent            Sun
   with friends — Summer — tanning
   and family           |
        |              Sunscreen
   Get togethers
              \
            Water sports
           /      |       \
     Tubing     Boating
       Waterskiing   Kneeboarding
```

From the original list, you may have created a mind map that looks like this SUMMER

with a sub topic attached to it, WATER SPORTS, with the words *boating, waterskiing, knee boarding, tubing* attached to it. Then attached to SUMMER you may also have the sub topic SUN TANNING attached to it, with the words *sunscreen, music, towels* attached to it. Then another sub topic attached to SUMMER may be WEATHER, and attached to that may have the words *hot weather, sunshine, rain, tornadoes*. Another sub category attached to the word *summer* might be TIME SPENT WITH FRIENDS AND FAMILY and attached to that might be *barbecues, parties, get togethers*.

## Using A Checklist to Edit your Non-Fiction Writing

The purpose of non-fiction writing is to communicate accurate and concrete information to an audience on a wide variety of different topics. The topics can range from different people, to different places, to different ideas, concepts, theories, events and even things.

When editing your non-fiction writing pieces, you must first begin by making sure your facts are accurate. A non-fiction piece must contain all true facts, or else it is considered fiction. Make sure that you have researched the information from a credible source before using it in your non-fiction writing piece.

Next, when evaluating your work, use an Editor's Checklist to make sure you have correctly edited all of your work and have it ready to continue on to the publishing stage.

## A Checklist for Non-fiction Writing

1. Have I checked the beginning and end punctuation of my sentences to make sure they are all completed correctly?
2. Have I checked to make sure my sentences make sense and are clear to the reader?
3. Have I checked the spelling to make sure everything is spelt correctly?
4. Are all my paragraphs complete and only covering one important topic?
5. Is my beginning engaging and does it clearly introduce my topic?
6. Is my ending complete and does it wrap up my entire writing piece in a clear way?

Once you have read through your story, each time completing one of the above checklist points, you should be ready to publish your work, in whatever way you choose to do so.

*Try This!*

Let's edit the following non-fiction piece together. Remember that each time you read through your piece you should be checking for one of the checklist points. We will read through this non-fiction writing piece 6 times.

a tornado is a funnel of fast spinning air. Tornadoes usually start in thunderstorms and sometimes come with hale. Tornadoes can move at a rapid pace of 16 - 32 km per hour (10 - 20 miles). They usually only last traveling on the ground for up to 10 kilometers (6 miles). usually last at maximum 1 hour or so, and that is usually if it is classified as a violent tornado it is not very eesy to tell which direction a tornado's path may be, as its direction may change in a matter of minutes due to it's spinning nature.

1. Have I checked the beginning and end punctuation of my sentences to make sure they are all completely correct?

**A** tornado is a funnel of fast spinning air. Tornadoes usually start in thunderstorms and sometimes come with hale. Tornadoes can move at a rapid pace of 16 - 32 km per hour (10 - 20 miles). They usually only last traveling on the ground for up to 10 kilometers (6 miles). **U**sually last at maximum 1 hour or so, and that is usually if it is classified as a violent tornado it is not very eesy to tell which direction a tornado's path may be, as its direction may change in a matter of minutes due to it's spinning nature.

2. Have I checked to make sure my sentences make sense and are clear to the reader?

A tornado is a funnel of fast spinning air. Tornadoes usually start in thunderstorms and sometimes come with hale. Tornadoes can move at a rapid pace of 16 - 32 km per hour (10 - 20 miles). They usually only last traveling on the ground for up to 10 kilometers (6miles). **Tornadoes** usually last at maximum 1 hour or so, and that is usually if it is classified as a violent tornado. It is not very easy to tell which direction a tornado's path may be, as its direction may change in a matter of minutes due to it's spinning nature.

3. Have I checked the spelling to make sure everything is spelled correctly?

A tornado is a funnel of fast spinning air. Tornadoes usually start in thunderstorms and sometimes come with **hail**. Tornadoes can move at a rapid pace of 16 - 32 km per hour (10 - 20 miles). They usually only last traveling on the ground for up to 10 kilometers (6 miles). Tornadoes usually last at maximum 1 hour or so, and that is usually if it is classified as a violent tornadoes. It is not very **easy** to tell which direction a tornado's path may be, as its direction may change in a matter of minutes due to **its** spinning nature.

4. Are all my paragraphs complete and only covering one important topic?

Because our example is only one paragraph long, it is best to just read over the paragraph to make sure it is all relevant to one topic. If not, then maybe a fact needs to be removed or in a larger text, moved to another paragraph where it fits. In this example, it is talking about tornadoes in general and the nature of them. Each sentence seems to fit this paragraph and no changes are necessary.

5. Is my beginning engaging and does it clearly introduce my topic?

**Tornadoes are one of the world´s fascinating natural disasters.** A tornado is a funnel of fast spinning air. Tornadoes usually start in thunderstorms and sometimes come with hail. Tornadoes can move at a rapid pace of 16 - 32 km per hour (10 - 20 miles). They usually only last traveling on the ground for up to 10 kilometers (6 miles). Tornadoes usually last at maximum 1 hour or so, and that is usually if it is classified as a violent tornado. It is not very easy to tell which direction a tornado's path may be, as its direction may change in a matter of minutes due to its spinning nature.

6. Is my ending complete and does it wrap up my entire writing piece in a clear way?

Tornadoes are one of the world´s fascinating natural disasters. A tornado is a funnel of fast spinning air. Tornadoes usually start in thunderstorms and sometimes come with hail. Tornadoes can move at a rapid pace of 16 - 32 km per hour (10 - 20 miles). They usually only last traveling on the ground for up to 10 kilometers (6 miles). Tornadoes usually last at maximum 1 hour or so, and that is usually if it is classified as a violent tornado. It is not very easy to tell which direction a tornado's path may be, as its direction may change in a matter of minutes due to its spinning nature. **Tornadoes can be dangerously unpredictable and destructive depending on its size and speed and how long it lasts for.**

Here is what the final paragraph might look like, once you have gone through each item to edit from the check list:

**Tornadoes are one of the world´s fascinating natural disasters.** A tornado is a funnel of fast spinning air. Tornadoes usually start in thunderstorms and sometimes come with **hail**. Tornadoes can move at a rapid pace of 16 - 32 km per hour (10 - 20 miles). They usually only last traveling on the ground for up to 10 kilometers (6 miles). **Tornadoes** usually last at maximum 1 hour or so, and that is usually if it is classified as a violent tornado. It is not very **easy** to tell which direction a tornado's path may be, as its direction may change in a matter of minutes due to its spinning nature. **Tornadoes can be dangerously unpredictable and destructive depending on its size and speed and how long it lasts for.**

# REVISE YOUR NON-FICTION WRITING TO EXPAND ON RELEVANT IDEAS

The purpose of non-fiction writing is to communicate accurate and concrete information to an audience searching for information on many different topics. The topics can range from different people, to different places, to different ideas, concepts, theories, events and even things. As long as the information is completely true, it is considered non-fiction.

It is important when you are writing a non-fiction piece, that you stay close to the topic you are writing about and the point or idea that you want to get across.

While you want to stay close to your topic and be as direct as possible when writing about a non-fiction topic, you also want to make sure that you are giving **enough information** about the topic being discussed. Sometimes you may have to **elaborate or expand** on the subtopic being discussed within a paragraph. Elaborating on the important topics, or details, will make sure your reader is getting the most important information about the topic being discussed.

*Example*
Let's say you were writing a report on the African Elephant. The paragraph below might be an example of what African Elephants look like.

African elephants are gray. They are big and tall and they have really big ears. Elephants are heavy in weight. They have a long trunk and two tusks.

---

This paragraph sounds like it has quite a bit of information in it, but we are still left questioning many things. The elephant is gray? What kind of gray? It's big and tall and heavy too, but how heavy or how tall? What are its ears like? What does the trunk look like and what is it used for?

*Example*
If we were to answer these questions in a report, our readers might be left with a lot fewer questions, than they would be when reading the vague first paragraph. Let's give this a try again.

African elephants are one of the largest animals in the world. If you were to measure them up to their shoulders they might measure up to four meters high! They are extremely heavy in weight and can weigh more than 14,000 pounds! That's huge! African Elephants are well known for their large ears that droop down and look something like the continent of Africa. African Elephants have a very long trunk that is used for breathing, smelling, eating and drinking. The trunk has over 100,000 different muscles in it! On either side of the trunk, the elephant has something called tusks, and these tusks are made out of ivory. Elephants are huge, unbelievable mammals to see.

Did you see how the second example of the same topic elaborated a lot more of the African Elephant's appearance, and gave the reader a more vivid idea of what the elephant might look like? This is what writers need to be aware of. They want to be able to paint the picture of what they are talking about into their readers' minds. By giving more specific details, you can make this happen for your readers.

## Now It's Your Turn to Try

Can you take this paragraph and add some more details to it, so it helps the reader to truly visualize what peacocks look like? Once you think you have a great paragraph, look at the solution below, as well.

Peacocks are colorful birds. There are typically the Blue Peacocks and the Green Peacocks. They both have lots of large feathers and lots of "eye" looking circles on their feathers.

Peacocks are very colorful birds. There are typically called Blue Peacocks or Green Peacocks. Depending on which peacock it is, the name gives away the color of body the peacock will have. Both peacocks have many large feathers that fan out from their body. Their feathers are 60% larger than the length of their bodies. On their feathers they have bright blue, gold, red as well as other hued circles, that many refer to as looking like a singular eye. These "eye" looking markings are found all over the feathers.

*5W.8    Recall relevant information from experiences or gather relevant information from print and digital sources; summarize or paraphrase information in notes and finished work, and provide a list of sources.*

## Use the Appropriate Graphic Organizer to Sort Information

A graphic organizer is a great tool for students to visually sort and organize information.

When sorting information, a commonly used graphic organizer is the Venn Diagram. A Venn Diagram is best used to sort two or more items, separating their differences on each side with the center consisting of the item's similarities. It looks likes circles overlapping each other about half way.

Below are a list of facts that relate to either a shark, a dolphin or both. A Venn Diagram would be an example of a graphic organizer to sort the information into groups.

## Characteristics of Sharks

- Tough, elastic skin
- More teeth
- Great sense of smell
- A scary appearance
- Are a fish

## CHARACTERISTICS OF DOLPHINS

- Smooth, rubbery skin
- Less teeth
- No sense of smell
- Friendly appearance
- Are mammals

## VENN DIAGRAM ORGANIZER

There are many kinds of graphic organizers which can help you sort information. The type of graphic organizer you use depends on the needs of you as a student and the task.

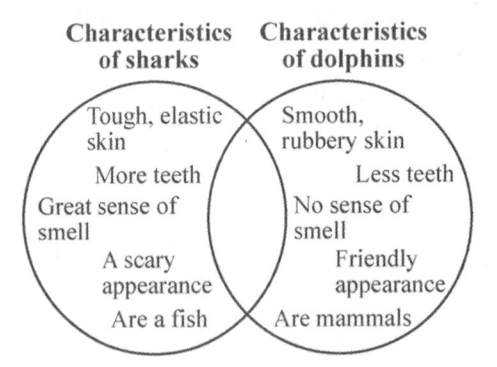

**Characteristics of sharks**
- Tough, elastic skin
- More teeth
- Great sense of smell
- A scary appearance
- Are a fish

**Characteristics of dolphins**
- Smooth, rubbery skin
- Less teeth
- No sense of smell
- Friendly appearance
- Are mammals

Other graphic organizers include the following:

- Plot diagrams
- Mind maps
- Thought webs
- Network trees
- Charts
- Tables

## USE KNOWLEDGE OF A RUBRIC TO ENHANCE WRITING

It is important for you to understand how a rubric works so you may use it to help enhance your writing. This enhancement can happen once you see the areas that need improvement, after doing a writing project and observing your scores on a rubric.

Let's look at how a rubric works, in order to determine where you can use improvement in your writing projects.

A rubric is a way to grade or monitor your own or someone else's project or assignment. A rubric usually has different categories or skills which the project focuses on, or requires. The rubric has a low level of achievement, with a description of what that low level might look like for each category. It will also show you a high level of achievement, with a description of what that high level might look like for the same categories. Depending on the rubric, there may also be a couple of other medium or proficent levels of achievement in the center of the rubric, with descriptions of what those levels might look like, as well.

| | |
|---|---|
| Level 1 | Represents a writing project that is not adequate and needs improvement. It does not stay on topic. Purpose is unclear and/or unsuitable. Information often confusing, incorrect, or inadequate. Order is confusing, topic sentences unclear. Style inappropriate for audience and purpose. No variation in sentence lengths, and little or no description. Several errors in paragraph structure, many spelling, punctuation errors. Project is mostly unreadable. |
| Level 2 | Represents a writing project that is adequate and needs some improvement. It is sometimes off topic, and the purpose is vague or not quite suitable. Information is sometimes confusing or inadequate. Order may be confusing. Some clear topic sentences, but no clear beginning, middle, and end. Style is not quite appropriate for audience and purpose. Some sentence lengths varied, description vague. Errors in paragraph structure, spelling, and punctuation. Somewhat readable. |
| Level 3 | Represents a writing project that is proficient and needs minimal improvements. It is mostly on topic, with a generally clear purpose, and is suitable. Information is mostly clear and seldom inadequate for purpose. Order generally makes sense, with mostly clear topic sentences, and a generally clear beginning, middle, and end. Style is generally appropriate, with most sentence lengths varied. Description general. Minor errors in paragraph structure, spelling, and punctuation. Readable. The project will need slight improvement to get to a level of excellence. |
| Level 4 | Represents a writing project that is at a level of excellence. It is always on topic, clear in purpose, and suitable for intended audience. Information is clear, correct, complete. The order makes sense, with clear topic sentences, and clear beginning, middle, and end. Style is appropriate, with varied sentence lengths. Description is vivid. Paragraph structure is correct, with no spelling or punctuation errors. Project is completely readable. |

Below is an example of a score-based rubric.

| Skill | Score Level (1 to 4) |
|---|---|
| Focus/Organization | 4 |
| Content | 4 |
| Style | 4 |
| Conventions | 4 |
| Total | 16 |

If there were 4 categories or skills to be assessed, then you would be graded out of 1 to 4 on each skill. If you did exactly what was asked of you in each category with no room for improvement you might score top marks of 4 in all for categories. 4 plus 4 plus 4 plus 4 would equal a total of 16 points. 16 points would be the maximum amount you could score.

Another example of scoring a rubric may not look so perfect! Let's say that in two skills you scored a 2 out of 4, in another skill you scored 3 out of 4, and the last skill you scored 4 out of 4. What would your total score be?

| Skill | Score Level (1 to 4) |
|---|---|
| Focus/Organization | 2 |
| Content | 2 |
| Style | 3 |
| Conventions | 4 |
| Total | 11 |

If you guessed 11 out of 16, you would be correct. How did we come to the number 11? We added the **two** scores of 2, plus 3, plus 4.
2 + 2 + 3 + 4 = 11

If you had this type of scoring on a rubric, you might choose to look at what area you scored lowest on. In this case you would look at the two skills you scored a 2 in and work to improve those areas of your writing.

*5W.6  With some guidance and support from adults, use technology, including the Internet, to produce and publish writing as well as to interact and collaborate with others; demonstrate sufficient command of keyboarding skills to type a minimum...*

## USE ELECTRONIC DICTIONARIES AND THESAURUSES

The purpose of this lesson is to introduce you to a few online websites that have electronic word searches (dictionaries) and thesauruses. Please keep in mind that these are online sources, which means you need to treat them with caution. They might not always have the best information or the most accurate and up to date data.

## USING AN ONLINE WORD SEARCH (DICTIONARY)

One of the most popular online dictionary and thesaurus websites is http://dictionary.reference.com/ but there are many more that you can use. Below you will find a list of online dictionaries along with a brief description for each one.

1. http://dictionary.cambridge.org/
   A great dictionary site that offers features like idioms, phrasal verbs and a learner's dictionary.
2. http://www.merriam-webster.com/dictionary/
   A great dictionary, a free translator, and even a medial dictionary that will read aloud most terms that you look up
3. http://www.thefreedictionary.com/
   A great site because even if you are not sure about the spelling of a word, you can type in the part that you know and it will figure out the rest. Another great feature of this site is that it can look up whole articles of information.
4. http://www.webster-dictionary.org/
   Webster dictionary is one of the most popular dictionaries out there. It is a reliable source of information. However, it is written at a higher level of complexity.
5. http://www.visuwords.com/
   This is an very helpful site that will look up the definition of a word. It is also both a thesaurus and a visual dictionary. Simply place your cursor over the word bubbles and the information will be shown.

## USING AN ONLINE THESAURUS

If you would like to look up a word in a thesaurus, there are many great sites for that too. Below you will find a list of online thesauruses and a brief description for each one.

1. http://thesaurus.com/
   One of the most commonly used sites. It is fast and very easy to use.
2. http://www.visualthesaurus.com/
   A great site that will map out your word with others that have similar ideas, and will also read them aloud. Finally, it will look up the words it suggests.
3. http://freethesaurus.net/
   A nice site that suggests many words for anything you decide to search for. It is easy to use and uses simple language.
4. http://www.wordsmyth.net/
   A great feature of Wordsmyth is that you can select the level of language you would like it to use, anything from beginner, children, to advanced!

## WHAT IS A BIBLIOGRAPHY?

When you look at the parts of the word, *bibliography*, it helps to know that "biblio" came from a Greek word meaning *book*, and "graph" came from a word meaning *write*. It means to write down your books.
A bibliography is a list of books, magazines, films, and websites that you have used for your research.

It is important to list every source that you use. This shows respect for the authors and websites that have shared their information with you. A bibliography for someone's research on New Orleans might look something like the one below.

## Bibliography

Downs, Tom, Edge, John. "New Orleans." The Lonely Planet, 2006.

Faulkner, William. *New Orleans Sketches*. College Press of Mississippi: New Orleans, 2002.

Gotham, Kevin. *Authentic New Orleans: Tourism, Culture, and Race in the Big Easy.* College Press: New York, 2007.

"New Orleans Before and After Katrina", New Orleans Office of Tourism, www.bigeasy.org. 2010.

## Create a Bibliography

The creation of a bibliography starts as soon as you begin preparing a report, speech, or any researched writing project. You need to keep track of where you are getting your information. That way you are showing respect for the work or ideas belonging to someone else. This is done simply by writing the name of the author and title of the work that you are using.

Things that you need to keep in mind are:

- author's name
- title of work
- publishing company
- location of publishing company
- date

There are also websites that can help you manage all the information you need for your bibliography. **Noodletools.com** is a great site that asks you to fill in a few information boxes. Then, it will create the reference for you in the proper format that is needed.

Below you will find an example of how a bibliography is written. You must also remember that entries in your bibliography are written in alphabetical order according to the author's last name.

*Example*
**Correct Order**: Author's last name, author's first name. "Title of piece of work." Publishing company: publishing company's location, year of publication.

Bennet, Lerone. *What Manner of Man: A Biography of Martin Luther King Jr.* Chicago: Johnson, 1964.

King Martin Luther Jr. *Why We Can't Wait*. New York: Harper and Row, 1963.

Martin Luther King, Jr. Wikipedia, the free encyclopedia:Wikipedia.org/wiki/Martin_Luther_King_Jr.

Smith, John. "Importance of being Humble." College of Calgary Press: Calgary, 2010.

## GATHER FACTS USING PRIMARY RESOURCES

*Primary resources* are valuable sources of information because they offer a believable inside view of a particular event. A primary source is an original source of information created at the time the event occurred.

Primary sources are valuable in gathering facts because they are not altered or changed. The facts that you gather are coming straight from someone who witnessed, first hand, the event in question.

*Example*
*The Diary of Anne Frank* and The Declaration of Independence are examples of primary resources.

Any original document, artifact, manuscript, diary or photograph is considered a primary resource.

---

*Example*
The following is a journal entry from an explorer of the Arctic circle on December 2, 1938:

"It was –38°C when our mission was aborted. Our ship hit an iceberg at 3:37 A.M.. No one witnessed it hit but we all felt it. The captain called the crew to the main deck to assess the damage. I stood at his side to support him as he broke the terrifying news. The ship has been punctured too many times and would soon capsize. We has less than 30 minutes to gather our things and evacuate the ship-the ship that had been my home for nearly 20 years. The life boats were almost prepared when the ship began sinking quickly. I witnessed two terrified men jump overboard into the icy water. Forty five men escaped the icy waters of the Arctic that early morning and only five men perished."

---

This journal entry is considered a primary resource because it was written by a man who not only witnessed the event at the time the event occurred, but also experienced it first hand.

If I were researching Arctic explorers and I came across this journal entry, it would provide me with valuable information about a tragic night that happened many years ago.

## GATHER FACTS USING SECONDARY RESOURCES

A secondary resource is an interpretation of a primary resource. It's the next best thing if the primary (original) resource isn't available.

Secondary resources are valuable resources because they are summaries and interpretations of events that are created after the event has occurred. The facts included in a secondary resource can contain more details, because the writer many have included information from many sources before evaluating what important details should be included.

*Example*

An encyclopedia, a biography, and a newspaper article about a particular person or event are examples of secondary sources.

Figure 2: Europe – 1919

If you were gathering facts on World War II, it might be useful to look at newspaper articles and books written after the war so that you have post war facts. The secondary resources may be created from many other reviews of the War, and not by a person who fought in it.

## ANALYZE DETAILS AND INFORMATION FROM REFERENCE MATERIAL

If you are asked to evaluate something you have read (a newspaper/magazine article or editorial cartoon), you need to describe the positive and negative qualities of the selection and then reach a conclusion about how good (or bad) the piece is.

As you evaluate the article, you will need to examine how well it is organized and whether the 5 W and 1 H questions are answered:

- Who is involved?
- What happened?
- When did it happen?
- Where did it happen?
- Why did it happen?
- How did it happen?

As you read the article, you will examine how well the information is supported by facts and opinions. The clearer the information is, the easier the article will be to read and understand.

## Barkerville Gazette

The lead, or first, paragraph of a newspaper article gives the main information.

### Dog Rescues Owner

Local artist Warren McComb is grateful that his pooch, Coyote, hates the smell of burning oil paint. McComb had fallen asleep on the sofa in his studio, shortly after 9 P.M. last evening, when he awakened to the frantic barking of his small dog in the smoke-filled room. Fortunately, there was enough visibility for him to grab the dog and exit to the patio, where he called 911. Firemen arrived in moments and quickly extinguished flames coming from a wastebasket.

Fire officials are still investigating the cause of the fire. Fire Marshall Kennie reports that the culprit may well be the brave dog. A charred and partially chewed lamp cord was discovered, still plugged in, right next to an overflowing wastebasket.

Warren McComb needs to redecorate his studio, but will not punish Coyote for chewing on the cord. "I'll just buy him some real bones," he promised with a grin.

*Analyze the Information*

If you use the 5 W's and 1 H questions to guide your analysis of the information in the news article, you will discover the following details:

- Who - Local artist Warren McComb and his dog, Coyote
- What - a fire
- When - shortly after 9 P.M. last evening
- Where - Warren McComb's studio
- Why - dog was chewing on lamp cord
- How - wire was exposed by chewing, and ignited contents of wastebasket

*5W.9a Draw evidence from literary or informational texts to support analysis, reflection, and research. Apply grade 5 Reading standards to literature.*

## MAKING INFERENCES WHILE READING
## WHAT IS INFERENCING?

Inferencing is making a guess, inferring, or drawing conclusions about what is happening in a story.

*Example*
If I was holding a pencil in my hand then asked you for a pencil sharpener, why do you think I asked for a pencil sharpener?

You might guess that I need to sharpen my pencil. This is making a inference, I did not tell you what I needed the sharpener for you just guess that since I was holding a pencil I wanted to sharpen it.

---

Authors sometimes do this in their writing, they do not tell their readers everything but rather have their readers make inferences about what might be happening.

## MAKING INFERENCES

Read the following scenarios and make an inference (guess) about what you think is happening or going to happen.

1. Before she left she put her raincoat on and grabbed her umbrella from the closet.
2. The children ran towards the pool with their swimsuits on.
3. Her bag was packed with her glove, bat and favorite ball.

What do you think was happening or going to happen next in the above scenarios?

Here are some possible answers:

1. Since she put on her raincoat and grabbed her umbrella before leaving we can infer that it was raining outside.

2. Since the children had on their swimsuits and were running towards the pool we can infer that they were going swimming.
3. Since her bag was packed with a glove, bat and ball we can infer that she was going to play baseball.

## MAKING INFERENCES ABOUT CHARACTERS

The author of a story that you may be reading does not always provide you with all the details of how a character might be feeling or what they may do next. Sometimes the author just provides you with little hints and you are left to infer the character's actual feelings or motives. Making conclusions about a character's feelings or motives is called inferencing.

# MAKING INFERENCES

*Example*
What can you infer about the characters in the following scenarios?

1. She reached for a tissue and took a deep breath as she wiped away her tears.
2. James' hands shook as he turned the nob and opened the door to the dark and deserted house.
3. The sun's rays were beating down as she wiped the sweat from her brow and panted across the finish line.

What inferences did you make about the above characters?

Here are some possible answers:

1. Reaching for a tissue, taking a deep breath and wiping tears away we can infer the character is sad.
2. Shaking hands opening a dark and deserted house we can infer that the character is nervous.
3. Sun's rays, wiping sweat, panting, and crossing the finish line we can infer that the character is hot and tired.

*5W.9b Draw evidence from literary or informational texts to support analysis, reflection, and research. Apply grade 5 Reading standards to informational texts.*

## SUPPORTING GENERALIZATIONS ABOUT TEXT WITH TEXTUAL EVIDENCE

Generalizations occur when the author makes a statement that goes beyond what the evidence supports. Generalizations usually contain words like *always*, *never*, *all*, *must*, *everyone*, and *nobody*. An example of a generalization would be to write the statement "All soccer players will tell you that their shoes are their most important equipment." The word *all* makes this a generalization because there are probably players for whom different pieces of equipment are more important. You cannot ask every single soccer player in the world what they think the most important piece of equipment is, so a more fair statement to make would be "Shoes are a very important piece of equipment for soccer players."

When you read a text, you can generalize or draw broader conclusions. Just make sure that you can support your conclusions or generalizations with evidence from the text.

*Example*
Tsunamis are caused by underwater earthquakes and volcanic eruptions, and they are the largest waves of all (**main idea**). Earthquakes occur when two **tectonic plates** collide or slide past each other. When an earthquake occurs under the ocean, the ocean bottom shakes. This movement causes the water above to become **displaced**. Waves of energy spread out in all directions from the source of the vibrations in ever-widening circles. As the tsunami approaches shore, the waves rub against the sea floor. **Friction** causes the waves to slow down and build from behind, creating huge piles of water that crash onto the shore.

All the other sentences support the main idea that tsunamis are caused by underwater earthquakes and volcano eruptions. The main idea is kind of a generalization in that it states a fairly broad main idea for the paragraph. You could support a few other generalizations, as well:

- Tsunamis will not occur in a land-locked area.
- Waves of energy spread in all directions from the source.
- Water only builds up as it slows down.
- People in coastal areas where tectonic plates meet could be in danger from tsunami activity.

---

## SUPPORTING CONCLUSIONS ABOUT TEXT WITH TEXTUAL EVIDENCE

After reading a piece of writing you should think about the text and come to a conclusion on what you have read. A conclusion is the main idea of the text.

Support your conclusion about a story using the following three steps:

1. Read the story
2. Think about what you have read and what the story means to you and form a conclusion.
3. Reread the story, and support your ideas with evidence from the story.

## READING THE PIECE OF WRITING

Read "The Clever Turtle", and try to come to a conclusion about what you have read.

---

### The Clever Turtle

*Come south of the equator, to the western coast of Africa, to where lies the land of Angola. Come to the village and sit around the evening fire and hear the old-time tales. Come help the storyteller weave a spell as he tells of the clever turtle.*

*One day, so goes the tale, a man left his village to tend to his field of maize. But he found only an open, empty place where before the young corn had stood straight and tall.*

*The man looked down at the poor broken stalks and saw a large turtle dozing in the sun. He caught the turtle and carried it back to the village.*

*The man said:* "What can we do to this turtle? It has crushed my corn."

*The people said:* "We should punish it. That is what we should do."

*The man said:* "How can we punish it?"

*The people said:* "Cook him for stew!"

*The turtle said:* "That's exactly what to do! I'd make a tasty turtle stew. But please, don't throw me into the river!"

*The man said:* "This turtle is not afraid of fire. What else can we do?"

*The people said:* "Tie him to a tree!"

*The turtle said:* "Do anything you like with me. Tie me to the strongest tree. But please, *please*, don't throw me into the river!"

*The man said:* "This turtle is not afraid of fire. This turtle is not afraid of rope. What else can we do?"

*The people said:* "Place him in a hole in the ground!"

*The turtle said:* "What is all this talk about? Dig the hole deep so I can't climb out. But please, *please*, PLEASE, don't throw me into the river!"

*The man said:* "This turtle is not afraid of fire. This turtle is not afraid of rope. This turtle is not afraid of earth. Now, what can we do?"

*The people said:* "Throw him into the river!"

*The turtle said:* "NO! Not the river! Can't you see? That river will be the end of me!"

*The people said:* "We have found a way. We will throw him into the river!"

*So the people carried the turtle to the river bank.*

*They threw him far out to where the water was the deepest. But suddenly the river water whirled and swirled and splattered and splashed, and up paddled the turtle as pleased as could be.*

*The man said:* "I think that turtle has tricked us."

*The people said:* "Indeed! That turtle has been more clever than we!"

*The turtle said:* "Born and bred in a river bed! Born and bred in a river bed! You just could not get the best of me!"

*Then the clever turtle swam away and was never ever seen near the village again.*

—*retold by* A.K. Roche

## WHAT THE STORY MEANS TO YOU

Think about the clues in the story, your own background knowledge, and form a conclusion.

*Example*
I think that this story is trying to teach us not to give up even in tough situations.

---

## REREADING THE STORY AND LISTING THE INFORMATION THAT SUPPORTS YOUR CONCLUSION

*Example*
The turtle gets captured and does not stop trying to get free until he does.

You can support your conclusion by the information in the following list:

- Every time the people suggest a way to punish the turtle, he shows no fear of what they suggest and tells them not to throw him in the river. The people say: "Cook him for stew!" The turtle says: "That's exactly what to do! I'd make a tasty turtle stew. But please, don't throw me into the river!"
- The turtle is being tricky by suggesting to the people not to throw him into the river, because that is what he really wants them to do. In reality, the turtle wants them to throw him into the river because that is where he was "Born and bred" (line 35).
- The people continue suggesting different ways to punish the turtle, but he continues to show no fear of what they suggest.
- Finally, the people believe that the turtle is really afraid of the river so they decide to punish him by throwing him into the river. The people say: Throw him into the river!" The turtle says: "NO! Not the river! Can't you see? That river will be the end of me!"
- The turtle gets away from the people. He never gives up until he is free.

# NOTES

# NOTES

# NOTES

# Practice Exercises

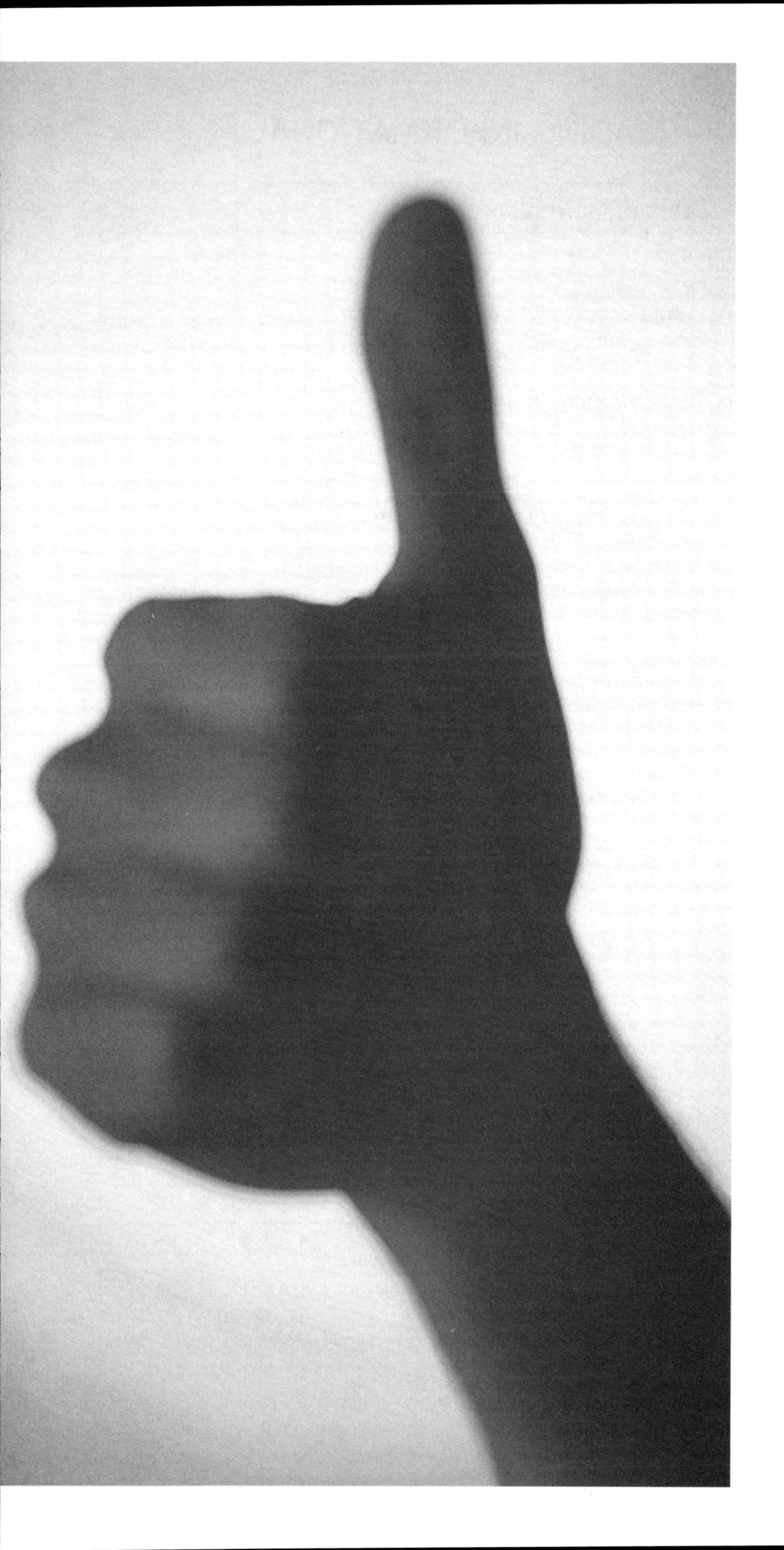

# EXERCISE #1—READING INFORMATIONAL

## Table of Correlations

| | Standard | Test #1 |
|---|---|---|
| **5RL** | **Reading Standards for Literature** | |
| 5RL.2 | Determine a theme of a story, drama, or poem from details in the text, including how characters in a story or drama respond to challenges or how the speaker in a poem reflects upon a topic; summarize the text. | 16, 22, 23, 24, 27, 28, 34, 35, 36, 39, 40, 42, 43, 44, 45, 48, 49 |
| 5RL.3 | Compare and contrast two or more characters, settings, or events in a story or drama, drawing on specific details in the text. | 17 |
| 5RL.9 | Compare and contrast stories in the same genre on their approaches to similar themes and topics. | 17 |
| 5RL.10 | By the end of the year, read and comprehend literature, including stories, dramas, and poetry, at the high end of the grades 4–5 text complexity band independently and proficiently. | 12 |
| **5RI** | **Reading Standards for Informational Text** | |
| 5RI.2 | Determine two or more main ideas of a text and explain how they are supported by key details; summarize the text. | 16, 22, 23, 24, 27, 28, 34, 35, 36, 39, 40, 42, 43, 44, 45, 48, 49 |
| 5RI.3 | Explain the relationships or interactions between two or more individuals, events, ideas, or concepts in a historical, scientific, or technical text based on specific information in the text. | 17 |
| 5RI.5 | Compare and contrast the overall structure of events, ideas, concepts, or information in two or more texts. | 33 |
| 5RI.8 | Explain how an author uses reasons and evidence to support particular points in a text, identifying which reasons and evidence support which point(s). | 17, 30, 31, 32 |
| 5RI.9 | Integrate information from several texts on the same topic in order to write or speak about the subject knowledgeably. | 17 |
| **5RF** | **Reading Standards: Foundational Skills** | |
| 5RF.3a | Know and apply grade-level phonics and word analysis skills in decoding words. Use combined knowledge of all letter-sound correspondences, syllabication patterns, and morphology to read accurately unfamiliar multisyllabic words in context... | 1, 2, 3, 5, 6, 7, 9, 13, 14, 21, 25, 37, 50, 51 |
| 5RF.4a | Read with sufficient accuracy and fluency to support comprehension. Read on-level text with purpose and understanding. | 29 |
| 5RF.4b | Read with sufficient accuracy and fluency to support comprehension. Read on-level prose and poetry orally with accuracy, appropriate rate, and expression on successive readings. | 29 |
| 5RF.4c | Read with sufficient accuracy and fluency to support comprehension. Use context to confirm or self-correct word recognition and understanding, rereading as necessary. | 2, 3, 5, 6, 7, 13, 14, 21, 25, 29, 51 |
| **5W** | **Writing Standards** | |
| 5W.9a | Draw evidence from literary or informational texts to support analysis, reflection, and research. Apply grade 5 Reading standards to literature. | 8, 10, 11, 20, 38, 53 |
| 5W.9b | Draw evidence from literary or informational texts to support analysis, reflection, and research. Apply grade 5 Reading standards to informational texts. | 8, 10, 11, 17, 20, 30, 31, 32, 38 |
| **5SL** | **Speaking and Listening Standards** | |
| 5SL.2 | Summarize a written text read aloud or information presented in diverse media and formats, including visually, quantitatively, and orally. | 22 |

| | | |
|---|---|---|
| 5SL.3 | Summarize the points a speaker makes and explain how each claim is supported by reasons and evidence. | 17, 22, 30, 31, 32 |
| **5L** | **Language Standards** | |
| 5L.1b | Demonstrate command of the conventions of standard English grammar and usage when writing or speaking. Form and use the perfect verb tenses. | 15 |
| 5L.1c | Demonstrate command of the conventions of standard English grammar and usage when writing or speaking. Use verb tense to convey various times, sequences, states, and conditions. | 15 |
| 5L.2d | Demonstrate command of the conventions of standard English capitalization, punctuation, and spelling when writing. Use underlining, quotation marks, or italics to indicate titles of works. | 4 |
| 5L.3b | Use knowledge of language and its conventions when writing, speaking, reading, or listening. Compare and contrast the varieties of English used in stories, dramas, or poems. | 17 |
| 5L.4a | Determine or clarify the meaning of unknown and multiple-meaning words and phrases based on grade 5 reading and content, choosing flexibly from a range of strategies. Use context as a clue to the meaning of a word or phrase. | 2, 3, 5, 6, 7, 13, 14, 21, 25, 51 |
| 5L.5c | Demonstrate understanding of figurative language, word relationships, and nuances in word meanings. Use the relationship between particular words to better understand each of the words. | 3, 13, 18, 19, 26, 41, 46, 47, 52 |

*Read the following passage and answer questions 1 to 4*

## Daniel Boone (1734–1820)

*The life of Daniel Boone is the stuff of American legend. Though many of the stories of Boone's exploits are fictional, the true events of his life are just as remarkable.*

Born in Pennsylvania in 1734, Daniel Boone was one of eleven children in a hearty and close-knit family. He was a gifted hunter, spending much of his childhood exploring the
5 wilderness. His love of solitude and his desire to be far from civilization remained constant throughout his life.

When he was a teenager, Boone's family relocated to North Carolina. Living in the wilds along the Yadkin River, Boone continued to develop his hunting skills. He also fought for the British in the French and Indian War. He began to hear to hear stories of a pristine
10 and captivating wilderness west of the Appalachian Mountains.

He first traveled over the mountains to present-day Kentucky on one of his long hunting expeditions in 1767, but he was not able to make an extended stay until 1769. Organizing a party that included five companions and many horses, Boone journeyed over the Blue Ridge Mountains and north to an old Indian trail, which led through a
15 gateway in the mountains called the Cumberland Gap.

Passing through the gap, Boone and his men left the frontier behind and entered a land untouched by Western settlement. Magnificent wooded vistas overflowing with game captured Boone's heart. He established a permanent camp, not returning to North Carolina until two years later, in 1771.

20 In North Carolina, Boone and his wife, Rebecca, had a growing family of their own. They encountered the increasing problem of too many settlers and hunters for the available land. Along with seven other families, the Boones set out through the Cumberland Gap to make a new home in Kentucky, but the party was attacked by Indians. Six people were killed, including Boone's eldest son, James. Heartbroken, the family temporarily
25 abandoned their journey.

But Boone's reputation as a formidable scout, hunter, and explorer continued to grow. He became known as a man who did not lose his head in a crisis and who learned from his experiences. Captured by Indians more than once, Boone always emerged unscathed. An avid reader, he carried one of his favorite books, *Gulliver's Travels,* on his Kentucky trips.

30 Many settlers began to share Boone's interest in Kentucky, and a land agent hired Boone in 1775 to make a road along the old Indian trail through the Cumberland Gap. With a crew of men, Boone cut away fallen trees, cleared underbrush, and built makeshift bridges. The resulting route, called the Wilderness Road, led all the way to the Kentucky River and attracted thousands of families seeking new homes.

35 Boone organized a settlement and fort called Boonesborough, on the Kentucky River. By the mid-1780s, over thirty thousand people had settled in the territory. After the American Revolution, Boone established a second settlement, now called Boone Station, north of the Kentucky River. He eventually moved even farther west to Missouri and lived his last years hunting and trapping on the long, quiet trips that he loved.

40 **The Abduction and Rescue of Jemima Boone**

One of the most celebrated and retold Daniel Boone stories centers on his daughter Jemima. In 1776, Boone and his family were living in the settlement of Boonesborough on the Kentucky River. Thirteen-year-old Jemima decided to take a canoe onto the river with two of her friends, fourteen- and sixteen-year-old sisters Fanny and Elizabeth
45 Callaway. Paddling farther away from the settlement than they should have, the three girls were surprised by a group of five Cherokee and Shawnee Indians. Indian resistance to frontier settlers had been growing rapidly, and the Cherokee and Shawnee were among the tribes angered by their displacement. Recognizing that one of the girls was the child of the famous pioneer Daniel Boone, the Indians jumped at the chance for
50 revenge. They sped off with the girls, but not before their shrieks alerted their families back at the settlement.

Hastily gathering a group of men to join him, Boone took off in pursuit of the Indians. The girls had done their best to leave a trail, snapping branches as they were dragged along. Nonetheless, Boone was ten miles behind the children. For three days, Boone and his
55 men fought their way through the brush, desperate to draw closer before the five Indians rejoined their war parties.

In an episode now dramatically re-created in paintings and stories, Boone and his party reached the Indians' encampment at sunset of the third day and crept up on it like panthers. In a flash of gunpowder, they overpowered and scattered the Indians, and the
60 three weeping girls were rescued. Terrified and exhausted, the girls explained that, though they had been pushed at a frightening pace, the Indians had otherwise treated them with kindness. The grateful and relieved men escorted the girls back home. The girls all married within a year of their capture. All three grooms were members of the rescue party that had brought them to safety.

65 —from *The Look-It-Up Book of Explorers* by Elizabeth Cody Kimmel

1. In the first paragraph, the phrase "close-knit family" means people who
   A. like to sew together
   B. live near each other
   C. are enemies of one another
   D. are very supportive of one another

2. In the sentence "When he was a teenager, Boone's family relocated to North Carolina,"[line 7] the word "relocated" means
   A. remained in the same place
   B. traveled across a river
   C. lived in the wilderness
   D. moved to a new place

3. A synonym for the word "magnificent," as it is used in the phrase "Magnificent wooded vistas overflowing with game,"[line 17] is
   A. large
   B. splendid
   C. palatial
   D. skillful

4. In the passage, *Gulliver's Travels* is italicized because it
   A. is the title of a book
   B. is written in another language
   C. was not the true title of the book
   D. was about another man's journeys

*Read the following passage and answer questions 5 to 8*

### Beetles

Beetles, beetles, beetles! You are surrounded by beetles! That's right! It is a fact that beetles would outnumber every other kind of animal at a worldwide animal convention. That's because fully one-quarter of all animals are actually beetles. You can pretty much find beetles anywhere in the world, even under water! Scientists have spent many hours
5 trying to figure out what makes beetles champions at surviving in such huge numbers. The answer seems to lie in an impressive beetle adaptation called the elytra.

The elytra is like a special suit of protective armor for beetles. Gradually, a hard casing, or shell, develops above the soft front wings of the beetles, meeting in a straight line down their backs. This elytra not only protects the fragile wings, but also prevents attacks
10 from both parasites (creatures which burrow inside something living to eat it) and predators (creatures which chew on something living from the outside). Because the elytra is hard, it holds moisture and coolness inside for beetles. Beetles don't even mind desert heat because the elytra provides them with their own personal air conditioners. Some beetles are further protected by their shape. They can be very flat and able to hide
15 in tiny, safe locations deep inside cracks or under rocks.

Do you think that one million years is a long time? Try 350 million years! That's how long scientists believe that beetles have been adapting and reproducing. During that time, beetles have produced some weird and wonderful world beetle champions. Some of these champions are described here for you.

20 **WORLD BEETLE CHAMPIONS**

**Largest**

The largest beetle would be the South American beetle known as *Titanus giganteus*. The name means "huge giant". This tropical beetle can measure more than 17 centimeters (6 ½ inches) in length, and can chop a pencil in half with mighty jaws called mandibles.

25 **Smallest**

The smallest beetle would be the featherwing beetle. It is barely visible at a length of one quarter of a millimeter (1/100 inch).

**Heaviest**

The champion heavyweight would be the goliath beetle, which weighs in at up to 100
30 grams (3 ½ ounces). Picture a large apple for comparison!

> **Longest**
>
> The champion of length is the Brazilian longhorn beetle. It stretches to an impressive record length of 20 centimeters (8 inches).
>
> **Strongest**
>
> 35 The mightiest beetle in the world is the African scarab or rhinoceros beetle. Because it is capable of lifting 850 times its own body weight, this beetle holds the record for being the world's strongest animal.

5. According to the passage, a "parasite" is a creature that
   A. depends on others for food and shelter
   B. feeds on the bodies of others
   C. lives on the bodies of others
   D. dislikes others

6. The elytra are a beetle's
   A. wing covers
   B. soft wings
   C. antennae
   D. legs

7. In this passage, the word "mandibles" refers to a beetle's
   A. eyes
   B. jaws
   C. horns
   D. antennae

8. What is the name of the world's heaviest beetle?
   A. Rhinoceros beetle
   B. Feathering beetle
   C. Longhorn beetle
   D. Goliath beetle

*Read the following passage and answer questions 9 to 12*

### Monsters from the Deep and Other Imaginary Beings

Moving day. Groan. All that stuff. For most of us, moving day doesn't happen too often. For Michael Kusugak, growing up in the far north, moving was a way of life. For the first six years of his life, Michael lived in the age-old Inuit tradition of traveling. The family traveled by dog-team in search of whales, seals and cariboo. In winter they lived in
5  igloos. In summer they pitched a tent. The nomadic life is not a life for collecting possessions. The family had only the essentials—furs, weapons and tools. But they also had something that required no space and had no weight, but which was essential to their survival. They had stories.

Small Michael would fall asleep every night listening to the stories of his parents and
10  grandmother. Legends, family stories, funny stories, stories with something to teach. He heard tales of the animals he knew—the bear, the cariboo, the squirrel. And he heard stories of imaginary beings.

When Michael grew up, he remembered a story told in the spring. In the far north spring can be a dangerous time for children as the sea ice begins to break up. To keep their
15  children away from the hazardous shore, parents tell stories of the Qallupilluit, a witchy undersea creature who kidnaps children. In *A Promise Is a Promise* (written with Robert Munsch), Michael Kusugak invents his own version of the Qallupilluit and puts it into the world where he lives now—a world of jeans, TV and computers.

—from *The Young Writer's Companion* by Sarah Ellis

9. The statement "The nomadic life is not a life for collecting possessions" **most likely** means that possessions
   A. can be stolen
   B. are too expensive
   C. make moving more difficult
   D. break too easily to withstand constant travel

10. Michael's family followed the seals in order to
    A. take pictures of them
    B. hunt them and sell them
    C. hunt them for food and skins
    D. find their way to warmer weather

11. According to the passage, Michael Kusugak's family traveled by
    A. horseback
    B. camper
    C. dog-team
    D. snowmobile

12. In the statement "He heard tales of the animals he knew,"[line 10] the word "tales" **most likely** refers to
    A. funny jokes
    B. bits of gossip
    C. legends or stories
    D. complicated explanations

*Read the following passage and answer questions 13 to 16*

### Joe's Junk

My name is Joe. All my life I have been a collector. I don't collect normal stuff like rocks or insects. I'm famous for my spectacular collection of junk.

"You trash it and I'll stash it!" That's my motto.

I am also a great inventor. My room is a workshop. I have a huge box of wire and some
5  old bicycle parts. I have a ball of used string you wouldn't believe. I also have two enormous jars of nuts and bolts. And that's only the beginning.

Naturally, my room is my favorite place.

But Mother sighs when she walks by my room. My father says, "Unfit for human habitation," whatever that means.

10 I have made some really super inventions with my junk. I made a new kind of family pet. It did not shed or eat much. It just rolled around the room going, "Squeak, squeak!" My aunt was at the house when I wound it up. When she heard it, she suddenly said she had to run.

One day I needed my skateboard. All the kids were going to the park. I wanted to go too,
15 but the kids got tired of waiting for me. I searched for three hours before I finally found my skateboard. It was in a box of "S" things with a Superman cape, metal springs, and 23 shoelaces. When I got through digging around, my room was in worse shape than before. Even I was disgusted!

Another day I came home and found a line of kids at the front door. My own brother,
20 Alvie, was selling tickets to the World's Largest Indoor Dump. My room, of course.

My folks finally said, "Clear it up or clear out!"

It took me some time to get around to the clean-up. One day I could hardly open the door of my room. I couldn't find my homework, which upset my teacher. I couldn't find any clean clothes, which upset my parents. But worst of all, I couldn't find the parts I needed
25 for my inventions, which upset me!

My parents were right. My collection of junk had to go. But where? And how?

Then it hit me. A garage sale was the perfect solution to my problems. I would have the Sale of the Century!

So I began to work. There was a lot to do. But when the weekend came, I had the
30 greatest bunch of bargains that I had ever seen!

At first it was hard to see my treasures go. But when I took a good look at my customers, I felt better. Many people were pulling broken wagons, just like mine. They looked like collectors, too. My junk was going to good homes. I could tell!

Well, I sold most of my terrific junk. I left the rest for the garbage collector. This pleased
35 my folks. But I got a really creepy feeling when I went into my room. I mean, it was
EMPTY! So when I saw that broken typewriter in the trash, I knew just where to put it.
Likewise for the garden hose. And I have the best idea for a new invention.

—*by* Susan Russo

13. The writer uses the word "enormous" in the phrase "two enormous jars of nuts and bolts" to show that the jars are
    A. long
    B. wide
    C. huge
    D. tall

14. In the sentence "Even I was disgusted!"[line 18] the word "disgusted" is closest in meaning to
    A. bitter
    B. bored
    C. fed up
    D. worn out

15. In which of the following tenses is the sentence "It took me some time to get around to the clean-up"[line 22] written?
    A. Past
    B. Future
    C. Present
    D. Continuous

16. Joe's mother **most likely** sighs when she walks by his room because she is
    A. worried that Joe's collection is too large
    B. displeased to see Joe's room so messy
    C. sad that Joe is not in his room
    D. tired and needing rest

*Read the following passage and answer questions 17 to 20*

### Just Imagine

Just imagine yourself in the most hostile place on earth. It's not the Sahara or the Gobi Desert. It's not the Arctic. The most hostile place on earth is the Antarctic, the location of the South Pole. North Pole, South Pole—what's the difference? The Arctic is mostly water—with ice on top, of course—and that ice is never more than a few feet thick. But
5  under the South Pole lies a continent that supports glaciers up to two miles in depth. Almost the entire southern continent is covered by ice. This mammoth icecap presses down so heavily that it actually distorts the shape of the earth. The ice never melts; it clings to the bottom of the world, spawning winds, storms, and weather that affect the whole planet.

10 And of all the weather it creates, the weather the Antarctic creates for itself is by far the worst. In the winter, the temperature can sink to 100 degrees below zero Fahrenheit. Cold air masses sliding down the sides of the glaciers speed up until they become winds of close to 200 miles per hour. When winter descends on the southern continent, the seas surrounding the land begin to freeze at the terrifying rate of two square miles every
15 minute, until the frozen sea reaches an area of 7 million square miles, about twice the size of the United States. It is truly the most hostile environment this side of the moon. Just imagine yourself stranded in such a place.

In 1915, a British crew of twenty-eight men *was* stranded there, with no ship and no way to contact the outside world. They all survived.

20 —from *Shipwreck at the Bottom of the World: The Extraordinary True Story of Shackleton and the* Endurance by Jennifer Armstrong

17. How is the Antarctic different from the Arctic? Provide three examples that show why the Antarctic is the most hostile place on Earth.

18. As it is used in the sentence "Just imagine yourself in the most hostile place on earth,"[line 1] the word "hostile" is a synonym of which of the following words?
    A. Angry
    B. Harsh
    C. Remote
    D. Extreme

19. As it is used in the sentence "This mammoth icecap presses down so heavily,"[line 6] the word "mammoth" is a synonym of which of the following words?
    A. Ancient
    B. Weighty
    C. Freezing
    D. Enormous

20. According to the comparison in the passage, about what is the area of the United States?
    A. 9.0 million square miles
    B. 4.5 million square miles
    C. 7.0 million square miles
    D. 3.5 million square miles

*Read the following passage and answer questions 21 to 24*

### from "Soft-Stone Sculpture"

*To create large stone sculptures like statues, artists cut into a huge block of rock with heavy tools until they have the shape they want. Here, you'll mix up a soft "stone" that's easy to carve.*

**Here's What You Need**

5   Vermiculite (from a plant nursery or garden supply store)
    Plaster of paris (from an art supply store)
    Bowl
    Water
    Small waxed cardboard milk or juice container
10  Newspaper
    Old blunt kitchen knife or grapefruit spoon
    Nail

**Here's What You Do**

Mix equal parts of vermiculite and plaster in a bowl. Stir in water until the mixture is like a
15  thick gravy. Pour it into the container. Let dry for 24 hours. Peel off the container.

Working on newspaper, use the knife or spoon to gently carve into the soft stone. Why not make your favorite animal? Or, create an abstract sculpture in a design or shape that's pleasing to you. Use the nail to add details.

**The Artist's Way: Michelangelo**

20  You may have heard of Michelangelo, who lived in Italy in the 1500s. He is famous for his huge, detailed painting that covers the ceiling of the Sistine Chapel at the Vatican in Rome.

Michelangelo was also a talented sculptor. He used a sharp metal tool called a *chisel* (there may be one in your house you could take a look at) to carve statues out of huge blocks of marble. He had very strong ideas about an image or idea being locked inside
25  the stone, and once said that he was trying to release the form from its rocky prison. Isn't that an interesting way to view sculpting?

> Michelangelo would often spend as long as eight months in the quarries (natural areas that stone is removed from) selecting a piece of stone for a statue. He carved one of his most famous sculptures, the 13' (4-m) *David*, from a block of stone that other sculptors
> 30 had rejected as being too tall and narrow.
>
> —from *Kids' Art Works: Creating with Color, Design, Texture &More* by Sandi Henry

21. "Old blunt kitchen knife or grapefruit spoon"

    The word "*blunt*" as used in the materials list for making soft stone means

    A. old
    B. dull
    C. sharp
    D. smooth

22. One of Michelangelo's most famous sculptures is called
    A. Michael
    B. Thomas
    C. David
    D. John

23. In this project, the nail is used to
    A. shape the soft stone
    B. hang the finished carving
    C. etch details into the carving
    D. poke a hole in the carving so that it can be hung

24. The stone from this recipe is good for trying out carving because it is
    A. the material all beginners use
    B. what Michelangelo carved in
    C. soft and easy to carve
    D. very inexpensive

*Read the following passage and answer questions 25 to 28*

### The Hot Dog Story: How the Hot Dog Linked Up with the Bun

*SPOTLIGHT ON INVENTION*
Substitute One Thing for Another to Create Something New

*Everyone who has ever taken a shower has an idea. It's the person who does something about it who makes a difference.*

5 —Nolan Bushnel,
inventor of Pong, the video game

In 1904 a salesman named Anton Feuchtwanger set up a frankfurter booth at the World's Fair in St. Louis. When customers ordered a frankfurter—a long spicy sausage—Anton handed them a pair of white gloves to wear so their hands would be clean and
10 grease-free. After they finished eating, customers were supposed to return the gloves, but many didn't, so Anton needed something to take their place. Something that didn't need to be returned. He asked his brother, a baker, to make longer-than-usual rolls. When someone ordered a frankfurter, he popped the meat onto the bun. No mess. No gloves. No returns. Soon everyone was selling frankfurters in buns.

15 But how did the frankfurter get to be called a "hot dog"? That too was a matter of one thing taking the place of another. Some people started calling the frankfurter the "dachshund sausage" because the long curved sausage reminded them of the dachshund—a long, lean dog. In 1906 a cartoonist named Tad Dorgan attended a baseball game in New York. He was fascinated by vendors shouting "Get your red hot
20 dachshund dogs!" After the game Dorgan dashed to his office, and sketched a cartoon of a real-looking dachshund in a bun smeared with mustard. He couldn't spell dachshund so instead he wrote 'Get your hot dogs!" The name stuck and is used to this day.

—from *Whose Bright Idea Was It?: True Stories of Invention* by Larry Verstraete

25. The word "INVENTION" appears in the beginning of the selection. To invent means to
    A. play a game of baseball
    B. create something new
    C. wear a pair of gloves
    D. bake a sausage

26. Another word for "salesman" is
    A. client
    B. vendor
    C. brother
    D. customer

27. Anton Feuchtwanger sold
    A. frankfurters
    B. mustard
    C. gloves
    D. buns

28. This passage **mostly** discusses the invention of a new
    A. drawing
    B. game
    C. term
    D. bun

*Read the following passage and answer questions 29 to 32*

### "Understanding Your Rabbit"

Your rabbit makes soft grunts, but these won't tell you its mood. Your rabbit will squeal when it is frightened. It also warns other rabbits of danger by thumping its back legs. A rabbit finds out a lot by sniffing. It can even tell from another rabbit's smell whether it is a friend or enemy. Watch your rabbit, and you will soon understand much of what it is doing.

**Keeping a lookout**
5   When your rabbit hears a strange sound, it stands up on its hind legs to see what is happening.

**Cuddling together**
Rabbit kittens are very friendly. The brothers and sisters huddle together in a heap when they are sleeping. This helps keep them warm.

10  **Marking what's mine**
Your rabbit rubs a special scent, which is made in its skin, onto everything in its hutch, grazing ark, and enclosure. If your rabbit lives with another rabbit, it rubs its friend's chin to leave the scent.

**Best of friends**
15  Your rabbit will show you that you are its friend. It rubs its head against you to leave its special scent. It may even wash you with its tongue!

**Signaling danger**
When a mother rabbit thinks that her kittens are in danger, she will stand in front of them. If she is very worried, she will thump the ground with her back leg. This tells the
20  kittens, and other nearby rabbits, to run for cover.

**Meeting the enemy**
A rabbit may become angry with another rabbit. It will stare straight at its enemy to let the other know that it is annoyed.

**Show of strength**
25  If the timid rabbit doesn't run away, both rabbits will scratch the ground with their front paws. They may run at each other.

### The fight
If neither rabbit is scared away, a fight begins. They charge forward and try to sink their teeth into each other's necks.

30 **The loser**
The weaker rabbit runs away when it is beaten. It will never forget the other rabbit's scent. Whenever it smells the other rabbit's scent, it will avoid it.

—from *Rabbits* by Mark Evans

29. A mother rabbit warns her babies that danger is coming by
    A. thumping the ground with her back leg
    B. scratching the ground with her claws
    C. running into a nearby hole
    D. jumping into the air

30. A rabbit stands on its hind legs when it wants to
    A. fight another rabbit
    B. snuggle for warmth
    C. show that it is friendly
    D. look around for danger

31. According to the passage, a rabbit scratches the ground with its front paws when it wants to
    A. dig a hole
    B. search for food
    C. scare another rabbit
    D. show that it is friendly

32. When a rabbit that has lost a fight smells the scent of the rabbit to which it lost, it will
    A. challenge it to another fight
    B. hide behind a bigger rabbit
    C. run away to avoid it
    D. offer it some food

*Read the following passage and answer questions 33 to 36*

### Chocolate Chip Cookie

Next time you bite into a chocolate chip cookie, thank Ruth Wakefield for taking a shortcut.

Ruth Wakefield and her husband Ken owned the Toll House Inn, a restaurant near Boston, Massachusetts. One day in 1933 she decided to prepare a batch of cookies. The recipe called for chocolate. Wakefield wanted to save time, so instead of melting
5 semi-sweet chocolate she broke the bar into pieces and tossed the bits into the batter, thinking that the chocolate would blend into the cookie dough as it baked. To her surprise and delight, the chocolate chunks softened slightly, but stayed whole.

Wakefield's "chocolate crispies" became a customer favorite at the Toll House Inn. As word spread, she started giving out her cookie recipe to anyone who was interested.

10 Meanwhile Nestlé, the chocolate manufacturer, noticed something odd. All across the country, sales of their semi-sweet candy bar had dropped. Everywhere, that is, except around Boston. Nestlé sent sales representative to investigate. When Nestlé learned of the popular Toll House cookie, they decided to keep making the bars. They even tried to help out.

15 First they scored the bar so that it broke into pieces more easily. Then they invented a special chopper to break the chocolate into small bits. Finally, in 1939, they started marketing packages of chocolate chips just for cookie making. The company got permission to print Ruth Wakefield's Toll House Cookie Recipe on the package. In exchange, they supplied her with a lifetime's worth of free chocolate.

20 —from *Whose Bright Idea Was It?: True Stories of Invention* by Larry Verstraete

33. The **main** reason this passage is considered an informational text is that it
   A. shows the value of creativity
   B. contains many facts
   C. is an amusing story
   D. is suspenseful

34. What trend did the Nestlé company notice everywhere in the country except in Boston?
   A. Nestlé cookies were very popular.
   B. Candy bar sales had increased.
   C. Sales of all candy bars had dropped.
   D. Sales of semi-sweet candy bars had dropped.

35. The shortcut that Ruth Wakefield took when baking her cookies was that she
   A. broke a bar of chocolate before melting it
   B. broke a bar of chocolate instead of melting it
   C. used a candy bar instead of chocolate chips
   D. used candy bar bits instead of cocoa powder

36. In this article, Nestlé is described as the company that
    A. sold the cookies
    B. made the cookies
    C. made the chocolate
    D. owned the Toll House Inn

*Read the following passage and answer questions 37 to 40*

### Amazing Black Holes

How many things can you see in the night sky? A lot! On a clear night you might see the Moon, some planets, and thousands of sparkling stars.

You can see even more with a telescope. You might see stars where before you only saw dark space. You might see that many stars look larger than others. You might see
5   that some stars that look white are really red or blue. With bigger and bigger telescopes you can see more and more objects in the sky. And you can see those objects in more and more detail.

But scientists believe there are some things in the sky that we will never see. We won't see them with the biggest telescope in the world, on the clearest night of the year.
10  That's because they're invisible. They're the mysterious dead stars called black holes.

You might find it hard to imagine that stars die. After all, our Sun is a star. Year after year we see it up in the sky, burning brightly, giving us heat and light. The Sun certainly doesn't seem to be getting old or weak. But stars do burn out and die after billions of years.

As a star's gases burn, they give off light and heat. But when the gas runs out, the star
15  stops burning and begins to die.

As the star cools, the outer layers of the star pull in toward the center. The star squashes into a smaller and smaller ball. If the star was very small, the star ends up as a cold, dark ball called a black dwarf. If the star was very big, it keeps squashing inward until it's packed together tighter than anything in the universe.

20  Imagine if the Earth were crushed until it was the size of a tiny marble. That's how tightly this dead star, a black hole, is packed. What pulls the star in toward its center with such power? It's the same force that pulls you down when you jump—the force called gravity. A black hole is so tightly packed that its gravity sucks in everything—even light. The light from a black hole can never come back to your eyes. That's why you see nothing but blackness.

25  So the next time you stare up at the night sky, remember: there's more in the sky than meets the eye! Scattered in the silent darkness are black holes—the great mystery of space.

37. The word "invisible" means
    A. damaged by another being
    B. seen with a telescope
    C. unseen by the eye
    D. hidden by magic

38. Which of the following statements **best** explains why people can see more detail when looking through a telescope?
    A. Telescopes magnify objects and make them appear larger.
    B. They make objects appear clearer at night.
    C. Telescopes change the color of objects.
    D. They improve people's eyesight.

39. According to the passage, a star dies when
    A. its gases run out
    B. it collides with other stars
    C. it has lived for a million years
    D. its outer layers begin to crumble into tiny pieces

40. Which of the following statements **best** explains the meaning of this quotation?
    A. Stars appear to be both red and blue.
    B. Telescopes are needed to see some stars.
    C. There are things in the sky that humans cannot see.
    D. Light from black holes can never come back to Earth.

*Read the following passage and answer questions 41 to 45*

### from "The Voyage of the Mayflower"

Pelted by rain under a black sky, the ninety-foot *Mayflower* rolled and pitched on mountainous waves. Its masts were bare because during a storm, a sailing ship must lower all its sails and drift with the wind to avoid capsizing or breaking apart.

5 Below the main deck, the passengers huddled in the dark. They could hear the wind howling and the waves thudding against the vessel's wooden sides and washing over the deck. Seawater dripped down on them through the canvas covering the deck gratings and seeped through the seams in the planking. The passengers were soaked and shivering; several were seasick besides. As frightened adults tried to comfort terrified children, they prayed for safety in the storm and an end to the long, terrible voyage.

10 Suddenly, above the din of the storm, they heard the noise of splitting timber. One of the beams supporting the deck had cracked! The ship was in danger of sinking. Then someone remembered a great iron screw brought from Holland. Carefully, the ship's carpenter positioned it beneath the beam and braced it. It would hold; the passengers and crew could reach land safely.

15 Crossing the Atlantic in 1620 was extremely risky. A wooden ship could leak or break apart in a storm. Since the sails could be raised only in fair weather, it was impossible to predict how long a voyage would last. To avoid the stormy autumn months, ships usually made the crossing in spring or summer. They almost never sailed alone.

Aware of these dangers, the Pilgrims had planned to cross the ocean in two ships in the summer of 1620. The English Separatists from Holland (who called themselves Saints) borrowed money from London businessmen and purchased a small ship, the *Speedwell*. For the Separatists' safety, and to help them establish a profitable colony, the businessmen recruited additional volunteers in London. The businessmen rented the *Mayflower*, a ship three times the size of the *Speedwell*, for these recruits, whom the Separatists called Strangers. The Saints and Strangers met for the first time in Southampton, England, a few days before the ships sailed on August 5.

The tiny *Speedwell* had been refitted with taller masts and larger sails so it could keep up with the *Mayflower*. These changes, however, caused the ship to leak badly at sea. On August 12, the ships put into Dartmouth. After the *Speedwell* was examined and repaired, they set off again on August 23. Two days later, the *Speedwell* began to leak again, and the vessels headed for Plymouth, England. There the ships' masters, carpenters, and principal passengers agreed that the *Speedwell* could not make the crossing.

Over the next few days, the sixty-seven Strangers on the *Mayflower* made room for thirty-five of the Saints from the *Speedwell*, along with their belongings and provisions. On September 6, the *Mayflower* set out from Plymouth alone. The one hundred two passengers, including thirty-four children, would not see land for sixty-six days.

The *Mayflower*, like all ships of the time, was built to carry cargo, not passengers. A few families crowded into the "great cabbin" in the stern. Most of the passengers, however, traveled in bunks or tiny "cabbins" below the main deck and above the hold, where cargo was stored. In this "'tween decks" area, they had only five feet of head room. Each person's living space was smaller than the mattress of a modern twin bed.

The Pilgrims suffered other discomforts. Many were seasick, particularly at the beginning of the voyage. In storms, they were constantly wet and cold. They could not bathe or wash and dry their clothes and bedding. For toilet purposes, they used buckets.

In fair weather, the adults and children who had recovered from seasickness could leave their dim, foul-smelling quarters for the wind and spray of the main deck. The adults took deep breaths of the cold, tangy air and stretched cramped muscles. The younger children, forbidden to run around, played quiet games. Damaris Hopkins, age three, and Mary and Remember Allerton, ages four and six, "tended the baby" (played with dolls). Six- and nine-year old brothers Wrestling and Love Brewster played "I Spy" and "Hunt the Slipper" with six- and seven-year-old Jasper and Richard More. Finger games such as cat's cradle and paper, scissors, stone were popular with eight-year-old Humility Cooper, Ellen More, John Cooke, John Billington, and Bartholomew Allerton. Elizabeth Tilley, age fourteen, and Mary Chilton and Constance Hopkins, both fifteen, helped prepare the meals.

For cooking, the passengers built charcoal fires in metal braziers set in sandboxes. There was so little space, however, that only a few people could cook at once. When storms made lighting fires dangerous, everyone ate cold meals.

After morning prayers, they ate a simple breakfast of cheese and ship's biscuit (hard, dry
60 biscuit). If cooking was allowed, they might have porridge. Their midday meal might
consist of ship's biscuit and cheese or, in fair weather, cooked "pease pottage," boiled
salt fish, pork, or beef and any freshly caught bonito or porpoise. Before retiring, they had
a light supper. Everyone, even the children, drank beer with their meals because it was
preferred to water.

65 Not until December 11, more than a month after first sighting land, did the Pilgrims
decide where they would build their colony. ...

—by Patricia M. Whalen

41. A synonym for the word "capsizing" is
    A. splitting up
    B. turning over
    C. cracking up
    D. breaking apart

42. The two finger games that were popular with the eight-year-olds on the ship were
    A. "dolls" and "I spy"
    B. "I spy" and "Hunt the Slipper"
    C. "Hunt the slipper" and "tended the baby"
    D. "cat's cradle" and "paper, scissors, stone"

43. Where did the Saints and Strangers meet for the very first time?
    A. London, England
    B. Southampton, England
    C. On board the *Speedwell*
    D. On board the *Mayflower*

44. The *Speedwell* was in Dartmouth for repairs for
    A. 10 days
    B. 11 days
    C. 12 days
    D. 13 days

45. The main reason that people would take the sort of risk that the Pilgrims took in order to go and live in America is to have
    A. a chance for a better life
    B. an opportunity to travel on a ship
    C. the possibility of having an adventure
    D. the adventure of exploring new places

*Read the following passage and answer questions 46 to 49*

### The St. Lawrence Beluga

Encountering a beluga whale is a real privilege. A somewhat ghostly animal, the beluga is a symbol of fragility and vulnerability. It knows the St. Lawrence like no other because it lives there year-round. The beluga herd in the St. Lawrence River is the only one in the world that does not live in the Arctic. The St. Lawrence provides habitat similar to the
5   Arctic: the salt water is nice and cold and there is lots of food.

There are many beluga herds in the Canadian North. The total beluga population is over 100,000. Other Arctic beluga herds live in northern Russia, Norway, Greenland, and Alaska.

A beluga has all the characteristics of a polar animal. Its white color acts as camouflage in the ice. It has a bumpy ridge extending along its back, instead of a dorsal fin, that
10  allows it to break through the ice to breathe without injuring itself. Belugas have a flexible neck, while all other whales have fused cervical vertebrae and cannot turn their head.

Belugas are highly social animals, which explains their extensive vocabulary. They have developed some of the most varied vocal repertoires in the animal kingdom. From its rounded forehead, a beluga sends out ultrasound waves to find its food.

15  The beluga herd in the St. Lawrence is not what it was a hundred years ago. At the turn of the last century, there were over 5,000 belugas in the River. Their numbers have dropped considerably since then. They were overhunted because it was thought that they were eating the salmon and cod that humans needed to survive. Authorities even offered a bonus of fifteen dollars for every beluga tail brought in, to encourage elimination
20  of the species as quickly as possible. The hunt was not brought to an end until the nineteen seventies. Now, there are between 700 and 1,200 in the St. Lawrence herd and the beluga is an endangered species.

Nowadays, because scientists have raised the alarm, the St. Lawrence beluga is protected. However, damage to its habitat and pollution continue to threaten its well-being.

25  The beluga is affected by various illnesses, but the link between disease and pollutants has yet to be found. Contaminants are not biodegradable, so the only way that belugas can get rid of them is through the female. A mother can reduce the level of pollutants in her body through her milk, but a newborn beluga starts life contaminated.

For all these reasons, the health of the St. Lawrence beluga is a concern. It will take
30  generations, many more studies, and a lot of determination to improve the situation. The beluga's health is definitely a reflection of the state of the St. Lawrence River.

—from *As Long As There Are Whales* by Evelyne Daigle, translated by Geneviève Wright

**46.** An antonym of the word "elimination," as it is used in the phrase "to encourage elimination of the species," is
   A. preservation
   B. eradication
   C. exclusion
   D. removal

47. In the statement, "Belugas are highly social animals, which explains their extensive vocabulary," [line 12] a synonym for the word "extensive" is
   A. noisy
   B. broad
   C. simple
   D. limited

48. Belugas were once overhunted because it was thought that they
   A. were eating salmon and seals
   B. had been polluting the water
   C. were eating salmon and cod
   D. had medicinal value

49. In this passage, the **main** theme that connects all of the information is that the
   A. beluga whale is an endangered species
   B. condition of the St. Lawrence River is poor
   C. authorities have allowed belugas to be killed
   D. belugas live in the St. Lawrence River all year

*Read the following passage and answer questions 50 to 53*

### Ancient Broom Games

Broom sports emerged almost as soon as broomsticks were sufficiently advanced to allow fliers to turn corners and vary their speed and height. Early wizarding writings and paintings give us some idea of the games our ancestors played. Some of these no longer exist; others have survived or evolved into the sports we know today.

5  The celebrated **annual broom race** of Sweden dates from the tenth century. Fliers race from Kopparberg to Arjeplog, a distance of slightly over three hundred miles. The course runs straight through a dragon reservation and the vast silver trophy is shaped like a Swedish Short-Snout. Nowadays this is an international event and wizards of all nationalities congregate at Kopparberg to cheer the starters, then Apparate to Arjeplog to
10 congratulate the survivors.

The famous painting *Günther der Gewaltig ist der Gewinner* ("Gunther the Violent is the Winner"), dated 1105, shows the ancient German game of **Stichstock**. A twenty-foot-high pole was topped with an inflated dragon bladder. One player on a broomstick had the job of protecting this bladder. The bladder-guardian was tied to the pole by a rope around his
15 or her waist, so that he or she could not fly further than ten feet away from it. The rest of the players would take it in turns to fly at the bladder and attempt to puncture it with the specially sharpened ends of their brooms. The bladder-guardian was allowed to use his or her wand to repel these attacks. The game ended when the bladder was successfully punctured, or the bladder-guardian had either succeeded in hexing all opponents out of
20 the running or collapsed from exhaustion. Stichstock died out in the fourteenth century.

In Ireland the game of **Aingingein** flourished, the subject of many an Irish ballad (the legendary wizard Fingal the Fearless is alleged to have been an Aingingein champion). One by one the players would take the Dom, or ball (actually the gallbladder of a goat), and speed through a series of burning barrels set high in the air on stilts. The Dom was to be thrown through the final barrel. The player who succeeded in getting the Dom through the last barrel in the fastest time, without having caught fire on the way, was the winner.

Scotland was the birthplace of what is probably the most dangerous of all broom games—**Creaothceann**. The game features in a tragic Gaelic poem of the eleventh century, the first verse of which says, in translation:

*The players assembled, twelve fine, hearty men,*
*They strapped on their cauldrons, stood poised to fly,*
*At the sound of the horn they were swiftly airborne*
*But ten of their number were fated to die.*

Creaothceann players each wore a cauldron strapped to the head. At the sound of the horn or drum, up to a hundred charmed rocks and boulders that had been hovering a hundred feet above the ground began to fall towards the earth. The Creaothceann players zoomed around trying to catch as many rocks as possible in their cauldrons. Considered by many Scottish wizards to be the supreme test of manliness and courage, Creaothceann enjoyed considerable popularity in the Middle Ages, despite the huge number of fatalities that resulted from it. The game was made illegal in 1762, and though Magnus "Dent-Head" Macdonald spearheaded a campaign for its reintroduction in the 1960s, the Ministry of Magic refused to lift the ban.

**Shuntbumps** was popular in Devon, England. This was a crude form of jousting, the sole aim being to knock as many other players as possible off their brooms, the last person remaining on their broom winning.

**Swivenhodge** began in Herefordshire. Like Stichstock, this involved an inflated bladder, usually a pig's. Players sat backwards on their brooms and batted the bladder backwards and forwards across a hedge with the brush ends of their brooms. The first person to miss gave their opponent a point. First to reach fifty points was the winner.

Swivenhodge is still played in England, though it has never achieved much widespread popularity; Shuntbumps survives only as a children's game. At Queerditch Marsh, however, a game had been created that would one day become the most popular in the wizarding world.

—from *Quidditch Through the Ages* by Kennilworthy Whisp (J. K. Rowling)

50. The annual broom race of Sweden takes place every
    A. year
    B. century
    C. 4 years
    D. 10 years

51. In the sentence "The game ended when the bladder was successfully punctured, or the bladder-guardian had either succeeded in hexing all opponents out of the running or collapsed from exhaustion,"[line 13] the word "hexing" means
    A. building a hexagon
    B. making fun of someone
    C. putting a spell on someone
    D. letting the air out of a balloon

52. A synonym of the word "vast," which is used in the phrase "the vast silver trophy is shaped like a Swedish Short-Snout,"[line 7] is
    A. immense
    B. polished
    C. weighty
    D. diverse

53. Magnus Macdonald **most likely** received the nickname "Dent-Head" because he
    A. fell off his broom
    B. was hit in the head with a spear
    C. had been hit so often by falling rocks
    D. had marks on his head from the cauldron straps

# EXERCISE #2—READING INFORMATIONAL

## Table of Correlations

| | Standard | Test #1 |
|---|---|---|
| **5RL** | Reading Standards for Literature | |
| 5RL.2 | Determine a theme of a story, drama, or poem from details in the text, including how characters in a story or drama respond to challenges or how the speaker in a poem reflects upon a topic; summarize the text. | 58, 68, 69, 73, 77, 80, 83, 84, 85, 98, 106 |
| 5RL.7 | Analyze how visual and multimedia elements contribute to the meaning, tone, or beauty of a text. | 67, 81, 82 |
| **5RI** | Reading Standards for Informational Text | |
| 5RI.2 | Determine two or more main ideas of a text and explain how they are supported by key details; summarize the text. | 58, 68, 69, 73, 77, 80, 83, 84, 85, 98, 106 |
| 5RI.7 | Draw on information from multiple print or digital sources, demonstrating the ability to locate an answer to a question quickly or to solve a problem efficiently. | 67, 81, 82 |
| 5RI.8 | Explain how an author uses reasons and evidence to support particular points in a text, identifying which reasons and evidence support which point(s). | 64, 92 |
| **5RF** | Reading Standards: Foundational Skills | |
| 5RF.3a | Know and apply grade-level phonics and word analysis skills in decoding words. Use combined knowledge of all letter-sound correspondences, syllabication patterns, and morphology to read accurately unfamiliar multisyllabic words in context... | 54, 59, 60, 61, 62, 63, 66, 70, 71, 74, 75, 78, 86, 87, 88, 91, 95, 96, 103 |
| 5RF.4a | Read with sufficient accuracy and fluency to support comprehension. Read on-level text with purpose and understanding. | 76 |
| 5RF.4b | Read with sufficient accuracy and fluency to support comprehension. Read on-level prose and poetry orally with accuracy, appropriate rate, and expression on successive readings. | 76 |
| 5RF.4c | Read with sufficient accuracy and fluency to support comprehension. Use context to confirm or self-correct word recognition and understanding, rereading as necessary. | 59, 60, 61, 62, 63, 70, 71, 74, 75, 76, 78, 86, 87, 88, 91, 95, 103 |
| **5W** | Writing Standards | |
| 5W.2a | Write informative/explanatory texts to examine a topic and convey ideas and information clearly. Introduce a topic clearly, provide a general observation and focus, and group related information logically; include formatting, illustrations, and... | 67, 82 |
| 5W.9a | Draw evidence from literary or informational texts to support analysis, reflection, and research. Apply grade 5 Reading standards to literature. | 65, 72, 93, 94, 102 |
| 5W.9b | Draw evidence from literary or informational texts to support analysis, reflection, and research. Apply grade 5 Reading standards to informational texts. | 64, 65, 92, 93, 94, 102 |
| **5SL** | Speaking and Listening Standards | |
| 5SL.2 | Summarize a written text read aloud or information presented in diverse media and formats, including visually, quantitatively, and orally. | 98, 106 |
| 5SL.3 | Summarize the points a speaker makes and explain how each claim is supported by reasons and evidence. | 64, 92, 98, 106 |

| 5L | Language Standards | |
|---|---|---|
| 5L.1b | Demonstrate command of the conventions of standard English grammar and usage when writing or speaking. Form and use the perfect verb tenses. | 55 |
| 5L.1c | Demonstrate command of the conventions of standard English grammar and usage when writing or speaking. Use verb tense to convey various times, sequences, states, and conditions. | 55, 79, 99 |
| 5L.4a | Determine or clarify the meaning of unknown and multiple-meaning words and phrases based on grade 5 reading and content, choosing flexibly from a range of strategies. Use context as a clue to the meaning of a word or phrase. | 59, 60, 61, 62, 63, 70, 71, 74, 75, 78, 86, 87, 88, 91, 95, 103 |
| 5L.5b | Demonstrate understanding of figurative language, word relationships, and nuances in word meanings. Recognize and explain the meaning of common idioms, adages, and proverbs. | 89, 90 |
| 5L.5c | Demonstrate understanding of figurative language, word relationships, and nuances in word meanings. Use the relationship between particular words to better understand each of the words. | 56, 57, 70, 97, 100, 101, 104, 105 |

*Read the following passage and answer questions 54 to 58*

## Built for the Water

### Why Are Whales So Big?

At four tons, the elephant is the biggest land animal we know of today. At seventy-five tons, the Brachiosaurus was one of the largest dinosaurs. But of all the animals that have ever lived on Earth, none has rivaled the blue whale in either size or weight. The
5  environment in which it lives has allowed it to reach gigantic proportions: the blue whale weighs approximately 100 tons!

Water supports weight much more easily than air. As a result, whales have expanded in size because they are not limited by gravity. They have a layer of blubber ten to twenty centimeters thick that makes them buoyant and allows them to live in weightlessness like astronauts.

10  ### Whale or Boat?

What do a boat and a whale have in common? The first boatbuilders must have been inspired by the shape of cetaceans. Whales are streamlined at both ends, which lets them glide through the water easily, with no resistance.

The pectoral fins (or flippers) on either side of the body help to stabilize them, like the
15  keel of a boat, and the horizontal tailfin (or flukes) propels them forward. Cetaceans are hydrodynamic, just like boats, which allows them to cut through waves.

### Diving to the Depths

Northern bottlenose whales are wonderful divers, as are sperm whales. They can stay submerged for up to seventy minutes at a time and can dive as deep as 800 meters!
20  Cetaceans are mammals, so they have lungs. Proportionally, their lungs are smaller than those of humans. So, how do they manage to beat all the diving records?

When a northern bottlenose whale comes to the surface to breathe, it exhales and then inhales ninety percent of all the air its lungs can contain, as opposed to seventy-five percent for humans. It has more available oxygen than we do because it is better at
25  emptying and refilling its lungs, not because its lungs contain more air.

The oxygen captured during inhalation is then stored in its blood in a protein called hemoglobin. Cetaceans have a higher volume of blood than humans, so they have more hemoglobin in their blood vessels and muscles. This means they can accumulate more oxygen reserves and stay under water longer!

30  —from *As Long As There Are Whales* by Evelyne Daigle, translated by Geneviève Wright

54. Like boats, whales are
    A. hydrodynamic
    B. hydroelectric
    C. hydrophobic
    D. hydraulic

Not for Reproduction

55. In the phrase "Cetaceans have a higher volume of blood than humans,"[line 27] the word "have" is in the
    A. past tense
    B. future tense
    C. present tense
    D. present perfect tense

56. An antonym of the word "forward" is
    A. downward
    B. backward
    C. upward
    D. toward

57. The whale's thick blubber makes it buoyant. A synonym for "*buoyant*" is
    A. fat
    B. heavy
    C. bumpy
    D. floatable

58. Northern bottlenose whales can dive as deep as
    A. 800 meters
    B. 900 meters
    C. 1,000 meters
    D. 1,100 meters

*Read the following passage and answer questions 59 to 65*

### Monsters from the Deep and Other Imaginary Beings

Moving day. Groan. All that stuff. For most of us, moving day doesn't happen too often. For Michael Kusugak, growing up in the far north, moving was a way of life. For the first six years of his life, Michael lived in the age-old Inuit tradition of traveling. The family traveled by dog-team in search of whales, seals and cariboo. In winter they lived in
5 igloos. In summer they pitched a tent. The nomadic life is not a life for collecting possessions. The family had only the essentials—furs, weapons and tools. But they also had something that required no space and had no weight, but which was essential to their survival. They had stories.

Small Michael would fall asleep every night listening to the stories of his parents and
10 grandmother. Legends, family stories, funny stories, stories with something to teach. He heard tales of the animals he knew—the bear, the cariboo, the squirrel. And he heard stories of imaginary beings.

When Michael grew up, he remembered a story told in the spring. In the far north spring can be a dangerous time for children as the sea ice begins to break up. To keep their
15 children away from the hazardous shore, parents tell stories of the Qallupilluit, a witchy undersea creature who kidnaps children. In *A Promise Is a Promise* (written with Robert Munsch), Michael Kusugak invents his own version of the Qallupilluit and puts it into the world where he lives now—a world of jeans, TV and computers.

—from *The Young Writer's Companion* by Sarah Ellis

59. An age-old tradition is something that
    A. is done to celebrate birthdays
    B. people do when they reach a certain age
    C. people are unable to do before a certain age
    D. has been done the same way for a long time

60. A caribou can **best** be described as
    A. a small bear
    B. an Arctic deer
    C. a tree-dwelling rodent
    D. a swimming mammal

61. The expression "age-old" means something that is
    A. new
    B. ancient
    C. done in old age
    D. done at a certain age

62. Michael's nomadic life is described in the first paragraph. From this description, the word "nomadic" means
    A. poor
    B. northern
    C. living in igloos
    D. traveling around

63. In the phrase "To keep their children away from the hazardous shore,"[line 14] the word "hazardous" means
    A. hazy
    B. haunted
    C. changing
    D. dangerous

64. In the passage, the Qallupilluit is described as a
    A. whale spirit
    B. sea serpent
    C. sort of mermaid
    D. witchy sea creature

65. As a young child, Michael Kusugak moved
   A. seldom
   B. never
   C. often
   D. once

*Read the following passage and answer questions 66 to 69*

### Finding a Puppy

THERE ARE LOTS OF WAYS to find a new puppy. If you would like a purebred dog, ask the local veterinarian for help, and contact the breed club for a list of recommended breeders with puppies for sale. The vet may also know of mixed-breed puppies looking for a home. You can also call a local animal shelter or rescue group. They often need to
5  find homes for unwanted puppies.

**Purebred puppies**

You can usually visit a breeder to look at a litter of puppies when the litter is about four weeks old. (You can't take the puppy you choose home until he is around nine weeks old.) Watch the mother of the puppies and see if she behaves in a nice way. Her puppies
10  may grow up to be just like her.

**Mixed breeds**

If you would like to own a mixed-breed puppy, try to meet one of his parents too, for an idea of how big he will grow. If you can't do this, look at the puppy's paws. If he has big paws, he will probably grow into a big dog.

15  **Puppy mills**

Avoid buying a puppy from a puppy mill. These are places where large numbers of puppies are bred purely for profit. The puppies can be unhealthy, and may have behavioral problems.

**A healthy puppy**

20  You can tell a lot about your puppy's personality and health at your first meeting. She should be lively and friendly, with a clean coat, even under her tail near her bottom. Remember to ask your vet to check your puppy's health, once you bring the pup home.

—from *Puppy Care: A Guide to Loving and Nurturing Your Pet* by Kim Dennis-Bryan

66. In the phrase "places where large numbers of puppies are bred purely for profit," the word "profit" means
   A. having fun
   B. looking good
   C. making money
   D. guarding homes

67. The author organized the information in this passage by
   A. the different types of puppies available
   B. the order of steps to go through to find a puppy
   C. several useful tips for choosing a suitable puppy
   D. a timeline of activities before bringing a puppy home

68. According to the author, when choosing a puppy, it is **most important** to make sure the puppy is
    A. healthy and purebred
    B. friendly and healthy
    C. purebred and friendly
    D. healthy and bright-eyed

69. Which of the following statements is one of the **main** ideas of this passage?
    A. Puppies are cute and lovable.
    B. A puppy can make an excellent family pet.
    C. Visiting puppies can be a lot of fun for your family.
    D. There are a lot of things to think about before choosing a puppy.

*Read the following passage and answer questions 70 to 73*

### Islands in the Mind

Robert Louis Stevenson was a strange little boy. He was so skinny that people said he looked as if his bones would poke through his clothes. The damp climate of his Scottish home made his weak lungs worse, and he was sick more often than he was well. An only child, he never attended school regularly and, apart from his cousins, he had few friends.
5   If you had seen him sitting in an Edinburgh park—pale, weak and overprotected by his stern nanny—you might have felt sorry for him.

Yet inside his head, Louis had a rich, exciting life. He could make a whole world out of anything—toy soldiers, Bible stories, tales his nanny told him, his own terrifying nightmares. He could even make a world out of his breakfast.

10  When Louis and his cousin Bob had breakfast together, they made kingdoms in their porridge. Bob sprinkled sugar on his porridge and explained how his kingdom was a harsh northern land covered with snow. Louis poured milk on his porridge to make an island with bays and coves—an island in terrible danger of being swamped by the milky sea.

Years later Louis was doodling one day with some watercolor paints. On his paper
15  appeared an island. Something about the shape of his doodle delighted Louis, and he started to imagine the characters who lived on this island and the adventures they might have.

So began a furious fifteen-day writing frenzy in which Louis wrote the first fifteen chapters of *Treasure Island*, a pirate adventure story that has been enjoyed by readers for more than one hundred years.

20  —from *The Young Writer's Companion* by Sarah Ellis

70. A synonym for the word **furious** in the phrase "a furious fifteen-day writing frenzy" is
    A. fierce
    B. angry
    C. enraged
    D. passionate

71. In the description of Robert Louis Stevenson as "pale, weak and overprotected by his stern nanny,"[line 5] the word "stern" means
    A. worrying
    B. old-fashioned
    C. strict and harsh
    D. loving and careful

72. Which of the following phrases from the passage suggests that Louis was lonely?
    A. "Robert Louis Stevenson was a strange little boy"
    B. "he was sick more often than he was well"
    C. "he never attended school regularly"
    D. "he had few friends"

73. As a child, Robert Louis Stevenson was inspired to make up stories by all of the following things **except**
    A. fairy tales
    B. nightmares
    C. toy soldiers
    D. bowls of porridge

*Read the following passage and answer questions 74 to 77*

### from Crabs for Dinner

One summer, my grandmother came for a visit all the way from Africa.

"Ghana," she said. "That's where I come from."

She brought us funny-looking clothes, the kind they wear in Ghana. I had a smock made of a rough cotton fabric with stripes of bright colors woven into it.

5   It was long and loose, almost like a dress. Grandma said it was meant to be worn over a pair of trousers.

"I'm never going to wear those," I said to my mom.

But Emily wore hers, a colorful batik dress with embroidery around the neck.

She looked so pretty that I decided to wear my smock. When I did, I thought I looked
10  "cool." Especially when I wore the striped cotton cap that came with the smock.

Grandma had lots of stories to tell. Stories her grandmother told her when she was young. I liked the ones about a cunning "Spider man" who got in and out of all kinds of trouble.

She always ended in a funny way, saying: "This story of mine whether good or bad, may pass away, or come to stay. It is your turn to tell your story."

15  So we took our turn and told her stories. And she liked them just as much as we liked hers.

A week before she left for Ghana, she invited my aunts and uncle to dinner.

"She's going to make soup and yucky crab," Emily said. "I'll bet she makes a lot of it. But I won't even take a bite."

She did make the soup, only she put in okra too.

20 "That's going to make it slimy," I said.

"Double Yuk," said Emily.

But dinner got cooked and dinner was served and grace was said.

Emily and I were eating hot dogs and the grown-ups were eating slime.

Uncle Robert rolled his eyes upward. "Mmm," he said. "Exquisite!"

25 I had never heard him use that word for Mom's soup.

"My word," Aunt Pauline said, "I had almost forgotten the original taste."

My mom simply said, "Delicious."

Even Aunt Araba paused from the sucking and crunching to say one word, "Authentic!"

I noticed that Grandma's soup smelled really good, much better than Mom's soup.
30 Suddenly I wanted to taste just a little bit of the fufu with crab and soup.

"Can I have a little, please?" I heard Emily ask.

"Why, of course!" Grandma replied.

If Emily doesn't die, I'll have some, I thought.

Emily took a bite and didn't die. Instead she took another bite.

35 "And how about you?" said Grandma.

"Yes, please," I said.

It tasted different, not like the soups I knew. It was spicy and hot and really good. It was thick and smooth and I thought I could taste the flavor of ginger.

I broke off a tiny piece of crab and sucked it just like Mommy did. It was all soft inside.
40 Then I crunched on it, really hard, just as my Aunt Araba did.

Then I ate a whole bowl of fufu and soup and a huge piece of crab. When I was done I rolled my eyes up to the sky and said aloud, "Exquisite!"

I am not even sure what that means, but probably it is a way of saying that sometimes grandmothers cook better than mothers.

45 —by Adwoa Badoe

74. When Aunt Araba calls Grandma's soup "Authentic," she means the soup is
    A. exquisite
    B. original
    C. bland
    D. fine

75. When Uncle Robert said the soup was "Exquisite," he meant that the soup was
    A. hearty
    B. delicious
    C. different
    D. slimy

76. The narrator's grandmother came from Ghana, which is in
    A. Australia
    B. America
    C. Africa
    D. Asia

77. The **main** idea or theme of this story is that it is
    A. fun to have large family gatherings
    B. important to keep cultural traditions alive
    C. a good idea to eat different types of food
    D. nice to have grandparents visit from other countries

*Read the following passage and answer questions 78 to 81*

### Chocolate Chip Cookie

Next time you bite into a chocolate chip cookie, thank Ruth Wakefield for taking a shortcut.

Ruth Wakefield and her husband Ken owned the Toll House Inn, a restaurant near Boston, Massachusetts. One day in 1933 she decided to prepare a batch of cookies. The recipe called for chocolate. Wakefield wanted to save time, so instead of melting
5   semi-sweet chocolate she broke the bar into pieces and tossed the bits into the batter, thinking that the chocolate would blend into the cookie dough as it baked. To her surprise and delight, the chocolate chunks softened slightly, but stayed whole.

Wakefield's "chocolate crispies" became a customer favorite at the Toll House Inn. As word spread, she started giving out her cookie recipe to anyone who was interested.

10  Meanwhile Nestlé, the chocolate manufacturer, noticed something odd. All across the country, sales of their semi-sweet candy bar had dropped. Everywhere, that is, except around Boston. Nestlé sent sales representative to investigate. When Nestlé learned of the popular Toll House cookie, they decided to keep making the bars. They even tried to help out.

15  First they scored the bar so that it broke into pieces more easily. Then they invented a special chopper to break the chocolate into small bits. Finally, in 1939, they started marketing packages of chocolate chips just for cookie making. The company got permission to print Ruth Wakefield's Toll House Cookie Recipe on the package. In exchange, they supplied her with a lifetime's worth of free chocolate.

20  —from *Whose Bright Idea Was It?: True Stories of Invention* by Larry Verstraete

78. In the statement "they scored the bar," the word "scored" means
    A. froze
    B. heated up
    C. flattened out
    D. marked lines into

79. Words in the first paragraph such as "broke," "blend," "tossed," and "baked" are all examples of
    A. words that describe verbs, or adverbs
    B. describing words, or adjectives
    C. naming words, or nouns
    D. action words, or verbs

80. In order to encourage people to buy Nestlé chocolate, the company printed the cookie recipe
    A. on their cookie packages
    B. in their cookie recipe book
    C. on their chocolate chip packages
    D. inside their candy bar wrappers

81. What is the **most likely** reason that the words "chocolate crispies" are in quotation marks in the sentence "Wakefield's 'chocolate crispies' became a customer favorite at the Toll House Inn" [line 8]?
    A. They are part of a direct quote.
    B. They are words in a foreign language.
    C. They are from the title of this passage.
    D. They are what Ruth Wakefield called her cookies.

*Read the following passage and answer questions 82 to 85*

### Stubborn Mary Shadd

*"No, Mary, you cannot go to school. It's against the law for Black children to go to school. Don't even let anyone know that you can read and write!"*

*"But why is it the law? Why is it wrong for me to read and write? It's not fair!"*

Mary Ann Shadd was a stubborn little girl. She longed to go to school and couldn't
5 understand why white children could go and she couldn't. However, Mary was born in Wilmington, Delaware, in 1823. At that time, most Black Americans were held in slavery. Only a few, like Mary's family, had always been free. Her parents, Abraham and Harriet Shadd, helped many people who were fleeing north to freedom from slavery. They hid them in their house until it was safe for them to move on to the next hiding place.

10 So Mary grew up knowing slavery was wrong, and that it led to unfair laws. That just made her even more determined to go to school. Now, many people at that time thought girls didn't need much education. Mary's family was different. They teased her for being so stubborn, but they did their best to help her. When Mary was ten years old, her parents moved their family to Pennsylvania. There, Mary and her brothers and sisters
15 could go to a school for Black children.

Mary learned quickly, and when she was sixteen, she became a teacher. She moved right back to Delaware, where she had not been allowed to go to school herself. There, she opened a school for Black children. She also began to write newspaper articles against the enslavement of Black people. Later she moved to other cities, going
20 wherever there was a need for teachers and schools for Black children.

### Mary Comes to Canada

In 1850, a new law was passed in the United States. This law meant that slave catchers could travel anywhere in the country, looking for runaway slaves. Sometimes they even took free Black people and sold them into slavery! So, many Black Americans decided to
25  flee to Canada, where slavery had not been legal since 1834. Mary knew that many new Black communities were springing up in Canada, and that they would need schools and teachers. She heard about a community near Windsor that needed both. She went there and opened a school.

Mary was a strict teacher, but she was fair. Her students were soon competing to show
30  Miss Shadd how well they could read, or write, or do arithmetic. They grew to love their new teacher. She cared so much about them that she bought firewood out of her own money and carried it to class to warm her little schoolroom.

Teaching school was only one of Mary's goals, though. She believed that Black Canadians should not live in separate communities and go to separate schools. She
35  thought that Canadians of all races should live together and build communities. This idea, known as *integration*, was not popular with many people at that time. When Mary supported integration, people became angry with her.

Mary also spoke out about equal rights. She said that people of all races were equal, and that men and women were, too. In those days, a lot of people didn't agree. Some even
40  believed that women should not speak in public. Mary's speeches made her even more unpopular than she was already. People began to say that she was odd, and that nobody should listen to her.

Mary didn't give up. She knew that newspaper articles were another way to share her ideas. In those days, there were no television or radio news reports to give information.
45  That made newspapers even more important than they are today. The trouble was, newspapers wouldn't print Mary's articles because she was unpopular and because she believed in equality for all people. So Mary set her mind to solving this problem, and when stubborn Mary did that, things happened!

### Mary Becomes an Editor

50  Mary decided to start a newspaper of her own. No woman had ever done that in Canada before. She knew that many people wouldn't buy her paper if they knew that its editor was a woman. So she got her friend, the Reverend Samuel Ward, to put his name on the paper as the editor. The first issue of her newspaper, the *Provincial Freeman*, was published in March, 1853. Mary used her paper to let people know about integration and
55  women's rights, and to publish news about events in Canada and around the world.

In 1854, Mary moved her newspaper to Toronto. There she listed her own name as the editor—but only as M. A. Shadd. The *Provincial Freeman* continued to sell many copies from Windsor to Toronto and beyond. At last, she revealed that M. A. Shadd was a woman. Many people were upset. In fact, the reaction was so strong that Mary decided
60  to move her paper to Chatham in 1855. There, she could be closer to her family, who had settled nearby. She also felt that the people in Chatham would understand what she was trying to do.

### Mary's New Life

In Toronto, Mary had made a friend who shared her goals and helped her with her
newspaper. Thomas Cary was a Toronto businessman. When his wife died, Mary agreed
to marry him and help raise his three children. They were married in 1856. In 1857, their
daughter was born. Mary now had four children to raise, but she didn't give up speaking,
writing, and teaching. She often traveled the country selling subscriptions to her
newspaper, gathering news reports, and giving public lectures. Thomas helped her by
looking after things at home and at the newspaper office while she was away.

### Stubborn to the End of Her Days

One day in 1858, Mary made news herself. Slave catchers from the United States were
becoming bold enough to come to Canada to drag people back to slavery. When a young
runaway slave was captured in Chatham, Mary soon heard about it. She sprang into
action. She rushed to the scene, snatched the boy from the slave catchers, and ran with
him to the courthouse. There she rang the courthouse bell until a large crowd had
gathered. Then she made a fiery speech, explaining what had happened. Soon she had
the crowd on her side, and the slave catchers had to give up and leave town.

In 1860, Mary's husband died, and soon afterward their second child was born. Life must
have been hard for Mary. She now had five children to support, but she didn't give up.
She earned money by writing for other newspapers, and kept on teaching. Somehow,
she managed to keep the *Provincial Freeman* going too. Then the Civil War broke out in
the United States, and Mary's life changed forever. She went to the United States to help
enlist American troops to fight against slavery. After the war, she stayed in the United
States to help educate the slaves who had been freed. Later, she became the first
woman in the United States to graduate from law school.

Mary and her family never moved back to Canada, but she will always be an important
part of Canadian history. Her life was an example of her values—education, self-respect,
and standing up for what you believe in. Do you ever wonder whether you can make a
difference to the people around you? Just remember stubborn Mary Shadd, who touched
the lives of so many people!

—by Karen Shadd-Evelyn

82. The first lines of this article are written in italics in order to show that
    A. slavery is unfair
    B. Mary could not go to school
    C. they are the introduction to the article
    D. they are conversation between two people

83. Mary Shadd was the first woman in the United States to graduate from
    A. law school
    B. primary school
    C. business school
    D. management school

84. Mary had to hide the fact that she could read and write because she
    A. lived in Delaware
    B. was a black American
    C. was not allowed to go to school
    D. had parents who were educated

85. Mary decided that the **best** way to get her ideas out to the public was through
    A. radio reports
    B. television news
    C. public speaking
    D. newspaper articles

*Read the following passage and answer questions 86 to 90*

### Cheetahs

The cheetah is the fastest mammal on land and can reach speeds of over 100 km/h over short distances. It usually chases its prey at only about half that speed, however. After a chase, a cheetah needs half an hour to catch its breath before it can eat.

5  The cheetah's excellent eyesight helps it find prey during the day. Sometimes, a cheetah perches on a high place and watches for prey. Cheetahs eat small- to medium-sized animals, such as hares, impalas, and gazelles.

When it spots prey, a cheetah begins to stalk. It creeps as close as possible before the attack. The cheetah is hard to see because its spotted coat blends with the tall, dry grass of the plains.

10 Suddenly, the cheetah makes a lightning dash. With a paw, it knocks its prey to the ground and then bites its throat.

Once found throughout Asia and Africa, cheetahs today are racing toward extinction. Loss of habitat and declining numbers of their prey combine to threaten the future of these cats.

86. When a cheetah stalks its prey, it
    A. crunches the bones of its dinner
    B. moves carefully and silently
    C. plays a trick on another animal
    D. roars very loudly

87. The word *prey* refers to
    A. an animal that is being hunted
    B. an animal that is hurt
    C. a small animal
    D. a hunter

88. To *perch* means to
   A. climb up to
   B. run beside
   C. lie under
   D. sit on

89. To say that cheetahs "are racing toward extinction"[line 12] means that cheetahs are
   A. trying to run faster than each other
   B. chasing after other animals
   C. increasing their speed
   D. decreasing in number

90. The phrase "makes a lightning dash"[line 10] means that the cheetah
   A. runs in a jagged pattern like a fork of lightning
   B. flees when it is stormy outside
   C. is very afraid of storms
   D. runs very fast

*Read the following passage and answer questions 91 to 94*

### Discovering the Mysteries of the St. Lawrence

As soon as the ice leaves the St. Lawrence, the sea breeze begins to blow more gently. This is a sign of spring and the time when sailors feel called to the sea. Docks in the small villages along the coastline are teaming with life. Everyone is getting their boats ready, anxious to weigh anchor after a long hibernation.

5  Offshore, the first whales appear, another sure sign of the change of season. They are humpback whales, weary after a long journey from the Caribbean. A mother and her calf have finally reached their destination and main feeding area after a three or four thousand kilometer trip.

The calf is discovering the St. Lawrence River for the first time, so it sticks close to its
10 mother. This is the first migration of its life. All these new sensations! Why did they have to leave clear, turquoise, tropical waters where it was born the winter before? Why launch off on this long expedition, where eddies and currents get colder and colder the farther north they go? In the freezing waters of the St. Lawrence, the young whale needs to be in constant communication with its mother. The water is so opaque, the
15 seaweed and plankton so dense, that it cannot afford to lose sight of her. It wonders where on earth its mother has brought it? The salty taste of the sea is the only thing it recognizes from home.

Odd-looking birds—seagulls, northern gannets, and cormorants—dive-bomb it every time it comes up for a breath, making it feel even more insecure.

20 The calf finds the currents in the St. Lawrence surprisingly powerful, just like the currents along the coast of North America. The tides weren't even that strong out at sea. And the sounds intrigue it. They're all so different, and from every direction. They come from boats sailing in the river; there are more boats here than on the ocean. Suddenly, through the currents, it spots a school of capelin. It has never seen so many fish in its
25 life! The mother heads straight for the cloud of small fish and swallows a huge quantity of them. The young whale will have to do the same one day, when it is no longer getting its mother's milk.

Everything is so new for this young humpback. It is suddenly beginning to see why its mother insisted on this great migration. They stopped along the way a few times to feed,
30 but now the calf understands that the icy, turbulent waters of the majestic St. Lawrence are actually one of the most extraordinary pantries on the planet.

—from *As Long As There Are Whales* by Evelyne Daigle, translated by Geneviève Wright

91. In the phrase "The water is so opaque," the word "opaque" means that the water of the St. Lawrence is
    A. icy cold
    B. crystal clear
    C. rough and wavy
    D. difficult to see through

92. According to the passage, the young whale and its mother have been traveling for
    A. three or four hundred miles
    B. three or four thousand miles
    C. three or four hundred kilometers
    D. three or four thousand kilometers

93. A baby whale is known as a
    A. whelp
    B. calf
    C. pup
    D. kit

94. What kind of whale is the young whale in this passage?
    A. Humpback
    B. Beluga
    C. Right
    D. Blue

*Read the following passage and answer questions 95 to 98*

## Are All Giants All Bad?

GIANTS ARE THOUGHT BY MOST HUMANS—probably unfairly—to be as dangerous and cruel as they are large. Whatever the truth, they have a troublesome history.

### Early Giants

The first giants were the Gigantes of ancient Greek mythology, born when the blood of Uranus (the Heavens) fell upon Gaea (Earth). The Gigantes fought the gods of Mount Olympus—Zeus, Hera, Apollo, and others. The Olympian gods needed the help of the hero Hercules to defeat them. The Gigantes were buried underneath mountains that then became volcanoes.

Another race of mythical Greek giants was known as the Cyclops. These monsters, who had only one eye, created the thunderbolts of Zeus. In Homer's epic poem *The Odyssey*, the hero Odysseus and his men encounter a Cyclops and barely escape.

Both these races of giants, like those that followed, were said to be vicious cannibals.

### British Giants

Among later giants, the legend of a pair named Gog and Magog spread throughout the world, changing a bit from place to place. In Britain the story survives in the form of two large statues in Guildhall in London, first erected in the 1400s and said to portray the last of a race of giants destroyed by the legendary founder of London. (The statues, public favorites, have been replaced twice: first after the Great Fire of 1666, then after an air raid during the Second World War.)

A slightly different British legend combines those giants into a single monster named Gogmagog, who lived near Cornwall. In that version, a brave soldier threw the giant off a cliff, which is still called Giant's Leap.

Another British giant of legend, Gargantua, became famous in the 1500s as the main character in comical adventures written by a Frenchman, François Rabelais. Gargantua was something like the gigantic American woodsman Paul Bunyan. He was so huge that a tennis court fit inside one of his teeth. It took the milk of 17,913 cows to quench his thirst. In some legends, he was employed by King Arthur, and was credited with defeating Gog and Magog.

### Giants and Magic

According to the early historian Geoffrey of Monmouth, Stonehenge, the mysterious circle of huge stones in southern England, originated with the giants of Ireland. As he records, Merlin had been asked for advice on building a war memorial. The wizard replied:

"If you want to grace the burial place of these men with some lasting monument, send for the Giants' Ring which is on Mount Killaraus in Ireland. In that place there is a stone
35 construction which no man of this period could ever erect, unless he combined great skill and artistry. The stones are enormous and there is no one alive strong enough to move them. If they are placed in position round this site, in the way in which they are erected over there, they will stand for ever….

"These stones are connected with certain religious secret rites and they have various
40 properties which are medicinally important. Many years ago the Giants transported them from the remotest confines of Africa and set them up in Ireland at a time when they inhabited that country. Their plan was that, whenever they felt ill, baths should be prepared at the foot of the stones; for they used to pour water over them and to run this water into baths in which their sick were cured. What is more, they mixed the water with
45 herbal concoctions and so healed their wounds. There is not a single stone among them that hasn't some medicinal virtue."

As Geoffrey tells it, the king took Merlin's advice and had the stones transported to their present site.

**A Secret Everyone Knows**

50 In Harry's world, most wizards are prejudiced against giants. Hagrid never told anyone his mother was the giantess Fridwulfa because he was worried about what they would think. For the same reason, the headmistress of Beauxbatons, Madame Olympe Maxime, is reluctant to admit she is also half-giant. But anyone with common sense would guess that secret from her name. Olympe refers to the original giants of Olympus,
55 and *maxime* means "great" or "very large" in French.

—from *The Magical Worlds of Harry Potter: A Treasury of Myths, Legends, and Fascinating Facts* by David Colbert

95. The quotation "the king took Merlin's advice and had the stones transported to their present site" means that the
    A. stones were given as a gift
    B. king sent to Africa for new stones
    C. king destroyed the present site in southern England
    D. stones were moved from Ireland to southern England

96. Geoffrey of Monmouth was an early historian. A historian is someone who
    A. tells fairy tales
    B. illustrates wars
    C. writes records of events
    D. creates comical adventures

97. In the phrase "there is a stone construction which no man of this period could ever erect,"[line 34] the word "period" is a synonym for
    A. end
    B. time
    C. chapter
    D. location

98. According to Merlin, the Giants' Ring in Ireland was used for
    A. transportation
    B. assemblies
    C. memorials
    D. healing

*Read the following passage and answer questions 99 to 102*

### from "The Court of King Arthur"

A long, long time ago, even before television was invented, there lived a knight called Sir Gadabout. This was in the days of the famous King Arthur and his Round Table. It was an exciting and mysterious time to live in, especially for a knight.

In a misty and remote corner of England stood the castle called Camelot, and there King
5  Arthur gathered the best knights in the land to sit at the Round Table. These knights had to be prepared to go out at a moment's notice and fight villains, dragons, people who drop litter—and generally keep the peace.

If you could travel in time and visit Camelot, you would find the gallant King Arthur, tall and brave, much loved and respected. By his side would be the Queen—Guinivere,
10  beautiful, graceful, and a dab hand at woodwork. Around them you would find all the great knights, whose names might seem odd to us now: Sir Lancelot, Sir Gawain, Sir Dorothy (his name seemed odd even then) and Sir Gadabout.

Now, although Sir Gadabout sat at the Round Table with the best of them, he wasn't quite one of the best knights in the land. It has to be said that he was indubitably the
15  Worst Knight in the *World*. In fact, the March edition of the magazine *Knights Illustrated* voted him the "knight most likely to chop his own foot off in a fight." …

His armor was held together purely by rust—and anyway, he'd grown out of it by the time he was eleven. His spear was bent and only good for throwing round corners, and his sword was broken in five places and fixed with lots of sticky tape; it wobbled
20  alarmingly in a stiff breeze. His horse, Pegasus, was knockkneed and about ninety years-old.

King Arthur felt sorry for Sir Gadabout, who was hard-working and polite. That was probably why the King allowed him to join the otherwise glorious company of the Round Table.

To be honest Sir Gadabout had not performed as many heroic deeds as the other knights. He'd hardly performed any, unless you count the time when he accompanied the
25  fearsome Sir Bors de Ganis on a mission to rescue the fair maid Fiona from the Isles of Iona. Then he got lost in the eerie mists and ended up in Tipton, some three hundred miles from where Sir Bors was having to get on with the rescue all alone.

Sir Gadabout did once get a dear old lady's cat down from a tree. It wasn't stuck, as it happened (but *he* wasn't to know that) and it only took Sir Tristram three hours to get Sir
30  Gadabout back down again…

—from *Sir Gadabout* by Martyn Beardsley

99. The phrase "his sword was broken" is written in the
    A. past tense
    B. future tense
    C. present tense
    D. past perfect tense

100. A homonym for the word "knight" is
   A. sir
   B. day
   C. night
   D. princess

101. The word "remote" is a synonym for
   A. hidden
   B. distant
   C. cold
   D. wild

102. The days of the famous King Arthur are described as
   A. exciting and mysterious
   B. fearsome and villainous
   C. adventurous and heroic
   D. dull and boring

*Read the following passage and answer questions 103 to 106*

### Ancient Broom Games

Broom sports emerged almost as soon as broomsticks were sufficiently advanced to allow fliers to turn corners and vary their speed and height. Early wizarding writings and paintings give us some idea of the games our ancestors played. Some of these no longer exist; others have survived or evolved into the sports we know today.

5   The celebrated **annual broom race** of Sweden dates from the tenth century. Fliers race from Kopparberg to Arjeplog, a distance of slightly over three hundred miles. The course runs straight through a dragon reservation and the vast silver trophy is shaped like a Swedish Short-Snout. Nowadays this is an international event and wizards of all nationalities congregate at Kopparberg to cheer the starters, then Apparate to Arjeplog to
10  congratulate the survivors.

The famous painting *Günther der Gewaltig ist der Gewinner* ("Gunther the Violent is the Winner"), dated 1105, shows the ancient German game of **Stichstock**. A twenty-foot-high pole was topped with an inflated dragon bladder. One player on a broomstick had the job of protecting this bladder. The bladder-guardian was tied to the pole by a rope around his
15  or her waist, so that he or she could not fly further than ten feet away from it. The rest of the players would take it in turns to fly at the bladder and attempt to puncture it with the specially sharpened ends of their brooms. The bladder-guardian was allowed to use his or her wand to repel these attacks. The game ended when the bladder was successfully punctured, or the bladder-guardian had either succeeded in hexing all opponents out of
20  the running or collapsed from exhaustion. Stichstock died out in the fourteenth century.

In Ireland the game of **Aingingein** flourished, the subject of many an Irish ballad (the legendary wizard Fingal the Fearless is alleged to have been an Aingingein champion). One by one the players would take the Dom, or ball (actually the gallbladder of a goat), and speed through a series of burning barrels set high in the air on stilts. The Dom was
25  to be thrown through the final barrel. The player who succeeded in getting the Dom through the last barrel in the fastest time, without having caught fire on the way, was the winner.

Scotland was the birthplace of what is probably the most dangerous of all broom games—**Creaothceann**. The game features in a tragic Gaelic poem of the eleventh century, the first verse of which says, in translation:

30 *The players assembled, twelve fine, hearty men,*
*They strapped on their cauldrons, stood poised to fly,*
*At the sound of the horn they were swiftly airborne*
*But ten of their number were fated to die.*

Creaothceann players each wore a cauldron strapped to the head. At the sound of the
35 horn or drum, up to a hundred charmed rocks and boulders that had been hovering a hundred feet above the ground began to fall towards the earth. The Creaothceann players zoomed around trying to catch as many rocks as possible in their cauldrons. Considered by many Scottish wizards to be the supreme test of manliness and courage, Creaothceann enjoyed considerable popularity in the Middle Ages, despite the huge
40 number of fatalities that resulted from it. The game was made illegal in 1762, and though Magnus "Dent-Head" Macdonald spearheaded a campaign for its reintroduction in the 1960s, the Ministry of Magic refused to lift the ban.

**Shuntbumps** was popular in Devon, England. This was a crude form of jousting, the sole aim being to knock as many other players as possible off their brooms, the last person
45 remaining on their broom winning.

**Swivenhodge** began in Herefordshire. Like Stichstock, this involved an inflated bladder, usually a pig's. Players sat backwards on their brooms and batted the bladder backwards and forwards across a hedge with the brush ends of their brooms. The first person to miss gave their opponent a point. First to reach fifty points was the winner.

50 Swivenhodge is still played in England, though it has never achieved much widespread popularity; Shuntbumps survives only as a children's game. At Queerditch Marsh, however, a game had been created that would one day become the most popular in the wizarding world.

—from *Quidditch Through the Ages* by Kennilworthy Whisp (J. K. Rowling)

103. In the sentence "The course runs straight through a dragon reservation and the vast silver trophy is shaped like a Swedish Short-Snout," a Swedish Short-Snout is **most likely** a
  A. pig
  B. dog
  C. parrot
  D. dragon

104. A synonym for the word "vary," as it is used in the phrase "to allow fliers to turn corners and vary their speed and height,"[line 1] is
  A. many
  B. count
  C. change
  D. maintain

105. A synonym for the word "evolved," as it is used in the sentence "Some of these no longer exist; others have survived or evolved into the sports we know today,"[line 3] is
   A. died
   B. changed
   C. enlarged
   D. disappeared

106. The broom game that never became widely popular was
   A. Stitchstock
   B. Shuntbumps
   C. Swivenhodge
   D. Creaothceann

# EXERCISE #1—READING LITERATURE

## Table of Correlations

| Standard | | Test #1 |
|---|---|---|
| **5RL** | Reading Standards for Literature | |
| *5RL.2* | *Determine a theme of a story, drama, or poem from details in the text, including how characters in a story or drama respond to challenges or how the speaker in a poem reflects upon a topic; summarize the text.* | 110, 117, 120, 125, 137, 138, 142, 144, 146, 148, 151, 154, 155 |
| *5RL.4* | *Determine the meaning of words and phrases as they are used in a text, including figurative language such as metaphors and similes.* | 130, 134 |
| *5RL.5* | *Explain how a series of chapters, scenes, or stanzas fits together to provide the overall structure of a particular story, drama, or poem.* | 126, 159 |
| *5RL.6* | *Describe how a narrator's or speaker's point of view influences how events are described.* | 124, 140 |
| *5RL.10* | *By the end of the year, read and comprehend literature, including stories, dramas, and poetry, at the high end of the grades 4–5 text complexity band independently and proficiently.* | 118, 126, 159 |
| **5RI** | Reading Standards for Informational Text | |
| *5RI.2* | *Determine two or more main ideas of a text and explain how they are supported by key details; summarize the text.* | 110, 117, 120, 125, 137, 138, 142, 144, 146, 148, 151, 154, 155 |
| *5RI.4* | *Determine the meaning of general academic and domain-specific words and phrases in a text relevant to a grade 5 topic or subject area.* | 130, 134 |
| *5RI.6* | *Analyze multiple accounts of the same event or topic, noting important similarities and differences in the point of view they represent.* | 124, 140 |
| *5RI.8* | *Explain how an author uses reasons and evidence to support particular points in a text, identifying which reasons and evidence support which point(s).* | 129 |
| **5RF** | Reading Standards: Foundational Skills | |
| *5RF.3a* | *Know and apply grade-level phonics and word analysis skills in decoding words. Use combined knowledge of all letter-sound correspondences, syllabication patterns, and morphology to read accurately unfamiliar multisyllabic words in context...* | 107, 108, 111, 115, 123, 127, 128, 131, 156, 157 |
| *5RF.4a* | *Read with sufficient accuracy and fluency to support comprehension. Read on-level text with purpose and understanding.* | 152, 153 |
| *5RF.4b* | *Read with sufficient accuracy and fluency to support comprehension. Read on-level prose and poetry orally with accuracy, appropriate rate, and expression on successive readings.* | 152, 153 |
| *5RF.4c* | *Read with sufficient accuracy and fluency to support comprehension. Use context to confirm or self-correct word recognition and understanding, rereading as necessary.* | 108, 111, 123, 127, 128, 131, 152, 153, 156, 157 |
| **5W** | Writing Standards | |
| *5W.3a* | *Write narratives to develop real or imagined experiences or events using effective technique, descriptive details, and clear event sequences. Orient the reader by establishing a situation and introducing a narrator and/or characters; organize...* | 124, 140 |

Reading Literature          Castle Rock Research

| | | |
|---|---|---|
| 5W.3b | Write narratives to develop real or imagined experiences or events using effective technique, descriptive details, and clear event sequences. Use narrative techniques, such as dialogue, description, and pacing, to develop experiences and events... | 125, 144 |
| 5W.9a | Draw evidence from literary or informational texts to support analysis, reflection, and research. Apply grade 5 Reading standards to literature. | 121, 122, 132, 133, 141, 145, 149, 150, 158 |
| 5W.9b | Draw evidence from literary or informational texts to support analysis, reflection, and research. Apply grade 5 Reading standards to informational texts. | 129, 132, 149 |
| **5SL** | Speaking and Listening Standards | |
| 5SL.2 | Summarize a written text read aloud or information presented in diverse media and formats, including visually, quantitatively, and orally. | 120, 137, 148 |
| 5SL.3 | Summarize the points a speaker makes and explain how each claim is supported by reasons and evidence. | 120, 129, 137, 148 |
| 5SL.6 | Adapt speech to a variety of contexts and tasks, using formal English when appropriate to task and situation. | 143 |
| **5L** | Language Standards | |
| 5L.1b | Demonstrate command of the conventions of standard English grammar and usage when writing or speaking. Form and use the perfect verb tenses. | 116, 119, 147 |
| 5L.1c | Demonstrate command of the conventions of standard English grammar and usage when writing or speaking. Use verb tense to convey various times, sequences, states, and conditions. | 112, 116, 119, 147 |
| 5L.4a | Determine or clarify the meaning of unknown and multiple-meaning words and phrases based on grade 5 reading and content, choosing flexibly from a range of strategies. Use context as a clue to the meaning of a word or phrase. | 108, 111, 123, 127, 128, 131, 156, 157 |
| 5L.5a | Demonstrate understanding of figurative language, word relationships, and nuances in word meanings. Interpret figurative language, including similes and metaphors, in context. | 139 |
| 5L.5c | Demonstrate understanding of figurative language, word relationships, and nuances in word meanings. Use the relationship between particular words to better understand each of the words. | 109, 113, 114, 135, 136, 157 |

*Read the following passage and answer questions 107 to 110*

### The Scooter

In my long life, I must declare,
I've gone a lot from here to there.
There is the bike and there's the car
And airplanes when you must go far.

5  In my mind fond memories lie
Of when I was a little guy.
With my big brother by my side
I made my solo scooter ride.

"A scooter's kind," so said my brother,
10 "You use one leg and rest the other."
It's an easy way to get downtown
Without your engine breaking down.

Serving as your travel tutor,
May I advise you get a scooter?
15 Try a scooter and you'll see
Your travels can be trouble free.

—*by* Grandpa Tucker

http://www.grandpatucker.com/scooter.html-ssi

107. When the speaker mentions being "a little guy," the stage of life he **probably** is referring to is
  A. adolescence
  B. adulthood
  C. childhood
  D. infancy

108. The word "*advise*" means to
  A. want something
  B. crave attention
  C. be wise
  D. inform

109. In the line "In my long life, I must declare,"[line 1] an antonym of the word "long" is
  A. short
  B. lengthy
  C. extended
  D. extensive

110. The speaker of the poem fondly remembers
  A. going downtown
  B. riding in an airplane
  C. buying his first scooter
  D. his first solo scooter ride

*Read the following passage and answer questions 111 to 114*

### How Brazilian Beetles Got Their Gorgeous Coats: A Story from Brazil

Long ago in Brazil, beetles had plain brown coats. But today their hard-shelled coats are gorgeous. They are so colorful that people often set them in pins and necklaces like precious stones. This is how it happened that Brazilian beetles got their new coats.

5 One day a little brown beetle was crawling along a wall. Suddenly a big gray rat darted out of a hole in the wall. When he saw the beetle, he began to make fun of her.

"Is that as fast as you can go? What a poke you are! You'll never get anywhere! Just watch how fast I can run!"

The rat dashed to the end of the wall, turned around, and ran back to the beetle. The beetle was still slowly crawling along. She had barely crawled past the spot where the rat 10 left her.

"I'll bet you wish you could run like that!" bragged the gray rat.

"You certainly are a fast runner," replied the beetle. Even though the rat went on and on about himself, the beetle never said a word about the things she could do. She just kept slowly crawling along the wall, wishing the rat would go away.

15 A green and gold parrot in the mango tree above had overheard their conversation. She said to the rat, "How would you like to race with the beetle? Just to make the race exciting, I'll offer a bright colored coat as a reward. The winner may choose any color coat and I'll have it made to order."

The parrot told them the finish line would be the palm tree at the top of the hill. She gave 20 the signal to start, and they were off.

The rat ran as fast as he could. When he reached the palm tree, he could hardly believe his eyes: there was the beetle sitting beside the parrot. The rat asked with suspicious tone, "How did you ever manage to run fast enough to get here so soon?"

"Nobody ever said anything about having to run to win the race," replied the beetle as 25 she drew out her tiny wings from her sides. "So I flew instead."

"I didn't know you could fly," said the rat with a grumpy look on his face.

The parrot said to the rat, "You have lost the contest. From now on you must never judge anyone by looks alone. You never can tell when or where you may find hidden wings."

Then the parrot turned to the brown beetle and asked, "What color would you like your 30 new coat to be?"

"I'd like it to be green and gold, just like yours," replied the beetle. And since that day, Brazilian beetles have had gorgeous coats of green and gold. But the rat still wears a plain, dull, gray one.

—from *How & Why Stories: World Tales Kids Can Read and Tell* by Martha Hamilton and
35  Mitch Weiss

111. "Then the parrot turned to the brown beetle…"

In the sentence above, the word "*then*" means almost the same thing as which of these other transition words?

A. Also
B. Next
C. However
D. Although

112. Which of the following words is a verb?
A. Fast
B. Gray
C. Green
D. Crawl

113. An antonym of the word "*suddenly*" is
A. unexpectedly
B. gradually
C. abruptly
D. quickly

114. A synonym for the word "*suspicious*" is
A. trusting
B. believing
C. skeptical
D. unguarded

*Read the following passage and answer questions 115 to 118*

## Very Last First Time

Eva Padlyat lived in a village on Ungava Bay in northern Canada. She was Inuit, and ever since she could remember she had walked with her mother on the bottom of the sea. It was something the people of her village did in winter when they wanted mussels to eat.

5 Today, something very special was going to happen. Today, for the very first time in her life, Eva would walk on the bottom of the sea alone.

Eva got ready. Standing in their small, warm kitchen, Eva looked at her mother and smiled.

"Shall we go now?"

"I think we'd better."

10 "We'll start out together, won't we?"

Eva's mother nodded. Pulling up their warm hoods, they went out.

Beside the house there were two sleds, each holding a shovel, a long ice-chisel and a mussel pan. Dragging the sleds behind them, they started off.

Eva and her mother walked through the village. Snow lay white as far as the eye could
15 see—snow, but not a single tree, for miles and miles on the vast northern tundra. The village was off by itself. There were no highways, but snowmobile tracks led away and disappeared into the distance.

Down by the shore they met some friends and stopped for a quick greeting.

They had come at the right time. The tide was out, pulling the sea water away, so there
20 would be room for them to climb under the thick ice and wander about on the seabed.

Eva and her mother walked carefully over the bumps and ridges of the frozen sea. Soon they found a spot where the ice was cracked and broken.

"This is the right place," Eva said.

After shoveling away a pile of snow, she reached for the ice-chisel. She worked it under
25 an ice hump and, heaving and pushing with her mother's help, made a hole.

Eva peered down into the hole and felt the dampness of the air below. She breathed deep to catch the salt sea smell.

"Good luck," Eva's mother said.

Eva grinned. "Good luck yourself."

30 Her eyes lit up with excitement and she threw her mussel pan into the hole. Then she lowered herself slowly into the darkness, feeling with her feet until they touched a rock and she could let go of the ice above.

In a minute, she was standing on the seabed.

Above her, in the ice hole, the wind whistled. Eva struck a match and lit a candle.

35 The gold-bright flame shone and glistened on the wet stones and pools at her feet.

She held her candle and saw strange shadow shapes around her. The shadows formed a wolf, a bear, a seal sea-monster. Eva watched them, then she remembered.

"I'd better get to work," she said.

40 Lighting three more candles, she carefully wedged them between stones so she could see to collect mussels. Using her knife as a lever, she tugged and pried and scraped to pull the mussels off the rocks. She was in luck. There were strings of blue-black mussel shells whichever way she turned.

Alone—for the first time.

Eva was so happy she started to sing. Her song echoed around, so she sang louder.
45 She hummed far back in her throat to make the echoes rumble. She lifted up long strings of mussels and let them clatter into her pan.

Soon her mussel pan was full, so she had time to explore. She found a rock pool that was deep and clear. Small shrimps in the water darted and skittered in the light from her candle. She stopped to watch them. Reaching under a ledge, she touched a pinky-purple
50 crab. The fronds of the anemones on the ledge tickled her wrist.

Beyond the rock pool, seaweed was piled in thick, wet, shiny heaps and masses. Eva scrambled over the seaweed, up and onto a rock mound. Stretching her arms wide, tilting her head back, she laughed, imagining the shifting, waving, lifting swirl of seaweed when the tide comes in.

55 The tide!

Eva listened. The lap, lap of the waves sounded louder and nearer. Whoosh and roar and whoosh again.

Eva jumped off the rock, stumbled—and her candle dropped and sputtered out. She had gone too far. The candles she had set down between the stones had burned to nothing.
60 There was darkness—darkness all around.

"Help me!" she called, but her voice was swallowed. "Someone come quickly."

Eva closed her eyes. Her hands went to her face. She could not bear to look.

She felt in her pockets. She knew she had more candles there, but she could not seem to find them.

65 The tide was roaring louder and the ice shrieked and creaked with its movement.

Eva's hands groped deeper. She took a candle out at last and her box of matches, but her fingers were shaking and clumsy. For a long, forever moment, she could not strike the match to light the candle.

The flame seemed pale and weak.

70 Eva walked slowly, fearfully, peering through the shadows, looking for her mussel pan.

At last, she found it and ran stumbling to the ice-hole. Then, looking up, Eva saw the moon in the sky. It was high and round and big. Its light cast a circle through the hole onto the seabed at her feet.

Eva stood in the moonlight. Her parka glowed. Blowing out her candle, she slowly began
75 to smile.

By the time her mother came, she was dancing. She was skipping and leaping in and out of the moonglow circle, darkness and light, in and out.

"Eva," her mother called.

"I'm here," she called back. "Take my mussel pan." Eva scrambled onto a rock and held
80 the pan up high to her mother. Then her mother's hands reached down and pulled her up, too, through the hole.

Squeezing her mother's hand, Eva saw the moon, shining on the snow and ice, and felt the wind on her face once more.

"That was my last very first—my very last *first* time—for walking alone on the bottom of
85 the sea," Eva said.

—*by* Jan Andrews

115. The word "tundra" refers to
　　A. a treeless frozen plain
　　B. land next to the sea
　　C. a mountain summit
　　D. prairie grassland

116. The sentence "We'll start out together, won't we?"[line 10] is an example of which verb tense?
　　A. Future
　　B. Present
　　C. Simple past
　　D. Present perfect

117. How many times had Eva been alone at the bottom of the sea before?
　　A. One
　　B. Two
　　C. None
　　D. Several

118. This story can be **best** described as
　　A. fiction
　　B. a letter
　　C. a poem
　　D. non–fiction

*Read the following passage and answer questions 119 to 122*

### Not Owls Too!

The reason Dad said: "Oh NO! Not owls too" was because I already had some pets.

There was a summerhouse in our back yard and we kept about thirty gophers in it. They belonged to Bruce and me, and to another boy called Murray. We caught them out on the prairie, using snares made of heavy twine.

5  The way you do it is like this: You walk along until you spot a gopher sitting up beside his hole. Gophers sit straight up, reaching their noses as high as they can, so they can see farther. When you begin to get too close they flick their tails, give a little jump, and whisk down their holes. As soon as they do that, you take a piece of twine that has a noose tied in one end, and you spread the noose over the hole. Then you lie down in the grass
10  holding the other end of the twine in your hand. You can hear the gopher all the while, whistling away to himself somewhere underground. He can hear you, too, and he's wondering what you're up to.

After a while he gets so curious he can't stand it. Out pops his head, and you give a yank on the twine. You have to haul in fast, because if the twine gets loose he'll slip his head
15  out of the noose and zip back down his hole.

We had rats too. Murray's dad was a professor at the college and he got us some white rats from the medical school. We kept them in our garage, which made my Dad a little peeved, because he couldn't put the car in the garage for fear the rats would make nests inside the seats. Nobody ever knew how many rats we had because they have so
20  many babies, and they have them so fast. We gave white rats away to all the kids in Saskatoon, but we always seemed to end up with as many as we had at first.

There were the rats and gophers, and then there was a big cardboard box full of garter snakes that we kept under the back porch, because my mother wouldn't let me keep them in the house. Then there were the pigeons. I usually had about ten of them, but
25  they kept bringing their friends and relations for visits, so I never knew how many to expect when I went out to feed them in the mornings. There were some rabbits too, and then there was Mutt, my dog—but he wasn't a pet; he was one of the family.

Sunday morning my father said:

"Billy, I think you have enough pets. I don't think you'd better bring home any owls. In any
30  case, the owls might eat your rats and rabbits and gophers…"

He stopped talking and a queer look came into his face. Then he said:

"On second thought—maybe we *need* an owl around this place!"

So it was all right.

—from *Owls in the Family*, by Farley Mowat

119. From the second to the third paragraph, the writer switches verb tenses from
   A. present to future
   B. future to present
   C. past to present
   D. present to past

120. In this story, the gophers belong to
    A. Bruce's dad
    B. Billy's family
    C. Bruce, Billy, and Murray
    D. Murray's brother and sister

121. The reason that Billy's father got a "queer" look on his face when he was talking about the owls was that
    A. Billy had outwitted him
    B. he had come to a sudden realization
    C. he realized there was no point in arguing
    D. the possibility of having more pets was frightening to him

122. At the beginning of this passage, the narrator is **most likely** feeling
    A. confident
    B. anxious
    C. relieved
    D. angry

*Read the following passage and answer questions 123 to 126*

### The Field Trip

The bus engine roared as we clambered on board
and took the first seats we could find.
Matthew had thought he'd have time for the bathroom,
but somehow we left him behind.
5   Pete put a beetle down Eleanor's back.
He just didn't think she would mind.
And Alex threw Tyler's new coat out the window
when Tyler said something unkind.

It rained down a fuss when we got off the bus.
10  Our teacher was soaked to the skin.
And then when she found she forgot all our lunches,
her patience began to wear thin.
She got so befuddled, she stepped in a puddle.
The water went up to her shin.
15  And I'd gladly say what she said when it happened,
but I know that swearing's a sin.

We moaned and we groaned as we started back home,
cranky, exhausted, and spent.
Sally was certain her stomach was hurtin'.
20 We soon understood what she meant.
My teacher might feel that this trip was a failure.
I'm sure that was not her intent.
I'll tell her we had the most wonderful time.
I just can't recall where we went.
25 —by Eric Ode

123. In the phrase "She got so befuddled, she stepped in a puddle," the word "befuddled" means
- A. tired
- B. dizzy
- C. confused
- D. concerned

124. The speaker of this poem is a
- A. principal
- B. student
- C. teacher
- D. parent

125. The reason that the students moan and groan on the way back home is that
- A. their stomachs hurt
- B. their trip was a failure
- C. they are starving and thirsty
- D. they are grumpy, tired, and worn out

126. This text can be **best** described as a
- A. personal narrative
- B. narrative poem
- C. funny limerick
- D. short story

*Read the following passage and answer questions 127 to 130*

### from "A Dive into the Sea"

Jason, Julia, and Rick were lying stomach-down on their towels, lining up some of the treasures they'd fished out of the sand: an assortment of colored rocks and shells, and a piece of wood with an iron bolt attached to it. To get the wood, Rick had swum out all the way to the very edge of the rocks, where the sea got deeper and the current started to
5  pull at him, like a hand grabbing at his legs. Rick felt it was wiser not to go farther out, and Julia happily agreed with him. There was no sense risking their lives when they had everything they needed right here.

Julia flipped onto her back to sunbathe while Rick and Jason explored the cove. They discovered a second stretch of beach, where there were traces of the small wooden pier.
10  A number of mooring lines hung from it. The walkways and boards had almost totally rotted away, but the remnants stood as evidence that old Ulysses had once, in fact, kept a boat here.

Jason was daydreaming about the old man's adventures as he and Rick went back to tell the news to Julia, who had become thoroughly bored with sunbathing. That was typical of
15  Julia. She could sit still for fifteen minutes, tops. She sat up and hugged her knees as Jason told her about what he and Rick had found. His telling made their adventure on the rocks take on mystical proportions.

While Jason spoke, Rick felt a raindrop on his face. He looked up. A dark cloud crossed overhead. "Rain," he announced.

20  Jason looked at the long series of steps that wound their way up toward home. A long, hard climb awaited them. "Should we start back up?" he asked.

"We'd better," Rick decided. "It may be only a shower, but you never know. We should be careful."

Julia agreed. Anything was better than sitting around in the rain.

The rain came harder now. The steps were more slippery than ever. Jason struggled to
25  keep up with his athletic sister and friend. In a burst of energy, he pushed them aside and sprinted up the stairs in twos and threes. He couldn't last at that pace, but at least he'd get a head start.

"See you up at the top, suckers!" he shouted.

Julia turned to Rick. "Come on, let's race," she urged.

30  But Rick surprised her. His face was calm, content. "Let him go," Rick said. "He gets to win while we take it nice and slow. Together."

Suddenly, Jason screamed. Rick and Julia looked up just in time to see him tumbling, falling, clawing for his life along the cliff.

—from *Ulysses Moore: The Door to Time* by Pierdomenico Baccalario, translated by
35  Edizioni Piemme

127. The purpose of a mooring line is **most likely** to
    A. catch fish
    B. drag a net
    C. tow a boat
    D. secure a boat

128. In the phrase "take on mystical proportions,"[line 17] the word "mystical" means
    A. secret
    B. severe
    C. strange
    D. supernatural

129. Rick returned to the shore after getting the piece of wood because
    A. Julia called him in
    B. Jason wanted to go exploring
    C. it was too dangerous to continue
    D. there was nothing more to retrieve

130. In the phrase "the current started to pull at him, like a hand grabbing at his legs,"[line 4] the expression "like a hand grabbing at his legs" is an example of
    A. simile
    B. metaphor
    C. hyperbole
    D. alliteration

*Read the following passage and answer questions 131 to 134*

### from The Lives of Christopher Chant

Christopher was called to Mama's dressing-room that afternoon. There was a new governess sitting on the only hard chair, wearing the usual sort of ugly grayish clothes and a hat that was uglier than usual. Her drab cotton gloves were folded on her dull bag and her head hung down as if she were timid or put-upon, or both. Christopher found her
5 of no interest. All the interest in the room was centered on the man standing behind Mama's chair with his hand on Mama's shoulder.

"Christopher, this is my brother," Mama said happily. "Your Uncle Ralph."

Mama pronounced it Rafe. It was more than a year before Christopher discovered it was the name he read as Ralph.

10 Uncle Ralph took his fancy completely. To begin with, he was smoking a cigar. The scents of the dressing-room were changed and mixed with the rich incense-like smoke, and Mama was not protesting by even so much as sniffing. That alone was enough to show that Uncle Ralph was in a class by himself. Then he was wearing tweeds, strong and tangy and almost fox-colored, which were a little baggy here and there, but blended
15 beautifully with the darker foxiness of Uncle Ralph's hair and the redder foxiness of his mustache. Christopher had seldom seen a man in tweeds or without whiskers. This did even more to assure him that Uncle Ralph was someone special. As a final touch, Uncle Ralph smiled at him like sunlight on an autumn forest. It was such an engaging smile that Christopher's face broke into a return smile almost of its own accord.

20 "Hallo, old chap," said Uncle Ralph, rolling out blue smoke above Mama's glossy hair. "I know this is not the best way for an uncle to recommend himself to a nephew, but I've been sorting the family affairs out, and I'm afraid I've had to do one or two quite shocking things, like bringing you a new governess and arranging for you to start school in autumn. Governess over there. Miss Bell. I hope you like one another. Enough to forgive
25 me anyway."

He smiled at Christopher in a sunny, humorous way which had Christopher rapidly approaching adoration. All the same, Christopher glanced dubiously at Miss Bell. She looked back, and there was an instant when a sort of hidden prettiness in her almost came out into the open. Then she blinked pale eyelashes and murmured, "Pleased to
30 meet you," in a voice as uninteresting as her clothes.

"She'll be your last governess, I hope," said Mama. Because of that, Christopher ever after thought of Miss Bell as the Last Governess. "She's going to prepare you for school. I wasn't meaning to send you away yet, but your uncle says—Anyway, a good education is important for your career and, to be blunt with you, Christopher, your Papa has made a
35 most *vexatious* hash of the money—which is mine, not his, as you know—and lost practically all of it. Luckily I had your uncle to turn to and—"

"And once turned to, I don't let people down," Uncle Ralph said, with a quick flick of a glance at the governess. Maybe he meant she should not be hearing this. "Fortunately, there's plenty left to send you to school, and then your Mama is going to recoup a bit by
40 living abroad. She'll like that—eh, Miranda? And Miss Bell is going to be found another post with glowing references. Everyone's going to be fine."

His smile went to all of them one by one, full of warmth and confidence. Mama laughed and dabbed scent behind her ears. The Last Governess almost smiled, so that the hidden prettiness half-emerged again. Christopher tried to grin a strong manly grin at
45 Uncle Ralph, because that seemed to be the only way to express the huge, almost hopeless adoration that was growing in him. Uncle Ralph laughed, a golden brown laugh, and completed the conquest of Christopher by fishing in a tweed pocket and tipping his nephew a bright new sixpence.

—by Diana Wynne Jones

131. As it is used in the quotation "Christopher, your Papa has made a most *vexatious* hash of the money," the word "vexatious" means
   A. troublesome
   B. enormous
   C. scary
   D. mean

132. Uncle Ralph hoped that Christopher and the new governess would get along so that
   A. they would forgive him for making big changes
   B. the governess could stay with the family
   C. the governess would teach Christopher
   D. Mama could go abroad

133. Which of the following statements describes how Christopher **most likely** feels about Uncle Ralph?
    A. He dislikes him because Uncle Ralph has brought a new governess.
    B. He admires Uncle Ralph but feels like he has been bribed by him.
    C. He admires him because Uncle Ralph is warm and confident.
    D. He likes Uncle Ralph but is suspicious of his motives.

134. The description of Uncle Ralph's smile as being "like sunlight on an autumn forest"[line 18] is an example of
    A. simile
    B. metaphor
    C. hyperbole
    D. personification

*Read the following passage and answer questions 135 to 138*

### Elephant and Hare

Hare and her friends had always lived peacefully among the tall grasses that grew on the shore of a clear blue lake. No one ever bothered them.

One day Elephant came crashing out of the jungle, followed by his herd. The elephants were thirsty and had been looking for water for a long time. When they saw the
5   shimmering blue lake, they were so excited, they stampeded through the grasses toward the water. They were in such a hurry, they didn't notice that they were trampling the burrows of Hare's friends beneath their huge feet.

After drinking and washing, Elephant led his herd back into the jungle to spend the night.
10  On their way, the elephants' enormous feet crushed many of the tender grasses that Hare and her friends used for food.

Hare was frantic with worry. She knew the elephants would return to the lake the next day, and the hares' homes and food would be destroyed completely. She thought very hard and finally came up with an idea.

15  "Don't worry," she told the other hares, "I have a plan."

A full moon was just peeking above the trees as Hare hopped to the jungle to talk to Elephant. She hopped right into the middle of the herd and started shouting as loud as she could, but no one paid any attention to her because her voice was tiny and hard for elephants to hear. When Hare was almost hoarse with shouting, Elephant flapped his
20  ears. He thought there was some kind of strange insect buzzing around his head. He flapped his ears again, but the noise wouldn't go away.

"What's that annoying sound?" he finally said.

"It's me!" shouted Hare.

Elephant looked down. He squinted at Hare and said, "Who are you?"

25 "I am a loyal subject of the all-powerful moon god," said Hare, bowing. "He has sent me to give you a message."

"Go on," said Elephant politely, although he didn't believe a word Hare was saying.

"When you and your herd went down to the lake today," said Hare, trying not to sound nervous, "you trampled the homes and food of the moon god's loyal subjects. This has
30 made the moon god extremely angry. He is so angry that he commands you to leave and never return."

"I don't believe in any moon god," scoffed Elephant. "Give me proof."

"Follow me to the lake then, and you will see the moon god for yourself," said Hare. "But watch where you're walking this time," she added.

35 When Elephant and Hare got to the edge of the lake, Hare pointed at the reflection of the full moon in the still water.

"There is the mighty moon god," she said. "Pay your respects by dipping your trunk in the lake.'

Elephant thought this was a silly thing to do, but he agreed. He stretched out his long trunk and touched the surface of the lake with it. Instantly, the water quivered and
40 rippled, making the moon's reflection burst into hundreds of shimmering pieces. Elephant threw back his trunk in fright.

"See how angry the moon god is?" shouted Hare.

"You're right," said Elephant, shaking with fear. "I promise I'll never annoy the moon god again!"

And with that, Elephant headed back to his herd in the jungle, being very careful indeed
45 not to step on any grasses or burrows on his way.

—retold by Jan Thornhill

135. A word that means almost the same as the word *loyal* is
   A. faithful
   B. mighty
   C. sleepy
   D. silly

136. An antonym of the word *destroyed* is
   A. abandoned
   B. damaged
   C. ruined
   D. fixed

137. To the elephants, Hare's voice sounded like
   A. a lion roaring
   B. an insect buzzing
   C. a trumpet blasting
   D. a mouse squeaking

138. According to Hare, the moon god's message was that the elephants should
   A. follow Hare
   B. leave and never return
   C. drink from a different lake
   D. avoid stepping on the burrows

*Read the following passage and answer questions 139 to 142*

### My Friend Jacob

My best friend lives next door. His name is Jacob. He is my very, very best friend.

We do things together, Jacob and I. We love to play basketball together. Jacob always makes a basket on the first try.

He helps me to learn how to hold the ball so that I can make baskets, too.

5   My mother used to say, "Be careful with Jacob and that ball. He might hurt you." But now she doesn't. She knows that Jacob wouldn't hurt anybody, especially his very, very best friend.

I love to sit on the steps and watch the cars go by with Jacob. He knows the name of every kind of car. Even if he only sees it for just a minute, Jacob can tell you the kind of car.

He is helping me be able to tell cars, too. When I make a mistake, Jacob never ever
10   laughs. He just says, "No no, Sam, try again."

And I do. He is my best best friend.

When I have to go to the store, Jacob goes with me to help me. His mother used to say, "You don't have to have Jacob tagging along with you like that, Sammy." But now she doesn't. Jacob helps me to carry, and I help Jacob to remember.

15   "Red is for stop," I say if Jacob forgets. "Green is for go."

"Thank you, Sam," Jacob always says.

Jacob's birthday and my birthday are two days apart. Sometimes we celebrate together.

Last year he made me a surprise. He had been having a secret for weeks and weeks, and my mother knew, and his mother knew, but they wouldn't tell me.

20   Jacob would stay in the house in the afternoon for half an hour every day and not say anything to me when he came out. He would just smile and smile.

On my birthday, my mother made a cake for me with eight candles, and Jacob's mother made a cake for him with seventeen candles. We sat on the porch and sang and blew out our candles. Jacob blew out all of his in one breath because he's bigger.

25   Then my mother smiled, and Jacob's mother smiled and said, "Give it to him, Jacob dear." My friend Jacob smiled and handed me a card.

HAPPY BIRTHDAY SAM
JACOB

He had printed it all himself! All by himself, my name and everything! It was neat!

30   My very best friend Jacob does so much helping me, I wanted to help him, too. One day I decided to teach him how to knock.

Jacob will just walk into somebody's house if he knows them. If he doesn't know them, he will stand by the door until someone notices him and lets him in.

"I wish Jacob would knock on the door," I heard my mother say.

35 So I decided to help him learn. Every day I would tell Jacob, but he would always forget. He would just open the door and walk right in.

My mother said probably it was too hard for him and I shouldn't worry about it. But I felt bad because Jacob always helped me so much, and I wanted to be able to help him.

I kept telling him, and he kept forgetting. So one day I just said, "Never mind, Jacob, 40 maybe it is too hard."

"What's the matter, Sam?" Jacob asked me.

"Never mind, Jacob," was all I said.

Next day, at dinnertime, we were sitting in our dining room when I and my mother and my father heard this real loud knocking at the door. Then the door popped open and Jacob 45 stuck his head in.

"I'm knocking, Sam!" he yelled.

Boy, I jumped right up from the table and went grinning and hugged Jacob, and he grinned and hugged me, too. He is my very, very, very best friend in the whole wide world!

—by Lucille Clifton

139. The expression "tagging along" means
   A. following someone
   B. playing a chasing game
   C. touching a person on the back
   D. putting a sticker on something

140. Who is telling the story?
   A. Sam
   B. Jacob
   C. The writer
   D. Jacob's mom

141. When Jacob knocks on Sam's door, Sam is
   A. frightened
   B. annoyed
   C. relieved
   D. proud

142. Why does Sam's mother warn him about getting hurt by Jacob?
   A. Because Jacob is not careful
   B. Because she thinks Jacob is mean
   C. Because she is worried about Sam's feelings
   D. Because Jacob is physically much bigger than Sam

*Read the following passage and answer questions 143 to 146*

## A Horse That Wore Snow Shoes

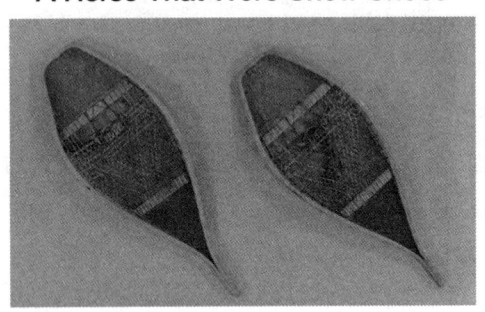

Mr. Brown had to go to his camp at Pine Tree Valley, which is in the midst of the mountains in California.

His men were cutting down the giant trees, and piling them in readiness for the Spring
5   freshet, or floods of the river, when the snows melted. Then they would slide them down the mountain sides to the little villages below.

There was a great deal of snow on the mountains, and Mr. Brown knew it would be hard work climbing to the camp, but Lady Gray was strong, and used to it.

Lady Gray was Mr. Brown's pet horse, and carried him everywhere. She was always
10  happy when her master was in the saddle.

But to-day the snow was very deep and soon Mr. Brown had to get off, throw away the saddle, and lead her. They had to stop very often, and lean against the trees and rocks for support, while they rested and regained their breath.

In places the snow was so deep and soft, that they sank above their knees. Late in the
15  afternoon they reached the camp nearly exhausted, and it was several days before they were able to return.

The snow was still deep and Mr. Brown knew he must go back on snow-shoes, but he was afraid Lady Gray would have to be left behind.

Finally one of the men suggested making her some snow-shoes. They cut four round
20  pieces of board, twelve inches across, and fastened them on with rope. Lady Gray seemed to understand what they were for and tried very hard to walk in them.

She was very awkward at first and could hardly stand up, but by practicing a little every day she was soon able to manage nicely.

So Mr. Brown and Lady Gray both returned on snow-shoes, and how every one did laugh
25  when they saw them.

But Lady Gray never could have done it if she had not tried.

143. When the story says that there was "a great deal of snow," it means that there was
   A. no snow
   B. a lot of snow
   C. a little bit of snow
   D. a chance of snow

144. Which of the following statements **best** describes Lady Gray's reaction to the snowshoes?
    A. She knew how to use them right away.
    B. She made a big effort to use them.
    C. Lady Gray refused to use them.
    D. Lady Gray was not impressed.

145. Which of the following statements about Lady Gray is **true**?
    A. She enjoyed sliding down the mountain.
    B. Lady Gray did not like her saddle.
    C. She was afraid of her master.
    D. Lady Gray liked Mr. Brown.

146. Which of the following words **best** describes Lady Gray as she learned to use snowshoes?
    A. Troublesome
    B. Cooperative
    C. Frustrating
    D. Helpful

*Read the following passage and answer questions 147 to 151*

### The Snake on Second Avenue

It wasn't my idea to have a snake for a pet. I don't like animals much, and as far as wild animals go—well, cats are too wild for me. But my mother's batty about animals. She watches nature shows on TV and writes letters to the editor complaining about inhumane traps. I find it a little tiresome, but mostly Mum's all right. She never complains when she
5  has to pick me up after ball practice, even though she thinks I should be bird-watching instead.

We were in Saskatoon for a dentist appointment the day we found the snake. It was a little garter snake, the kind we have in the garden at home—green with yellow stripes. There was one thing unusual about this one, though. It was on Second Avenue right outside a shoe store. The snake looked really scared and I don't blame it. It was too
10  small to be made into shoes, but that wasn't its biggest worry. From the look of the crowd gathered around it on the sidewalk, the busy street would have been safer.

We noticed the crowd from the end of the block. As we got closer we could hear a kid scream over and over, "Kill it! Kill it!" I don't know why the kid didn't just leave.

As soon as Mum heard the kid yell she doubled her speed. I ran along with her because I
15  was pretty curious about what all the people were staring at. A mouse? A Martian? A kid playing hooky?

Mum pushed her way through the crowd and I followed. The snake was coiled up on the sidewalk. Everyone seemed to be arguing about how to kill it.

"Oh, the poor thing!" exclaimed Mum. She went straight to the snake and picked it up. It
20  was already so frightened that it didn't even try to get away. It just wrapped its tail around her wrist and poked its tongue in and out.

There was a horrified silence. Even the kill-it kid stopped yelling.

"It's just a garter snake," said Mum, quite loudly. "It's not poisonous and it's not a constrictor. The only things it can damage are insects." She paused, then said, "And I'm
25  going to take it home. Please excuse me." She didn't have to push her way out. The crowd just separated in front of her. She seemed to have forgotten me so I followed along behind, watching the snake move in her hands and wondering what it felt like.

We'd reached the car before I noticed where we were. "Hey, Mum!" I exclaimed. "I thought we were going to buy me some jeans."

30  "With a snake?" she asked. "We're going home now. You'll have to hold the snake."

I wish she'd waited till we were in the car. I don't want you to think I'm chicken, but the first time I hold a snake, I'd like advance warning.

Terrified that I might drop it, I just blinked and grabbed the thing around the neck. I was surprised at how it felt—not slimy at all, but hard and dry on the top and soft underneath.
35  Its head was amazingly small, but it still kept sticking its tongue out. I stuck mine out at it, then climbed into the car.

Mum started the engine and said, "I've heard that garter snakes make good pets."

I groaned, but I knew there was no point in arguing. And really, it wasn't so bad. I could probably write a science report on it and amaze all the teachers. After all, there are
40  worse things than living in the same house as a snake. At least it wasn't a cat.

—by Adele Dueck

147. The past tense of the word *kill* is
    A. kills
    B. killen
    C. killed
    D. killing

148. Which of the following statements is the **best** summary of the passage?
    A. I used to dislike all animals, but then I met a snake that I liked.
    B. Most people think that snakes are scary, but I think they are way better than cats.
    C. When Mom and I were shopping one day, my mom rescued a scared snake from possibly being attacked by a crowd of people, which brought a quick end to our shopping trip.
    D. I am not usually wild about animals, but when my mother and I came across a snake that needed our help, I actually found him to be pretty interesting and ended up with a new pet.

149. The narrator describes garter snakes as
    A. yellow with green stripes
    B. green with yellow stripes
    C. green with yellow spots
    D. yellow with green spots

150. What will the narrator **most likely** do at the end of the story?
   A. Give up playing ball
   B. Keep the snake as a pet
   C. Get an A on a science report
   D. Find other animals to have as pets

151. Before being handed the snake, the narrator would have liked
   A. a chance to clean his or her hand
   B. advance warning
   C. to be given a choice
   D. some advice

*Read the following passage and answer questions 152 to 155*

### from "Curvy Beak, Pointy Claws"

I, Nate the Great, am a detective. Right now I am a clickety-clack rocking-back-and-forth detective. I am on a train. My dog, Sludge, is with me. He is a detective too. We are on a case. We are bodyguards. For an owl. Her name is Hoot. She belongs to my cousin Olivia Sharp.

5

The case started this morning. Sludge and I were visiting Olivia in San Francisco. Olivia is also a detective. This morning she said, "Hoot needs to take a train to a special owl doctor in Los Angeles." "A plane is faster," I said. "Hoot doesn't like to fly," she said. "I, Nate the Great, say that is a good enough reason for an owl to see a doctor." Olivia
10 tossed her boa around her neck. She always wears a boa. "Glad you think so," she said.

Then she tossed her boa around my neck, looked me straight in the eye, and said, "You'll take Hoot on the train for me. I know I can count on you." Olivia pulled me over to a covered birdcage. She lifted the cover. I looked into two huge staring eyes.

15  Then I saw a big head, a curvy beak, and sharp pointy claws. "What big eyes she has!" I said. "Yes, and she's easy to feed," Olivia said. "She eats mice." "You have told me, Nate the Great, more than I want to know." But Olivia wasn't finished.

—from *Nate the Great on the Owl Express* by Marjorie Weinman Sharmat and Mitchell Sharmat

152. The purpose of Nate's train trip is to
   A. visit his cousin in Los Angeles
   B. visit his cousin in San Francisco
   C. take an owl to a doctor in Los Angeles
   D. take an owl to a doctor in San Francisco

153. Which characters are riding on the train?
   A. Nate the Great and Hoot
   B. Nate the Great and Sludge
   C. Sludge, Hoot, and Nate the Great
   D. Olivia, Sludge, Hoot, and Nate the Great

154. Olivia tells Nate that Hoot eats
   A. snakes
   B. bugs
   C. mice
   D. rats

155. Nate thinks Hoot should see a doctor because the owl
   A. eats mice
   B. wears a boa
   C. dislikes flying
   D. likes to ride on trains

*Read the following passage and answer questions 156 to 159*

**Matilda: Who told Lies, and was Burned to Death**

Matilda told such Dreadful Lies,
It made one Gasp and Stretch one's Eyes;
Her Aunt, who, from her Earliest Youth,
Had kept a Strict Regard for Truth,
5   Attempted to Believe Matilda:
The effort very nearly killed her,
And would have done so, had not She
Discovered this Infirmity.
For once, towards the Close of Day,
10  Matilda, growing tired of play,
And finding she was left alone,
Went tiptoe to the Telephone,
And summoned the Immediate Aid
Of London's Noble Fire-Brigade.
15  Within an hour the Gallant Band
Were pouring in on every hand,
From Putney, Hackney Downs, and Bow,
With Courage high and Hearts a-glow
They galloped, roaring through the Town,
20  "Matilda's House is Burning Down!"
Inspired by British Cheers and Loud
Proceeding from the Frenzied Crowd,
They ran their ladders through a score
Of windows on the Ball Room Floor;
25  And took Peculiar Pains to Souse
The Pictures up and down the House,
Until Matilda's Aunt succeeded
In showing them they were not needed
And even then she had to pay
30  To get the Men to go away!
It happened that a few Weeks later
Her Aunt was off to the Theater
To see that Interesting Play
*The Second Mrs. Tanqueray.*
35  She had refused to take her Niece

To hear this Entertaining Piece:
A Deprivation Just and Wise
To punish her for Telling Lies.
That Night a Fire *did* break out—
40 You should have heard Matilda Shout!
You should have heard her Scream and Bawl,
And throw the window up and call
To People passing in the Street—
(The rapidly increasing Heat
45 Encouraging her to obtain
Their confidence)—but all in vain!
For every time She shouted "Fire!"
They only answered "Little Liar!"
And therefore when her Aunt returned,
50 Matilda, and the House, were Burned.
—by Hilaire Belloc

156. In the line "Discovered this infirmity," the word "*Infirmity*" means
- A. fault
- B. hospital
- C. strength
- D. ill health

157. In the line "A Deprivation Just and Wise,"[line 37] the word "*Deprivation*" is a synonym of
- A. punishment
- B. remorse
- C. removal
- D. gift

158. After Matilda's phone call to the fire brigade, her aunt **most likely** feels
- A. secure
- B. amazed
- C. frustrated
- D. disoriented

159. This poem can **most accurately** be called a
- A. ballad
- B. sonnet
- C. lyric poem
- D. narrative poem

# EXERCISE #2—READING LITERATURE

## Table of Correlations

| Standard | | | Test #1 |
|---|---|---|---|
| **5RL** | | Reading Standards for Literature | |
| 5RL.2 | | Determine a theme of a story, drama, or poem from details in the text, including how characters in a story or drama respond to challenges or how the speaker in a poem reflects upon a topic; summarize the text. | 163, 174, 175, 179, 184, 185, 186, 196, 200, 208, 212 |
| 5RL.4 | | Determine the meaning of words and phrases as they are used in a text, including figurative language such as metaphors and similes. | 191, 204 |
| 5RL.5 | | Explain how a series of chapters, scenes, or stanzas fits together to provide the overall structure of a particular story, drama, or poem. | 167, 192 |
| 5RL.6 | | Describe how a narrator's or speaker's point of view influences how events are described. | 201, 210 |
| 5RL.10 | | By the end of the year, read and comprehend literature, including stories, dramas, and poetry, at the high end of the grades 4–5 text complexity band independently and proficiently. | 167, 192 |
| **5RI** | | Reading Standards for Informational Text | |
| 5RI.2 | | Determine two or more main ideas of a text and explain how they are supported by key details; summarize the text. | 163, 174, 175, 179, 184, 185, 186, 196, 200, 208, 212 |
| 5RI.4 | | Determine the meaning of general academic and domain-specific words and phrases in a text relevant to a grade 5 topic or subject area. | 191, 204 |
| 5RI.6 | | Analyze multiple accounts of the same event or topic, noting important similarities and differences in the point of view they represent. | 201, 210 |
| 5RI.8 | | Explain how an author uses reasons and evidence to support particular points in a text, identifying which reasons and evidence support which point(s). | 169, 194 |
| **5RF** | | Reading Standards: Foundational Skills | |
| 5RF.3a | | Know and apply grade-level phonics and word analysis skills in decoding words. Use combined knowledge of all letter-sound correspondences, syllabication patterns, and morphology to read accurately unfamiliar multisyllabic words in context... | 164, 165, 172, 173, 176, 180, 189, 197, 205, 206 |
| 5RF.4a | | Read with sufficient accuracy and fluency to support comprehension. Read on-level text with purpose and understanding. | 160, 181, 193 |
| 5RF.4b | | Read with sufficient accuracy and fluency to support comprehension. Read on-level prose and poetry orally with accuracy, appropriate rate, and expression on successive readings. | 160, 181, 193 |
| 5RF.4c | | Read with sufficient accuracy and fluency to support comprehension. Use context to confirm or self-correct word recognition and understanding, rereading as necessary. | 160, 165, 172, 173, 176, 181, 189, 193, 197, 205, 206 |
| **5W** | | Writing Standards | |
| 5W.3a | | Write narratives to develop real or imagined experiences or events using effective technique, descriptive details, and clear event sequences. Orient the reader by establishing a situation and introducing a narrator and/or characters; organize... | 201, 210 |
| 5W.3b | | Write narratives to develop real or imagined experiences or events using effective technique, descriptive details, and clear event sequences. Use narrative techniques, such as dialogue, description, and pacing, to develop experiences and events... | 186 |

| | | |
|---|---|---|
| 5W.9a | Draw evidence from literary or informational texts to support analysis, reflection, and research. Apply grade 5 Reading standards to literature. | 162, 170, 171, 178, 183, 187, 188, 195, 199, 202, 203, 211 |
| 5W.9b | Draw evidence from literary or informational texts to support analysis, reflection, and research. Apply grade 5 Reading standards to informational texts. | 169, 178, 194, 199 |
| **5SL** | **Speaking and Listening Standards** | |
| 5SL.2 | Summarize a written text read aloud or information presented in diverse media and formats, including visually, quantitatively, and orally. | 185 |
| 5SL.3 | Summarize the points a speaker makes and explain how each claim is supported by reasons and evidence. | 169, 185, 194 |
| **5L** | **Language Standards** | |
| 5L.3a | Use knowledge of language and its conventions when writing, speaking, reading, or listening. Expand, combine, and reduce sentences for meaning, reader/listener interest, and style. | 161, 177 |
| 5L.4a | Determine or clarify the meaning of unknown and multiple-meaning words and phrases based on grade 5 reading and content, choosing flexibly from a range of strategies. Use context as a clue to the meaning of a word or phrase. | 165, 172, 173, 176, 189, 197, 205, 206 |
| 5L.5a | Demonstrate understanding of figurative language, word relationships, and nuances in word meanings. Interpret figurative language, including similes and metaphors, in context. | 182, 198 |
| 5L.5c | Demonstrate understanding of figurative language, word relationships, and nuances in word meanings. Use the relationship between particular words to better understand each of the words. | 166, 168, 190, 207, 209 |

*Read the following passage and answer questions 160 to 163*

### from "Why the Sea Is Salt: A Scandinavian Folk Tale"

In ancient times there were two brothers, one rich and the other poor. Christmas day was approaching, and the poor man had not a bit of meat nor a morsel of bread to make his Christmas feast; so he went to his brother and asked for a trifling gift. The brother was ill-natured, and when he heard his brother's request he looked very surly. But as it was
5  Christmas time, when even the worst people give gifts, he took a fine ham down from the chimney, where it was hanging to smoke, threw it at him, and bade him begone and never to return.

The poor man was very glad to have such a fine ham and, thanking his brother, put it under his arm and went his way.

10  He had to pass through a great wood on his way home; and, when he reached the thick of the wood, he saw an old man, with a long white beard, hewing timber. "Good evening," said the young man.

"Good evening," returned the old one, raising himself up from his work. "That is a fine ham you are carrying." And at this the poor man told him all about it.

15  "It is lucky for you," said the old man, "that you have met me; for I can put you in the way of making a splendid bargain with that ham. Now, if you will take it into the land of the dwarfs, the entrance of which lies just under the roots of this tree which I am chopping down, you can get any money for it; because the dwarfs are very fond of ham, and hardly ever get any. But, mind what I say: you must not sell it for money. Let them offer you ever
20  so much; but demand for it the 'old handmill which stands behind the door.' When you come back, I'll show you how to use it; for that mill is something particular, I can tell you."

The poor man thanked his new friend, and said he would take his advice. The old man showed him the door under a stone below the roots of the tree, where he entered the subterranean land of the dwarfs. No sooner had he set foot within it, than the fragrant
25  smell of his ham attracted the dwarfs from all parts; and such a throng came about him as nobody could believe, offering him queer, old-fashioned money, and gold and silver ore, if he would but sell them the ham.

The poor man, however, refused all their tempting offers, as the old man in the wood had bade him, and said that he had no particular wish to sell his ham, which was intended for
30  his Christmas dinner. Seeing that they had all set their hearts on it, however, he said he would exchange it, not sell it; and they could have it for the old handmill behind the door.

At these words the dwarfs, poor little things, looked as if they were shot. They all fled back, and then stood stock still, holding up their little old hands, and looking quite perplexed.

"You don't agree to my bargain then," said the poor man; "so I'll bid you all a good-day!"
35  And with that he swung his fine smoked ham around, so that the fragrance of it reached all the remoter parts of dwarf-land. And soon other little troops with spades, and pickaxes, and shovels, came up from their work of digging out the ore, and they were all eager for the ham, again offering gold and silver by the barrowful. But again the poor man was resolute: he would only barter his ham for the old handmill behind the door.

40  "Let him have it," said several of the newly arrived dwarfs, "It is quite out of order, and he won't know how to use it. Let him have it and we'll have the ham."

And so in the end it was settled. The dwarfs had the smoked ham, and the poor man had the old handmill. Carrying it in his hand, for it was a little thing, not a quarter the size of the ham, he went back again to the old man with the long white beard in the wood; and the old man was as good as his word, and showed him exactly how he was to use it—for there was a very particular trick about it.

All this had taken up a deal of time, and it was midnight when the poor man reached home.

"Where in the world have you been?" said his wife. "Here I have sat waiting and waiting, and we have not so much as two sticks in the house to make the porridge-pot boil, even if we had anything to put in it for our Christmas supper."

The house was dark and cold; but the man, with a cheery word, bade her wait and see what he had been about. Groping his way to the table he set down the little handmill and began to grind. As he ground, out there came, first, candles, because in his own mind he said they must come—grand lighted candles, and plenty of them, and a fire in the grate, and a porridge-pot boiling over it. Then he ground out a tablecloth, and dishes, and spoons, and knives, and forks. Down they went clattering and ringing into a big basket which he had ground out to receive them. The poor man himself was astonished at his good luck, as you may believe. As to his wife, I could not possibly tell you the state of amazement and joy she was in.

Well, they had a good supper; nor did they go to bed all that night, but instead, ground out of the mill everything they could possibly think of to make their house and themselves warm and comfortable—bedding, and furniture, and clothes, and plenty to eat and drink. And so they had a merry Christmas eve and morning.

The poor man's house was not far from the church, and next day when the people went there they could hardly believe their eyes, to see what a change there was in the place. Such a smoke came out of the chimney; there was glass in the windows instead of a wooden shutter, and the man himself, dressed in a fine suit of clothes, was seen devoutly praying in the church.

"There is something very comical in all this," said everybody.

"Something very comical indeed!" said the rich brother, when three days afterward he received an invitation from the formerly poor brother to a grand feast.

What a feast it was! There was a grand table, almost bigger than the house would hold, covered with a cloth as white as snow, and glittering with gold and silver. And such dishes! How the poor man and his wife ever thought of them is more than I can tell. You may imagine the astonishment of the rich brother. He could not, in his great house and with all his wealth, set out such a table.

"Where in the name of fortune," exclaimed he to his brother, "have you got all these things from? Why, the day before Christmas Eve you were as poor as a church mouse!"

The formerly poor man told his brother how he had exchanged the ham for a little old handmill, which, however, had the magical power of grinding out whatever one wished. With that he put the mill on the table, and ground out boots and shoes, and coats and cloaks, and stockings and blankets, and woolen petticoats and waistcoats. He bade his wife hand them out as fast as ever she could to crowds of poor people, who had gathered round the house to peep in and get a sight of the wonderful dinner which the poor brother had made for the rich one.

The sight of this wonderful mill raised such a desire in the mind of the rich brother to possess it, that he let the other have no peace, day or night. He offered money, land, anything for it; and at last, in hay-harvest, he got him to consent to his having the use of it for one day, meaning in his own mind—for he was not an honest man—never to let his
90 brother have it again and to become himself richer than a king.

It was hay-harvest, as I said, when he fetched the mill. That he might have it all to himself, he sent his servants and his wife into the hay-fields, and bade them not to come back till night. You may think how pleased he was when, after a long walk to his brother's and back before breakfast, he shut the door, and being quite alone in the house, thought
95 first of all, to save time and trouble, that he would grind out his breakfast—his favorite breakfast of milk-soup and herrings.

So the mill began to grind; and grind it did. Milk-soup and herring in shoals and streams. He caught it in basins, and jugs and cans, and buckets and tubs, and kettlefuls and potfuls; and then, when all were full, it ran over the floor. It was no use trying to stop it or
100 turning the handle the other way.

Out came the milk-soup and herrings till the kitchen floor swam, and put out the fire, and filled the cellar, and ran out of doors in gallons!

The man felt half mad! What could he do? The beds swam, the tables and the chairs swam in the milk-soup and knocked against the herrings. Oh, dear! Oh, dear! He was up
105 to his knees in this abominable milk-soup; and more, and more, and more, and more came streaming out! It was enough to drive him wholly mad! He could not stop it! …

160. The poor man's problem is that he
    A. can never return to his brother
    B. has to travel through the woods
    C. is ill-natured and has no friends
    D. has nothing for his Christmas feast

161. The statement "Oh, dear!"[line 104] is an example of a
    A. greeting
    B. fragment
    C. simple sentence
    D. compound sentence

162. The story reveals that the rich brother's personality is
    A. warm-hearted
    B. ill-natured
    C. pleasant
    D. mature

163. The old man's specific advice to the poor man was to
    A. sell the ham to the dwarfs
    B. trade the ham for some ore
    C. share the ham with the dwarfs
    D. trade the ham for the handmill

*Read the following passage and answer questions 164 to 167*

### A Snake Named Rover

   Mom wouldn't let me have a dog
    "With all the mess they make!"
   So, if I couldn't have a dog,
   I said I'd like a snake.

5  My mother gasped quite audibly,
    But Dad approved the plan.
   "A snake," he gulped, "a real live snake…
   Well, sure, I guess you can."

   We went to Ralph's Repulsive Pets
10 And bought a yard of asp.
   It coiled inside a paper bag
    Held firmly in my grasp.

   I put him in a big glass tank
   And dubbed my new pet Rover,
15 But all the fun of owning it
    Was very quickly over.

   For all he did was flick his tongue
    Once or twice each minute,
   While nervous Mom rechecked the tank
20 To make sure he was in it.

   Then one fine day, we don't know how,
   My Rover disappeared.
   My father told me not to fret,
    But Mom was mighty scared.

25 We searched the house from front to back
    And gave the yard a sweep.
    By midnight we had given up
    And tried to get some sleep.

   At three AM my dad arose
30 To answer nature's call.
   I heard him scream, I heard him swear,
    And then I heard him fall.

   For Dad had found the wayward pet
   I'd given up for dead
35 Curled up inside his slipper,
   Lying right beside his bed.

> Now Rover's living back at Ralph's
> With frogs, and newts, and guppies,
> And now I have a dog named Spot—
> 40  She'll soon be having puppies.
>
> —by Maxine Jeffris

164. The phrase "a yard of asp" refers to
   A. some rolled cloth
   B. some insects
   C. a courtyard
   D. a snake

165. In the line "My father told me not to fret,"[line 23] the word "fret" means
   A. cry
   B. worry
   C. fear
   D. move

166. In the quotation "I heard him scream, I heard him swear,"[line 31] the word "scream" means almost the same thing as which of the following words?
   A. Cry
   B. Laugh
   C. Shriek
   D. Whisper

167. Which of the following types of poems describes this poem **best**?
   A. Haiku
   B. Limerick
   C. Rhyming poem
   D. Free verse poem

*Read the following passage and answer questions 168 to 171*

### Why the Evergreen Trees Never Lose Their Leaves

Winter was coming, and the birds had flown far to the south, where the air was warm and they could find berries to eat. One little bird had broken its wing and could not fly with the others. It was alone in the cold world of frost and snow. The forest looked warm, and it made its way to the trees as well as it could, to ask for help.

5   First it came to a birch tree. "Beautiful birch tree," it said, "my wing is broken, and my friends have flown away. May I live among your branches till they come back to me?"

"No, indeed," answered the birch tree, drawing her fair green leaves away. "We of the great forest have our own birds to help. I can do nothing for you."

"The birch is not very strong," said the little bird to itself, "and it might be that she could
10  not hold me easily. I will ask the oak." So the bird said, "Great oak tree, you are so strong, will you not let me live on your boughs till my friends come back in the springtime?"

"In the springtime!" cried the oak. "That is a long way off. How do I know what you might do in all that time? Birds are always looking for something to eat, and you might even eat up some of my acorns."

15 "It may be that the willow will be kind to me," thought the bird, and it said, "Gentle willow, my wing is broken, and I could not fly to the south with the other birds. May I live on your branches till the springtime?"

The willow did not look gentle then, for she drew herself up proudly and said, "Indeed, I do not know you, and we willows never talk to people whom we do not know. Very likely
20 there are trees somewhere that will take in strange birds. Leave me at once."

The poor little bird did not know what to do. Its wing was not yet strong, but it began to fly away as well as it could. Before it had gone far a voice was heard. "Little bird," it said, "where are you going?"

"Indeed, I do not know," answered the bird sadly. "I am very cold."

25 "Come right here, then," said the friendly spruce tree, for it was her voice that had called.

"You shall live on my warmest branch all winter if you choose."

"Will you really let me?" asked the little bird eagerly.

"Indeed, I will," answered the kind-hearted spruce tree. "If your friends have flown away, it is time for the trees to help you. Here is the branch where my leaves are thickest and softest."

30 "My branches are not very thick," said the friendly pine tree, "but I am big and strong, and I can keep the North Wind from you and the spruce."

"I can help, too," said a little juniper tree. "I can give you berries all winter long, and every bird knows that juniper berries are good."

So the spruce gave the lonely little bird a home; the pine kept the cold North Wind away
35 from it; and the juniper gave it berries to eat. The other trees looked on and talked together wisely.

"I would not have strange birds on my boughs," said the birch.

"I shall not give my acorns away for any one," said the oak.

"I never have anything to do with strangers," said the willow, and the three trees drew
40 their leaves closely about them.

In the morning all those shining, green leaves lay on the ground, for a cold North Wind had come in the night, and every leaf that it touched fell from the tree.

"May I touch every leaf in the forest?" asked the wind in its frolic.

"No," said the Frost King. "The trees that have been kind to the little bird with the broken
45 wing may keep their leaves."

This is why the leaves of the spruce, the pine, and the juniper are always green.

—by Florence Holbrook

168. A synonym for the word "kind" as used in the sentence, "'It may be that the willow will be kind to me,' thought the bird.", is
   A. nice
   B. angry
   C. bossy
   D. playful

169. The willow tree's answer to the bird's request for help was
   A. "Come right here"
   B. "Indeed, I do not know you"
   C. "We of the great forest have our own birds to help"
   D. "Birds are always looking for something to eat, and you might even eat up some of my acorns"

170. How did the bird feel when the spruce offered it a home?
   A. eager
   B. shocked
   C. hopeless
   D. uncertain

171. After the cold North Wind visited in the night, the birch, oak, and willow trees **probably** felt
   A. wise
   B. strong
   C. foolish
   D. prudent

*Read the following passage and answer questions 172 to 175*

## The Legend of the Bluebonnet

"Great Spirits, the land is dying. Your People are dying, too," the long line of dancers sang. "Tell us what we have done to anger you. End this drought. Save your People. Tell us what we must do so you will send the rain that will bring back life."

For three days, the dancers danced to the sound of the drums. And for three days, the
5 People called Comanche watched and waited. Even though the hard winter was over, no healing rains came.

Drought and famine are hardest on the very young and the very old. Among the few children left was a small girl named She-Who-Is-Alone. She sat by herself watching the dancers. In her lap was a doll made from buckskin. It was a warrior doll. The eyes, nose,
10 and mouth were painted on with the juice of berries. It wore beaded leggings and a belt of polished bone. On its head were brilliant blue feathers from the bird who cries "Jay-jay-jay." She loved her doll very much.

"Soon," She-Who-Is-Alone said to her doll, "the shaman will go off alone to the top of the hill to listen for the words of the Great Spirits. Then, we will know what to do so that once
15 more the rains will come. The Earth will be green and alive and the People will be rich again."

As she talked, she thought of the mother who made the doll. She thought of the father who brought the blue feathers. She thought of the grandfather and the grandmother she had never known. They were all like shadows. It seemed long ago that they had died from the famine. The People had named her and cared for her. The warrior doll was the
20 only thing she had left from those distant days.

"The sun is setting," the runner called as he ran through the camp. "The shaman is returning."

The People gathered in a circle and the shaman spoke.

"I have heard the words of the Great Spirits," he said. "The People have become selfish. For years, they have taken from the Earth without giving anything back. The Great Spirits
25 say the People must sacrifice. We must make a burnt offering of the most valued possession among us. The ashes of this offering shall then be scattered to the four points of the Earth, the Home of the Winds. When this sacrifice is made, drought and famine will cease. Life will be restored to the Earth and to the People!"

The People sang a song of thanks to the Great Spirits for telling them what they must do.

30 "I'm sure it is not my new bow that the Great Spirits want," a warrior said.

"Or my special blanket," a woman added. Everyone went to the tepees to talk and think over what the Great Spirits had asked. Everyone, that is, except She-Who-Is-Alone. She held her doll tightly to her heart.

"You," she said, looking at the doll. "You are my most valued possession. It is you the
35 Great Spirits want." She knew what she must do.

As the council fires died out and the tepee flaps began to close, the small girl returned to the tepee, where she slept, to wait. The night outside was still except for the distant sound of the night bird with the red wings. Soon everyone in the tepee was asleep, except She-Who-Is-Alone.

40 Under the ashes of the tepee fire, one stick still glowed. She took it and quietly crept out into the night. She ran to the place on the hill where the Great Spirits had spoken to the shaman. Stars filled the sky. There was no moon.

"O Great Spirits," She-Who-Is-Alone said, "here is my warrior doll. It is the only thing I have from my family who died in this famine. It is my most valued possession. Please accept it."

Then, gathering twigs, she started a fire with the glowing firestick. The small girl watched as the twigs began to catch and burn. She thought of her grandmother and grandfather, her mother and father, and all the People—their suffering, their hunger. Before she could change her mind, she thrust the doll into the fire.

She watched until the flames died down and the ashes had grown cold. Then, scooping up a handful, She-Who-Is-Alone scattered the ashes to the Home of the Winds, the North and the East, the South and the West. And there she fell asleep until the first light of the morning sun woke her.

She looked out over the hill. Stretching out from all sides, where the ashes had fallen, the ground was covered with flowers—beautiful flowers, as blue as the feathers in the hair of the doll, as blue as the feathers of the bird who cries "Jay-jay-jay."

When the People came out of their tepees, they could scarcely believe their eyes. They gathered on the hill with She-Who-Is-Alone to look at the miraculous sight. There was no doubt about it, the flowers were a sign of forgiveness from the Great Spirits.

As the People sang and danced their thanks to the Great Spirits, a warm rain began to fall. The land began to live again. From that day on, the little girl was known by another name—"One-Who-Dearly-Loved-Her-People."

Every spring, the Great Spirits remember the sacrifice of a little girl. They fill the hills and valleys of the land, now called Texas, with the beautiful blue flowers.

Even to this very day.

—by Tomie DePaola

172. The word "famine" refers to a
    A. long period without food
    B. long period without rain
    C. terrible storm
    D. prairie fire

173. In the phrase "must make a burnt offering,"[line 25] the word "offering" refers to a
    A. type of fuel
    B. gift to the gods
    C. special kind of food
    D. ceremonial decoration

174. The warrior doll is the little girl's
    A. companion
    B. protector
    C. shaman
    D. trophy

175. Which of the following statements **best** describes why the warrior doll is the girl's most valued possession?
    A. She thinks it is better than the warrior's bow.
    B. She thinks it is splendidly decorated.
    C. It is all she has left of her family.
    D. It is the nicest thing she owns.

*Read the following passage and answer questions 176 to 179*

### Not Owls Too!

The reason Dad said: "Oh NO! Not owls too" was because I already had some pets.

There was a summerhouse in our back yard and we kept about thirty gophers in it. They belonged to Bruce and me, and to another boy called Murray. We caught them out on the prairie, using snares made of heavy twine.

5  The way you do it is like this: You walk along until you spot a gopher sitting up beside his hole. Gophers sit straight up, reaching their noses as high as they can, so they can see farther. When you begin to get too close they flick their tails, give a little jump, and whisk down their holes. As soon as they do that, you take a piece of twine that has a noose tied in one end, and you spread the noose over the hole. Then you lie down in the grass
10 holding the other end of the twine in your hand. You can hear the gopher all the while, whistling away to himself somewhere underground. He can hear you, too, and he's wondering what you're up to.

After a while he gets so curious he can't stand it. Out pops his head, and you give a yank on the twine. You have to haul in fast, because if the twine gets loose he'll slip his head
15 out of the noose and zip back down his hole.

We had rats too. Murray's dad was a professor at the college and he got us some white rats from the medical school. We kept them in our garage, which made my Dad a little peeved, because he couldn't put the car in the garage for fear the rats would make nests inside the seats. Nobody ever knew how many rats we had because they have so
20 many babies, and they have them so fast. We gave white rats away to all the kids in Saskatoon, but we always seemed to end up with as many as we had at first.

There were the rats and gophers, and then there was a big cardboard box full of garter snakes that we kept under the back porch, because my mother wouldn't let me keep them in the house. Then there were the pigeons. I usually had about ten of them, but
25 they kept bringing their friends and relations for visits, so I never knew how many to expect when I went out to feed them in the mornings. There were some rabbits too, and then there was Mutt, my dog—but he wasn't a pet; he was one of the family.

Sunday morning my father said:

"Billy, I think you have enough pets. I don't think you'd better bring home any owls. In any
30 case, the owls might eat your rats and rabbits and gophers…"

He stopped talking and a queer look came into his face. Then he said:

"On second thought—maybe we *need* an owl around this place!"

So it was all right.

—from *Owls in the Family*, by Farley Mowat

176. A "snare" can be **best** described as a
   A. cage
   B. noose
   C. metal trap
   D. large rock

177. The sentence "He can hear you too, and he's wondering what you're up to",[line 11] is an example of a
   A. compound sentence
   B. sentence fragment
   C. simple sentence
   D. run-on sentence

178. Which animals does the narrator describe having the **most** of?
   A. Dogs
   B. Rabbits
   C. Pigeons
   D. Gophers

179. Billy and his friends acquired the white rats from
   A. the prairie
   B. Billy's garage
   C. the storehouse
   D. Murray's father

*Read the following passage and answer questions 180 to 184*

### from "A Dive into the Sea"

Jason, Julia, and Rick were lying stomach-down on their towels, lining up some of the treasures they'd fished out of the sand: an assortment of colored rocks and shells, and a piece of wood with an iron bolt attached to it. To get the wood, Rick had swum out all the way to the very edge of the rocks, where the sea got deeper and the current started to
5  pull at him, like a hand grabbing at his legs. Rick felt it was wiser not to go farther out, and Julia happily agreed with him. There was no sense risking their lives when they had everything they needed right here.

Julia flipped onto her back to sunbathe while Rick and Jason explored the cove. They discovered a second stretch of beach, where there were traces of the small wooden pier.
10  A number of mooring lines hung from it. The walkways and boards had almost totally rotted away, but the remnants stood as evidence that old Ulysses had once, in fact, kept a boat here.

Jason was daydreaming about the old man's adventures as he and Rick went back to tell the news to Julia, who had become thoroughly bored with sunbathing. That was typical of
15  Julia. She could sit still for fifteen minutes, tops. She sat up and hugged her knees as Jason told her about what he and Rick had found. His telling made their adventure on the rocks take on mystical proportions.

While Jason spoke, Rick felt a raindrop on his face. He looked up. A dark cloud crossed overhead. "Rain," he announced.

20  Jason looked at the long series of steps that wound their way up toward home. A long, hard climb awaited them. "Should we start back up?" he asked.

"We'd better," Rick decided. "It may be only a shower, but you never know. We should be careful."

Julia agreed. Anything was better than sitting around in the rain.

The rain came harder now. The steps were more slippery than ever. Jason struggled to
25  keep up with his athletic sister and friend. In a burst of energy, he pushed them aside and sprinted up the stairs in twos and threes. He couldn't last at that pace, but at least he'd get a head start.

"See you up at the top, suckers!" he shouted.

Julia turned to Rick. "Come on, let's race," she urged.

30  But Rick surprised her. His face was calm, content. "Let him go," Rick said. "He gets to win while we take it nice and slow. Together."

Suddenly, Jason screamed. Rick and Julia looked up just in time to see him tumbling, falling, clawing for his life along the cliff.

—from *Ulysses Moore: The Door to Time* by Pierdomenico Baccalario, translated by
35  Edizioni Piemme

---

180. In which of the following words is the first syllable emphasized when the word is spoken?
    A. Assortment
    B. Proportion
    C. Adventure
    D. Mystical

181. Rick is Julia's
    A. father
    B. friend
    C. cousin
    D. brother

182. The author uses the phrase "tumbling, falling, clawing"[line 32] to create
    A. the illusion of motion
    B. a sense of foreboding
    C. suspense and mystery
    D. the sound of something falling

183. When Jason recited his story of what he and Rick had found, how did he **most likely** tell the tale?
    A. In a matter-of-fact manner
    B. With an abundance of pauses
    C. Using accurate descriptive details
    D. With exaggerations and embellishments

184. When Rick says "He gets to win while we take it nice and slow,"[line 30] he is showing that he
    A. is not competitive
    B. likes a challenge
    C. is a good loser
    D. likes Julia

*Read the following passage and answer questions 185 to 188*

### from Ronia, The Robber's Daughter

AND THEN SPRING CAME LIKE A SHOUT OF JOY TO THE WOODS AROUND Matt's Fort. The snow melted, streaming down all the cliff faces and finding its way to the river. And the river roared and foamed in the frenzy of spring and sang with all its waterfalls a wild spring song that never died. Ronia heard it every waking hour and even in her
5  nightly dreams. The long, terrible winter was over. The Wolf's Neck had long been free of snow. There was a turbulent stream rushing down it now, and the water splashed around the horses' hooves when Matt and his robbers came riding early one morning through the narrow pass. They sang and whistled as they rode out. Oh, ho, at last their splendid robbers' life was beginning again!

10  And at last Ronia was going to her woods, which she had missed so much. The moment the snow melted and all the ice thawed away, she should have been there to see what was happening in her domain, but Matt had stubbornly kept her at home. The spring forests were full of dangers, he claimed, and he would not let her go until it was time for him to set out with his robbers.

15  "Off you go then," he said, "and don't drown yourself in some treacherous little pool."

"Oh, yes, I shall," Ronia said. "To give you something to make a fuss about at last."

Matt gazed gloomily at her. "My Ronia," he said with a sigh. Then he flung himself into the saddle, led his robbers down the slopes, and was gone.

As soon as Ronia saw the last horse's rump disappear through the Wolf's Neck, she
followed at a run. She, too, was singing and whistling as she waded in the cold water of
the brook. Then she was running, running, until she reached the lake.

And there was Birk, as he had promised. He was stretched out on a flat rock in the
sunshine. Ronia did not know if he was asleep or awake, so she picked up a stone and
tossed it into the water to see if he heard the splash. He did, and he sprang up and came
toward her.

"I've been waiting a long time," he said, and once again she felt that little spurt of joy
because she had a brother who waited and wanted her to come.

And here she was now, diving headfirst into spring. It was so magnificent everywhere
around her, it filled her, big as she was, and she screeched like a bird, high and shrill.

"I have to scream a spring scream or I'll burst," she explained to Birk. "Listen! You can
hear spring, can't you?"

They stood silently, listening to the twittering and rushing and buzzing and singing and
murmuring in their woods. There was life in every tree and watercourse and every green
thicket; the bright, wild song of spring rang out everywhere.

"I'm standing here feeling the winter run out of me," said Ronia. "Soon I'll be so light I can fly."

—by Astrid Lindgren

185. Which of the following sentences **best** summarizes this passage?
    A. This story is about a little girl who likes to swim in streams.
    B. Ronia is a robber's daughter who loves experiencing spring in the forest.
    C. Ronia likes to play in the forest with her brother Birk.
    D. This story is about a girl who hates the winter.

186. Which of the following sentences **best** indicates how Matt and the robbers feel about spring?
    A. "They sang and whistled as they rode out."[line 8]
    B. "Matt and his robbers came riding early one morning"
    C. "And at last Ronia was going to her woods, which she had missed so much."[line 10]
    D. "Then he flung himself into the saddle, led his robbers down the slopes, and was gone."[line 17]

187. Ronia's comment "Oh, yes, I shall"[line 16] is made in
    A. jest
    B. fury
    C. agreement
    D. amazement

188. Matt, who is the leader of the robbers, is **most likely** Ronia's
    A. brother
    B. father
    C. husband
    D. neighbor

*Read the following passage and answer questions 189 to 192*

### Red Fox at Dawn

The fox glides like a flame through frozen fields of morning,
On black velvet feet.
His jet-black pointed ears prick up as he hears
The first cocks crow on far off farms.
5   He pauses, listening,
Then yawns a delicate yawn and licks his chops
And swiftly flows into the glowing dawn,
Passing like a comet out of sight,
Trailing his tail—a plume of firelight—
10  As bright tongues lick across the morning sky,
And all the frosted grass bursts into life
With rubies, garnets, diamonds sparkling.
The red fox slips across red jeweled fields,
On feet of night.
15  —by Dahlov Ipcar

189. In the phrase "Trailing his tail—a plume of firelight," the word "plume" refers to a
   A. fluffy tail
   B. puff of smoke
   C. moving column
   D. bushel of feathers

190. A synonym for the word "delicate," as it is used in the phrase "yawns a delicate yawn,"[line 6] is
   A. slight
   B. smooth
   C. splendid
   D. sensitive

191. Which of the following phrases contains a simile?
   A. "glides like a flame"[line 1]
   B. "yawns a delicate yawn"[line 6]
   C. "slips across red jeweled fields"[line 13]
   D. "swiftly flows into the glowing dawn"[line 7]

192. This poem is an example of which type of poetry?
   A. Limerick
   B. Cinquain
   C. Diamante
   D. Free verse

*Read the following passage and answer questions 193 to 196*

### from A Toad for Tuesday

"Skis? What are skis?" said Morton.

"Something a traveling rabbit told me about last summer, and I know just how to make them."

Morton's jaw dropped open, but he didn't say a word. He knew that once Warton's mind was made up there was no changing it.

5   For the next three days Warton worked very hard. He made his skis from strong oak tree roots. When he was done they were as handsome a pair of skis as anyone could want. They were sturdy and straight and polished to such a smoothness they felt like silk. He had also made ski poles to push with from porcupine quills and salamander leather.

On Wednesday morning he was ready to leave for Aunt Toolia's. It took quite a while to
10   bundle up in all his warm clothes. The last thing he put on was a little pack Morton had made for him. In it were several lunches, for it would be at least three or four days' travel to Aunt Toolia's home. There were also a few other things which Warton thought he might need, such as an extra pair of mittens and furry slippers. And on the bottom was the box of beetle brittle for Aunt Toolia.

15   He said goodbye to his brother who was already washing the breakfast dishes.

"Goodbye," said Morton, "and be very, very careful."

Warton started up through the long tunnel that led to the top of the old stump they lived under. When he stepped out he was dazzled. The brilliant snow glistened and glittered, and the deep blue sky was filled with puffy white clouds that drifted over the tall
20   evergreens. Snowbirds twittered gaily as they hopped from branch to branch.

"This is positively beautiful," thought Warton. "But I must be going. It's a long way to Aunt Toolia's, and I'm curious to try my new skis."

He reached down and strapped them on and then gave a strong push. Immediately, the skis became tangled, sending him tumbling into a hill of snow. He hopped up quickly and
25   tried again. This time he went much farther, until he ran straight into a squirrel who was digging in the snow. Once again he hopped up, and after apologizing, off he went again.

Now he was going along quite well. The more he skied the more he enjoyed it. All bundled up in his four coats, three sweaters, two pairs of mittens, and his cap with the ear flaps, the little toad looked like a tiny ball skimming over the woodland snow.

30   After he had gone quite a way and when the sun was directly overhead he decided to have some lunch. He saw a perfect place to eat—a large, flat stump sticking out of the snow.

Stepping out of his skis and giving a big jump, he landed on top. He brought out one of his lunches and poured some hot acorn tea. He ate two sandwiches and was just about to bite into a slice of mosquito pie when he heard a strange sound.

35   It sounded very much like a far-off hiccup. Warton looked around, but he saw nothing. He started to take another bite and again he heard it. This time it seemed to come from below the stump. He hopped over to the edge and cautiously peeked down.

There, sticking out of the snow, were two furry brown legs with tiny white feet and little toes that wiggled and jiggled every time the hiccup was heard. Warton hopped down and
40   began clearing away the snow as fast as he could. When he was done he found that he had uncovered a brown and white furred deer-mouse. His big dark mouse eyes were filled with gratitude.

> "Oh, thank you," the mouse said with relief. "That was …hic …most uncomfortable. It seems that whenever I become upside down I get the hiccups. I was afraid I would
> 45 remain that way till the snow melts in the spring."
>
> "How did you manage to get stuck upside down?" asked Warton with a blink.
>
> "I was on top of the …hic …stump having a little snooze in the noon sun as I often do. But this time …hic …I had a dream that I was a merry-go-round, and before I could wake up I rolled right off the edge of the stump."
>
> 50 "I think I have just the thing for you," Warton said, "if you'll hop back up with me."
>
> When they did, Warton gave the mouse some hot tea and right away the hiccups disappeared.
>
> "Thank you again," said the mouse. "That's much better."
>
> —by Russell E. Erickson

193. The smoothness of the finished skis is compared to
    A. wax
    B. silk
    C. stone
    D. butter

194. The writer describes Warton as a "tiny ball skimming over the woodland snow"[line 29] because Warton is
    A. tumbling down the hill
    B. rolling around in the snow
    C. tucked up into a ball shape so he can ski faster
    D. wearing so many layers he looks like a round ball

195. When Warton leaves to begin his journey, his brother Morton **most likely** feels
    A. worried
    B. excited
    C. jealous
    D. lonely

196. Warton used porcupine quills and salamander leather to make a
    A. pair of skis
    B. small backpack
    C. pair of ski poles
    D. box for the beetle brittle

*Read the following passage and answer questions 197 to 200*

## The Snake on Second Avenue

It wasn't my idea to have a snake for a pet. I don't like animals much, and as far as wild animals go—well, cats are too wild for me. But my mother's batty about animals. She watches nature shows on TV and writes letters to the editor complaining about inhumane traps. I find it a little tiresome, but mostly Mum's all right. She never complains when she
5  has to pick me up after ball practice, even though she thinks I should be bird-watching instead.

We were in Saskatoon for a dentist appointment the day we found the snake. It was a little garter snake, the kind we have in the garden at home—green with yellow stripes. There was one thing unusual about this one, though. It was on Second Avenue right outside a shoe store. The snake looked really scared and I don't blame it. It was too
10  small to be made into shoes, but that wasn't its biggest worry. From the look of the crowd gathered around it on the sidewalk, the busy street would have been safer.

We noticed the crowd from the end of the block. As we got closer we could hear a kid scream over and over, "Kill it! Kill it!" I don't know why the kid didn't just leave.

As soon as Mum heard the kid yell she doubled her speed. I ran along with her because I
15  was pretty curious about what all the people were staring at. A mouse? A Martian? A kid playing hooky?

Mum pushed her way through the crowd and I followed. The snake was coiled up on the sidewalk. Everyone seemed to be arguing about how to kill it.

"Oh, the poor thing!" exclaimed Mum. She went straight to the snake and picked it up. It
20  was already so frightened that it didn't even try to get away. It just wrapped its tail around her wrist and poked its tongue in and out.

There was a horrified silence. Even the kill-it kid stopped yelling.

"It's just a garter snake," said Mum, quite loudly. "It's not poisonous and it's not a constrictor. The only things it can damage are insects." She paused, then said, "And I'm
25  going to take it home. Please excuse me." She didn't have to push her way out. The crowd just separated in front of her. She seemed to have forgotten me so I followed along behind, watching the snake move in her hands and wondering what it felt like.

We'd reached the car before I noticed where we were. "Hey, Mum!" I exclaimed. "I thought we were going to buy me some jeans."

30  "With a snake?" she asked. "We're going home now. You'll have to hold the snake."

I wish she'd waited till we were in the car. I don't want you to think I'm chicken, but the first time I hold a snake, I'd like advance warning.

Terrified that I might drop it, I just blinked and grabbed the thing around the neck. I was surprised at how it felt—not slimy at all, but hard and dry on the top and soft underneath.
35  Its head was amazingly small, but it still kept sticking its tongue out. I stuck mine out at it, then climbed into the car.

> Mum started the engine and said, "I've heard that garter snakes make good pets."
>
> I groaned, but I knew there was no point in arguing. And really, it wasn't so bad. I could probably write a science report on it and amaze all the teachers. After all, there are
> 40 worse things than living in the same house as a snake. At least it wasn't a cat.
>
> —by Adele Dueck

197. In the statement "my mother's batty about animals", the word "*batty*" means
   A. interested
   B. afraid
   C. nosey
   D. crazy

198. The author uses the phrase, "mother's batty about animals"[line 2] to show that the mother
   A. is very fond of animals
   B. finds animals annoying
   C. feels animals take too much time
   D. does not care much about animals

199. Which animal is "too wild" for the boy?
   A. snakes
   B. dogs
   C. cats
   D. rats

200. According to the mother, the only things a garter snake can damage are
   A. insects
   B. people
   C. birds
   D. rats

*Read the following passage and answer questions 201 to 204*

## Becca's Diary

Becca's diary: April 2, 1920
Onboard *Expedient*

Our new home is better than I'd imagined. We have cabins five and six; Mrs. Ives describes it as a suite, but it is just two small rooms connected by a narrow door. She
5   thought we'd like to be close to each other. I think when I know her a bit better, I shall ask for a different cabin, as far away from brother Doug and his lucky socks as I can get.

My cabin is self-contained, and I rather like it. I felt a small pang of homesickness for my bedroom in Lucknow, but this will be fine until Mother and Father return from their expedition to the Sinkiang. A mahogany bunk curves along one side. Underneath it are
10  three drawers for clothes. There's a small desk beside the door, which is where I'm writing this, with bookshelves jutting out above. All the fittings are beautifully finished, and the wood gleams in the soft glow of the oil lamp (there is no electric light in this part of the ship). Doug's cabin is the mirror of mine, but he's furious because I have a brass plaque on my door that says GUNNERY OFFICER!

15  We both have a present from the captain. Mine is a gramophone and some records. Doug has got some paints and watercolor paper, which he's mucking around with now. Our interests are known to our uncle, it seems—I suspect via the dreaded Aunt Margaret. Perhaps life aboard ship won't be as bad as I feared.

We are housed in what used to be the officers' quarters. It's a small corridor with eight
20  cabins off it, all polished to an astonishing sheen. Mr. and Mrs. Ives occupy the cabins opposite ours. The rest of the crew are in the mess deck at the other end of the ship, so it's quiet down here—just the steady heartbeat thump of the engines.

Mrs. Ives is the ship's cook and is married to the ship's coxswain. She's left us an enormous tray of pies and puddings. Unfortunately this heat has made me thirsty rather
25  than hungry, but Dustbin Douglas has made light work of his share and is eyeing up mine.

Before leaving us on our own, Mrs. Ives repeatedly warned us that we are not allowed to wander off, as there are many dangerous parts of the ship. I think she couldn't wait to get her hands on the bandaged man we saw being stretchered aboard, who, she told us, was now resting in the sickbay. So we've been left to unpack and settle in. One small
30  triumph is that we at least now know where we are headed—Mrs. Ives told us we are bound for the South China Sea on some sort of research expedition. Researching what exactly, she wasn't clear. Suddenly I realize how little we know about our uncle and his curious ship.

35  —*by* Joshua Mowll

201. This passage is written in the voice of which character?
   A. Doug
   B. Becca
   C. Mrs. Ives
   D. The captain

202. The reason that Becca does not like her cabin is that it is
    A. too small
    B. self-contained
    C. beautifully furnished
    D. next to Doug's cabin

203. Which of the following positions does Mrs. Ives have on the ship?
    A. Cook
    B. Doctor
    C. Captain
    D. Coxswain

204. The phrase "just the steady heartbeat thump of the engines"[line 22] is an example of
    A. a simile
    B. hyperbole
    C. a metaphor
    D. alliteration

*Read the following passage and answer questions 205 to 208*

### from Coram Boy

It was not just because he seemed a gentleman that made Alexander different. Although the boys joked about him, they never laid a finger on him, and Thomas soon realised they respected him after all, for no one doubted that Alexander had the finest voice of them all and, more than that, was the most musically gifted. Even the bishop treated him
5   with awe and called him "our little genius." Not only did Alexander have the voice of an angel, but he played the harpsichord and virginal precociously well and had composed obsessively from the age of six. His anthems and choral pieces were often sung at services and concerts.

At first, Thomas was disappointed to find himself ordered to sit next to this surly,
10  uncommunicative boy in the schoolroom. Strange that Alexander, who had advised Thomas to make the boys laugh, seemed impervious to jokes and wise-cracking. When Thomas tried to get even a smile out of his companion, his attempt was received with a blank uncomprehending stare. But Thomas was gifted at algebra, and when he saw Alexander drifting helplessly over a calculation, he offered to help him. Alexander
15  grudgingly accepted his assistance and, in due course, reciprocated by helping Thomas with Latin, Greek and French. Then, when Thomas took up the violin, he soon showed himself to be such a skillful performer, Alexander began writing pieces for him. Without realising it, they had become friends.

—by Jamila Gavin

205. In the phrase "Alexander grudgingly accepted his assistance", the word "*grudgingly*" means
    A. happily
    B. willingly
    C. resentfully
    D. indifferently

206. In the phrase "his attempt was received," [line 12] the word "*attempt*" means
   A. skill
   B. effort
   C. advice
   D. knowledge

207. A synonym for the word "*ordered*" is
   A. commanded
   B. instructed
   C. requested
   D. asked

208. The bishop refers to Alexander as their little
   A. star
   B. angel
   C. genius
   D. musician

*Read the following passage and answer questions 209 to 212*

### Gramma's Apron

Gramma's gone, but not forgotten,
that's her apron hanging there.
It still hangs in Grampa's kitchen.
Sometimes he looks at it and stares.

5  When Gramma wore her apron
it was magical to see.
The pockets held such treasures
for the grandkids just like me.

Saw it shine up Grampa's fender once
10  just as pretty as you please,
and it wiped my brother's cheek off
one time when he sneezed.

It took cookies from the oven,
it rushed to wipe a tear,
15  got a grain of sand out of your eye,
made a lap for the stories we'd hear.

It wiped spills up from the countertop
when she was baking pies,
a symbol of her love and care
20  and it showed, too, in her eyes.

> Sometimes I'm sad to look at it
> when I see my Grampa stare.
> Gramma's gone, but not forgotten.
> That's her apron hanging there.
>
> 25 —by C. J. Heck

209. Which of the following pairs of words are synonyms?
    A. Stories and treasures
    B. Gone and forgotten
    C. Apron and kitchen
    D. Look and stare

210. The speaker of the poem is
    A. Grampa
    B. Gramma
    C. a daughter
    D. a grandchild

211. Grampa **most likely** leaves the apron hanging in the kitchen because
    A. he uses it frequently
    B. nobody else wants it
    C. it reminds him of Gramma
    D. that is where aprons are kept

212. Gramma's love and care showed in her
    A. eyes
    B. apron
    C. kitchen
    D. treasures

# EXERCISE #1—LANGUAGE ARTS

## Table of Correlations

| Standard | | Test #1 |
|---|---|---|
| 5RL | Reading Standards for Literature | |
| 5RL.4 | Determine the meaning of words and phrases as they are used in a text, including figurative language such as metaphors and similes. | 263, 264 |
| 5RL.10 | By the end of the year, read and comprehend literature, including stories, dramas, and poetry, at the high end of the grades 4–5 text complexity band independently and proficiently. | 265 |
| 5RI | Reading Standards for Informational Text | |
| 5RI.4 | Determine the meaning of general academic and domain-specific words and phrases in a text relevant to a grade 5 topic or subject area. | 263, 264 |
| 5RF | Reading Standards: Foundational Skills | |
| 5RF.3a | Know and apply grade-level phonics and word analysis skills in decoding words. Use combined knowledge of all letter-sound correspondences, syllabication patterns, and morphology to read accurately unfamiliar multisyllabic words in context... | 213, 214, 215, 216, 217 |
| 5RF.4c | Read with sufficient accuracy and fluency to support comprehension. Use context to confirm or self-correct word recognition and understanding, rereading as necessary. | 213, 214 |
| 5W | Writing Standards | |
| 5W.1c | Write opinion pieces on topics or texts, supporting a point of view with reasons and information. Link opinion and reasons using words, phrases, and clauses. | 257, 258, 259, 260, 261 |
| 5W.2c | Write informative/explanatory texts to examine a topic and convey ideas and information clearly. Link ideas within and across categories of information using words, phrases, and clauses. | 257, 258, 259, 260, 261 |
| 5W.9a | Draw evidence from literary or informational texts to support analysis, reflection, and research. Apply grade 5 Reading standards to literature. | 262 |
| 5L | Language Standards | |
| 5L.1a | Demonstrate command of the conventions of standard English grammar and usage when writing or speaking. Explain the function of conjunctions, prepositions, and interjections in general and their function in particular sentences. | 227 |
| 5L.1b | Demonstrate command of the conventions of standard English grammar and usage when writing or speaking. Form and use the perfect verb tenses. | 222, 232, 234, 235, 238 |
| 5L.1c | Demonstrate command of the conventions of standard English grammar and usage when writing or speaking. Use verb tense to convey various times, sequences, states, and conditions. | 218, 219, 220, 221, 222, 223, 224, 225, 226, 227, 228, 229, 230, 231, 232, 233, 234, 235, 236, 237, 238 |
| 5L.1e | Demonstrate command of the conventions of standard English grammar and usage when writing or speaking. Use correlative conjunctions. | 227 |
| 5L.2a | Demonstrate command of the conventions of standard English capitalization, punctuation, and spelling when writing. Use punctuation to separate items in a series. | 239, 240 |

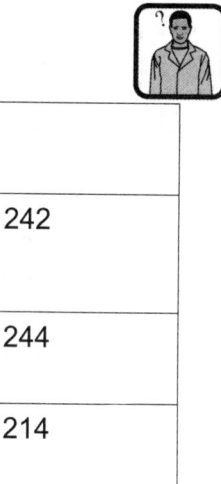

| | | |
|---|---|---|
| 5L.2b | Demonstrate command of the conventions of standard English capitalization, punctuation, and spelling when writing. Use a comma to separate an introductory element from the rest of the sentence. | 241 |
| 5L.2c | Demonstrate command of the conventions of standard English capitalization, punctuation, and spelling when writing. Use a comma to set off the words yes and no, to set off a tag question from the rest of the sentence, and to indicate direct address. | 241, 242 |
| 5L.2e | Demonstrate command of the conventions of standard English capitalization, punctuation, and spelling when writing. Spell grade-appropriate words correctly, consulting references as needed. | 243, 244 |
| 5L.4a | Determine or clarify the meaning of unknown and multiple-meaning words and phrases based on grade 5 reading and content, choosing flexibly from a range of strategies. Use context as a clue to the meaning of a word or phrase. | 213, 214 |
| 5L.4c | Determine or clarify the meaning of unknown and multiple-meaning words and phrases based on grade 5 reading and content, choosing flexibly from a range of strategies. Consult reference materials, both print and digital, to find the... | 245, 246, 247, 248, 249 |
| 5L.5c | Demonstrate understanding of figurative language, word relationships, and nuances in word meanings. Use the relationship between particular words to better understand each of the words. | 250, 251, 252, 253, 254, 255, 256 |

213. Which of the following sentences is written most clearly and correctly?
    A. Protects skin sunscreen from the harsh sun.
    B. Sunscreen protects skin from the harsh sun.
    C. From the harsh sun protects skin sunscreen.
    D. Sunscreen from the harsh sun protects skin.

214. Which of the following sentences is written most clearly and correctly?
    A. Who is the guest speaker at the year-end banquet?
    B. At the year-end banquet is the guest speaker who?
    C. Is the guest speaker at the year-end banquet who?
    D. Is the guest speaker who at the year-end banquet?

*Use the following information to answer the next question.*

| If the teacher asks her students to **redo** their work, she wants them to do it _____. |

215. Which of the following choices correctly completes the given sentence?
    A. better
    B. again
    C. quickly
    D. with a friend

216. Which of the following prefixes can be added to the front of the word *certain* to make a word that means "not sure"?
    A. In-
    B. Un-
    C. Dis-
    D. Mis-

217. In the sentence "We have to unfold the map before we can read it," the word "unfold" means to
    A. open up
    B. fold again
    C. fold in half
    D. roll in a tube

218. Which of the following sentences contains the correct subject and verb agreement?
    A. Julie and Tom is going to the park.
    B. Sandy are doing her homework.
    C. Michael and Alice likes to eat apples.
    D. Samantha is babysitting her little brother.

219. Read the sentence below. There may be a mistake in capitalization, punctuation, or usage. Which of the alternatives is written most clearly and correctly? If there is no mistake, choose *Correct as is*.

yes i have even seen the red road's

- A. Yes I have even seen the red roads,
- B. Yes, I have even seen the red roads.
- C. Yes, I has even seen the red roads.
- D. Correct as is.

220. Read the sentence below. There may be a mistake in capitalization, punctuation, or usage. Which of the alternatives is written most clearly and correctly? If there is no mistake, choose *Correct as is*.

Answers the phone quickly?

- A. Answer the phone quickly!
- B. Answer, the phone quickly!
- C. Answers the Phone quickly.
- D. Correct as is.

221. Read the sentence below. There may be a mistake in capitalization, punctuation, or usage. Which of the alternatives is written most clearly and correctly? If there is no mistake, choose *Correct as is*.

Finish your homework before you go outside!

- A. Finishes your homework before you go outside?
- B. finish your homework before you go outside
- C. finishes your homework before you go outside,
- D. Correct as is.

222. In the following sentence, which tense is used for the verb *rained*?

It rained on my birthday.

- A. Past tense
- B. Future tense
- C. Present tense
- D. Perfect tense

223. Sarah loved walking through the woods on sunny days.

Which word in the sentence above is a verb?

- A. Woods
- B. Sarah
- C. Through
- D. Walking

224. Which of the following sentences is written using correct capitalization, punctuation, and usage?
- A. Against his fathers wish, Kobi continue's to play violent computer game's.
- B. Against his father's wishes, Kobi continues to play violent computer games.
- C. Against his fathers wish's Kobi continues to play violent computer games.
- D. Against his father's wishes Kobi continue to play violent computer games.

225. Read the sentence below. There may be a mistake in capitalization, punctuation, or usage. Which of the alternatives is written correctly? If there is no mistake, choose *Correct as is*.

Furthermore planets and moons stays in orbit because of the force called gravity.

- A. Furthermore planet's and moon's stay in orbit because of the force called gravity.
- B. Furthermore, planets and moons stay in orbit because of the force called gravity.
- C. Furthermore, Planets and Moons stayed in orbit because of the force called gravity.
- D. Correct as is.

226. Read the sentence below. There may be a mistake in capitalization, punctuation, or usage. Which of the alternatives is written correctly? If there is no mistake, choose *Correct as is*.

As earth turned, the part facing the sun is lit up, and the part away from the sun was dark.

- A. As Earth turns, the part facing the sun is lit up, and the part away from the sun is dark.
- B. As Earth turns, the part facing the sun was lit up, and the part away from the sun is dark.
- C. As earth turn, the part facing the sun are lit up, and the part away from the sun are dark.
- D. Correct as is.

*Use the following information to answer the next question.*

Read the sentence below. If there is a mistake in sentence structure, choose the alternative that is written most clearly and correctly. If there is no mistake, choose *Correct as is*.

227. At last weekend the hockey tournament, Paul scored six goals for his team.
- A. At the hockey tournament last weekend, Paul scored six goals for his team.
- B. The hockey tournament at last weekend, scored Paul six goals for his team.
- C. Last weekend at the hockey tournament, six goals scored Paul for his team.
- D. Correct as is.

228. Which of the following sentences is written most clearly and correctly?
- A. The farm dog chased the sheep into the pen.
- B. Chased the sheep the farm dog into the pen.
- C. The pen into the farm dog the sheep chased.
- D. The dog farm chased sheep the pen into the.

*Use the following information to answer the next question.*

My cousin Billy always plays with a blue rubber ball.

229. What is the verb in the given sentence?
- A. cousin
- B. plays
- C. Billy
- D. ball

*Use the following information to answer the next question.*

Can you see your brother <u>running</u> across the lawn?

230. What is the correct way to write the underlined word in the given sentence?
    A. ran
    B. will run
    C. was running
    D. Leave as is

*Use the following information to answer the next question.*

A <u>cat spending</u> most of the day sleeping.

231. What is the correct way to write the underlined words in the given sentence?
    A. cat spend
    B. cat spends
    C. cat was spend
    D. Leave as is

*Use the following information to answer the next question.*

Beat the eggs and _____ them to the batter.

232. Which of the following choices correctly completes the given sentence?
    A. add
    B. added
    C. did add
    D. are adding

*Use the following information to answer the next question.*

_____ to look both ways before you cross the street.

233. Which of the following choices correctly completes the missing part of the given sentence?
    A. Remember
    B. Remembered
    C. Did remember
    D. Am remembering

*Use the following information to answer the next question.*

Last night I _____ in a tent in the backyard.

234. Which of the following choices correctly completes the given sentence?
    A. slept
    B. sleep
    C. had slept
    D. will sleep

*Use the following information to answer the next question.*

I am late because I did not hear the alarm and I _____ in.

235. What is the correct way to complete the missing part of the given sentence?
 A. slept
 B. do sleep
 C. will sleep
 D. am sleeping

*Use the following information to answer the next question.*

_____ uses a backpack to carry his books.

236. Which of the following subjects **cannot** be used to complete the given sentence?
 A. A student
 B. Our teacher
 C. All students
 D. My big brother

*Use the following information to answer the next question.*

_____ to your room and stay there!

237. What is the correct way to write the missing part of the given sentence?
 A. go
 B. gone
 C. went
 D. am going

*Use the following information to answer the next question.*

Sometimes we _____ to school together in the morning.

238. Which of the following choices correctly completes the given sentence?
 A. walk
 B. walks
 C. are walking
 D. done walking

239. Which of the following sentences has the commas correctly placed within the list?
 A. On the weekend, we enjoy, hiking fishing and boating.
 B. On the weekend, we enjoy hiking, fishing and boating.
 C. On the weekend we enjoy hiking, fishing, and, boating.
 D. On the weekend we enjoy hiking, fishing, and boating.

240. Which of the following sentences uses commas in the correct places?
    A. At Disneyland, we saw cartoon characters, went on the roller coaster and tried many kinds of foods.
    B. At Disneyland we saw, cartoon characters, went on the roller coaster and tried many kinds of foods.
    C. At Disneyland we saw cartoon characters, went on the roller coaster, and tried many kinds of foods.
    D. At Disneyland, we saw cartoon characters went on the roller coaster, and tried many kinds of foods.

241. Which of the following sentences is written correctly?
    A. No I still think that riding a bike without a helmet is not very safe.
    B. No, I still think that riding a bike without a helmet is not very safe.
    C. No I still think that, riding a bike without a helmet is not very safe.
    D. No, I still think that, riding a bike without a helmet is not very safe.

242. Which of the following sentences is written correctly?
    A. I love my mother because she is loving caring and supportive.
    B. I love my mother because she is loving, caring, and supportive.
    C. I love my mother because she is loving, caring, and, supportive.
    D. I love my mother because, she is loving, caring, and supportive.

243. Read the sentence carefully. Which of the underlined words is spelled incorrectly? If all the words are spelled correctly, choose *No mistake.*

    My grandmother <u>always</u> has the most <u>beautifull</u> garden in the <u>neighborhood</u>.

    A. always
    B. beautifull
    C. neighborhood
    D. No mistake

*Use the following information to answer the next question.*

| The brave ___*i*___ rescued the ___*ii*___ maiden from the dragon. |

244. Which of the following charts correctly completes the given sentence?

   A.
   | *i* | *ii* |
   |---|---|
   | night | fair |

   B.
   | *i* | *ii* |
   |---|---|
   | night | fare |

   C.
   | *i* | *ii* |
   |---|---|
   | knight | fair |

   D.
   | *i* | *ii* |
   |---|---|
   | knight | fare |

A student read the following dictionary entry for the word *rack*:

> rack (rak) • *noun* **1** A framework, usually with hooks or rails, for holding or hanging things. **2** A pair of antlers. **3** A joint of meat that includes the ribs.
>
> • *verb* **1** To strain or stretch. *She racked her brain to remember where she put her keys.*

245. According to this entry, which definition for the word *rack* is the **most common**?
    A. Definition 1 (noun)
    B. Definition 2
    C. Definition 3
    D. Definition 1 (verb)

246. Which of the following guide words would **most likely** appear on the page containing this dictionary entry?
    A. Racket—Radar
    B. Rabbit—Racing car
    C. Race—Racquetball
    D. Rabble—Racehorse

> **snap** • *verb* (**snapped, snap•ping**)
> **1** to break suddenly with a cracking noise. **2** to grab or try to grab something suddenly with the teeth. **3** to speak in a short, sharp, or annoyed way.
>
> • *noun* **1** a device that closes or opens something and often makes a sharp noise **2** a short period of cold weather **3** a sharp or cracking sound

247. Which of the following sentences uses *snap* in the same way as in the third verb definition in the given dictionary entry?
    A. The slender branch snapped under his weight, and he fell.
    B. The hungry dog snapped the sandwich out of my hand.
    C. "That is a silly question," she snapped at her sister.
    D. He snapped up his coat and went into the storm.

248. Which of the following sentences uses *snap* in the same way as the third noun definition?
    A. Can you help your little sister do up the snaps on her jacket?
    B. Tent doors usually have snaps or zippers to open and close them.
    C. The weather has been warm except for one short cold snap last week.
    D. When I heard the snap, I knew that the mouse had been caught in the trap.

249. Which of these words would you find on the dictionary page with the guide words *star—strong*?
   A. Stork
   B. Stunt
   C. Style
   D. Stuff

250. In the sentence "Mandy saw her former music teacher at the mall," the word "former" means
   A. interesting
   B. talented
   C. new
   D. past

251. An antonym for the word **difficult** is
   A. easy
   B. long
   C. angry
   D. confused

252. An antonym for the word *cluttered* is
   A. lost
   B. closed
   C. hidden
   D. organized

253. A synonym for the word *freezing* is
   A. cold
   B. warm
   C. isolated
   D. tropical

254. Which of the following words is an antonym for the word *fat*?
   A. Tall
   B. Thin
   C. Heavy
   D. Round

255. Which of the following words is an antonym for the word *always*?
   A. Ever
   B. Now
   C. Never
   D. Sometimes

256. Which of the following pairs of words are synonyms?
    A. Pail, pale
    B. Sad, funny
    C. Heavy, light
    D. Well, healthy

257. Read the sentence carefully. Which of the underlined words is spelled incorrectly? If all the words are spelled correctly, choose "No mistake".

    He could not <u>comprehend</u> the lack of <u>compassion</u> <u>demonstrated</u> by others.

    A. comprehend
    B. compassion
    C. demonstrated
    D. No mistake

258. Which of the following sentences is written most clearly and correctly?
    A. Jennifer received a perfect score on her spelling test yesterday.
    B. Jennifer a perfect score on her spelling test yesterday received.
    C. On her spelling test yesterday, a perfect score received Jennifer.
    D. A perfect score received Jennifer on her spelling test yesterday.

259. Read the sentence below. If there is a mistake in sentence structure, choose the alternative that is written most clearly and correctly. If there is no mistake, choose *Correct as is*.

    The yellow buttercup to the sun gently turned its face.

    A. To the sun gently turned its face the yellow buttercup.
    B. The yellow buttercup gently turned its face to the sun.
    C. Gently turned its face the yellow buttercup to the sun.
    D. Correct as is.

260. Read the sentence below. If there is a mistake in sentence structure, choose the alternative that is written most clearly and correctly. If there is no mistake, choose *Correct as is*.

    At our house is family games night every Friday.

    A. Is family games night at our house every Friday.
    B. Every Friday is family games night at our house.
    C. Friday every is family games night at our house.
    D. Correct as is.

261. Which of the following sentences is written most clearly and correctly?
    A. From their living room window, could see they the skyline.
    B. The skyline from their living room window, they could see.
    C. From their living room window, they could see the skyline.
    D. Could they see from their living room window the skyline.

262. In a fable, the characters are often
   A. toys
   B. robots
   C. ghosts
   D. animals

263. A figure of speech that uses the words *like* or *as* to compare two unlike things is known as
   A. onomatopoeia
   B. alliteration
   C. a metaphor
   D. a simile

*Use the following information to answer the next question.*

When I woke up, I felt as sleepy as a bear before hibernation.

264. The given sentence contains an example of
   A. a simile
   B. a metaphor
   C. personification
   D. onomatopoeia

265. A story about Greek gods and goddesses is called a
   A. fable
   B. myth
   C. folktale
   D. fairy tale

# ANSWERS AND SOLUTIONS — EXERCISE #1—READING INFORMATIONAL

| | | | |
|---|---|---|---|
| 1. D | 15. A | 29. A | 43. B |
| 2. D | 16. B | 30. D | 44. B |
| 3. B | 17. See solution | 31. C | 45. A |
| 4. A | 18. B | 32. C | 46. A |
| 5. A | 19. D | 33. B | 47. B |
| 6. A | 20. D | 34. D | 48. C |
| 7. B | 21. B | 35. B | 49. A |
| 8. D | 22. C | 36. C | 50. A |
| 9. C | 23. C | 37. C | 51. C |
| 10. C | 24. C | 38. A | 52. A |
| 11. C | 25. B | 39. A | 53. C |
| 12. C | 26. B | 40. C | |
| 13. C | 27. A | 41. B | |
| 14. C | 28. C | 42. D | |

**1. D**

The term "close-knit" refers to members of a family, community, or group who are supportive and loyal to one another. Examining both parts of the hyphenated word will help you to understand the meaning.

**2. D**

The word *located* means to be in or to have put something in a particular place. To be relocated means to be moved to a new place. The context suggests that Boone's family moved.

**3. B**

A synonym is a word that means the same thing or almost the same thing as another word. A synonym of the word "Magnificent" as it is used in the given phrase is *splendid*. "Palatial" and "skillful" are sometimes synonyms for magnificent, but they do not express the meaning that is used in the phrase.

**4. A**

*Gulliver's Travels* is italicized because it is the title of a book. All titles of books should be italicized.

**5. A**

In this passage, "parasites" are defined as creatures that eat beetles from the inside out. This means the creature lives inside a beetle's body while it is feeding, and it receives both food and shelter from its host. The passage describes parasites as living inside the bodies of others rather than on them.

**6. A**

The elytra are the hard casings of a beetle's forewings that cover and protect a beetle's hind wings, which are used for flying.

**7. B**

In this passage, the word mandibles refers to the jaws of the biggest beetle in the world, the "*Titanus giganteus.*"

**8. D**

The world's heaviest beetle is the goliath beetle.

**9. C**

It is better for nomadic people, who are constantly packing up and moving from place to place, not to have too many possessions with them slowing them down.

Answers and Solutions      Castle Rock Research

10. C

Michael's family is described as living in the traditional Inuit ways. They moved from place to place, carrying only essential furs, weapons, and tools. They needed to hunt to provide for all their other needs, such as food, clothing, oil for lamps, and so on.

11. C

The passage states that the family "traveled by dog-team in search of whales, seals, and cariboo." The reader can infer that dog teams would most likely be used only in the winter, and that the family would travel by foot or some other means in the other seasons.

12. C

In this passage, the narrator describes "tales of the animals he knew." In cultures where groups of people moved around to find food, such animal stories were also known as legends. These stories were handed down by tradition. The other alternatives can also be described as tales, but they are not the kind of tales referred to in the passage.

13. C

The word "enormous" means extremely large. The jars are huge.

14. C

When Joe is through digging around in his room, it is in worse shape than before. At this point in the story, Joe says, "Even I was disgusted!" He is fed up with the mess in his room.

15. A

The word "took" is the past tense of the verb *to take*. The phrase suggests that it took time before Joe actually started cleaning up his junk.

16. B

Joe describes his bedroom as a workshop where he stashes everything he finds. To sigh means to draw in or let out a very long, deep, loud breath. Joe's mom sighs because she is displeased to see Joe's room stashed with junk and looking so messy.

17.

| Points | Rationale |
|---|---|
| 4 | The response clearly and thoroughly identifies information in the text to show that the Antarctic is the most hostile place on Earth and links this to clear, relevant examples and inferences about how it differs from the Arctic. Relevant examples and details are provided from the passage, and the response provides clear evidence of comprehension. |
| 3 | The response adequately identifies information in the text to show that the Antarctic is the most hostile place on Earth and links this to examples and inferences about how it differs from the Arctic. Relevant examples and details are provided from the passage, and the response provides adequate evidence of comprehension. OR One section of the question may have been answered clearly and thoroughly, while the other section of the question was not answered or was not answered clearly. |
| 2 | The response uses limited supporting information from the passage. There is limited use of information identified from the passage. There may be major misinterpretations. The response provides evidence of basic understanding. OR The response adequately addresses one part of the task but does not address the other part. |

| Points | Rationale |
|---|---|
| 1 | The response uses inadequate information to describe the hostile environment of the Antarctic. It provides limited to no supporting information from the passage, and that information may be incorrect. The response provides evidence of minimal understanding.<br>OR<br>The limited response addresses one part of the task but does not address the other part. |
| 0 | The response is totally incorrect and shows no evidence that the student understands the task. The response may be off topic, completely irrelevant, or missing. |

18. B

The word "hostile" has multiple meanings, but in this context it means forbidding, inhospitable, or harsh.

19. D

The word "mammoth" means of very great size, and synonyms include the word *enormous*.

20. D

The comparison given in the passage is that "the frozen sea reaches an area of 7 million square miles, about twice the size of the United States." If the area of the United States is approximately half the size of the frozen sea, it is about 3.5 million square miles.

21. B

When a knife is blunt, it is no longer sharp. It is dull.

22. C

Under the heading "The Artist's Way," the writer refers to the statue David as one of Michelangelo's most famous sculptures.

23. C

According to the instructions, the nail can be used to add details to the carving.

24. C

The author suggests in the opening that this recipe makes something soft and easy to carve. You can infer that this would make it ideal for a beginner trying out carving for the first time.

25. B

To invent means to create something new.

26. B

At the baseball game, vendors were shouting, "Get your red hot dachshund dogs" to sell their hot dogs. *Vendor* is another word for "salesman."

27. A

Anton Feuchtwanger was a salesman who sold frankfurters at a booth at the World's Fair in St. Louis.

28. C

This passage mostly discusses the invention of the term "hot dog."

29. A

If a mother rabbit senses danger, she will stand in front of her kittens. If she is very worried, she will thump the ground with her back leg. This tells the kittens that they should run for cover.

30. D

Rabbits stand on their hind legs so they can see farther and look for danger.

31. C

The writer states that a rabbit scratches the ground with its front paws when it wants to scare off another rabbit.

32. C

A rabbit never forgets the scent of another rabbit that has beaten it in a fight. Whenever it smells the stronger rabbit's scent, the weaker rabbit will avoid it.

33. **B**

    Informational text is a type of non-fiction that conveys or explains information. One of its main characteristics is that it provides facts about a particular subject.

34. **D**

    Nestlé observed that sales of semi-sweet candy bars had dropped everywhere, except around Boston.

35. **B**

    To save time, Ruth Wakefield broke a bar of chocolate into bits instead of melting it. She thought the bits would melt in the oven and blend into the batter. This is an example of taking a shortcut—choosing a faster or shorter way to do something or get somewhere.

36. **C**

    The author introduces Nestlé as the manufacturer, or maker, of the chocolate that was being used in the cookies.

37. **C**

    Something described as visible can be seen by the eye, and the prefix *-in* means *not*. Something described as "invisible" cannot be seen by the eye.

38. **A**

    The passage states that when using a telescope, you "might see stars where before you only saw dark space." It goes on to say that with "bigger and bigger telescopes you can see more and more objects in the sky." These objects are normally difficult to see because they are far away. People can see them with a telescope because the telescope magnifies objects and makes them appear larger.

39. **A**

    The passage explains that "when the gas runs out, the star stops burning and begins to die."

40. **C**

    In the quotation, the words "meets the eye" refers to what comes into human sight, or what human eyes can see. The given quotation means there are things in the sky that humans cannot see with their eyes.

41. **B**

    A synonym is a word with a similar meaning. The term "capsizing," as used in the story, "The Voyage of the Mayflower" means turning over.

42. **D**

    The two finger games "cat's cradle" and "paper, scissors, stone" were played by the eight-year-olds.

43. **B**

    They met for the first time in Southampton, England, a few days before the two ships sailed on August 5.

44. **B**

    The *Speedwell* was put into Dartmouth harbor on August 12th and left again on August 23rd. That is an interval of 11 days.

45. **A**

    Most of the early settlers in America and Canada came in order to escape persecution or hardships in their daily lives. They saw this as an opportunity to make a new beginning for themselves and to improve on their quality of life. The people who came across the Atlantic in order to explore did not travel with their families on the Mayflower. The dangers of crossing the ocean and the expense outweighed the desire to have a trip on a ship, and while the experience would have been an adventure, that is not the reason why the Pilgrims made the journey.

46. **A**

    An antonym is a word with the opposite meaning. The word *preservation* means to maintain something or keep something alive, which is the opposite of the word "elimination."

47. **B**

    A synonym is a word that means the same thing as another word. Extensive means broad or expansive.

**48. C**

Authorities assumed that the belugas were eating the salmon and cod that people needed to survive.

**49. A**

The writer expresses fear and concern about the beluga whale's being an endangered species.

**50. A**

The race takes place every year. The word "annual" refers to something that happens every year.

**51. C**

Since the passage discusses magical people, sports, and creatures, it is safe to assume that the word "hexing" refers to the act of putting a spell on someone.

**52. A**

A synonym is a word that has the same meaning as another word. The word "vast" is used to describe something very large. A synonym of "vast" is immense.

**53. C**

The most likely explanation for the nickname "Dent-Head" is that, as a Creaothceann player, Magnus Macdonald was hit by a number of falling rocks, and these permanently damaged his head.

# ANSWERS AND SOLUTIONS — EXERCISE #2—READING INFORMATIONAL

| 54. A | 68. B | 82. C | 96. C |
| --- | --- | --- | --- |
| 55. C | 69. D | 83. A | 97. B |
| 56. B | 70. D | 84. B | 98. D |
| 57. D | 71. C | 85. D | 99. D |
| 58. A | 72. D | 86. B | 100. C |
| 59. D | 73. A | 87. A | 101. B |
| 60. B | 74. B | 88. D | 102. A |
| 61. B | 75. B | 89. D | 103. D |
| 62. D | 76. C | 90. D | 104. C |
| 63. D | 77. B | 91. D | 105. B |
| 64. D | 78. D | 92. D | 106. C |
| 65. C | 79. D | 93. B | |
| 66. C | 80. C | 94. A | |
| 67. C | 81. D | 95. D | |

**54. A**
Whales are hydrodynamic, which means that, like boats, they can cut through waves.

**55. C**
The word "have" is in the present tense.

**56. B**
An antonym of the word "forward" is *backward*.

**57. D**
A synonym is a word that means the same thing as another word. In this case, the word "buoyant" means "floatable" like a fishing buoy.

**58. A**
Northern bottlenose whales can dive as deep as 800 meters.

**59. D**
An age-old tradition is a custom that has been handed down or done in the same way for a very long time.

**60. B**
A caribou is an Arctic deer with large antlers.

**61. B**
The expression "age-old" means very old or ancient.

**62. D**
The word "nomadic" describes a lifestyle in which people are constantly moving or traveling from place to place.

**63. D**
The word "hazardous" means dangerous. In this case, it refers to the melting ice on the shoreline, which would be very dangerous, especially for children.

**64. D**
The Qallupilluit is described as a "witchy undersea creature who kidnaps children."

**65. C**
For Michael, moving was "a way of life." His family probably moved every season to be closer to the animals they depended upon for food, clothing, and shelter.

**66. C**
The author describes puppy mills as "places where large numbers of puppies are bred purely for profit," meaning that puppy mills are concerned only with making money.

SOLARO Study Guide – ELA 5

**67. C**
The author has chosen to organize this passage into five separate pointers or tips on what to consider when choosing a puppy, including where to look, things to check for in purebred and mixed breed puppies, reasons to avoid puppy mills, and how to make sure your puppy is healthy.

**68. B**
The author emphasizes the importance of checking for signs of good health and observing the dog's behavior.

**69. D**
The article focuses on some different things to consider when choosing a puppy, such as the breed, the mother's behavior, the breeder, and the puppy's health. The other statements, while they may be true, are not relevant to this passage.

**70. D**
The word furious can be used to mean several different things. In this context, it means excited, passionate, or intense. Its most common usage is as a synonym for angry, but that is not how it is used in this passage. Stevenson is excited about writing a story based on his imaginary island.

**71. C**
A stern person is hard, harsh, grim, strict, and/or unbending.

**72. D**
The fact that he had few friends probably meant that Louis was lonely.

**73. A**
The author specifically describes Robert Louis Stevenson imagining worlds and stories based on nightmares, toy soldiers, and bowls of porridge, as well as Bible stories. There is no reference to fairy tales at all in the passage.

**74. B**
When Aunt Araba says that Grandma's soup is authentic, she means that the soup tastes like the original African soup she probably remembers from Ghana.

**75. B**
The word *exquisite* usually refers to things that are beautiful or delicate. From the passage it is possible to guess that Uncle Robert is referring to the taste of the soup, not how it looks. In this context, Uncle Robert says "Exquisite" to mean delicious.

**76. C**
The narrator's grandmother visited her family from Ghana, which is a country in Africa.

**77. B**
Grandmother brought the children traditional clothes ("the kind they wear in Ghana"); she told "stories her grandmother told her when she was young," including "Spider man" stories; and she cooked Ghanaian food, proclaimed by one aunt to be "authentic." It is inferred throughout the story that Grandmother wanted to keep the family's customs and traditions alive among her extended family who had emigrated to America.

**78. D**
In the statement "they scored the bar," the word "scored" means they marked, or indented, lines into the candy bar. The scored lines made the bars easier to break into pieces because along the lines the chocolate was thinner and weaker.

**79. D**
"Broke," "blend," "tossed," and "baked" are all verbs, which indicate actions.

**80. C**
The writer explains that Nestlé began making and selling chocolate chips just for baking cookies and that they printed the recipe on the package.

**81. D**
The words "chocolate crispies" are in quotation marks to indicate that this is what Ruth Wakefield called her cookies.

82. **C**

The first lines are italicized in order to show that they are the introduction to the non-fiction article that follows. The italicized lines provide what is likely the main reason Mary Shadd became an advocate for education for blacks. The italicized introduction is a fictitious conversation, while the remainder of the article is non-fiction.

83. **A**

Mary Shadd was the first woman in the United States to graduate from law school.

84. **B**

The introduction states "It's against the law for Black children to go to school. Don't even let anyone know that you can read and write!" These statements imply that the law forbidding black children from going to school was because the state did not want black children to be educated. Mary was not allowed to go to school, but this was because she was a black American.

85. **D**

Because Mary's ideas were considered odd, fewer people would have attended her public speeches; therefore, she decided that "newspaper articles were another way to share her ideas." As the passage mentions, "In those days, there were no television or radio news reports."

86. **B**

The word *stalk* means to follow or track.
To catch its prey, a cheetah must not be seen. This way, it can surprise the other animal. The cheetah must blend in with the grass and be very quiet and cautious.

87. **A**

The word *prey* refers to an animal that is caught for food. The cheetah is a hunter that must hunt and kill its prey to survive.

88. **D**

The word *perch* means to rest or balance on. The passage states that the cheetah "perches on high places." This means that it sits up high in order to see far distances.

89. **D**

The word "extinction" comes from the word extinct, which means destroyed or wiped out. To say that cheetahs "are racing toward extinction" means that the number of cheetahs in the world is getting smaller very quickly.

90. **D**

A dash is a quick run or sprint in one direction. The expression means that the cheetah runs fast like a lightning flash.

91. **D**

The water is described as being full of seaweed and plankton, which means that it is difficult or impossible to see through. Something that is opaque is something that does not let light through.

92. **D**

The solution is found in this sentence from the second paragraph: "A mother and her calf have finally reached their destination and main feeding area after a three or four thousand kilometer trip."

93. **B**

The second paragraph describes the whales as a mother and her calf.

94. **A**

The arrival of humpback whales is described in the second paragraph of the passage.

95. **D**

The word "transported" means to have carried something from one place to another.
The "present site" is the place where the large stones currently sit, which is in southern England.

96. **C**

A historian is someone who writes or compiles records of events that have taken place.

## 97. B

A synonym is a word that means the same thing as another word. *Time* is a synonym for the word "period," meaning an age.

## 98. D

Merlin said that the stones in the Giants' Ring in Ireland "are connected with certain religious secret rites and they have various properties that are medicinally important." Giants would come to the Giants' Ring for healing.

## 99. D

The phrase "his sword was broken" is in the past perfect tense.

## 100. C

A homonym for the word "knight" is *night*. A homonym is a word that sounds the same as another word but has a different meaning.

## 101. B

A synonym is a word that means the same thing as another given word. When a place is remote, it is distant or far-removed.

## 102. A

According to the passage, the days of the famous King Arthur were "an exciting and mysterious time to live in."

## 103. D

Since the sentence describes how the course runs through the middle of a dragon reservation, this suggests that a Swedish Short-Snout is probably a dragon.

## 104. C

The sentence indicates that broomstick fliers had to be able to turn corners and adjust their speed and height. The appropriate synonym for the word "vary" is change.

## 105. B

In the context of the sentence, a synonym for the word "evolved" is *changed*. The writer is saying that some of the ancient broom games have changed into sports that are familiar in the present day.

## 106. C

While it is still played in England, Swivenhodge never became widely popular.

# ANSWERS AND SOLUTIONS — EXERCISE #1—READING LITERATURE

| | | | |
|---|---|---|---|
| 107. C | 121. B | 135. A | 149. B |
| 108. D | 122. B | 136. D | 150. B |
| 109. A | 123. C | 137. B | 151. B |
| 110. D | 124. B | 138. B | 152. C |
| 111. B | 125. D | 139. A | 153. C |
| 112. D | 126. B | 140. A | 154. C |
| 113. B | 127. D | 141. D | 155. C |
| 114. C | 128. D | 142. D | 156. A |
| 115. A | 129. C | 143. B | 157. A |
| 116. A | 130. A | 144. B | 158. C |
| 117. C | 131. A | 145. D | 159. D |
| 118. A | 132. A | 146. B | |
| 119. C | 133. C | 147. C | |
| 120. C | 134. A | 148. D | |

**107. C**

When he talks about being "a little guy," the speaker is referring to his childhood.

**108. D**

The word "advise" means to counsel, inform, or provide guidance.

**109. A**

An antonym (opposite) of the word "long" is short.

**110. D**

The "fond memories" the narrator refers to in the second stanza are of his first solo scooter ride.

**111. B**

"*Then*" is closest in meaning to the word "next." It shows timing of events.

**112. D**

The word crawl implies movement and is a verb.

**113. B**

An antonym (opposite) of the word "*suddenly*" is gradually.

**114. C**

Skeptical and suspicious both mean to be doubtful or distrusting. The rat is suspicious of the beetle when he sees the beetle is waiting for him at the palm tree.

**115. A**

Clues in the passage indicate that tundra is wide, cold, and treeless.

**116. A**

The contraction "we'll" combines the words *we* and *will*. The use of the auxiliary verb *will* indicates a future event that will happen sometime later on.

**117. C**

Today was the first day for Eva to walk on the bottom of the sea alone.

**118. A**

Fiction is imaginative writing that is not necessarily based on facts. Someone who has collected mussels from the bottom of the sea might have inspired this story, but the story itself is still made up.

**119. C**

In the second paragraph, the writer uses the words "kept," "belonged," and "caught," which means he is speaking in the past tense. In the third paragraph, the writer uses the words "walk," "tie," and "give," so he is speaking in the present tense. Therefore, the tense switches from past to present.

**120. C**

The speaker in this story is Billy. He says the gophers "belonged to Bruce and me, and to another boy called Murray." The three boys own the gophers.

**121. B**

Billy's father got a queer look on his face because he had suddenly realized that the owls might be useful to him. Billy's father thought Billy already had too many pets, and he realized that the owls would probably help solve this problem by eating some of Billy's rats, gophers, and rabbits.

**122. B**

The narrator is anxious to know whether his father will let him bring home an owl to add to his pets. By the end of the passage, he would be feeling relieved. He probably would not be feeling confident that his father would let him keep the owl, because he already had so many animals and his father's initial reaction was quite negative. There is nothing to suggest that the narrator is feeling angry.

**123. C**

The word "befuddled" means the same as the word *confused*. Both words refer to someone being baffled by the events he or she has gone through. The teacher in the poem becomes so confused and muddled that she accidentally steps in a puddle that is "up to her shin".

**124. B**

The name of the speaker is not revealed, but it is clear that the speaker is on the field trip with the class. He or she refers to the teacher as "my teacher" and is telling a story about the field trip experience.

**125. D**

The poem states that the students are moaning and groaning, and it explains that they are "cranky, exhausted, and spent." This means they are grumpy, tired, and worn out.

**126. B**

A narrative is a story or tale. Although this passage is a poem, it is one that tells a story. Hence, it is a narrative poem.

**127. D**

The word *moor* means to tie or fasten a watercraft with ropes. A pier or dock might have several rings with ropes that can be used to keep the boats close to the pier. Jason and Rick can see pieces of these old lines hanging from the rotten pier.

**128. D**

The word "mystical" means supernatural. When Jason tells Julia about his and Rick's discovery of the second beach, he makes their adventure on the rocks take on mystical, or supernatural, proportions.

**129. C**

Rick returned to the shore because the current had become too strong and he felt it would have been dangerous to stay in the water: "the current started to pull at him, like a hand grabbing at his legs. Rick felt it was wiser not to go farther out, and Julia happily agreed with him. There was no sense risking their lives when they had everything they needed right here."

**130. A**

A simile is a comparison between two objects using the words *like* or *as*. In the phrase "the current started to pull at him, like a hand grabbing at his legs," the expression "like a hand grabbing at his legs" is a simile comparing the current to a grabbing hand.

Answers and Solutions

Castle Rock Research

131. **A**

As it is used in the quotation, the word "vexatious" means annoying or troublesome. Christopher's father had made a troublesome mess of the money, and Mama needed Uncle Ralph's help to sort out the mess.

132. **A**

Uncle Ralph hoped Christopher and the new governess would get along well enough that they would forgive Uncle Ralph for implementing such big changes.

133. **C**

Christopher likely admires Uncle Ralph because he is warm and confident. He likes the way Uncle Ralph looks and how he seems to care for the people around him.

134. **A**

A comparison using *like* or *as* is known as a simile. In this case, Uncle Ralph's smile is compared to sunlight shining on an autumn forest.

135. **A**

The word "faithful" means almost the same as the word "loyal".

136. **D**

The word "fixed" is an antonym of the word *destroyed*.

137. **B**

The elephants could barely hear Hare because Hare was so small and they were so large. To their ears, Hare's voice sounded like an insect buzzing.

138. **B**

Hare told the elephants that the moon god was very angry with them for trampling the burrows and grasses. She said that the moon god's message was that the elephants must leave and never return.

139. **A**

The expression "tagging along" means following someone, especially in going from one place to another.

140. **A**

We can tell Sam is telling the story because it is told using the pronoun "I" and the other characters speak to the storyteller by calling him "Sam."

141. **D**

Sam knows that people will feel better about Jacob if he does not always barge in to their houses without knocking. Sam knows how hard it is for Jacob to remember things, so when Jacob finally remembers to knock, Sam is very proud.

142. **D**

In the story we learn that Jacob blew out all of his candles in one breath "because he's bigger." The fact that Jacob is physically much bigger than Sam is important to the story because it suggests more about Jacob's differences from Sam.

143. **B**

In this context, the expression "a great deal" means a large amount. There was a lot of snow on the mountains.

144. **B**

Lady Gray must have found it very unusual to have snowshoes on her feet. The story says that she was "very awkward at first" when the snowshoes were fastened on. However, she "tried very hard to walk in them," and she was "practicing a little every day." That means she made a big effort to use the snowshoes.

145. **D**

The story says that Lady Gray "was always happy when her master was in the saddle."

146. **B**

It was difficult for Lady Gray to walk in snowshoes, and many animals might not have been as happy to try as she was. Lady Gray seemed to understand what the problem was, and she practiced walking in her snowshoes so that Mr. Brown would not have to leave her behind. She was cooperative.

**147. C**

The past tense of the word *kill* is *killed*.

**148. D**

The best summary explains the narrator's attitude at the beginning of the passage, summarizes the action, and then briefly tells the reader how the narrator's attitude changed as a result of the action. The other alternatives address only one of these elements, either the author's attitude or the action, but not both.

**149. B**

The narrator describes this snake as similar to the garter. Snakes that he has seen in his garden: "green with stripes."

**150. B**

When the narrator states "And really, it wasn't so bad," he or she is referring to keeping the garter snake as a pet. The narrator plans to observe the snake and write an amazing science report, but there is no evidence that he or she will receive an A. There is also no evidence to suggest that the narrator will get other pets or give up playing ball.

**151. B**

The narrator would have liked to receive advance warning from his or her mother before being handed the snake.

**152. C**

Nate explains that he has to take Hoot the owl to a doctor in Los Angeles. He describes himself as being on the train acting as a bodyguard to the owl. He has left his cousin Olivia behind in San Francisco.

**153. C**

Nate introduces himself and says that he is riding on the train with Sludge. He goes on to say that they are acting as bodyguards for Hoot, which must mean that Hoot is with them. This is confirmed again when Olivia asks Nate to take Hoot on the train.

**154. C**

Near the end of the passage, Olivia tells Nate that Hoot eats mice.

**155. C**

Nate the Great is surprised to hear that an owl does not like to fly. He thinks all owls should like flying, so he tells Olivia that Hoot should see the doctor for that problem. Nate might not like the fact that Hoot eats mice, but he probably understands that this is normal for an owl. It is Olivia who wears the boa, not Hoot. Hoot may or may not like riding on trains, but Olivia only tells Nate that Hoot does not like flying.

**156. A**

In the context of this poem, the word "*infirmity*" means fault. Matilda's Aunt discovered Matilda's fault, which was her tendency to tell lies.

**157. A**

A synonym of the word "*Deprivation*" is punishment. Not being able to attend the play was a punishment for Matilda since she had been telling lies. Her aunt tried to discipline her by having her lose out on something fun.

**158. C**

The aunt is likely frustrated for a variety of reasons: Matilda's lies have left her with a damp house to clean, and the aunt is required to pay the fire brigade to stop their enthusiastic aid.

**159. D**

This poem can be best described as a narrative poem. A narrative poem tells a story with a beginning, a middle, and an end.

# ANSWERS AND SOLUTIONS — EXERCISE #2—READING LITERATURE

| | | | |
|---|---|---|---|
| 160. D | 174. A | 188. B | 202. D |
| 161. B | 175. C | 189. A | 203. A |
| 162. B | 176. B | 190. A | 204. C |
| 163. D | 177. A | 191. A | 205. C |
| 164. D | 178. D | 192. D | 206. B |
| 165. B | 179. D | 193. B | 207. A |
| 166. C | 180. D | 194. D | 208. C |
| 167. D | 181. B | 195. A | 209. D |
| 168. A | 182. A | 196. C | 210. D |
| 169. B | 183. D | 197. D | 211. C |
| 170. A | 184. D | 198. A | 212. A |
| 171. C | 185. B | 199. C | |
| 172. A | 186. A | 200. A | |
| 173. B | 187. A | 201. B | |

**160. D**

The poor man's problem is stated directly at the beginning of the story when it says that he "had not a bit of meat nor a morsel of bread to make his Christmas feast."

**161. B**

The statement "Oh, dear!" is a common expression, but an incomplete thought. Thus, it is a fragment.

**162. B**

In a folktale, there is often an underlying moral to the story. The rich brother is obviously greedy, selfish, and ill-natured, which sets the stage for the story.

**163. D**

The old man emphasized that the poor man was not to sell the ham to the dwarfs. The old man specifically instructed the poor man to request the old handmill in exchange for the ham.

**164. D**

An asp is a type of snake.

**165. B**

To fret is to worry or feel upset. In this poem, the meaning is reinforced by the following line, which describes the mother being scared despite the father's reassurances. The narrator is not scared, but only worried that Rover has apparently escaped from his glass tank.

**166. C**

The word *shriek* means almost the same thing as the word "scream."

**167. D**

The poem does not follow the specific structures of a haiku or a limerick. It does have a rhyming scheme, thus it cannot be described as free verse. It is a rhyming poem.

**168. A**

A synonym for the word "kind" is nice. Using the context of the sentence, the word "kind" could be replaced by the word *nice*.

**169. B**

When the bird asks the willow for help, the willow replies, "Indeed, I do not know you, and we willows never talk to people whom we do not know."

SOLARO Study Guide – ELA 5

### 170. A
The word that best describes how the bird felt when the spruce offered it a home is

### 171. C
After the birch, oak, and willow trees had all their leaves blown off and their true characters revealed, they may have felt foolish for not helping the bird.

### 172. A
A famine is a severe shortage of food, often brought on by drought.

### 173. B
An offering is something offered in worship or devotion. In this story, the little girl offers her doll to the gods in order to stop the drought and famine.

### 174. A
She-Who-Is-Alone talks to her doll when there is no one else for her to talk to. The doll is like a friend and companion.

### 175. C
The doll is the little girl's most valued possession because it is all she has left to remind her of her parents.

### 176. B
A snare is a noose, usually formed with heavy twine. Snares are used for capturing small game.

### 177. A
The sentence "He can hear you too, and he's wondering what you're up to," contains two main clauses. It is a compound sentence.

### 178. D
The author describes having a dog and about 30 gophers and 10 pigeons. He says he also has "some" rabbits, but he does not say exactly how many. He probably does not have anywhere near 30 rabbits, because they are mentioned as if they were not very important or significant. Moreover, 30 rabbits would require a lot of space and feeding.

### 179. D
Billy and his friends got the rats from Murray's father, who was a professor at the college and got the rats from the medical school.

### 180. D
*Mystical* is the only word that has the first syllable emphasized. The others all have the second syllable emphasized.

### 181. B
Rick is Julia's friend. The sentence "Jason struggled to keep up with his athletic sister and friend" suggests that Julia and Jason are brother and sister and Rick is a friend.

### 182. A
Repeating the *-ing* endings in the words "tumbling," "falling," and "clawing" creates a sense of repetitive motion. When the words are read aloud, they help the reader to visualize the tumbling motion of rocks as they roll down a hill. This visualization of the motion of the falling rocks creates a stronger sense of the story's action. In order to create the sound of something falling, the writer would probably use words that suggest sounds more than motion, such as "clattering," "thundering," or "crashing".

### 183. D
The narrator says that Rick's tale took on "mystical proportions." This suggests that Rick made the adventure seem exciting and mysterious, probably with exaggerations and embellishments.

### 184. D
Rick indicates that he would much rather walk slowly with Julia than race against Jason. This shows that he likes her.

185. B

A good summary will briefly introduce the main characters and explain the main idea and events from the story. The best summary introduces Ronia as a robber's daughter, gives the setting, and sums up the main action. The other alternatives focus on smaller details from the story.

186. A

The singing and whistling indicates that Matt and his robbers are happy that spring has arrived. This behavior suggests that the robbers are pleased to be out in the forest.

187. A

Ronia makes this comment in jest. Matt expresses concern that Ronia may accidentally drown herself, and she teases Matt to let him know that she thinks he worries too much about her.

188. B

According to the title of the passage, Ronia is a daughter of a robber. Since Matt is the leader of the robbers and the person who forbids Ronia to go into the forest, he is probably also her father.

189. A

In the phrase "Trailing his tail—a plume of firelight," the word "plume" refers to the fox's fluffy tail, which is red and resembles firelight.

190. A

A synonym is a word that means the same thing as another word. A synonym for the word "delicate" is *slight*.

191. A

A simile is a comparison between two objects using the words *like* or *as*. In the phrase "glides like a flame," the fox's movement is compared to a flame.

192. D

This type of poem, with no regular pattern or rhymes, is known as free verse.

193. B

The writer describes Warton's skis as being "polished to such a smoothness they felt like silk."

194. D

Warton is wearing so many layers of clothing that he looks like a round ball. He is all bundled up in "four coats, three sweaters, two pairs of mittens, and his cap with the ear flaps." With all that clothing on, the little toad would look quite round.

195. A

When Warton first tells Morton of his idea to make skis, "Morton's jaw dropped open," which indicates that Morton is worried about Warton's plan. When Warton finally leaves on his journey, the last thing Morton tells him is to "be very, very careful." These context clues indicate that Morton is uneasy and worried about Warton skiing to Aunt Toolia's house.

196. C

The passage states that Warton "made ski poles to push with from porcupine quills and salamander leather."

197. D

In this statement, the word "batty" means crazy. The narrator's Mum is crazy about animals: she loves them.

198. A

The word "batty" is used figuratively to mean, fond of, crazy about, or very enthusiastic about animals.

199. C

The narrator says that he does not "like animals much, and as far as wild animals go—well, cats are too wild for me."

200. A

When Mum rescues the snake from the crowd, she says, "The only things it can damage are insects."

201. **B**

The title of the passage, "Becca's Diary," identifies the narrator as Becca.

202. **D**

Becca wants to ask Mrs. Ives to move her to a cabin as far away as possible from her brother Doug's cabin.

203. **A**

Mrs. Ives is referred to as the ship's cook in line: "Mrs. Ives is the ship's cook".

204. **C**

A metaphor is a figure of speech in which a word or phrase for one object or idea is used in place of another to suggest a similarity between them. Thus, the steady thump of the ship's engine is being compared to a human heartbeat.

205. **C**

Resentfully is a synonym for "*grudgingly*".

206. **B**

Effort is a synonym for the word "*attempt*".

207. **A**

Commanded is a synonym for the word "*ordered.*"

208. **C**

Because of Alexander's exceptional musical abilities, the bishop called him "our little genius."

209. **D**

The words *look* and *stare* are synonyms.

210. **D**

The speaker identifies himself as a grandchild in the lines "The pockets held such treasures / for the grandkids just like me."

211. **C**

The last stanza of the poem infers that Grampa probably leaves the apron hanging in the kitchen because it reminds him of Gramma and keeps her memory alive.

212. **A**

The speaker says that the apron was "A symbol of her love and care / and it showed, too, in her eyes." That Gramma was a loving and caring person is a main idea of the poem.

# ANSWERS AND SOLUTIONS — EXERCISE #1—LANGUAGE ARTS

| 213. B | 227. A | 241. B | 255. C |
| 214. A | 228. A | 242. B | 256. D |
| 215. B | 229. B | 243. B | 257. D |
| 216. B | 230. D | 244. C | 258. A |
| 217. A | 231. B | 245. A | 259. B |
| 218. D | 232. A | 246. C | 260. B |
| 219. B | 233. A | 247. C | 261. C |
| 220. A | 234. A | 248. D | 262. D |
| 221. D | 235. A | 249. A | 263. D |
| 222. A | 236. C | 250. D | 264. A |
| 223. D | 237. A | 251. A | 265. B |
| 224. B | 238. A | 252. D | |
| 225. B | 239. D | 253. A | |
| 226. A | 240. C | 254. B | |

**213. B**

The correct response is "Sunscreen protects skin from the harsh sun." The alternative "Protects skin sunscreen from the harsh sun" has no subject and is an incomplete sentence. The other choices have an awkward word order that does not make sense or is not clear.

**214. A**

The correct response is "Who is the guest speaker at the year-end banquet?" When asking a question using *who* as the subject, it should be the first word in the sentence.

Who (pronoun subject) is the guest speaker (verb phrase, verb + complement) at the year-end banquet (adverb phrase of location)?

**215. B**

The prefix *re-* means "again," so it changes the meaning of the word *do* to "do again."

**216. B**

The prefix *un-* means "not." If you add the prefix *un-* to the word *certain*, it changes the meaning of the word to "not certain" or "not sure."

**217. A**

If the prefix *-un* is added to the word *fold*, it changes the meaning of the word. The word "unfold" means to open up.

**218. D**

The correct response is: "Samantha is babysitting her little brother." If the subject is singular, the verb must also be singular. If the subject is plural, the verb must also be plural.

**219. B**

The correct response is: "Yes, I have even seen the red roads." The first word and the word *"I"* are capitalized in this sentence. This sentence is not in the form of a question; therefore, a period is used as the end punctuation. There is a comma after the word *"yes"* before leading into the rest of the sentence. There are no apostrophes in this sentence because there are no contractions or words showing possession. The verb must match the subject (first person singular: "I have").

### 220. A

The correct response is: "Answer the phone quickly!" This sentence is an imperative; therefore, an exclamation point is used as the end punctuation. The verb must match the subject (second person: "[you] answer"). No comma is needed.

### 221. D

The sentence is "Correct as is." The first word in this sentence is capitalized. This sentence is an imperative; therefore, an exclamation point is used as the end punctuation. The verb must match the subject (second person: "[you] finish").

### 222. A

The verb "rained" is in the past tense.

### 223. D

The word *walking* is a verb.

### 224. B

A comma is needed after the introductory phrase "Against his father's wishes."
The apostrophe in the word "father's" indicates possession. No other apostrophes are needed. The verb must match the subject (third person singular: "he continues").

### 225. B

The correct response is: "Furthermore, planets and moons stay in orbit because of the force called gravity." Only the first word in this sentence is capitalized. A comma is needed after the introductory word "Furthermore." There are no apostrophes in this sentence because there are no contractions or words showing possession. The verb must match the subject (third person plural: "they stay"). The action in this sentence appears to take place in the present; therefore, the verb "stay" is in the present tense.

### 226. A

The correct response is: "As Earth turns, the part facing the sun is lit up, and the part away from the sun is dark." As a planet's name, the word "Earth" is capitalized. The verbs must match the subjects (third person singular: "it turns" and "it is"). The verbs in this sentence must be in tense (in this case, the present tense) agreement: "turns…is."

### 227. A

The correct order is:

| Subordinate Clause | |
|---|---|
| Subordinating Conjunction | At |
| Subject (Noun) Phrase | The hockey tournament |
| Adverbial Phrase of Time | last weekend, |
| Main Clause | |
| Subject (Noun) Phrase | Paul |
| Verb Phrase (Verb + Adjective + Noun) | scored six goals |
| Adverbial Phrase of Purpose | for his team |

### 228. A

The correct response is "The farm dog (subject or noun phrase, article + adjective + noun) chased the sheep (verb phrase, verb + article + noun) into the pen (adverbial phrase of location, preposition + article + noun)."

### 229. B

The word "plays" is the verb in the given sentence.

### 230. D

The sentence is correct. "Running" is the present tense of *run*.

### 231. B

The correct response is "cat spends."

### 232. A

The correct response is "add." This imperative sentence should be written "Beat the eggs and add them to the batter."

Answers and Solutions

233. A

This is an imperative sentence; therefore, the correct choice is "Remember."

234. A

The sentence is referring to something that happened in the past. The alternative "slept" is the past tense of *sleep*.

235. A

The sentence is referring to something that happened in the past. The word *slept* is the past tense of *sleep*.

236. C

"All students" is plural, so it does not agree with the verb. The verb is singular, so the subject must also be singular. "All students" would only agree with the verb *use,* and *his* would have to change to *their*.

237. A

This is an imperative sentence. The missing word is the verb *go*. The correct way to write the sentence is "Go to your room and stay there!"

238. A

This sentence is referring to something that is happening in the present. The correct way to complete this sentence is "Sometimes we walk to school together in the morning."

239. D

The sentence that has the commas correctly placed within the list is "On the weekend we enjoy hiking, fishing, and boating."

240. C

The sentence that uses commas in a series correctly is "At ;Disneyland we saw cartoon characters, went on the roller coaster, and tried many kinds of foods."

241. B

At the beginning of a sentence, a comma should be placed after introductory words. Therefore, the following sentence is correct: No, I still think that riding a bike without a helmet is not very safe.

242. B

The following sentence is correct: I love my mother because she is loving, caring, and supportive. This sentence has commas correctly placed after the descriptive words.

243. B

The correct spelling of the suffix that means "full of" is *ful*. The word meaning "full of beauty" is correctly spelled *beautiful*.

244. C

The following chart correctly completes the given sentence:

| i | ii |
|---|---|
| knight | fair |

245. A

It is standard practice for a dictionary to list the most common use of a word first.

246. C

Guide words indicate the first and last words found on an alphabetically ordered page. When placed in alphabetical order, the word *rack* would be found between the guide words *race* and *racquetball*.

247. C

The correct response is "'That is a silly question,' she snapped at her sister."

248. D

The sentence "When I heard the snap, I knew that the mouse had been caught in the trap." uses *snap* in the same way as the third noun definition.

249. A

A dictionary uses guide words to help you find the word you are looking for. The word *stork* falls alphabetically between the words *star* and *strong*.

250. D

In this sentence, the word former means past.

251. **A**

An antonym is a word that means the opposite of another word. The opposite of difficult is easy.

252. **D**

An antonym is a word that means the opposite of another word. An antonym for the "cluttered" is organized.

253. **A**

A synonym is a word that means the same, or almost the same, as another word. Freezing and cold are synonyms.

254. **B**

The opposite, or antonym, of the word *fat* is thin.

255. **C**

The opposite, or antonym, of the word *always* is never.

256. **D**

Two words that are similar in meaning (i.e., synonyms) are *well* and *healthy*.

257. **D**

All of the words are spelled correctly.

258. **A**

The correct response is "Jennifer (subject or noun phrase) received (verb phrase) a perfect score (object or noun phrase) on her spelling test (prepositional phrase as adjective) yesterday (adverb of time)."

259. **B**

The correct response is:

| Subject (Noun) Phrase | Verb Phrase (verb & object) | Adverbial Phrase of Location |
|---|---|---|
| The yellow buttercup | gently turned its face | to the sun. |

260. **B**

The correct response is:

| Subject (Noun) Phrase | Verb Phrase (verb & object) | Adverbial Phrase of Location |
|---|---|---|
| Adjective & Noun | | |
| Every Friday | is family games night | at our house. |

261. **C**

The correct response is "From their living room window (adverbial phrase of location), they (subject or noun phrase) could see the skyline (verb phrase, verb + object or auxiliary + verb + article + object/noun).

262. **D**

The characters in a fable are often animals.

263. **D**

A figure of speech that uses the words *like* or *as* to compare two unlike things is known as a simile.

264. **A**

A simile is a figure of speech that uses the words *like* or *as* to compare two unlike things. The sentence contains the simile "felt as sleepy as a bear," which compares someone who is sleepy to how a bear must feel before hibernation.

265. **B**

Myths tell stories about gods and goddesses.

# Writing

# EXERCISE #1—WRITING

## EXTENDED (LONGER) WRITING PIECE (55 MINUTES)

Look at the picture carefully. What do you think is about to happen? Write an exciting story about what happens.

The activity will take about 55 minutes to complete.

## Overview

*Time*

| | |
|---|---|
| 2 minutes | Overview and directions for the student |
| 3 minutes | Writing topic |
| 2 minutes | Criteria |
| 8 minutes | Planning |
| 35 minutes | Written work |
| 5 minutes | Look back on your writing |

## Directions to the Student

1. You do not need to use all of the pages provided.
2. Remember to write double-spaced (on every other line) so you have room to go back to your writing and make changes and corrections.
3. You may use a dictionary or thesaurus.
4. You will be marked on the "Written Work" pages only (not the planning).

## Writing Topic

Your writing should be about **two** to **four** pages long.

### Criteria (Story/Narrative)

| | |
|---|---|
| Check your work for the following things: | |
| Did I write an exciting story about the picture? | ☐ |
| Is my story complete and easy to follow? | ☐ |
| Does my story include details to make it interesting to the reader? | ☐ |
| Did I choose words and ideas to make my reader feel something (happy, sad, surprised, excited) and are the words appropriate? | ☐ |
| Does my story have a beginning, middle, and end? | ☐ |
| Does my story have interesting characters (e.g., dialogue, description)? | ☐ |
| Have I made corrections in spelling, punctuation, and use of words? | ☐ |

### Planning

*My purpose*

To write an interesting story about the picture.

*My audience*

The teachers who will mark my writing.

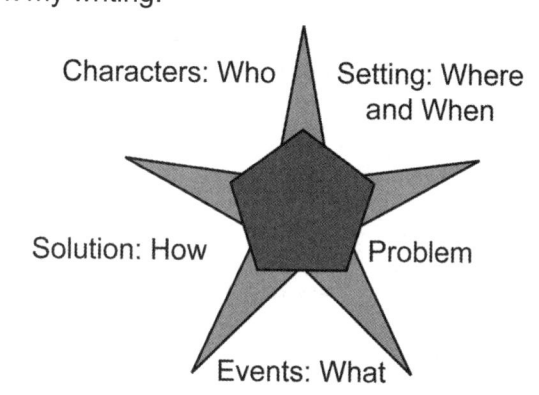

- Characters: Who
- Setting: Where and When
- Problem
- Events: What
- Solution: How

*Written Work*

Take 35 minutes to write your story. Use the criteria and your planning page as a guide when you write. Be careful to include words and actions that are appropriate for all readers.

*Look Back on Your Writing*

Take 5 minutes to look back on your writing.

Carefully go through your writing and make any changes or corrections. Use the criteria at the top of this page to guide you.

# SAMPLE RESPONSES—EXERCISE #1

## EXAMPLE OF WRITING RESPONSE PROFICIENT

One day me and my brothers went camping. When my mom and dad had gone for a walk we stayed by the camp fire, we did'nt see the alians coming out of there space ship to us. Then we saw them and I said WOW look at those creters and Tyler said they are alians from out of space. They walked across the river and came to us and said we want to be your friend because we have just landed on earth and we are hungary. Tyler went into the tent and came out with some hot dogs and we poked them with sticks and put them in the fire and cooked them and then we gave them to the alians to eat. They really liked them! And they eat 4 each. Then the alians told us about there plannet and it was awsome because everything on it is green. It is called the green plannet. Then the alians said they had to go and thanked us and walked back to there space ship and it just vanished. When mom and dad came back we told them about the alians and they said how exiting and we all went to bed.

## RATIONALE FOR RESPONSE SATISFACTORY

### Content

The majority of the events, actions, and ideas are appropriate for the context established by the writer (three children are camping when they see aliens approach them from their spaceship).

Details are general, but are appropriate for the story (e.g., "They walked across the river and came to us," "we have just landed on earth and we are hungry," and "aliens told us about their planet").

The writing generally holds the reader's interest and provides some support for a main idea, as it tells about the children meeting and communicating with the aliens.

### Organization

The beginning directly presents information about events (e.g., "One day me and my brothers went camping"), characters (e.g., "me and my brothers"), and setting (e.g., "we stayed by the camp fire").

Connections and/or relationships between events, actions, details, and/or characters are generally maintained (e.g., "said we want to be your friend because we have just landed on earth" and "the aliens said they had to go and thanked us").

The ending ("When mom and dad came back we told them about the alians and they said how exiting and we all went to bed") is predictable and contrived but is connected to events and actions.

**Sentence Structure**

Sentence structure is generally controlled, but run-on sentences are present (e.g., "we stayed by the camp fire, we di'dnt see the alians coming" and "they said how exiting and we all went to bed").

Sentences may vary in type and length (e.g., "Then the alians told us about there planet and it was awsome because everything on it is green" and "It is called the green planet").

Some variety of sentence beginnings (e.g., "One day...," "When my mom...," and "Tyler went...") is evident.

**Vocabulary**

Words chosen (e.g., "mom and dad had gone for a walk" and "Then we saw them") tend to be common or ordinary.

Expressions (e.g., "they are alians from out of space" and "we poked them with sticks and put them in the fire and cooked them") are usually more general than specific.

Words and expressions (e.g., "WOW" and "it was awsome") generally enhance the writing.

**Conventions**

Conventional end punctuation and capitalization are usually correct.

Many familiar words (e.g., "camping," "friend," and "vanished") are spelled correctly; errors (e.g., "did'nt," "creters," "hungary," and "there") suggest uneven control of spelling rules; unfamiliar words (e.g., "alians" and "plannet") are generally spelled phonetically.

Errors (e.g., "how exiting") are sometimes intrusive and may affect the clarity of communication.

**EXAMPLE OF WRITING RESPONSE PROFICIENT**

**The Aliens**

I felt very excited because we were going camping for the first time this summer. We all got ready and packed the tents and things and then we drove to our very favorite place. It was in the woods and a rushing river was near by and we could catch fish and swim in the river. After setting up the tent and putting our sleeping bags inside and having a apple mom and dad lighted the fire and then went to find more wood so we could cook hot dogs and roast marshmellows for supper. Tracy and me were just sitting there by the fire when we saw a bright shiny light across the river. The light turned into a space ship and it landed and out of it came three little green aliens with big round heads and antenas sticking out of the top of their heads. "Look at that!" I yelled at Tracy. "WOW!!" she said. "What do they want? I wondered. They walked across the river and did'nt seem to notice that it was very cold and they came towards us. We were very frightend but they were nice and one of them beamed us a message that said we just landed on this planet and we are lost and hungry. Do you know where we are? I said "You are on earth and we can give you some apples and hot dogs if you like." They said "Yes please and if we are on earth we know how to get back to our planet by flying though the milky way." After they had eaten their food they thanked us and went back to their space ship and we watched them take off with a WOOSH and then they dissapeared into the darkness.

## RATIONALE FOR RESPONSE PROFICIENT

### Content

Events, actions, and ideas are appropriate for the context established by the writer (children are camping when they see a space ship and aliens land on the other side of the river).

Details (e.g., "we could catch fish and swim in the river," "we saw a bright shiny light," and "The light turned into a space ship") are specific and generally effective.

The writing engages the reader's interest and presents a supported main idea (e.g., "We just landed on this planet").

### Organization

The beginning ("I felt very excited because we were going camping for the first time this summer. We all got ready and packed the tents and things and then we drove to our very favorite place. It was in the woods and a rushing river was near by and we could catch fish and swim in the river.") clearly establishes events, characters, and setting, and provides direction for the writing.

Connections and/or relationships between events, actions, details, and characters are maintained (e.g., "mom and dad lighted the fire and then went to find more wood," "out of it came three little green aliens," and "We were very frightend").

The ending ("After they had eaten their food they thanked us and went back to their space ship and we watched them take off with a WOOSH and then they dissappeared into the darkness") provides an appropriate finish for event and actions.

### Sentence Structure

Sentence structure is controlled (e.g., "Tracy and me were just sitting there by the fire when we saw a bright shiny light across the river").

Sentence type and sentence length (e.g., "What do they want?" and "We were very frightend but they were nice and one of them beamed us a message that said we just landed on this planet and we are lost and hungry") are usually varied and effective.

Sentence beginnings (e.g., "After setting up...," "The light turned...," and "Do you know") are often varied.

### Vocabulary

Well-chosen words (e.g., "rushing river" and "a bright shiny light") are often used.

Expressions (e.g., "three little green aliens with big round heads and antenas sticking out of the top of their heads" and "beamed us a message") are usually specific and effective.

Words and expressions (e.g., "WOW!!," "get back to our planet by flying though the milky way," and "WOOSH") are descriptive and often enhance the writing.

**Conventions**

End punctuation and capitalization are essentially correct.

Familiar words are spelled correctly; spelling errors (e.g., "frightend" and "dissapeared") are "slips"; unfamiliar words (e.g., "marshmellows" and "antenas") may be spelled phonetically.

Errors that are present (e.g., "Tracy and me," "did'nt seem," and "the milky way") rarely affect the clarity of communication.

### EXAMPLE OF WRITING RESPONSE EXCELLENT

#### What a Camping Trip!

"Now remember to stay close to the camp sight and don't let the fire go out" said Dad when he and Mom set off for their usual night time walk. My brothers and me were used to this, every night after supper Mom and Dad went for a walk and left us to look after our things. Tonight was different. There was a bright full moon in the sky and the stars were extra bright and sparkling. Suddenly what looked like a falling star came crashing down to earth just across the river. "Wow! Awesome!" we cried out in amazement. We realized it was not a falling star because it was shaped like a space ship and climbing slowly down a ladder came three crimson red aliens. They had large heads with one big bulgeing eye, two legs that were so long they looked like spiders and two arms that had eight fingers on each hand. They skipped towards the bubbling river and noisily splashed across the cold water. When they reached our camp sight they beamed a message to us through their big eye and said "We are friendly aliens and we wonder if you would like to come for a ride in our space ship." "YES! YES!" we shouted together. "This is so exciting and amazing." "But…but…but what about Mom and Dad?" asked my little brother. "Don't worry." said one of the aliens. "We will have you back before your parents return."

We rushed as fast as a speeding bullet to get our shoes and jackets and then we went with the aliens across the river to their space ship. I had to help Bobby up the ladder because he couldn't reach the steps but we made it and once the door was shut we blasted off. We felt like we were on a speed boat but suddenly everything became smooth and we glided over the earth. We looked out the window and saw the rocky mountains and lakes and then we were over the ocean and could see dolphins and hump back whales swimming in the sea. We climbed higher and higher until the earth was a big round blue globe below us. It was truly miraculous and just like the pictures that I had seen in books. All too quickly we were back on earth beside the gurgling river and across from our camp sight. We thanked the aliens for an awesome adventure and said we would never forget them and we would tell everyone that aliens are really friendly and nice. They said "See you next year and we will take you for another ride into space!" We got back to the camp before Mom and Dad and decided to keep our visit with the aliens a secret.

### Content

Events, actions, and ideas are consistently appropriate for the context established by the writer (three children see a space ship with aliens descend to Earth, and they travel with the aliens for a visit to outer space)

Details (e.g., "came crashing down to earth just across the river" and "they beamed a message to us through their big eye") are specific and consistently effective, and the reader experiences the excitement felt by the writer of the arrival of the aliens.

The writing captivates the reader's interest and presents a well-supported main idea ("We are friendly aliens and we wonder if you would like to come for a ride in our space ship").

### Organization

The beginning captures the reader's attention ("'Now remember to stay close to the camp sight and don't let the fire go out' said Dad when he and Mom set off for their usual night time walk. My brothers and me were used to this, every night after supper Mom and Dad went for a walk and left us to look after our things.") clearly establishes events, characters, and setting, and provides direction for the writing.

Connections and/or relationships between events, actions, details, and characters are consistently maintained (e.g., "it was shaped like a space ship and climbing slowly down a ladder came three crimson red aliens," "we were over the ocean and could see dolphins and hump back whales swimming," and "We climbed higher and higher until the earth was a big round blue globe below us").

The ending ("We thanked the aliens for an awesome adventure and said we would never forget them and we would tell everyone that aliens are really friendly and nice. They said "See you next year and we will take you for another ride into space!" We got back to the camp before Mom and Dad and decided to keep our visit with the aliens a secret.") ties events and actions together.

### Sentence Structure

Sentence structure is consistently controlled (e.g., "'But…but…but what about Mom and Dad?'").

Sentence type and sentence length (e.g., "Tonight was different" and "I had to help Bobby up the ladder because he couldn't reach the steps but we made it and once the door was shut we blasted off") are varied and effective.

Sentence beginnings (e.g., "Now remember…," "Suddenly what looked…," "We rushed…," and "All too quickly…") are consistently varied.

**Vocabulary**

Well-chosen words (e.g., "bright full moon in the sky and the stars were extra bright and sparkling" and "skipped towards the bubbling river and noisily splashed across") are used effectively.

Expressions (e.g., "came crashing down," "Wow! Awesome!," "YES! YES!," and "was truly miraculous") are consistently precise and effective.

Words and expressions (e.g., "three crimson red aliens," "large heads with one big bulgeing eye, two legs that were so long they looked like spiders and two arms that had eight fingers on each hand," "as fast as a speeding bullet," and "the gurgling river") are used to create vivid images and enhance the writing.

**Conventions**

End punctuation and capitalization are correct.

Most words, familiar and unfamiliar, are spelled correctly; spelling errors (e.g., "camp sight" and "bulgeing") are understandable "slips."

Errors that are present (e.g., "My brothers and me" and "rocky mountains") do not affect the clarity or effectiveness of communication.

# EXERCISE #2—WRITING

## EXTENDED (LONGER) WRITING PIECE (55 MINUTES)

In this activity, you will write a story after looking carefully at the picture. Imagine you see a fairground on an island. You cannot imagine how to reach the fairground. Write an interesting story about what happens.

## Overview
### Time

| | |
|---|---|
| 2 minutes | Overview and directions for the student |
| 3 minutes | Writing topic |
| 2 minutes | Criteria |
| 8 minutes | Planning |
| 35 minutes | Written work |
| 5 minutes | Look back on your writing |

## Directions to the Student

5. You do not need to use all of the pages provided.

6. Remember to write double-spaced (on every other line) so you have room to go back to your writing and make changes and corrections.

7. You may use a dictionary or thesaurus.

8. You will be marked on the "Written Work" pages only (not the planning).

## Writing Topic

Your writing should be about **two** to **four** pages long.

### Criteria (Story/Narrative)

| | |
|---|---|
| Check your work for the following things: | |
| Did I write an exciting story about the picture? | ☐ |
| Is my story complete and easy to follow? | ☐ |
| Does my story include details to make it interesting to the reader? | ☐ |
| Did I choose words and ideas to make my reader feel something (happy, sad, surprised, excited) and are the words appropriate? | ☐ |
| Does my story have a beginning, middle, and end? | ☐ |
| Does my story have interesting characters (e.g., dialogue, description)? | ☐ |
| Have I made corrections in spelling, punctuation, and use of words? | ☐ |

### Planning

*My purpose*

To write an interesting story about the picture.

*My audience*

The teachers who will mark my writing.

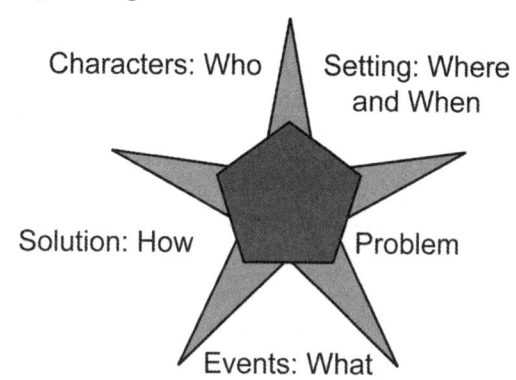

Characters: Who
Setting: Where and When
Solution: How
Problem
Events: What

*Written Work*

Take 35 minutes to write your story. Use the criteria and your planning page as a guide when you write. Be careful to include words and actions that are appropriate for all readers.

*Look Back on Your Writing*

Take 5 minutes to look back on your writing.

Carefully go through your writing and make any changes or corrections. Use the criteria at the top of this page to guide you.

# SAMPLE RESPONSES—EXERCISE #2

**SAMPLE OF WRITING RESPONSE: SATISFACTORY**

### The Islands fair

"Aaaaahhhh" I heard in a scream as the faris wheal suddenly came to a pause. All the fair workers were running to get the kids of the faris wheal. When all the kids had returned to the ground all the fair workers called a meeting to find out what coused the faris wheal to stop. At the end of the meeting they finally suspected that the faris wheal was sabatoshed by one of the fair workers that was on deyty yesterday at the faris wheal. So it is eather Bob or Jarramy that was at the faris wheal yesterday but what could they have done to make it break down like that and just pause and not start again there has to be an explanaition for it, it cannot just have broken down on it's own and just without anyone taking a part of a machine from it causing it to break down and go into a pause. I'm going to go find the Janator and see if he can fix the faris wheal said one of the workers. When he found the Janator the Janator took a look at it and sadly said "I'm sorry but there is no way I can fix it there is too many damages so more than one thing happen to it, it is also very old and has been used a lot, so it's probably worn out, I think its time for a new faris wheal."

About a year later they got the money to buy a turbo speed one and it never broke down and all the kids loved it.

**RATIONALE FOR RESPONSE SATISFACTORY**

### Content

The majority of the events, actions, and ideas are appropriate for the context established by the writer (a fairground has a Ferris wheel for children to ride).

Details are general, but are appropriate for the story (e.g., "find out what coused the faris wheal to stop" and "so it's probably worn out").

The writing generally holds the reader's interest and provides some support for a main idea (it refers to the Ferris wheel that has broken down, but the idea of sabotage is not followed through).

### Organization

The beginning directly presents information about events, characters, and setting (e.g., "'Aaaaahhhh' I heard in a scream as the faris wheal suddenly came to a pause. All the fair workers were running to get the kids of the faris wheal").

Connections and/or relationships between events, actions, details, and/or characters are generally maintained (e.g., "fair workers called a meeting to find out what coused the faris wheal to stop" and "there is no way I can fix it there is too many damages").

The ending ("About a year later they got the money to buy a turbo speed one and it never broke down and all the kids loved it") is predictable and contrived but is connected to events and actions.

### Sentence Structure

Sentence structure is generally controlled but sentence run-ons are present (e.g., "So it is eather Bob or Jarramy that was at the faris wheal yesterday but what could they have done to make it break down like that and just pause and not start again there has to be an explanaition for it, it cannot just have broken down on it's own and just without anyone taking a part of a machine from it causing it to break down and go into a pause").

Sentences may vary in type and length (e.g., "I heard in a scream as the faris wheal suddenly came to a pause" and "I'm going to go find the Janator and see if he can fix the faris wheal said one of the workers").

Some variety of sentence beginnings (e.g., "All the fair…," "At the end…," and "I'm going…") is evident.

### Vocabulary

Words chosen (e.g., "were running" and "no way I can fix it") tend to be common or ordinary.

Expressions (e.g., "what could they have done to make it break down" and "the Janator took a look at it and sadly said") are usually more general than specific.

Words and expressions (e.g., "'Aaaaahhhh'," "sabatoshed," and "has to be an explanaition") generally enhance the writing.

### Conventions

Conventional end punctuation and capitalization are usually correct.

Many familiar words (e.g., "suddenly," "finally suspected," "machine," and "damages") are spelled correctly; errors (e.g., "faris wheal," "coused," "deity," "eather," and "explanaition") suggest uneven control of spelling rules; unfamiliar words (e.g., "sabatoshed" and "Janator") are generally spelled phonetically.

Errors (e.g., "anyone taking a part of a machine from it causing it to break down and go into a pause," "there is too many damages so more than one thing happen to it," and "I think its time") are sometimes intrusive and may affect the clarity of communication.

## SAMPLE WRITING RESPONSE: PROFICIENT

### The Island

"Mom are we there yet?" Britt asked.

"10 minutes until we are at the beach honey" Mom said. We were going to mexico beach and it was 10 hours drive from our house. My mom finally stopped the car and said "We are here!" We unpacked all our things and put them into the hotel room. Everything was real close which was good so we headed off to the beach. I wasn't really a good swimmer so I could only go as deep as my belly button. I had a little swim splashing around in the shallow water and when I dried off I noticed another island. It had a ferris wheel, carousel, a big top tent and one big roller coaster. There were some kids on the island and they were going down a very big water slide. It looked so much fun and I wanted to go on the island but I knew my mom wouldn't let me because I couldn't swim. After some time Mom went back to the hotel so I quickly went into the water up to my neck. Then I just started sinking. I was down at the bottom of the ocean when BOOM a big dark thing went over me and a boy picked me up. I shut my eyes tight and the boy bought me to a chair and sure enough I was on that island. My eyes shot open. This island was paradise. 2000 hours on this island is like 5 seconds in my world so no way would my mom get all worried. I met other kids and made three friends, Taka, Lana and Louis who rescued me. We had so much fun going on the rides and my favourite was the water slide because it was the longest and fastest I have ever seen and we got soaking wet every time we went on it.

After some time I began to get homesick. It hadn't even been 1 second in my world but I just wanted to go home because I had had my fun. I wanted Louis Lana and Taka to come and see my world. Their parents said it was ok with them. Louis taught me how to swim. Lana taught me different things you can do in the water like handstands and playing tag and Taka showed me how to do all kinds of dives. I showed them the outer world and things like cars and airplanes and Mcdonalds and the hotel we were staying in and they thought it was so amazing. I told them I'm so happy to have you for my friends because I never had true friends before. My life was complete and my mom didn't even know I went in the waters and about my new friends. My water friends went back to there home (island). Me and my mom went to the beach more often.

### RATIONALE FOR RESPONSE PROFICIENT

**Content**

Events, actions, and ideas are appropriate for the context established by the writer (a young girl discovers a fantasy island where she meets friends and has many experiences).

Details (e.g., "2000 hours on this island is like 5 seconds in my world" and "we got soaking wet every time we went on it") are specific and generally effective, and the reader is caught up in the island's fantasy world where time stands still.

The writing engages the reader's interest and presents a supported main idea (stating that "This island was paradise" because time as we know it does not exist).

### Organization

The beginning ("'Mom are we there yet?' Britt asked. '10 minutes until we are at the beach honey' Mom said. We were going to mexico beach and it was 10 hours drive from our house. My mom finally stopped the car and said 'We are here!' We unpacked all our things and put them into the hotel room. Everything was real close which was good so we headed off to the beach. I wasn't really a good swimmer so I could only go as deep as my belly button. I had a little swim splashing around in the shallow water and when I dried off I noticed another island") clearly establishes events, characters, and setting, and provides direction for the writing.

Connections and/or relationships between events, actions, details, and characters are maintained (e.g., "It had a ferris wheel, carousel, a big top tent and one big roller coaster," "We had so much fun going on the rides," and "It hadn't even been 1 second in my world but I just wanted to go home because I had had my fun").

The ending ("My life was complete and my mom didn't even know I went in the waters and about my new friends. My water friends went back to there home (island). Me and my mom went to the beach more often") provides an appropriate finish for events and actions.

### Sentence Structure

Sentence structure is controlled (e.g., "My mom finally stopped the car and said 'We are here!'").

Sentence type and sentence length (e.g., "'Mom are we there yet?'" and "I had a little swim splashing around in the shallow water and when I dried off I noticed another island") are usually varied and effective.

Sentence beginnings (e.g., "My mom finally…," "After some time…," "This island was…," and "Louis taught me…") are often varied.

### Vocabulary

Well-chosen words (e.g., "paradise," "we got soaking wet," and "I began to get homesick") are often used.

Expressions (e.g., "as deep as my belly button," "down at the bottom of the ocean," "BOOM a big dark thing," and "My life was complete") are usually specific and effective.

Words and expressions (e.g., "splashing around in the shallow water," "My eyes shot open," and "no way would my mom get all worried") are descriptive and often enhance the writing.

### Conventions

End punctuation and capitalization are essentially correct.

Familiar words are spelled correctly; spelling errors (e.g., "the boy bought me" and "to there home") are "slips."

Errors that are present (e.g., "mexico," "real close," and "Me and my mom") rarely affect the clarity of communication.

The length and complexity of the response has been considered.

## Sample Writing Response: Excellent

### Thrillville

John and Linda were at the beach with their parents for their summer vacation when their mom and dad were called home because their grandma was sick. Linda was 17 so she said she could look after John. After their parents said goodbye and be good John and Linda headed for the beach. It was a beautiful hot sunny day and they played in the water and lay in the sun. John was watching some sail boats flying across the lake as the wind caught their sails when suddenly he noticed a small island in the middle of the lake that he hadn't seen before. "Hey look Linda" he yelled. "What is it?" asked Linda. "There is an island on the lake and there is a fair on the island. Can we go?" John said. "Sure" said Linda it sounds like fun. "But how will we get there?" "Let's rent a canoe and we can paddle there." said Linda. It did'nt take them long to find the canoes for rent and to head for the island. They both were good paddlers because they always went canoeing with their mom and dad. When they arrived at the island they paid $5 to go into the fair and John ran straight towards the ferris wheel. "Wait up John!" called Linda. They both got in line and when they got on the ferris wheel started up and hummed quietly as it went around and around. When they reached the top they had amazing views of the whole area. They could see the hotel and on the other side of the lake there was a gigantic forest and green hills and lots of smaller lakes and they could see the road they drove on to get to the beach. After the ferris wheel they decided to go to the big tent where the circus was because they wanted to see what animals they had. The circus was SUPER because of the acrobats who climbed to the top of the tent and swung on bars and leaped from one swing to another catching each other in mid air. The trapeeze acts looked dangerous and risky but no one fell and the clowns were hillarius. After that Linda demanded that they go on the biggest roller coaster ever built. Once they were locked in the roller coaster started the slow steep climb to the very top. John hated the roller coaster because he thought that they would break but Linda loved them. At the top John closed his eyes and held on tight to Linda's hand. He could feel them going through the loop-d-loop when suddenly …he opened his eyes and they were back on the straight track. All of a sudden it stopped. Everyone started yelling and screaming and then the guy who runs the ride said "The generator has shut down. It should be back in a few minutes. Stay in your seats please. "I knew it would break!" said John. Finally the generator started up again and they returned to earth. Now it was nearly dark so Linda and John got their canoe and went back to the hotel and had supper. The next morning they went to the beach and they couldn't believe their eyes because the island and the fair had dissapeared. They wondered if it had been a dream.

## RATIONALE FOR RESPONSE EXCELLENT

**Content**

Events, actions, and ideas are consistently appropriate for the context established by the writer (a boy and a girl see a fair on an island in the middle of the lake and paddle across in order to go to the fair).

Details (e.g., "they payed $5 to go into the fair and John ran straight towards the ferris wheel" and "swung on bars and leaped from one swing to another catching each other in mid air") are specific and consistently effective, and the reader is caught up in fair activities that the children find on the island.

The writing captivates the reader's interest and presents a well-supported main idea (stating that "'There is an island on the lake and there is a fair on the island. Can we go?'" John said. 'Sure' said Linda it sounds like fun").

**Organization**

The beginning captures the reader's attention, clearly establishes events, characters, and setting ("John and Linda were at the beach with their parents for their summer vacation when their mom and dad were called home because their grandma was sick. Linda was 17 so she said she could look after John") and provides direction for the writing (e.g., "There is an island on the lake and there is a fair on the island").

Connections and/or relationships between events, actions, details, and characters are consistently maintained (e.g., "They both were good paddlers because they always went canoeing with their mom and dad," "When they reached the top they had amazing views of the whole area," and "At the top John closed his eyes and held on tight to Linda's hand").

The ending ("Now it was nearly dark so Linda and John got their canoe and went back to the hotel and had supper. The next morning they went to the beach and they couldn't believe their eyes because the island and the fair had dissapeared. They wondered if it had been a dream") ties events and actions together.

**Sentence Structure**

Sentence structure is consistently controlled (e.g., "It was a beautiful hot sunny day and they played in the water and lay in the sun").

Sentence type and sentence length (e.g., "But how will we get there?" and "They could see the hotel and on the other side of the lake there was a gigantic forest and green hills and lots of smaller lakes and they could see the road they drove on to get to the beach") are varied and effective.

Sentence beginnings (e.g., "John and Linda were…," "When they reached…," "Finally the generator…," and "Now it was…") are consistently varied.

**Vocabulary**

Well-chosen words (e.g., "circus was SUPER," "looked dangerous and risky," and "clowns were hillarius") are used effectively.

Expressions (e.g., "sail boats flying across the lake as the wind caught their sails," "ferris wheel started up and hummed quietly," "amazing views," and "catching each other in mid air") are consistently precise and effective.

Words and expressions (e.g., "a gigantic forest and green hills and lots of smaller lakes" and "going through the loop-d-loop") are used to create vivid images and enhance the writing.

**Conventions**

End punctuation and capitalization are correct.

Most words, familiar and unfamiliar, are spelled correctly; spelling errors (e.g., "did'nt" and "dissapeared") are understandable "slips." The words "trapeeze" and "hillarius" are spelled phonetically.

Errors that are present (e.g., "'Sure' said Linda it sounds like fun" and "John hated the roller coaster because he thought that they would break") do not affect the clarity or effectiveness of communication.

# Appendices

# CREDITS

A Dive into the Sea—by Pierdomenico Baccalario, found in *The Door to Time*, Scholastic Inc., 2006

*A Horse That Wore Snow Shoes*—Anonymous, found on apples4the teacher.com,

A Secret for Two—by Quentin Reynolds, found in *Experiences*, Wiley Publishers, 1975

*A Snake Named Rover*—by Maxine Jeffris, Meadowbrook press, 1991

*A Toad for Tuesday*—by Russell E. Erickson, Beech Tree Books, 1974

*Amazing Black Holes*—Anonymous, www.longman.com/ae/marketing/sfesl/tests/grade4.html

An Invite from Uncle—by Aaron Taouma, found in *Home: New Short Stories from New Zealand Writers*, Random House

Ancient Broom Games—by J.K Rowling, found in *Quidditch Through the Ages*, Raincoast Books, 2001

Are All Giants All Bad?—by David Colbert, found in The Magical Worlds of Harry Potter, Lumina Press, 2001

*Becca's Diary*—by Joshua Mowll, Candlewick Press 2005

Built for the Water—by Evelyne Daigle, found in *As Long as there Are Whales*, Tundra Books, 2004

*Cheetahs*—National Geographic for Kids website

Chocolate Chip Cookie—by Larry Verstraete, found in *Whose Bright Idea Was It? True Stories of Invention*, published by Scholastic Canada, 1997

*Coram Boy*—by Jamila Gavin, Nick Hern Books, 2000

*Crabs for Dinner*—by Adwoa Badoe, Sister Vision Press, 1995

*Curvy Beak, Pointy Claws*—by Marjorie Weinman Sharmat, Dell yearling, 1993

Daniel Boone (1734–1820)—by Elizabeth Cody Kimmel, found in *The Look-It-Up Book of Explorers*, Random House Children's Books, 2004

Discovering the Mysteries of the St. Lawrence—by Evelyne Daigle, found in As Long as there Are Whales, Tundra Books, 2004

Elephant and Hare—by Jan Thornhill,found in *Crow and Fox and Other Animal Legends*, Greey de Pencier Books, 1993

Finding a Puppy—by Kim Dennis-Bryan, found in *Puppy Care*, Penguin Group (UK), 2004

Gramma's Apron—by C.J.Heck, found in *Barking Spiders and Other Such Stuff*, SterlingHouse Publisher Inc., 2006

How Brazilian Beetles Got Their Gorgeous Coats: A Story From Brazil—by Martha Hamilton and Mitch Weiss, found in *How & Why Stories: World Tales Kids Can Read and Tell*, August House Inc., 1999

*I Survived the Titanic*—by Jennifer A. Kirkpatrick, National Geographic Kids News website

Islands in the Mind—by Sarah Ellis, found in *The Young Writer's Companion*, Groundwood Books/Douglas & McIntyre, 1999

*Joe's Junk*—by Susan Russo, Henry Holt and Co., 1986

Just Imagine—by Jennifer Armstrong, found in *Shipwreck at the Bottom of the World*, Crown Publishers, 1998, rights random house

Matilda: Who Told Lies, and was Burned to Death—by Hilaire Belloc, found in *Poems for Boys and Girls Book 3*, The Copp Clark Publishing Co. Limited, 1956

Monsters from the Deep and Other Imaginary Beings—by Sarah Ellis, found in *The Young Writer's Companion*, Groundwood Books, 1999

My Friend Jacob—by Lucille Clifton, Dutton Juvenile, 1980

Nim's Island—by Wendy Orr, Scholastic Inc., 1999

Not Owls Too!—by Farley Mowat, found in Owls in the Family, McClelland & Stewart Ltd., 1961

*Pygmalion, Act I*—by George Bernard Shaw, Public Domain

Red Fox at Dawn—by Dahlov Ipcar, found in *The Beauty of the Beast: Poems from the Animal Kingdom*, Alfred A. Knopf Inc., 1997

*Ronia, the Robber's Daughter*—by Astrid Lindgren, published by Penguin Group, 1981.

Soft-Stone Sculpture—by Sandi Henry, found in *Kids' Art Works! Creativity with Color, Design, Texture & More*, Williamson Publishing Co., 1999

*Stars*—Marjorie Pickthall, Public

The Birthday Wall—by C.J.Heck, found in *Barking Spiders and Other Such Stuff*, SterlingHouse Publisher Inc.

The Clever Turtle—by A.K. Roche, found in *The A.K. Roche Collection*, Prentice Hall, 1969

*Stubborn Mary Shadd*—by Karen Shadd-Evelyn

# SOLARO Study Guides
# Ordering Information

Every SOLARO Study Guide unpacks the curriculum standards and provides an overview of all curriculum concepts, practice questions with full solutions, and assignment questions for students to fully test their knowledge.

Visit www.solaro.com/orders to buy books and learn how SOLARO can offer you an even more complete studying solution.

**SOLARO Study Guide—$29.95 each plus applicable sales tax**

SOLARO
Study Guides

| SOLARO Common Core State Standard Titles ||
|---|---|
| Mathematics 3 | Algebra I |
| Mathematics 4 | Algebra II |
| Mathematics 5 | Geometry |
| Mathematics 6 | English Language Arts 3 |
| Mathematics 7 | English Language Arts 4 |
| Accelerated Mathematics 7 (Int.) | English Language Arts 5 |
| Accelerated Mathematics 7 (Trad.) | English Language Arts 6 |
| Mathematics 8 | English Language Arts 7 |
| Accelerated Mathematics I | English Language Arts 8 |
| Mathematics I | English Language Arts 9 |
| Mathematics II | English Language Arts 10 |
| Mathematics III | English Language Arts 11 |
| Accelerated Algebra I | English Language Arts 12 |

**To order books, please visit**
www.solaro.com/orders

Volume pricing is available. Contact us at orderbooks@solaro.com